D0930696

NICOLAS GUEUDEVILLE AND HIS WORK
(1652-172?)

ARCHIVES INTERNATIONALES D'HISTOIRE DES IDEES

INTERNATIONAL ARCHIVES OF THE HISTORY OF IDEAS

99

AUBREY ROSENBERG

NICOLAS GUEUDEVILLE AND HIS WORK (1652-172?)

NICOLAS GUEUDEVILLE AND HIS WORK
(1652-172?)

by

AUBREY ROSENBERG

1982
MARTINUS NIJHOFF PUBLISHERS
THE HAGUE / BOSTON / LONDON

Distributors:

for the United States and Canada
Kluwer Boston, Inc.
190 Old Derby Street
Hingham, MA 02043
USA

for all other countries
Kluwer Academic Publishers Group
Distribution Center
P.O. Box 322
3300 AH Dordrecht
The Netherlands

Library of Congress Cataloging in Publication Data

Rosenberg, Aubrey.
  Nicolas Gueudeville and his work (1652-172?)

  (Archives internationales d'histoire des idées
International archives of the history of ideas ;
99)
  Bibliography: p.
  Includes index.
  1. Gueudeville, Nicolas, ca. 1654-ca. 1721.
2. Authors, French--18th century--Biography.
I. Title. II. Series: Archives internationales
d'histoire des. idées ; 99.
PQ1987.G49Z85   848'.409   81-11319
                                AACR2

ISBN 90-247-2533-x (this volume)
ISBN 90-247-2433-3 (series)

PRINTED IN THE NETHERLANDS

ACKNOWLEDGEMENTS

No study of this kind would be possible without the cooperation of librarians and archivists in many parts of the world. Those who have helped me are too numerous to mention individually, but I must offer my profound gratitude to Dr. J.J. van der Roer-Meyers, Gemeente Bibliotheek, Rotterdam, Dr. I.H. van Eeghen, Gemeentelijke Archiefdienst, Amsterdam, and Monsieur Jacques-Yves de Sallier Dupin, Bibliothèque Municipale, Nantes.

I should also like to acknowledge the help of Professors J.M. Bigwood and K.R. Thompson of the Classics department, University of Toronto, Drs. H.M.B. Jacobs of the Gemeentearchief, The Hague, Dr. A.J. Veenendaal Jr. of the Bureau der Rijkscommissie voor Vaderlandse Geschiedenis and Professor D.J. Roorda of the University of Leiden. I am grateful to Drs. M.M. Hutcheson and J. Svilpis of the Centre for Reformation and Renaissance Studies, University of Toronto, for tolerating my excessive intrusions on their time, and to Mrs. E. Scharbach who assisted me, as she has done many times before, by typing my scrawl, and by interpreting Dutch texts. Finally, I should like to express my heartfelt thanks to my colleague, Professor D.W. Smith, who has helped me once again, especially in the field of bibliography. This book was made possible by a Canada Council Leave Fellowship, 1977–1978, and has been published with the help of a grant from the Canadian Federation for the Humanities, using funds provided by the Social Sciences and Humanities Research Council of Canada.

A NOTE ON THE TEXT

Unless otherwise indicated, the spelling is modernized except in the descriptions of title-pages. In these descriptions the use of large capitals is not noted.

LIST OF ABBREVIATIONS FOR LIBRARIES

A-Athenaeum; Ar-Arsenal; B-Beinecke; BC-Bibliothèque Classée; BI-Bibliothèque de l'Institut; BL-British Library; BN-Bibliothèque Nationale; C-Central; CA-Calvet; CU-Catholic University; ETH-Swiss Federal Insitute of Technology; FU-Free University; H-Humboldt University; HA-Herzog August; I-Inguimbertine; ISG-Insituut voor Sociale Geschiedenis; JH-Johns Hopkins; KM-Karl Marx; L-Land; Li-Library; M-Municipal; Ma-Mazarine; McM-McMaster University; N-National; Ne-Newberry; P-Public; R-Royal; RC-Renaissance Centre; RF-Rosenbach Foundation; Ro-Rocheguide; S-State; SMC-St. Michael's College; SMU-Southern Methodist University; So-Sorbonne; St.J.-St. John's College; TF-Thomas Fisher; TI-Taylor Institution; U-University; UC-University College; UCa-University of California; UnC-Union College; UTS-Union Theological Seminary; V-Vassar; VC-Victoria College; WLC-William L. Clements.

TABLE OF CONTENTS

To Yvonne and Michelle

INTRODUCTION

It is generally agreed that great men transcend their time while ordinary men remain rooted in it. This is why, if we want to know what life was like in days gone by, we must study those who were most representative of their age, those individuals who, though they may have achieved a modicum of fame or notoriety, are now, because of their limited abilities and outlook, largely forgotten.

The great figures involved in the political and religious controversies that took place in Holland[1] towards the end of the seventeenth century and the beginning of the eighteenth, men such as Bayle, Jurieu, Le Clerc and others who were in the forefront of what has been aptly termed as the "crise de la conscience européenne," these figures have been the object of extensive investigation. The minor personages of this period, on the other hand, have received little attention. For this reason, in a previous study,[2] I examined the life and work of one of these minor figures, and tried to show how he was representative of those French Huguenots who came to Holland in the latter half of the seventeenth century, who settled in relatively remote places, and who made an effort to integrate themselves and gain acceptance in Dutch provincial society.

The majority, however, like most refugees and first-generation immigrants, tended to stay together. They settled in the major cultural, political and commercial centres of Amsterdam, Rotterdam, Leiden and The Hague, where they could continue to speak their own language and carry on their customs, and where there was no obligation to assimilate. There was, nonetheless, the necessity to earn a living. Many of these French Huguenots possessed no readily marketable skills, and they had to make the most of their native abilities, supplemented by whatever education they had been able to acquire before their exile. Fortunately, Holland, during the last quarter of the seventeenth century, had become the intellectual centre of Europe. As a result, the book trade was at its height, so there were great opportunities and a great demand for the talented, and the not so talented, in the republic of letters:

Many Huguenots with a knowledge of French and Latin were able to win a temporary meal-ticket, and to make the vital, initial break-through into the world of letters... by taking on work as proof correctors or/and translators. Opportunities for translating were numerous, not only translating books, but also, in the expanding world of journalism, translating foreign news.[3]

It was in this world of letters that the great names I have mentioned made their outstanding contributions to the process that would later be known as the Enlightenment. But for every Bayle or Le Clerc there were scores of lesser lights whose achievements only occasionally rose above the level of the mediocre, and whose reputations died with them. These men were followers not leaders. They were the unknown soldiers who helped to undermine the political and religious conventions of their time.

To represent these unsung warriors I have chosen, for this present study, Nicolas Gueudeville, a Benedictine monk who renounced his religion and settled in Holland towards the end of the century. At first glance it seems perverse to choose an ex-monk to represent a certain class of Huguenots, but it should be remembered that the *moines défroqués,* of whom there was an abundance in Holland at this time, were welcomed into the Walloon Churches where, in the manner of converts, they frequently displayed a hatred of France and Catholicism more violent than that expressed by the Huguenots themselves.

Gueudeville is also representative because of his energy and versatility. During the course of his career he was involved in all kinds of polemical literature including journalism, literary criticism, editing and contributing to the work of others. He also did popular translations of classical and Renaissance authors. In short, he participated in all those activities by which so many of his compatriots earned their daily bread.

Although the name of Gueudeville is now relatively unknown, in his own day he was a notorious figure in the republic of letters, and numbered amongst his friends some of the most prominent writers of his time. But, because he was an imitator rather than an original thinker, his works have fallen into obscurity. Nevertheless, his life and work are so typical of so many exiles of the period that, through the study of this one obscure individual, we are able to gain some appreciation of an important aspect of the French Huguenot experience in Holland.

I. THE LIFE

Up to now, there have been no detailed biographies of Gueudeville for the simple reason that almost nothing is known about him. It is not known for certain, for example, when he was born or when he died, and there is very little information about the intervening period. The standard biographical works, which often copy from each other and thus compound the inaccuracies, contain brief notices embodying the usual mixture of fact and fiction. Archival research, the discovery of his first publication, hitherto unknown, a study of his writings and those of his contemporaries, have enabled me to add something to the knowledge of Gueudeville's life and personality. There is obviously a lot more to be discovered but, for the present, we must be content with the following.

The origins of the Gueudeville or Gueutteville family are somewhat obscure. At least two branches that may be related to the family of Nicolas Gueudeville, have been identified. One branch had settled in Rouen in the sixteenth century, and another is found, also in the sixteenth century, in Dieppe. This latter branch seems to have been Protestant, and several of its members moved to Amsterdam before and after the Revocation of the Edict of Nantes.[1]

Nicolas, himself, was born in 1652, to a Catholic family in Rouen. According to Pierre Bayle, with whom Gueudeville was to become friendly, his father was a doctor. Apart from this, little is known of his family except that their circumstances were poor or, as Gueudeville puts it in the preface to his *Les Motifs de la conversion,* he was "né d'un père qui avait laissé à une famille nombreuse, plus de réputation que de bien." At all events, it was as much for the benefit of his body as for his soul that, in 1671, Gueudeville made his vows in the Benedictine monastery at Jumièges, near Rouen.[2]

Young Nicolas seems to have realized fairly quickly that he was temperamentally unsuited to the rigours of the monastic life, but he was determined to uphold his vows:

je sortis de l'enfance pour entrer dans le cloître. . . sans avoir jamais rien vu; je jurai solennellement de ne plus rien voir, et. . . le premier usage que je fis de ma liberté, ce fut de me l'interdire pour toujours. Aussi ne fus-je pas longtemps à m'apercevoir que j'avais fait un mauvais marché. J'aurais bien voulu m'en dédire, et je l'aurais fait sans scrupule, étant persuadé que Dieu est trop juste pour y avoir eu part, et qu'il est trop bon pour m'obliger à le tenir. Mais, tout moine que j'étais, je me piquais un peu de ce qu'on appelle honnête homme, et, dans cette seule vue, je résolus de finir sous le harnois, et de traîner mon lien jusqu'à la mort, de la moins mauvaise grâce que je pourrais.[3]

But God, and the writings of Jurieu, opened his eyes to the falseness of the Catholic religion, and he could no longer tolerate his situation. As a result, he lost his faith, and was quite prepared to lapse into a life of godlessness and libertinage when, by an act of divine providence, he met a Protestant and was saved:

Dieu me procura la connaissance d'une personne de la Religion. Je m'ouvris à elle, et je ne sais qui de nous alla plus vite, elle pour m'offrir la liberté, moi pour la lui demander. Elle y travailla d'abord avec assez de chaleur, mais quelques incidents que le public se passera bien de savoir, ayant reculé la chose, on en donna avis au couvent, et il fallut sortir sans délai d'un corps qui avait autant de passion de me retenir que j'en avais de le quitter.[4]

Who this person was, and what was the nature of Gueudeville's relationship with him or her, we shall probably never know. At all events, on August 25 1688, Gueudeville made a clandestine and permanent exit from the monastery of Saint-Martin-de-Sées, near Alençon, to which he must have moved from Jumiéges.[5] It is not clear how he made his escape but, according to the biographers, he did so in true Stendhalian fashion, "en escaladant les murs."

If the identity of his assistant and his mode of escape are unclear, the events after his flight, and the circumstances of his arrival in Holland, the following year, are equally vague and providential:

Où j'ai été et ce que j'ai fait depuis ce temps-là, il importe fort peu. Ce qui mérite d'être su, et ce qui surprendra sans doute, quoique ce soit la vérité toute pure, c'est qu'à Pâques dernier, ayant fait quarante lieues de chemin, tout exprès pour venir chercher à Paris les moyens de me rendre dans l'aimable et bienheureux pays où je suis, ne connaissant pas une âme de la Religion dans cette grande ville, n'ayant pas une ligne de recommandation à personne, concevant bien d'ailleurs que je ne pouvais m'ouvrir d'une affaire si délicate sans risque de la vie, cependant, dès le lendemain de mon arrivée, croyant n'acheter qu'une bagatelle, et ne pensant à rien dans le moment, je m'aperçus avec un étonnement que je ne puis exprimer, que j'avais trouvé en un demi-jour, et sans y penser, ce que d'autres n'ont pas trouvé en deux ans: je veux dire un expédient le plus propre qu'on pût voir passer, comme, en effet, je suis passé quelques semaines après, sans argent, et malgré Mars et Thémis, j'entends malgré les déclarations de la justice et de la guerre.[6]

It sounds as if he had managed to obtain a passport or some kind of authorization that would allow him to pass freely from France to Holland, but perhaps there is some other explanation for this almost miraculous stroke of fortune. In any case, it is difficult to know how much reliance one can place on this account of why he lost his faith and fled the country. After all, the explanation presented above was the one he gave to the Dutch authorities on the occasion of his conversion, but, according to Lenglet Dufresnoy, who knew him in Holland, Gueudeville, once he was established, told a different story:

[Gueudeville] ne voyait qu'en riant tous ces prétendus évangéliques qui allaient par cohorte en Hollande, où lui-même s'était retiré il y avait déjà longtemps, pour pratiquer, disaient-ils, la parole de Dieu avec plus de pureté qu'on ne le fait dans cette Eglise Romaine, cette prostituée, cette Babylone antichrétienne, ce cloaque de tous les vices où l'on est si contraint qu'on n'y souffre pas, quand on le sait, qu'un pauvre moine se livre à la vie joyeuse, ni même qu'il se marie honnêtement quand il a une fois donné sa parole d'honneur de ne le pas faire. Il y en alla un grand nombre après la paix de Ryswick, touchés du saint zèle d'avoir une espèce de sacrement de plus; et M. Gueudeville ne pouvait s'empêcher de dire, "voilà encore un fripon de plus parmi nous." On fut avec raison scandalisé de ce discours, car ce sont là les vérités qui offensent; on lui en parla, et avec une droiture qui le devait faire estimer dans son infortune; il dit, sans s'étonner, à un Seigneur même de l'Etat, "que tous ces petits moines, ces gens à froc, cette prêtraille que vous voyez si âpres à suivre l'Evangile, sont autant de fripons qui sortent du papisme, où ils n'ont pu vivre régulièrement, pour venir faire trophée ici de leurs désordres. Et vous pouvez m'en croire, disait-il, car si moi-même je n'eus pas fait quelque friponnerie, vous ne me verriez pas ici."[7]

From what we learn about Gueudeville's attitude to any religion not based on reason alone, this latter account has the ring of authenticity, and the probability is that he left France more to save his skin than his soul.

What we do know for certain is that, in 1689, he made his way to Rotterdam which, because of its location as a port, had become an important centre for refugees from France, especially from such places as Dieppe, Bordeaux, La Rochelle, and other coastal areas. These refugees, most of whom arrived in a destitute state, were offered spiritual and material aid by the Walloon Churches and the city magistrates. In Rotterdam Gueudeville renounced his religion and was accepted into the Walloon Church where, on July 18, he delivered an address which he published under the title, *Les Motifs de la conversion* (see chaper 2).

When Gueudeville first came to Rotterdam, the open hostilities between Bayle and Jurieu had not yet begun. Since Jurieu was a titular pastor of the Church in which Gueudeville perhaps hoped eventually to obtain a post, and since Jurieu's fulminations against Louis XIV and Catholicism accorded with his own sentiments, Gueudeville probably cultivated his support.[8] But, in 1691, when Jurieu opposed the nomination to ordinary pastor of Jacques Basnage whose candidacy was favoured by Bayle, Gueudeville must have allied himself with Jurieu's enemies.[9] Basnage, like Gueudeville, was originally from Rouen, and about the same age. Bayle, too, had spent a little time in Rouen, so there was perhaps some common ground. It is not possible to prove that Gueudeville's friendship with Basnage and Bayle began at this time, but we do know that the former was godfather to one of Gueudeville's twin daughters, born in 1696. At all events, the friendship with Basnage and Bayle was to prove extremely valuable in that it would earn him favourable reviews in the *Histoire des ouvrages des savants* of which Henri Basnage de Beauval, brother of Jaques, was the editor.

Little is known of Gueudeville's first few years in Holland. On June 10 1691 he married, in the French Church in The Hague, Marie Blèche, a recently arrived Protestant refugee, living with the prominent Masclary family, who had escaped to Holland as a result of the Revocation of the Edict of Nantes. Over the next few years Marie gave birth to four children.[10] Nothing is known of them, although there is a suggestion that only one survived to maturity.[11] According to Bayle, Gueudeville earned his livelihood "à enseigner le latin chez lui, et à tenir des pensionnaires," but, being an energetic and ambitious individual, he soon tired of this occupation and sought to make a career and a name for himself by writing.[12]

It was not only the Huguenots but also the *moines défroqués* who availed themselves of the literary opportunities in Holland. In a series of portraits of the different kinds of authors to be found in Holland, La Barre de Beaumarchais describes the ex-monk in a manner that clearly reveals just how typical Gueudeville was of his breed. The portrait is so apt that it deserves to be quoted almost completely.

L'un, se livrant à une ferveur passagère, a quitté le monde, sans l'avoir vu et sans le connaître. La douce oisiveté qu'il voyait régner dans un monastère, l'embonpoint et le teint fleuri des moines, lui ont fait comprendre que rien n'était plus heureux qu'une vie qui n'est troublée par aucun besoin, ni fatiguée par aucun travail, ni du corps, ni de l'esprit. Cet état lui a paru un charmant asile contre la pauvreté dont il était menacé. Ajoutez à tout cela une petite dose d'enthousiasme dévot. Il a pris l'habit, a fait profession après avoir soupiré tout un an après ce grand jour, et il a enfin prononcé le voeu solennel et irrévocable. Il est sorti du monde par une porte qu'il s'est lui-même fermée : il y rentre bientôt par une autre. Les objets l'ébranlent, sa règle les lui interdit; c'est pour cela qu'ils font sur son coeur une plus vive impression. . .

Le beau sexe, auquel notre jeune homme s'est trop hâté de renoncer, le revendique. Des visites un peu fréquentes font parler; le Supérieur, homme incommode, en est averti; on le suit déjà, et au premier jour il pourrait bien être mis en pénitence. Quel remède? Un voyage au pays étranger lui rendra la liberté qu'il regrette. De quoi y subsistera-t-il? Voici l'embarras; mais il a ouï dire qu'en Hollande il y a un grand commerce de librairie; le voilà déterminé. Arrivé à la Haye, ou à Amsterdam, il se produit en qualité d'auteur, et, huit jours après, il aura déjà un manuscrit tout prêt à mettre sous la presse.[13]

It is true that Gueudeville arrived in Rotterdam, not The Hague or Amsterdam, and that he did not immediately present himself as an author. But it is also true that, after his arrival, he wasted no time in publishing *Les Motifs de la conversion*.

His real writing career, however, did not begin until 1699 when, in May of that year, he moved from Rotterdam to The Hague where, in the following month, he began publishing anonymously a monthly, political periodical, *L'Esprit des cours de L'Europe,* in which, for the next ten years, he waged an incessant war against the Pope and Catholicism, against Louis XIV and France. In 1701, Gueudeville's periodical so offended the French ambassador to The Hague that the Dutch authorities were requested to suppress it. The Dutch managed to satisfy the ambassador without actually complying with his request.[14]

The publication of Fénelon's *Télémaque,* in 1699, provoked a number of critical commentaries among which was Gueudeville's anonymous *Critique générale des avantures de Télémaque.* This appeared in several parts from 1700 to 1702. The year 1705 saw Gueudeville involved in promoting the cause of natural religion through his anonymous editing of the works of the baron de Lahontan, and, in the same year, he began his collaboration in a massive publishing project entitled the *Atlas historique* (1705–1720).[15]

Through his authorship of *L'Esprit des cours,* especially as a result of the French ambassador "affair," and his outrageous attacks on the Pope and Louis XIV in his journal and the critique of *Télémaque,* Gueudeville achieved a degree of fame or notoriety that extended far beyond the borders of Holland, but, if his writings brought him fame they did nothing for his fortune, for, despite the quantity and diffusion of his works, Gueudeville, like most' struggling authors, was at the mercy of his publishers, and was consequently ill-paid. In 1706, on the grounds that he was desperately poor, he applied to the States-General for a grant of two hundred guilders. The request was refused.[16] When Bayle died, later that year, Gueudeville lost a most influential friend, and the one he most admired and imitated.[17]

In 1709 he published anonymously *Dialogues des morts d'un tour nouveau,* and collaborated, in 1713, on a geographical work entitled *Nouveau Théâtre du monde.*[18] Neither of these publications seems to have been a commercial success, and one can only suppose his financial state remained precarious.

In 1713 he embarked on a new career, that of translator, and, with his translation of Erasmus' *Moriae encomium,* scored an immediate success. Indeed, so popular was this translation that it appeared in twenty-two editions throughout the eighteenth century. To what extent Gueudeville benefited financially from this venture I am unable to say, but since he followed this success with a popular translation of More's *Utopia,* in 1715, one is inclined to think he received sufficient inducement to enable him to pursue his translating activities.[19] Although these translations were a commercial success, they were not highly regarded by the *savants,* as we shall see.

In 1716 Gueudeville contributed a series of commentaries to a book by Jean Aymon, entitled *Maximes politiques du Pape Paul III.*[20] In 1719 he published a ten-volume translation of the plays of Plautus, and, in 1720, a six-volume version of Erasmus' *Colloquia.*[21] It was soon after this, in 1721 or 1722, that, according to Jean Le Clerc, Gueudeville died in a miserable state.[22]

Despite an extensive search of the archives I have been unable to find any record of Gueudeville's death. What is particularly disconcerting is that translations under his name continued to appear. In 1726 there was published a three-volume translation of works by Agrippa von Nettesheim, and, in 1728, a translation of a medical treatise by Insulanus Menapius under the title, *L'Eloge de la fièvre quarte*.[23] If Le Clerc is correct it must be assumed these works were published posthumously in the hope of profiting from Gueudeville's reputation.

Not only is the date of his death uncertain, but also the cause. Again, if Le Clerc is correct, it is possible that excessive use of alcohol was a contributing factor since, "sur la fin de sa vie [il] s'enivrait d'eau-de-vie comme il avait fait de vin, quand il en avait eu. Il est mort à peu près comme il avait vécu, aussi bien que Gabillon, autre moine défroqué, qui ne valait pas mieux que lui. J'ai cru devoir cela. . . afin qu'on ne crût pas que cette sorte de gens est fort approuvée parmi les Protestants."[24] Perhaps it was in a drunken state that "un jour, Gueudeville fut tellement abandonné de Dieu, qu'il voulut se noyer dans un canal de La Haye, mais . . . le sieur Vander Aa, Fameux libraire de cette ville, l'en empêcha."[25]

It appears, then, that Gueudeville ended his life as he had begun, with "plus de réputation que de bien," and with a "réputation", at least in the scholarly world, of dubious worth.

Given the paucity of information about Gueudeville's life it is extremely difficult to know what sort of a person he was, and we must resort mainly to conjecture and speculation. What little evidence we have from those who knew him personally would suggest he was a man of great energy, a forceful personality who lived life to the full, whenever he had the opportunity to do so. According to Bayle, "il est certain qu'on ne peut avoir plus de feu ni plus d'imagination qu'en a cet auteur." Bayle also described him as "fort agréable en conversation," and as one "[qui] ne hait pas les plaisirs." Le Clerc, as we have seen, was less impressed. For him, Gueudeville was a "moine défroqué" who wrote books "en style burlesque plutôt que sérieux, et pleins d'impertinences, qui n'ont pu plaire qu'à des gens de mauvais goût." Lenglet Dufresnoy deplored his opinions but admired his frankness.[26]

Most of what we know about Gueudeville has been provided by the man himself in his writings. We have, therefore, a rather biased picture of his character. He generally liked to portray himself as an utterly reasonable and down-to-earth individual, with no special talents or virtues. He once described himself as "ni théologien, ni savant, ni bel esprit, et je ne connais. . . que le blanc et le noir."[27] He was, however, firmly rooted in the sceptical *moraliste* tradition, and when he was not inveighing against Louis XIV or the Pope, he criticized mankind in general, and ridiculed the follies of human nature.

There was one thing on which he prided himself, and that was his talent for badinage. Indeed, as we shall see, it was not so much the content but the humorous and forceful style of his writings that endeared him to his public. Gueudeville claimed to write primarily to entertain. If he also managed to instruct so much the better. He addressed his works to "tout lecteur qui prend quelque goût à mon badinage (car je n'écris ni pour les Catons, ni pous les savants, ni pour les beaux esprits)."[28]

Nothing is known of Gueudeville's education prior to his entry into the Benedictine order, but it is not unreasonable to assume that, being the son of a doctor, however poor, he would have received more than a rudimentary schooling, and that his ability must have been of a sufficiently high standard for him to be accepted by the scholarly Benedictines. He tells us himself that he knew no Greek, that he had no pretensions to being a scholar, and that his main desire was to appeal to the ordinary reading public.[29] In short, he saw himself as a popular interpreter of the world of letters. Since he was poor he possessed no private library, and his main source of reference was Bayle's dictionary. Gueudeville, however, unlike many of his contemporaries, made no attempt to disguise his sources, and openly acknowledged the debt to his friend: "Je déclare, donc, une fois pour toutes, que je prends souvent dans le gros ouvrage de ce fameux auteur; ce riche et inépuisable trésor fait toute ma bibliothèque . . ."[30] We can see from the following account by La Barre de Beaumarchais of how aspiring authors contrive to appear learned, that although Gueudeville was typical in his exploitation of Bayle, he distinguished himself by his candour:

[Ce secret] consiste 1. a avoir par achat ou par emprunt. . . un Dictionnaire de Moréri, et surtout celui de Bayle; voilà en quoi doit consister la bibliothèque d'un jeune savant, ou du moins celle d'un jeune homme qui veut jeter de la poudre aux yeux de ses lecteurs. 2. A savoir en détacher, habilement ou non, des morceaux frappants ou curieux, et avec cela seul, on se met d'abord, et à peu de frais, en possession de l'érudition vaste et profonde qui a coûté tant de sueurs et de veilles aux grands hommes que l'on dépouille. Surtout il faut bien se garder d'indiquer ni les articles ni les pages d'où est tiré ce que l'on emprunte. On trouve dans les oeuvres de Bayle des citations toutes digérées; il ne faut que savoir lire et transcrire ce qu'on écrit. . .

Un peu de critique des auteurs cités fait bien, et donne bonne idée du discernement de celui qui cite; cela se trouve encore tout préparé dans le Dictionnaire de Bayle.[31]

Finally, there is the question of the extent to which Gueudeville was the "libertin déclaré" that Le Clerc termed him. Since the charge of atheism was not infrequent, and was levelled at a variety of religious beliefs, it is not easy to say how sincere Gueudeville was in his protestations of faith. Naturally, when he first came to Holland he embraced the Calvinist doctrine with apparent enthusiasm, but he clearly had no alternative. However, much later in his career, when he had rejected the metaphysical aspects of religion, he described himself as "chrétien par la grâce de Dieu, et comme tel j'adore une providence agissante avec pleine connaissance de cause, et ne faisant rien que pour de bonnes raisons," although he also, on another occasion, referred to himself as "moi qui ne suis

point né pour le mystère, et qui ne saurais percer au-delà des apparences."[32]
It is probable that Gueudeville believed in God, but in the "natural" God of
the deists and the noble savage. But he could not afford to declare his beliefs
openly, and so, while his attack on Catholicism is explicit and avowed, his
criticism of revealed religion is implicit and clandestine.

II. THE FIRST PUBLICATION

On July 18 1689, to mark his acceptance into the Walloon Church at Rotterdam, Gueudeville delivered an oration which he then published under the title, *Les Motifs de la conversion.*[1] In the dedication of this book Gueudeville claims he made his speech at the request of the church authorities. It is only fitting, he says, that he should offer them this work as a small token of his gratitude. However small it is as a token, it is quite lengthy for an oration, and could not reasonably have been delivered in under an hour and a half. While it is true that sermons of this length were not uncommon in the seventeenth century it is not my impression that such discourses were a requirement of acceptance into the Church. Perhaps Gueudeville was invited to make some statement which, on publication, he then augmented and embellished with a variety of digressions, a practice frequently employed by pastors who published their sermons.

According to the title-page, the work was published "Aux dépens de l'auteur", but in the dedication Gueudeville makes reference to this poverty:

Je suis ravi d'avoir trouvé cette occasion pour rendre justice à votre charité, et pour la rendre aussi publique que vous tâchez de la tenir secrète. Quand ma pauvreté ne me serait pas glorieuse je ne la confesserais pas moins, et j'ai tant de joie d'avoir trouvé en vous les vrais successeurs des premiers Chrétiens, que j'aurais quelque espèce de chagrin si une fortune plus heureuse m'avait empêché de l'éprouver.

It is doubtful, therefore, that Gueudeville would have been able to defray the costs of publication, and highly unlikely that the Church would have supplied funds for such a venture. Probably he gave the text to a publisher who printed a limited quantity, using the proceeds of his sales to cover the costs of publication. It is also possible that, since this type of work was quite popular among the refugee communities, the publisher took a chance on recovering his expenses on the understanding that, if any loss were incurred, Gueudeville would make up the deficiency.

The oration itself is undistinguished but of great interest for the study of the man and his work since it constitutes the first of his attacks on the Catholic church, attacks that will be one of the principal features of his writings throughout his life. It is also worthy of note because it gives no hint of

11

Gueudeville's later rejection of all religions not based on reason alone. Obviously Gueudeville, at this critical stage of his life, had to speak and act as if he were a devout Calvinist. The problem, as we have seen, is to know whether he really was, in 1689, a true believer, or whether he was simply an opportunist. What is not to be doubted is his detestation of Catholicism in all its aspects. In the dedication he refers to the Roman Church which, unlike the Walloon Churches, "fait gloire de se multiplier pas les amorces et par la violence, et qui, bien plus jalouse de sa propre gloire que de celle de Dieu, se soucie fort peu du salut de ses sujets pourvu qu'elle en grossisse le nombre."[2]

The theme is taken from chapter 12, verse 36, of Saint John: "Tandis que vous avez la lumière, croyez en la lumière, afin que vous soyez des enfants de lumière." After speaking of the advantages of light as a physical entity Gueudeville turns to a consideration of the benefits conferred by the light of grace, and relates how God opened his eyes to the true religion. Three things made him renounce Catholicism:

J'ai reconnu qu'elle n'a pas la lumière dans ce qu'elle croit; j'ai reconnu qu'elle ne croit pas à la lumière qu'elle a; et enfin j'ai reconnu que ses enfants ne sont point enfants de lumière. L'Eglise Romaine n'a point la lumière dans ce qu'elle croit, vous le verrez pas la fausseté de ses dogmes. Elle ne croit point à la lumière qu'elle a, vous en jugerez par la manière dont cile traite la parole de Dieu. Et enfin, ses enfants sont de ténèbres puisque son culte étant profane, et n'étant point la véritable Eglise, elle ne peut produire des enfants de lumière (p. 7).

Before his eyes were opened, Gueudeville saw only that there were two religions, each accusing the other of schism and heresy. The method of their attacks was, however, different. One side resorted to force and violence while the other relied "sur son bon droit et sur ses raisons." He knew there could be only one true church, one source of light, but did not know which route to follow. His birth and education, the authority and grandeur of the Catholic religion, all conspired to keep him a Catholic, but he began to try to view things objectively until, eventually, "cette Eglise me parut comme un abîme dont la face était couverte de ténèbres." In order to illustrate this statement Gueudeville elects to consider two doctrines of the Church: "la Transsubstantiation et la justification par les oeuvres":

Le Seigneur a dit, "Ceci est mon corps, et ceci est mon sang." Voilà l'Achille, le bouclier et le retranchement de ceux de Rome. Voilà ce grand sujet pourquoi l'on a dressé tant de gibets, allumé tant de feux, fait couler des fleuves de sang, massacré un si grand nombre de personnes, commis tant de violences et de perifidies. Voilà le grand sujet pourquoi, dans ces malheureux jours, une patrie encore plus malheureuse, a reçu une triste et terrible secousse qu'elle semblait n'avoir pas lieu de craindre. Patrie qui est devenue à ses enfants pire que les cachots et que les prisons, Patrie qui a eu la douleur de se voir abandonnée par la plus saine et la plus fidèle portion des siens. Mais Patrie qui, bien loin de songer sérieusement à guérir la plaie et à réparer la brèche qu'elle s'est faite, aime mieux suivre son funeste penchant. . . (pp. 14—15).

Gueudeville reminds the congregation of the various interpretations of the biblical quotation, adds some thoughts of his own, and concludes that the bread and wine are but symbolic representations of the divinity.

He then passes to a discussion of the Catholic belief that good deeds contribute to the achievement of salvation. He regards this as unmitigated arrogance and an insult to the divine power. As if God would permit man to participate in the granting of grace!:

Voyez, mes frères, dans quel abîme d'impiété l'on se précipilé quand on a fermé une fois les yeux à la bonne lumière. Que le démon fait bien son compte avec cette orgueilleuse doctrine! Il a introduit la Transsubstantiation pour abolir le culte du vrai Dieu, et il a institué le mérite pour détruire sa bonté; il combat l'amour divin par l'amour propre, en flattant ce dernier d'un pouvoir que nous n'avons pas (pp. 39—40).

In the true Church we were ever conscious of our sins, and we know that while grace can mitigate the evil of our ways it can never endow us with merit. Good works are implicit in salvation, but they accompany it and do not precede it. They are the sign and not the cause of it. Our salvation is in Jesus and not in ourselves. This ends the first part of Gueudeville's demonstration, namely, that the Roman Church "n'a point de lumière dans ce qu'elle croit."

He now goes on to show that "cette Eglise ne croit point à la lumière qu'elle a." He does this by arguing that Catholics pay little attention to the word of God, which is another way of saying the light of God, by which we know and love Him. The word of God is the source of all truth. Catholics claim, however, that the word of God is too obscure to serve as a guide, that it is insufficient to guarantee salvation, and that it is not the highest authority:

Non, mes frères, on ne vous en impose point, et l'on n'a nul dessein de vous aigrir ni de vous envenimer contre les Chrétiens de Rome; mais seulement de vous précautionner contre leurs erreurs. Quand on vous dit que la parole de Dieu est suspecte à cette Eglise. . . la chose n'est que trop certaine; et quand Dieu n'aurait parlé que pour nous tendre des pièges, et que pour nous couvrir la face des abîmes et des précipices qu'il aurait résolu de nous cacher pour nous y précipiter plus aisément, il est certain qu'on ne pourrait pas lire sa parole avec plus de circonspection qu'on le fait dans cette Eglise (pp. 48—49).

It is a contradiction in terms to say that God, the source of all light, is obscure. The Catholics argue that the obscurity comes not from God but from the weakness and limitations of the human mind. But this is a ridiculous argument because God's commandments are clear and simple and accessible to all. The word of God is obscure only to those who do not want to see clearly. The Holy

Scriptures contain all we need to know for our salvation, and we require no arbiters or intermediaries to help us achieve it. We are not in the hands of men but of God. The Roman Church, however, claims to be the sole and infallible interpreter of the Scriptures:

C'est ainsi, Seigneur, que les hommes se font un plaisir d'être tes juges. C'est ainsi que ta parole est accoutumée à comparaître devant leurs tribunaux, et à subir leurs sentences et leurs arrêts (pp. 60—61).

But from where and from whom do these so-called judges derive their wisdom and authority? The Scriptures are full of examples of false prophets, of men who claimed to be divinely inspired but who were simply charlatans. Even in the case of the genuine messengers of God there is no mention of infallibility. If these judges do not derive their authority from God they must find it in the Scriptures which they interpret in such a way as to reinforce their false claims to infallibility. On this basis they profess to damn all those who do not agree with their interpretation, and who wish to read the Scriptures for themselves and in their own way:

N'est-il pas étrange que des gens qui, pour la plupart, nagent dans le plaisir sensuel et regorgent des délices du monde; qui ne sont pasteurs que pour tondre et pour dégraisser un troupeau, et qui n'estiment leur prétendue vocation qu'autant qu'elle les fait de grands seigneurs, n'est-il pas, dis-je, étrange que ces gens s'attribuent sur les âmes un droit que les Apôtres ne connaissaient point. . . (pp. 68—69).

How fortunate we are and how different from the Christians of Rome. They inhabit a world of darkness and fear while we live in light and joy. They gather only brambles and thorns while we pick flowers and fruit. They find in their path only scruples and worries while we find peace and pleasure. They speak only to men but we speak directly to God. Here ends the second part of Gueudeville's demonstration which has shown that "l'Eglise Romaine ne croit point à la lumière qu'elle a."

He now turns to the third and final argument, that "l'Eglise Romaine ne produit point des enfants de lumière." If we go out at night it is dark and we cannot see. If we shut out all the light at midday we are in the same situation as at night. In the first case the light is too far away to be of use, and in the second case we have put ourselves in a place where light cannot penetrate. The Catholic Church is in the latter situation because God is too far away from the Church as a result of its profane and idolatrous cult, and because, not being the true Church, it is not a suitable place for illumination. We are commanded to worship only God and no other. This is why we are forbidden all graven images or other symbols, for fear that the common people may come to mistake the representation for the reality. The Roman Church, however, disregards this fundamental commandment, and fills its cult with all kinds of irrelevant and profane rituals and ceremonials. Our hearts are wholly devoted to God to whom we owe all our love. This love cannot be divided. In the Roman Church, however, the adoration is given not to God but to men and to objects:

Cet homme qu'on y adore comme s'il était Dieu, et qui est ordinairement si corrompu dans ses moeurs qu'on le regarde comme un prodige et comme une merveille quand il l'est un peu moins que les autres, tel qu'est celui qui règne aujourd'hui,[3] a-t-il un grand crédit, auprès de Dieu? Est-ce ce bois, cette pierre, ce métal et toutes ces matières inanimées devant lesquelles on est assez fou de répandre son corps et son âme?. . . Entrez dans les temples de cette communion, vous n'y entendrez presque parler que des saints. Si l'on y chante c'est l'office d'un saint; si l'on y prêche c'est l'éloge d'un saint; si l'on y dit la messe c'est en l'honneur d'un saint. . . Quelles extravagances ne commet-on point autour de leurs images? On les pare comme des poupées, on leur fleurit la tête et les mains, on brûle de la cire entre leurs orteils, on les racle et on en emporte la poussière comme si chaque grain valait une pierre précieuse. . . Que dirai-je de ces présents dont on les accable? Pour peu qu'un saint se mêle de miracles il est hors de pair, et son image. . . devient comme une boutique de foire. . . Mais c'est grand dommage que ces pauvres statues n'aient besoin de rien. . . Ne croyez pas pourtant qu'elles soient toujours insensibles à tant de bienfaits. Non, non; elles suspendent quelquefois leur gravité. On les a vu rire, baisser la tête, avancer la main, dire des douceurs. . . (pp. 81–85)

What has all this to do with the worship of God? What kind of a God would pay attention to such trivialities and such nonsense that transgress the fundamental laws? What kind of religion is this that so imposes on the weakness and ignorance of the masses, not only by appealing to their idolatrous and superstitious tendencies but by conducting services in a language they do not understand, thus forcing them to depend entirely for their prayers on the priests?

Since there is only one God there can be only one Church. The Pope claims to be the head of the only true Church. What sort of man is the Pope? He calls himself the servant of servants but acts like the master of masters. He says he is the vicar and lieutenant of one whose kingdom is not of this world, but he claims sovereign power over all the other earthly powers. He glories in being the successor of a poor man, and he is one of the richest monarchs in Europe. He says his sole concern is with matters of salvation, and he is actively involved in every temporal affair. He claims to act on behalf of the prince of peace, yet no one is more bellicose. He says he is infallible, but will not permit any scrutiny of his doctrine. He is just a man who behaves like God. The whole edifice of the papacy is founded on the injunction to Saint Peter to build the Church, an injunction that has been used to justify everything that has been done. What resemblance is there between the Popes and Saint Peter?

. . . à combien d'entre eux, principalement depuis sept ou huit siècles, pourra-t-on dire sans mentir ou se tromper, Tu es Pierre? Sera-ce à des incestueux, à des parricides, à des empoisonneurs, à des fourbes, à des hypocrites, à des athées, à des libertins consommés? Ce ne sont point des injures que je substitue en la place de la raison, ce sont choses de fait... Pierre avait-il un vaste et riche domaine, de magnifiques palais, des ameublements superbes, une grosse épargne, grand nombre d'officiers, des troupes de soldats? Si Pierre était un chef c'était un chef de douceur et non pas un tyran. Il cherchait à gagner les coeurs, il ne les violentait pas. Il persuadait les esprits, il ne leur ôtait pas les moyens de se persuader. Il était altéré du salut des âmes, il ne respirait pas le sang humain. Il offrait la vie à ceux qui la voulaient, mais il ne procurait le bannissement ni la mort à personne (pp. 92–93)

The successors of Peter, instead of following in his footsteps, have taken a path in entirely the opposite direction, and, therefore, have no right to use the Scripture as a justification for their actions, and to pose as the inheritors of the true faith. The real and only cornerstone of the Church is Jesus Christ from whom all the apostles derived their wisdom and authority. A Church built on any other formation cannot be the true Church.

Gueudeville ends his homily on a personal note by saying how fortunate he is to have discovered the true Church, and how grateful he is for being accepted into it. He closes with a prayer in which he thanks God for all his mercies, for bringing light to the world, and for rescuing him from the darkness. He regrets sincerely all his sins, and hopes they will be forgiven.

As I have suggested, Gueudeville probably never gave this oration. But if he did, and if he delivered it with the appropriate modulations and cadences, it would have made a profound impression on a congregation of whom may had suffered personally at the hands of the French "inquisition." In spite of the fact that Gueudeville was celebrating his conversion it must have seemed to many that he had always been one of them, that he, too, had been persecuted because of his faith, rather than because of the lack of it. At all events, once he was accepted into the Church Gueudeville behaved as if he were a Huguenot like the others, and, in later life, would refer to himself as such.[4]

In his address are all the elements of his later, relentless attacks on Catholicism. The energy, the biting satire, the questionable taste, these dominant characteristics of his style are all here in embryo. There is no hint that he was insincere in his conversion to Calvinism but, in the light of his later pronouncements on metaphysical questions, and considering he was a man "[qui] ne hait pas les plaisirs", one finds it hard to believe he could have wholeheartedly embraced this new-found religion.

If Gueudeville hoped the publication of his discourse would provide him an entrée into the world of letters he was destined to be disappointed. It was not until ten years later, when he embarked on his journalistic career, that he once again had the pleasure of seeing his ideas in print. After that, and until his death, hardly a year would pass without the publication of some work from his pen, although, in several cases, he was obliged to forego the pleasure of seeing his name on the title-page.

III. L'ESPRIT DES COURS DE L'EUROPE

When Gueudeville moved from Rotterdam to The Hague, in May 1699, he must already have been negotiating with the publishers for some time, since the following month saw the first issue of a new monthly political periodical, *L'Esprit des cours de l'Europe*[1] in which, until 1710, Gueudeville would anonymously wage a relentless battle against France and the Pope, and through which he would achieve considerable notoriety as a polemicist, satirist, and as a generally scurrilous individual who delighted in the irreverent and the obscene.

If it seems surprising that Gueudeville should so suddenly have passed from the status of a lowly teacher of Latin to that of author and editor of a journal, we should remember that, in those days, journalism was in its infancy, and that its products, though popular, enjoyed little prestige. Moreover, most of the early periodicals in Holland were directed by French Huguenots who used the medium to carry on the war against Louis XIV.[2]

In a number of recent articles and books, writers have drawn attention to the importance of the monthly political periodicals that flourished in Europe towards the end of the seventeenth century and the first half of the eighteenth.[3] Their popularity, diffusion and influence were enormous, and, as one critic has pointed out, those published in the Dutch republic were the most sought after:

In England and in Ireland, periodicals existed which were mere compilations drawn from Dutch originals. In Spain and Italy... the Dutch periodical had no rivals during the first half of the eighteenth century... Even in Germany... the supremacy of Dutch periodicals appears to have been unassailable, at least in the first half of the eighteenth century.[4]

But, in spite of the acknowledged importance of these political journals, most of them have not been the object of any detailed study, and little is known of their background and development.

When *L'Esprit des cours de l'Europe* first appeared it was published jointly by Etienne Foulque and by François and Jonas L'Honoré.[5] The expression, "les cours de l'Europe" was a conventional one that figured in the titles of many works.[6] The format of the periodical was also based on accepted practice:

... très vite s'établissent de véritables règles pour le nouveau genre: chaque relation doit suivre un ordre chronologique et géographique strict. Les règles

17

exigent aussi une certaine clarté et un traitement systématique des sujets. C'est pour cela qu'on traite seulement d'un pays à la fois... suivant de préférence le même ordre. On peut commencer par Rome ou par la France, mais c'est toujours la France qui se taille la part du lion et le plus grand nombre de pages.[7]

The preface, in which Gueudeville commented on the demand for such periodicals: "La politique est le grand goût du temps. C'est la matière à la mode", and solemnly promised "de ne jamais blesser la bienséance et de ne jamais envisager personne dans la satire", was equally conventional.[8]

In the second issue, in July, it was announced that the periodical would be published on the 15th of each month.[9] The August issue contained a new preface in which it was announced that the first two months had been used to test public reaction. The author now undertook to deal with the most important events, and invited readers to write to him. It is not clear what occasioned this second start at such an early stage. Perhaps it was simply a promotional device, perhaps a contract had now been signed, or perhaps Gueudeville had established some connections on whom he could rely for a steady source of information. A comparison of the subsequent issues with those of June and July, however, reveals no marked differences in content or style.

The demand for L'Esprit des cours must have grown fairly rapidly since, by November 1699 at the latest, a pirated edition appeared on the market.[10] The journal appeared regularly until the issue of April 1701 in which Gueudeville made some characteristically sarcastic observations on Louis XIV's declaration, of March 12, of a general capitation tax.[11] What happened next is not entirely clear but, according to Guillaume de Lamberty,[12] these comments offended the French envoy, the count de Briord, who sent his equerry to Gueudeville with instructions to assault him, but the equerry was prevented from doing so by Gueudeville's neighbours. Whereupon the count asked the States-General to suspend publication of the periodical. In order to circumvent this censorship it was continued without cessation under a new name, Nouvelles des cours de l'Europe.[13]

Lamberty's account seems somewhat fanciful and, furthermore, was written long after the event. Even if Briord did make the initial representations to the States-General, it was the ambassador d'Avaux who took charge of the matter. In a letter to secretary Torcy, dated April 14 1701, d'Avaux explained that he was doing his best to have the periodical suppressed without any publicity that would involve French prestige. On May 12 he wrote again to say that the Grand Pensionary, Heinsius, had acceded to his request.[14] The French were obviously unaware that the periodical was continuing under a new name since, on October 19 1701, the count de Pontchartrain wrote to d'Argenson, Lieutenant-General of police, " Je parlerai à M. d'Avaux sur les expédients qu'on pourrait prendre pour empêcher qu'on ne recommence d'imprimer en Hollande l'Esprit des cours et les autres mauvais livres dont l'impression est si fréquente en ce pays-là."[15] The fact that Gueudeville was allowed to continue his periodical by this elementary piece of subterfuge is an indication of the value placed by the Dutch authorities on such organs of propaganda.

The May issue came out under three different title-pages, all bearing the new title, one with the name Etienne Foulque, another with François L'Honoré, and another with "Imprimé pour l'auteur." In June there were again three title-pages but this time, the one bearing the name of François L'Honoré also carried the old title, *L'Esprit des cours de l'Europe*. I am unable to explain this anomaly. It is just possible that the publishers feared that readers would not recognize the periodical under its new name, and took the risk, probably small, of reminding them of its continued existence.[16] According to Bayle, Lamberty himself took over the periodical for three months after the d'Avaux complaint, but I have been unable to find any evidence to support this. The style and content of the periodical seem unchanged during this period, although the articles on France are reduced and quite innocuous.

No doubt the news of the journal's "suppression" had provided a healthy stimulus to sales, since in the issue of May 1702 it was announced (with pride or chagrin, it is not always easy to tell) that a very inferior pirating of the periodical had been going on for some months in Liège.[17] In October 1702 it was announced that, due to the author's indisposition, the periodical would be published on the first of the month instead of the fifteenth. On October 19 1703, Etienne Foulque sold his copyright for 250 guilders, and 8400 copies for 630 guilders, to the brothers L'Honoré.[18] Towards the end of that year, François L'Honoré moved to Amsterdam where he set up in business with the Châtelain family into which he married.[19] From November, the periodical reverted to its original title, and was published solely under the name of Jonas L'Honoré who, on December 31 1704, entered into a limited partnership with T. Johnson of The Hague.[20] This agreement was terminated on October 9 1705, about two weeks before Jonas L'Honoré declared bankruptcy.[21]

It is not clear why Jonas L'Honoré went bankrupt or to what extent the bankruptcy is to be attributed to his management of *L'Esprit*. According to the rival and hostile author of *La Clef du Cabinet des princes de l'Europe*, Jonas L'Honoré simply overestimated the periodical's popularity:

S'il en eût débité cinq à six milles exemplaires chaque mois, comme fait l'imprimeur de *la Clef du Cabinet*, il ne se serait pas vu exposé à cette faillite, d'autant mieux que son profit n'aurait pas été diminué par les frais considér-ables qu'on est obligé de faire pour l'entretien des correspondances étrangères, lui qui ne travaille que sur les matériaux de sa féconde imagination.[22]

From October 1705, title-pages no longer bear the publisher's name, and only the words "Imprimé pour l'auteur" appear. However, at the end of the October issue, it was announced that the periodical would in future be published in Amsterdam by François L'Honoré. In the January 1706 issue it was announced that the periodical would be available from François L'Honoré on the 25th of each month and on the 28th at all other Dutch booksellers.

It is possible that, when François L'Honoré took over the journal, sales had declined. It also seems likely that there were new financial arrangements that were less advantageous to Gueudeville. At least this would explain Gueudeville's request to the States-General for 200 guilders on the ground that he was desperately poor.[23] Perhaps a further indication of declining sales is to be found in the announcement in the December issue that, beginning in January 1707, the periodical would be published every four months instead of monthly.[24] And this was how the periodical was published until the issue of September-December 1710 after which, with no prior warning, it ceased publication.

We can only speculate as to why publication stopped when it did. The most obvious and likely explanation is that the publisher decided to terminate the periodical because it was no longer a paying proposition. It is possible, however, that the decision was Gueudeville's. There is, as we shall see, some evidence that he never really felt comfortable in his role as journalist and that, as the years went by, he became increasingly dissatisfied with his position.

The situation of a journalist at this time was a somewhat unenviable one. Journalists were mostly from the lower end of the social scale, and they were generally poor and poorly paid.[25] Some of them were knowledgeable about politics and had useful connections, but many conformed more to La Barre de Beaumarchais' description: "A peine savent-ils qu'il y a en Angleterre un parlement, ou s'ils le savent, ils en jugent sur le pied du parlement de Rennes, de Bordeaux, ou de Toulouse; aussi faut-il leur rendre justice, ils se mêlent peu de cette étude et font sagement."[26]

The greatest problem, especially in wartime, related to the obtaining of reliable and accurate information. The problem was most acute for those who published a gazette, two or three times a week. But even for the more leisurely monthly periodicals there was a dearth of reliable sources. While it is true that a journalist working in The Hague was close to the centre of an elaborate network of information gathering under the direction of Heinsius and his aides, and that prominent Huguenots such as Jurieu, for example, and some journalists themselves, were in constant touch with their colleagues in France, Switzerland, and elsewhere,[27] not all journalists were privy to this secret information, and the Dutch authorities gave to the press only such information as would further the Allied cause. Information from professional agents had to be paid for, and not every publisher or editor could afford this luxury, especially when the news obtained by these means often turned out to be incorrect.[28]

Not that it was particularly difficult for the author of a monthly political periodical to fill his columns. All he had to do was copy what was available in the gazettes, and then elaborate by means of commentaries.[29] The problem was that he felt himself to be neither a purveyor of news, since the news he dealt with was already stale, nor a historian, since there was not sufficient time or distance from the events to see them objectively. All the editors of monthly political periodicals felt the untenability of their position, but none more keenly than Gueudeville who, because of his essentially sceptical nature, baulked at relaying the half-truths and falsehoods that constituted the world of journalism, especially during the War of the Spanish Succession.[30]

Gueudeville was much influenced in his attitude by Pierre Bayle who was journalism's severest critic, and he seems to have taken to heart Bayle's call for "un honnête homme":

On ne saurait assez blâmer l'institution de la gazette, de la façon qu'on la compose présentement. C'est le fléau et la peste de l'histoire. Car ceux qui en voudront composer une, d'ici à cent ans, s'imagineront que pour y procéder en bonne conscience, il faudra consulter les auteurs contemporains, comme ceux qui ont eu la plus de facilité pour s'instruire du vrai de la chose. Mais que sont, je vous prie, les auteurs contemporains, sinon des rhapsodeurs et des compilateurs de la gazette? ou bien, y a-t-il un honnête homme, soit en Hollande, soit en France, qui voulût présentement se hasarder d'écrire du combat de Senef autrement qu'ont fait les Gazettes?[31]

Although Gueudeville very much wanted to make his periodical an accurate journal of record, although he endlessly proclaimed his dedication to truth, he soon found it impossible to live up to these ideals, often because he had no information, sometimes because the information was false or contradictory,[32] and sometimes because the information he had he was not permitted to publish. There is some evidence, as we shall see, that it was this last consideration that contributed to the journal's demise.

Gueudeville had already had some hint of the power of authority during the d'Avaux "affair" in 1701, for, although he had been allowed to continue the periodical under another name, he had probably been ordered to moderate his tone:

Quel devrait être l'unique but de l'impression, cet art merveilleux par lequel un seul homme communique à tant d'autres ses plus intimes pensées? . . .Dévoiler la vérité, la montrer toute nue à ceux qui ne la connaissent pas; la représenter telle qu'elle est à ceux qui ont déjà le bonheur de la connaître. . . Si ce n'est pas faire une chute trop ridicule que d'appliquer à un fantôme d'auteur, tel que je suis, cette haute maxime dont l'usage manque à tant d'illustres têtes, j'avouerai ingénuement que toute mon ambition serait de la mettre en pratique. Non, je ne souhaiterais plus que de pouvoir raisonner ces Nouvelles des cours avec un désintéressement épuré de toute prévention. . . je voudrais encore, hélas que ne l'est-il permis, mesurer tous les faits à la règle de la pure justice, et peser chaque chose au poids de l'équité. Mais puisque la vérité est persécutée jusque dans son asile il faut céder au torrent et ne point passer les bornes que la bienséance et l'autorité prescrivent à la liberté de dire ce qu'on pense. (October 1701, 686–689)

Although Gueudeville firmly believed it was more important to tell the truth than support a cause, in 1703 he had not yet found any conflict between his moral principles and the obligation to be an organ of propaganda:

Il est d'un devoir capital de faire des voeux pour le parti dans lequel on se trouve engagé. Grâce à Dieu je n'ai rien à me reprocher là-dessus, et personne ne souhaite avec plus d'ardeur que moi la prospérité des incomparables souverains à l'abri desquels je me procure, à la pointe d'une faible plume, un nécessaire des plus modiques. Mais j'aime la vérité par dessus tout, et j'en fais le plus doux fruit de cette liberté dont j'ai le bonheur de jouir dans la plus agréable, et la plus humaine république qui soit sur la terre. Je me fais donc une loi inviolable d'alléguer le pour et le contre sur tous les événements. (August-September 1703, 193)

But anyone who consistently places truth above the cause is bound eventually to find himself in conflict with the authorities. In what specific ways Gueudeville gave offence I am unable to say. It is noticeable that he often refused to take sides on certain issues, and he also frequently dwelt on enemy victories instead of glossing them over in the manner of some journalists.[33] Perhaps it was his hints at dissension in the allied ranks, caused by the continual vetoing of Marlborough's campaign plans, that got Gueudeville into trouble.[34] Whatever the reasons, it is clear that his periodical was subject to censorship:

L'expérience fait voir que les narrateurs les plus favorables au parti sont les plus recherchés, et les plus au goût du souverain qui quelquefois fait pleuvoir sur eux des récompenses et des gratifications. Les nouvellistes qui s'attachent scrupuleusement au vrai n'y trouvent pas leur compte; on les rejette, on fronce le sourcil contre eux, on les soupçonne de penchant pour l'ennemi, et même de quelque chose de plus mauvais dès qu'ils annoncent un fait chagrinant avec toutes les circonstances dont il est revêtu. Croyez-moi, en toutes sortes de genres les hommes aiment qu'on les trompe agréablement; et les maîtres des hommes savent bien dans le maniement d'un état mettre à profit cette disposition naturelle des sujets. Quand le temps a montré que l'événement est beaucoup moins bon, ou beaucoup plus mauvais qu'on ne l'avait cru, on se fâche alors contre les Stratoclès de profession, contre les historiens à semaine ou à mois, qui ont leurs raisons pour dire toujours trop ou trop peu; mais on n'en revient pas moins à ces doux imposteurs; et on ne saurait s'empêcher de les croire plus que les écrivains sincères, par la seule raison qu'ils vous disent ce que vous souhaitez. (January–April 1709, 111–113)

It is worth remembering that, far from receiving any "récompenses" or "gratifications," Gueudeville, for reasons unstated, had been refused 200 guilders by the States-General.

There is also some evidence that is was not simply the items Gueudeville wanted to publish that were a source of concern but also his mode of expression. Gueudeville's style was very forceful and satirical. What he referred to as his "badinage" others found to be vicious and in the worst possible taste.[35] Perhaps he was required to do a certain amount of rewriting before his articles were considered acceptable. There is certainly some suggestion of difficulties with the publisher:

Le but de notre confraternité n'est ni de vous apprendre sûrement ce qui se passe, ni de raisonner juste; c'est de vivre avec le libraire, et de tâcher, à quoi je n'ai pu encore réussir, que le libraire vive avec nous. Ainsi, quand nous ne vous donnons que des nouvelles de forge, et que des commentaires en l'air, vous ne sauriez en bonne conscience nous rien reprocher; nous sommes dans notre chemin une fois, et nous suivons le maître statut de notre ordre... (January— April 1709, 54)

But perhaps the above passage simply refers to financial difficulties between Gueudeville and L'Honoré.

Gueudeville, then, finding himself in an impossible situation, in a world where truth was of little consequence, took refuge in a kind of jocular scepticism. By this approach he managed to distance himself from his untenable position. He solved the problem of being in the contradictory situation of wanting to tell the truth, and, for a variety of reasons, being unable to do so, by indulging in contradictions. Sometimes, as we have seen, he would speak of the journalist's responsibility to history, to accurate documentation, at other times he ridiculed this obligation.[36] Sometimes he celebrated the freedom of the press, and sometimes, as already noted, he complained of the restrictions.[37] One of his last statements about the periodical is characteristic of his frivolous yet honest approach:

On s'est moqué plusieurs fois de mon opuscule; j'ai toujours été du sentiment de mes censeurs; mais jamais ils n'ont été plus de mon goût que lorsqu'ils ont plaisanté mon titre ou plutôt celui des libraires, car il n'est assurément pas le mien. En effet, rien n'est plus risible que de voir nommer *L'Esprit des cours de l'Europe* un tissu de nouvelles publiques, presque toutes rouillées et assez assaisonnées de réflexions, de tirades, et de citations la plupart forcées, qui fatiguent le lecteur sans lui rien apprendre. (January — April 1708, 21)

Within the approximately fourteen thousand pages of Gueudeville's periodical there is a great variety of material. What he describes as "un tissu de nouvelles publiques" includes not only reports and comments on the major events of the day, supported by such official documents as diplomatic correspondence, terms of treaties, capitulations, proceedings of the English parliament, lists of those killed in battle, maps, etc., [38] but also a multitude of digressions on all sorts of subjects from women's fashions and hair styles, women in general, gambling, doctors and the art of medicine, interspersed with reflections on such questions as whether the earth belongs to all, whether war can ever be justified, the nature and significance of death, and so on.[29] All the material in the periodical is constantly supported by references to and quotations from classical and other sources, with Bayle's *Dictionnaire historique* being the chief source of reference.[40] Many of the events in the wars of the day are found by Gueudeville to have a parallel in the history of Greece or Rome, or in the struggles for political and religious power that developed during the Renaissance.[41]

The two dominant preoccupations of Gueudeville's periodical are politics and religion, which, in Gueudeville's mind, are "liées. . . par une enchaînure si étroite" that it is almost impossible to consider them separately:

De tout temps les princes n'ont employé la religion qu'autant qu'elle a accommodé leurs affaires; le culte divin est trop utile pour négliger de s'en servir; c'est par là qu'ils s'attirent le plus la vénération du peuple, qu'ils contiennent les sujets dans l'obéissance, qu'ils les animent contre l'ennemi; en un mot, la religion est un moyen très efficace en la main du prince pour enchaîner la liberté au dedans, et pour s'agrandir au dehors; aussi les souverains en sont-ils grands zélateurs tant qu'ils y trouvent honneur et profit.[42]

When the interests of religion conflict with those of politics, it is the temporal power that usually prevails.

Although all religions are fundamentally divisive, so that it is better for a state to have good citizens than defenders of the faith[43] (as Bayle had suggested in his remarks about a community of atheists), the religion that Gueudeville held most responsible for all the troubles in the world was the Catholic religion embodied in the person of the Pope. While Gueudeville attacks the Catholic religion and its representatives in many articles, and at the slightest or with no provocation, it is particularly in his articles on Rome that he concentrates his invective. Indeed, there is good evidence that it was these articles, more than any other, that established the notoriety of the periodical:

Je sais que mes articles de la cour de Rome ne sont pas du goût de bien des gens; les Catholiques en sont scandalisés jusqu'à s'en faire un cas de conscience et de confessional, et même certain genre de Protestants radoucis, et qui font profession de n'aimer pas la fronde, s'en lassent et s'en rebutent. (October 1705, 447)

It should be noted, of course, that because Gueudeville had been a monk for so many years he felt himself more qualified and competent to comment in this sphere than in any other.

However much offence Gueudeville's anti-Catholic diatribes gave, it appears that censorship was not applied in this area, since he wrote that "s'il m'était permis de parler aussi librement des autres cours que de celle de Rome, mon livre tiendrait sa promesse, du moins ne serait-il pas si charlatan ni si menteur."[44] Thus he attacked everything to do with Catholicism — popes, cardinals, monks, nuns, and especially the Jesuits, all of whom were accused of hypocrisy, lechery, cruelty, in the service of a gigantic fraud. Gueudeville was particularly pleased whenever he detected divisions within the Church, and so he frequently reported, with delight, such items as the censure of Fénelon for his espousal of quietism, and the condemnation of the Jesuit missionaries in China.[45]

Gueudeville defended his attacks on the grounds that the Pope was the Protestants' greatest enemy:

On m'a reproché que mon avant-garde était ordinairement composé de calomnies contre les Papes: ce sont, au sentiment de mon plus redoutable adversaire. . . des armes rouillées qui ne sont plus d'usage. . . enfin ces gazettes, aussi surannées qu'elles sont scandaleuses, font mal au coeur et donnent du dégoût aux honnêtes gens de l'une et de l'autre communion. . . Sur quoi obliger un Protestant à laisser le Papat en repos? L'évêque de Rome a-t-il donc changé d'esprit et de sentiment? A-t-il rien diminué de ses prétentions? Est-il moins notre persécuteur, moins notre ennemi déclaré? Quoi? il sera permis à ces saints pères d'être alertes contre notre liberté de conscience, d'employer les caresses et les supplices pour nous rappeler dans leurs chaînes, de nous damner tous sans miséricorde si nous ne retournons sous leur joug, et l'on nous fera un crime de railler ces usurpateurs. . .? (December 1705, 583)

Although Gueudeville expressed some sympathy for the Pope's difficult position as mediator between the Habsburg and Bourbon claims to Spain and its possessions, especially in Italy, he mistrusted the Pope's declarations of neutrality, and suspected him of playing off one side against the other in a characteristically jesuitical manner:

[Le pape] se partage entre la religion et la politique, mais celle-ci l'embarrasse beaucoup plus que l'autre. Quelque forte que puisse être l'ardeur de son zèle il n'a rien à craindre pour sa souveraineté dans ce culte. . . l'ignorance, la superstition, la barbarie, véritables appuis de son autorité sans bornes, sont trop enracinées dans le monde pour en sortir si tôt. . . Il n'en va pas ainsi de la souveraineté temporelle de cette fausse divinité à deux visages, de ce Janus du Christianisme. Un Pape s'alarme dès qu'il voit la guerre à sa porte, et il a raison . . . Ainsi voyons-nous le Pontife. . . beaucoup plus occupé à pacifier l'Italie qu'à réformer les abus dont sa commune est toute défigurée. (April 1701, 421)

The Pope was threatened by the fighting between French and Imperial troops in Italy and, according to Gueudeville, he secretly favoured the claims of France and Spain (June 1702, 594; December 1703, 549). In the early stages of the war, for example, when Cardinal Grimani asked the Pope to allow the Germans to make their winter quarters in Ferrara, he refused on the grounds that this would be a violation of his neutrality (October 1702, 360). When the tide turned, however, he was obliged to change his tactics. In 1706, when Prince Eugène demanded passage through papal territories, the Pope acquiesced (December 1706, 609). Gueudeville's attitude towards the Pope's strategy is perhaps best summed up in a long reflection of somewhat dubious and contorted logic, in the issue of May—August 1708:

Je suppose que les cours de Vienne et de Barcelone, déjà justement irritées contre celle de Rome, ont fait de nouvelles instances auprès de celle-ci pour l'engager à reconnaître la royauté de Charles III, du moins par rapport à la possession du royaume de Naples. . . Pourquoi Clément XI, qui voudrait persuader. . . que son coeur pontifical est vraiment neutre. . . n'accordera-t-il pas au roi Charles, ce qu'il a accordé au roi Philippe lorsque le roi Philippe était dans le cas du roi Charles?. . . Il y a une grande différence, dites-vous. Le Pape avait reconnu le droit du duc d'Anjou à la monarchie d'Espagne, et sur ce pied-là il ne pouvait pas se dispenser de le traiter en monarque. Mais le Pape n'a reconnu jusqu'à présent dans le roi Charles qu'un archiduc d'Autriche. . .

Cette objection a quelque chose d'imposant, mais elle ne séduira que ceux qui ne voudront pas l'approfondir. . . Le Saint Père. . . eut grand tort de prendre si chaudement l'affirmative pour la raison de France en reconnaissant le duc d'Anjou pour successeur légitime de Charles II. . . Je veux croire que. . . Sa Sainteté. . . ait cru de bonne foi que l'Empereur ne s'opposerait point à ce fatal testament qui coûte tant de sang à l'Europe. . . Pour avoir reconnu Philippe V. . . sans mauvaise intention contre la maison d'Autriche, en devait-il moins reconnaître la royauté de Charles III? Clément XI, s'il s'était déclaré absolument neutre entre les Espagnols. . . Autrichiens et Français, n'aurait qu'édifié les deux partis; et s'attirant leur estime et leur confiance, il se fût mis en état de travailler à la réunion par un démembrement.

Enfin, le Pape ne reconnaît point Philippe V pour roi de Naples, puisqu'il lui a refusé constamment l'investiture de ce royaume. Le Pape ne reconnaît donc pas Philippe V pour le légitime possesseur de la monarchie d'Espagne, car, s'il le reconnaissait pour tel, Sa Sainteté n'aurait pu, sans commettre une injustice visible et criante, refuser à Philippe ce que Philippe avait droit de demander. . . Ainsi, puisque le Pape. . . , par cette exception des royaumes de Naples et de Sicile, avait fait voir qu'il doutait de la validité du testament, cela ne devait-il pas l'engager à faire les choses égales, et à traiter l'archiduc comme il avait traité le duc d'Anjou? (May—August 1708, 237—246).

The Pope found himself in similar difficulties with respect to the war in the north, where Charles XII of Sweden opposed the claims of the Saxon king Augustus to the Polish throne. Charles, who supported the rival claims of Stanislaus, made it his objective to depose Augustus and put Stanislaus on the throne. In this ambition he was supported by the Cardinal Primate. At first, the Pope watched with interest but without comment. When it became evident, however, that Augustus, a convert to Catholicism, would be deposed, the Pope declared his hand in favour of Augustus, and this produced yet another minor schism in the Church. (March 1704, 277)

Gueudeville's own attitude to the northern war was mainly one of incomprehension. Not only was the news from the north slow to arrive but, when it did, it was unreliable, contradictory, incomprehensible or false.[46] In October 1700, Gueudeville regarded the war between Sweden and Poland as a relatively minor skirmish, and was hopeful that "leur désunion ne durera pas longtemps; la paix du Holstein fait espérer celle de Livonie; on se flatte que les puissances qui ont produit la première influeront efficacement pour la seconde, et quoique la médiation ne soit plus armée, l'on ne s'en promet pas moins un succès heureux." Gueudeville, like everyone else (except the victims), praised the daring and successful exploits of the Swedish king, and celebrated the victory at Narva.[47] But, when it emerged that Charles, bent on the total destruction of his real and supposed enemies, would not accept peace at any price, Gueudeville, like many others, became disenchanted:

On n'oserait dire que le roi de Suède soit aussi prêt à désarmer. Ce monarque semble encore donner beaucoup à sa vengeance et à son ressentiment. Son glorieux succès dans la guerre la lui fait goûter de plus en plus. Un héros bien persuadé de sa bonne cause ne désarme pas aisément... Les héros, cependant, sont sujets à l'illusion comme les autres; la valeur peut les aveugler; les heureux succès les trompent quelquefois... (May 1702, 557)

Although Gueudeville followed the northern campaigns, and devoted a good deal of space to them in his periodical, he felt himself to be most incompetent in this area, partly because of the information problem referred to above, but also because he was less interested, less emotionally involved in the issues at stake. Most of his long reflections on the state of affairs refer to the War of the Spanish Succession.

At the beginning of 1701, despite the events of the previous year, the death of the Spanish king and the declaration of the duke of Anjou as sole heir to the throne, Gueudeville was still hopeful that a major conflict could be avoided. It was still in Louis XIV's best interests, he argued, to keep the peace. He certainly would not want to increase the power of Spain to the detriment of France. He was helping to negotiate a settlement in the war between Poland and Sweden; if he had violated the Partition Treaty this was solely to maintain peace. In Gueudeville's view, the real threat to peace came not from France but from Austria who was determined to promote her own claims to the Spanish throne. Whether Gueudeville really was optimistic that peace could be maintained, or whether he was merely indulging in wishful thinking, it is difficult to say. But he ended his reflections on a note of caution:

.... attendons le temps; il éclaircira nos conjectures, et il développera peut-être le ridicule de nos creuses spéculations; ce qu'il y a d'indubitable, c'est qu'une couronne contestée par un puissant prince et défendue par un autre encore plus puissant, peut produire des événements extraordinaires... (January 1701, Réflexions sur l'état présent de l'Europe)

In May 1702, despite the French occupation of the Spanish Netherlands in the previous year, and the immediate threat to the United Provinces, Gueudeville still spoke of the situation as one mainly to do with reconciling the rival claims of France and Austria. The aim of the war was "d'opposer au prince que l'on craint un autre prince qui ne soit pas moins à craindre, afin qu'aucun des deux ne puisse se saisir de tout." The irony of the fact that war had not yet been officially declared was not lost on Gueudeville — "On s'assiège, on se bat, on se pille, on court les uns sur les autres, on se pirate, et cependant on observe les traités, et l'on commerce. Cette nouvelle méthode de s'entregorger de bonne amitié ne sera vraisemblablement pas de longue durée" (538). By the time war was officially declared fighting was taking place in Italy, the Netherlands and Germany, with the added complication for the allies of the Hungarian revolt against Austria.

By the middle of 1704 the enemy had won significant victories against the Emperor, and was holding its own in Italy and The Netherlands. Although Portugal had defected to the allies, and an Anglo-Dutch fleet had captured Gibraltar, the imminent collapse of the Empire seemed to herald defeat on all fronts. However, the joint forces of Marlborough, Louis of Baden and Eugène of Savoy, in a series of campaigns at Schellenberg, Donauworth and Hochstedt, turned near-defeat into a victory that seemed to change the whole course of the war:

La maison d'Autriche penchait, toute prête à tomber; et la chute de cet ancien et massif édifice aurait infailliblement écrasé la liberté de l'Europe... La jonction du maréchal de Tallard avec l'Electeur ne suffisait que trop pour faire renaître nos alarmes; le duc de Bavière lui-même revenu de son étourdissement était aussi fier qu'auparavant... et l'on fait dire à ce prince, "encore quelques jours, et je punirai l'insolence de mes ennemis"... La journée de Hochstedt ruina tous les vastes projets de ce prince... La Bavière est réduite, et le plus utile allié des deux couronnes n'est plus qu'un haut officier qui leur est à charge; les Hauts Alliés ont chassé l'ennemi d'un autre électorat; ils ont enlevé de bonnes forteresses; ils ont établi pour leurs troupes des quartiers à souhait; enfin ils ont fait tout ce qu'il leur a plu sur le Rhin, sur la Moselle, sur la Saar... (January 1705, 41—50)

But, for a variety of reasons, the allies failed to follow up their advantage, and 1705 proved to be a year of relative inactivity during which the enemy had time to regroup and rearm. Despite allied successes in the years that followed, culminating in the battle of Malplaquet, and despite peace overtures from both sides, when Gueudeville's periodical ceased publication in 1710, peace seemed as far away as ever. The last peace conference on which Gueudeville commented was that of Geertruydenberg, in the spring of 1710. When France rejected the allied proposals, Gueudeville observed ironically:

Il est de certains peuples qui ont absolument besoin de guerre pour se civiliser, pour s'enrichir, et même (ce qui est un paradoxe) pour s'humaniser. Le monarque, chargé par le droit de la naissance ou par celui des suffrages, ou par celui de l'épée, lequel on prétend (je ne sais ni ne veux savoir pourquoi) être aussi légitime que les deux autres droits... du gouvernement d'une telle nation, peut-il mieux remplir ses engagements qu'en tenant le plus qu'il lui est possible ses sujets sous les armes?... L'obligation essentielle du prince est de rendre ses sujets heureux... Sur ce principe-là... ce prince ne doit-il pas, pour l'acquit de sa conscience, s'attacher surtout à la profession de guerrier et de conquérant? Votre principe est faux, direz-vous; un monarque pacifique, pour peu qu'il sache régner, peut rendre ses sujets heureux. Je serais trop embarrassé à répondre. (May—August 1710, 284—286)

Gueudeville's reflections on the progress of the war were governed not only by his loyalty to the allied cause, his detestation of France and his hatred of Catholicism, but also by his ideas on the nature of government and politics. He subscribed to the Grotius doctrine of natural law and the social contract. His knowledge and interpretation of Grotius were probably received second hand through the writings of Bayle, Jurieu and Locke.[48] Gueudeville believed that man is "né pour être libre", that monarchy "est originairement un contrat passé entre un seul homme et toute une nation, et agréé de Dieu", and that "dans cet âge d'or les rois vivaient pour les peuples."[49] But the golden age was no more, partly because of the ambition of kings but also because of the apathy and gullibility of the people:

Jetez les yeux sur quelque état purement monarchique; on n'y connaît plus ces vains fantômes de liberté, de repos, d'abondance, d'égard et de tendresse pour les peuples. Le souverain s'empare impunément de tout, et sa volonté est le seul mobile du gouvernement. Avec tout cela les peuples sont-ils mécontents? Au contraire, ne sont-ils pas absolument dévoués au prince, enivrés de sa gloire, passionnés pour sa grandeur et pour sa prospérité personnelle, s'estimant trop heureux qu'il s'élève à leur dépens, pourvu que le bruit de sa puissance étonne l'univers, qu'ils aient la joie de pouvoir s'écrier, oh que nous avons un grand roi! (September 1703, 157)

The people, then, are "insensibles à l'esclavage. . . et pourvu qu'on ne leur reproche point leurs chaînes, ils les portent tranquillement et sont doux comme des agneaux."[50] In spite of this, however, Gueudeville, as M. Yardeni has pointed out, was not opposed to monarchy.[51] On the contrary, he considered the English system to be ideal. Indeed, if there were any defect in this system it was that parliament tended to play too great a role in matters not affecting the basic principles of the contract:

Le prince et le parlement ne sont-ils pas de même avis? Le sentiment du prince est préférable à celui du parlement pourvu qu'il ne s'agisse de rien qui puisse renverser les lois et détruire la liberté, car alors l'assemblée représentative est plus croyable que le roi. . . (January 1701, 87)

Gueudeville, therefore, was an advocate of benevolent monarchy and of the republican system as practised in the United Provinces. If he had to choose between absolute monarchy and a weak republic he would choose the former, on the grounds that absolute monarchy at least guarantees peace and security, while the latter leads to civil war (March 1706, 266).

Despite Gueudeville's detestation of absolute monarchy with its concomitant enslavement of the people, he did not, at least in theory, advocate rebellion as a solution to the problem. The only revolution of which he wholeheartedly approved was the bloodless one by which William became king of England:

Si toutes les révolutions étaient aussi peu sanguinaires et aussi heureuses que celle qui arriva le siècle dernier chez les Insulaires nos voisins, la question n'aurait plus rien pour moi de problématique... mais rien n'est plus rare qu'un tel événement, et je doute qu'en fait de politique on ait jamais vu un dessein de cette nature s'exécuter avec aussi peu de résistance et d'opposition. (March 1705, 305)

But Gueudeville's theories did not hold up against the harsh reality of the bloody rebellion in the Cévennes. He could not but approve of the Protestant uprising against the brutal persecution by Louis XIV. Gueudeville deeply regretted the suppression of the Camisards, and looked forward to further uprisings.[52] His theories suffered a similar setback when faced with the Hungarian problem. Even though Gueudeville condemned the Hungarian revolt against the Austrians, his condemnation was not wholly unqualified:

Pour surcroît d'infortune, les propres sujets de sa Majesté Impériale grossissent le nombre de ses ennemis. Les Hongrois trouvent l'occasion favorable et la font valoir. Supposé qu'on les ait opprimés, ont-ils tort de se remuer dans un temps propre à crier liberté, sont-ils blâmables d'embrasser la conjoncture du monde la plus heureuse pour secouer le joug? Je laisse la solution de ce problème à quelque habile jurisconsulte républicain et neutre; je dirai seulement que les scruples d'honneur sont peu de chose lorsqu'il s'agit de recouvrer son droit naturel.[53]

Gueudeville was not unaware of the contradictions between his theory and practice, and this was one of the reasons he tried to remain neutral in the face of such problems. His neutrality, however, did not extend to the battles that journalists conducted amongst themselves. For wars are waged not only on battlefields but also in the columns of the press, and Gueudeville took an active part in the invective and abuse that journalists regularly hurled at each other in their weekly and monthly publications:

Quelqu'un a dit que, pendant la guerre, les nouvellistes des partis opposés se battent à la plume comme les soldats au mousquet ou à l'épée. Cette pensée-là est plus heureuse qu'elle ne paraît... c'est effectivement une espèce de guerre que les journalistes, que les écrivains des événements publics dans des causes difficiles se font entre eux. Toujours aux prises les uns avec les autres, ou du moins ne convenant jamais de toutes les circonstances, c'est à qui aura gagné le plus, c'est à qui aura le moins perdu. (May–August 1709, 332–333)

Gueudeville's four principal enemies were Eusèbe Renaudot of the French *Gazette,* Donneau de Visé of the *Mercure Galant,* Claude Jordan, the anonymous author of *La Clef du Cabinet des Princes,* and Jean de la Chapelle, the anonymous author of *Lettres d'un Suisse.*[54] Since Jordan and La Chapelle did not cross swords with Gueudeville until 1705, the bulk of his attacks were addressed to Renaudot and Donneau de Visé, either directly or by implication.

A common accusation by both sides was that the enemy government hid the truth from its people. Thus, for example, Donneau de Visé, in response to accounts in the Dutch press of the battle of Luzzara, wrote:

Les Hollandais... persuadés qu'il est à propos de tromper leurs peuples qui souffrent impatiemment la guerre où ils se trouvent engagés, ont fait mettre dans leurs nouvelles publiques que nous avions eu six mille hommes de tués, que les Impériaux n'avaient pas eu deux mille hommes tués on blessés, qu'ils avaient gagné le champ de bataille... Ainsi toutes les relations ne peuvent surprendre que le menu peuple de Hollande à qui l'on cache la vérité pour lui faire supporter patiemment la dépense à laquelle il est obligé de contribuer pour les frais de la guerre présente. (August 1702, 361–366)

In response to accounts in the *Gazette* of the battle of Hochstedt, Gueudeville adopted a similar tactic, finding that "par ces insignes et visibles faussetés, on veut cacher aux peuples la grandeur du mal, et leur tenir toujours en haleine pour la contribution et la bursalité" (September 1704, 357).

In describing the miserable conditions of the winter quarters of the Imperial army in 1701, Donneau de Visé observed that "lorsqu'ils travaillent à s'y retrancher ils bâtissent une forteresse pour la peste." He went on to express the hope that "leurs retranchements soient bons afin qu'elle [la peste] ne sorte pas." Gueudeville's reply to this was:

Voilà ce qui s'appelle se distinguer en pointe, se surpasser en belle pensée, et bien choisir son sujet pour s'égayer... Que dirons-nous du souhait? Il est inhumain, barbare, dénaturé, mais en récompense il est fin, délicat, spirituel. Désirer sans façon que la peste crève cinquante mille hommes qui ne sont coupables de rien, et qui font leur devoir en obéissant à leur maître, c'est renoncer publiquement à l'humanité, c'est donner une affreuse idée de son naturel. (November 1701, 850–851)

But if de Visé was guilty of inhumanity on a large scale, Gueudeville was not entirely innocent on a personal level. When he learned of de Visé's impending blindness Gueudeville commented, "il est rare qu'un encenseur de profession ait les yeux bons; la fumée qu'il donne sans cesse l'aveugle et lui fait voir toujours trouble." And, when de Visé was completely blind, he observed that "le bon et illustre Monsieur Devisé... qui n'a jamais eu les yeux de jugement trop bons, commence à les perdre après avoir perdu les yeux de la tête."[55]

Over the years Gueudeville employed a wide range of expressions, such as "rhapsodiste", "petit écrivain... hardi en hyperboles", "l'oracle du prophète Mercure", with which to mock and ridicule de Visé. A characteristic passage describes the man and his journal:

Or, comme bien savez, ce Sieur de Visé est un auteur des plus graves. Il est le héraut et le crieur public du bel esprit dans le royaume. Tous ceux qui veulent traffiquer quelque petite production de cabinet, ou quelque exhalaison de noblesse et de généalogie contre un peu d'encens et de fumée, s'adressent au Sieur de Visé; il n'y a pas jusqu'aux deviseurs d'énigmes qui ne soient couchés de leur long sur le registre de ce greffier du Parnasse. Sa plume est consacrée aux éloges; flatterie ou justice, mensonge ou vérité, c'est ce qui ne l'inquiète point du tout; il loue indifféremment à titre d'office, et encore plus par droit d'aubaine. (March 1705, 361)

Even after his death de Visé was not free from attack. In 1711 there appeared an anonymous pamphlet in which he was portrayed in Hades, nervously awaiting the arrival of "les auteurs de *Mercure historique*, de *L'Esprit des Cours*, de *la Clef du Cabinet des Princes*, du *Journal des Savants*, des *Quintessences.* . ."[56]

Gueudeville reserved some of his harshest language for Jean de la Chapelle, "un certain masque déguisé en Suisse" whom he correctly identified as being in the pay of France, an "avocat au pain et aux gages du despotisme", "cet auteur qui nous traite de calomniateurs et de serpents, lorsque lui-même vomit son venin sur la maison d'Autriche."[57] When secretary Torcy offered to silence Gueudeville, La Chapelle preferred to use Gueudeville's attacks to make some replies of his own.[58] In September 1705 he devoted the whole of his thirty-sixth letter to Gueudeville and his periodical. After describing Gueudeville as "le lynx de tous les faiseurs de libelles et de lardons de Hollande", he went on to ridicule his style, a feature that Gueudeville considered his greatest gift and the key to his success as a journalist. La Chapelle then proceeded to attack the content of *L'Esprit des cours*:

L'auteur place à la tête de chacun de ses journaux, comme un avant-garde invincible, une longue suite de ces plaisanteries surannées contre l'Eglise Catholique et son chef; jeux frivoles dont vous m'avez cent fois dit que les gens sages, les gens d'esprit de votre religion étaient eux-mêmes dégoûtés, honteux que l'ignorance des premiers Protestants eût ajouté foi à tant d'exagérations, et de fables ridicules.

Après cette vieille bande, marche un recueil rare et curieux, de tout ce que les colporteurs de Paris ont crié et vendu dans les rues il y a plus de six mois. . . Edits, déclarations, arrêts du Conseil sur des matières triviales, fausses relations, nouvelles usées; tout cela *brodé* par le compilateur, lui fournit mille railleries fines, à ce qu'il croit, et relevées par ce sel que Lucilius jetait à plaines mains dans Rome.

Just as La Chapelle ridiculed Gueudeville's style, and accused him of publishing plagiarized, outdated and trivial news, so Gueudeville, in turn, levelled the same charges at Claude Jordan:

. . . il écrit avec une noblesse si populaire, la moindre femmelette pourrait atteindre à l'élévation de son style. D'ailleurs, j'ai de la reconnaissance pour ce docte personnage et je dois beaucoup à son érudition. Sans lui j'aurais oublié quantité de nouvelles de gazettes, quoiqu'insérées déjà dans mon pédantesque journal, et sans le secours de ses profondes recherches j'ignorerais encore l'histoire importante du célèbre chien de Jean de Nivelles. (July 1705, 178)[59]

Claude Jordan, in turn, described Gueudeville as someone "qui ne travaille que sur les matériaux de sa féconde imagination."[60]

Wars and periodicals eventually come to an end. It seems that Gueudeville knew his periodical was going to cease publication, for, in the January—April issue of 1710, he inserted a passage in which he suggested he was about to be silenced for having written according to the dictates of his conscience. In this critical hour he is quite alone, having been deserted by all those he thought were his friends:

... qu'il est doux de pouvoir disposer de sa conscience sans en être regardé de mauvais oeil! C'est un plaisir que je suis bien éloigné d'avoir. Mes anciens frères (je vous dis cela sous le secret de l'imprimerie, et j'espère que vous n'en abuserez point) mes anciens frères m'ont en horreur; et mes frères de vingt et un an, ou vingt et un ans, car je ne sais lequel vaut mieux, ne me détestent pas moins. Je vois bien qu'il faut *me préparer au martyre de la liberté de conscience;* je ne sais pas ce qu'il vaut dans l'autre monde, mais je sais bien que cette palme-là est infâme en ce monde-ci. Le bon Dieu veuille me donner sa grâce! (January—April, 120)

With the issue of September—December 1710, in its eleventh year, the periodical finished as unceremoniously as it had begun, and Gueudeville's journalistic career came to an end.[61] Some of the monthly political periodicals lasted much longer than *L'Esprit des cours de l'Europe.* The *Mercure galant* became the *Mercure de France,* and is still going strong. *La Clef du Cabinet des princes* changed its name several times but did not cease publication until 1776. The *Mercure historique et politique* finished in 1782, and the *Letters historiques* lasted from 1692 to 1729. In its day, however, no periodical caused a greater stir than *L'Esprit des cours,* and no journalist was more notorious than Gueudeville.

In his edition of Lahontan's *Dialogues,* attributed to Gueudeville, Gilbert Chinard said of *L'Esprit des cours de l'Europe*:

Il y aurait une bien amusante étude à faire de ce petit journal, curieux, bilieux et haineux dans lequel l'éditeur se plaisait à réunir nouvelles authentiques et racontars qui circulaient sous le manteau, et attaquaient particulièrement les Jésuites, le pape et la cour de Versailles. Anecdotes démontrant l'immoralité des Français, maris complaisants, battus, quelquefois à moitié assassinés et contents, attaques contre les juges, contre les dépenses exagérées du roi, contre l'application de la torture à de simples suspects ou à des innocents, scandales publics et privés, on trouve tout chez ce Saint-Simon de bas étage à qui il ne manquait que le génie pour mériter une place dans la littérature.[62]

While I cannot claim to have written "une bien amusante étude" I have tried to bring out the flavour and variety of the journal to which Chinard referred.

Today, *L'Esprit des cours de l'Europe* is largely forgotten. As an accurate record of the events of the time it is not of great worth. But for students of the history of journalism, and as a reflection of the preoccupations and opinions of the day, it remains a valuable document.

IV. THE CRITIQUE OF FENELON'S *TELEMAQUE*

Having launched his onslaught on Louis XIV, in *L'Esprit des cours de l'Europe*, Gueudeville soon found a wonderful opportunity to increase the intensity by using archbishop Fénelon's latest publication as a vehicle for his attack on absolute monarchy. As soon as the *Suite du quatrième livre de l'Odyssée d'Homère ou les Avantures de Télémaque fils d'Ulysse* began to appear in Paris, in April 1699, it was banned by the authorities. This measure had the usual effect of drawing attention to the work which was then brought out in France in a number of clandestine editions, and in The Netherlands by Adrian Moetjens of The Hague.[1]

Despite the fact that it was published anonymously, and supposedly without his permission, it seemed to be generally known that Fénelon was the author. The critics lost no time in airing their views. On May 18, Bossuet described the work as "peu sérieux, peu digne d'un prêtre."[2] In June, Basnage de Beauval, in a short but important review, set down what were to become the main criticisms of the work:

Personne n'a balancé à donner les Avantures de *Télémaque* à Mr. l'Archevêque de Cambrai. La renommée l'avait annoncé par avance. On admire qu'un prélat élevé à la dévotion la plus sublime, et la plus épurée, possède si parfaitement le langage des poètes. Son livre est un précis d'Homère, et de Virgile, et un poème épique en forme: il n'y manque que la mesure des vers. Les politiques spéculatifs prétendent y trouver un sens mystique, et ne sauraient s'imaginer que les graves leçons que le sage Mentor fait au jeune Télémaque, ne soient faites que pour gouverner la petite île d'Ithaque. Les grandes maximes qu'on y débite, semblent ne convenir qu'à un prince destiné à régir un plus grand empire. Le fils d'Ulysse pour régner dans une bicoque telle que l'île d'Ithaque, n'avait pas besoin qu'on le fît ressouvenir tant de fois, que *les rois ne sont faits que pour les peuples*; Qu'ils *sont assujettis aux lois*, que *le roi est l'homme de son peuple*: Et qu'il *est plus juste qu'un seul serve à la félicité des peuples, que non pas les peuples servent par leur misère à flatter l'orgueil d'un seul.* C'est ce qui fait que les gens qui raffinent sur tout, y cherchent un sens mystérieux, et allégorique. Vous en croirez ce qu'il vous plaira. . .

Quoi qu'il en soit il y a là beaucoup d'adresse, et d'artifice. L'art surpasse la matière. Souvenez-vous toujours que c'est une prose poétique sans quoi le style vous paraîtra trop enflé, et peut-être un peu trop guindé. Il chausse trop haut le cothurne. Il y a des descriptions brillantes et hyperboliques, qu'on ne pardonne qu'aux poétes. Je ne sais même si elles ne reviennent pas trop souvent, et si l'esprit ne se lasse point de figures, et d'expressions métaphoriques, quand elles ont des retours si fréquents et si réguliers. Vous n'y trouvez point de ruisseau qui ne murmure, ou qui ne serpente agréablement dans une prairie; point de tempête qui ne fasse écumer les flots, et mugir la mer irritée, etc.[3]

Basnage de Beauval, then, drew attention to three points — the inappropriateness of such a work by an archbishop, the political implications, and the defects of style. Other critics took up these points and added to them. In August, in his correspondence, Bayle referred to a second volume recently brought out by Moetjens, and the promise of a third. Some people, according to Bayle, were less impressed with the second volume, and "bien des gens ont peine à se persuader qu'il soit de Mr. de Cambrai."[4] In October, Noailles, bishop of Châlons, wrote to his brother, the archbishop of Paris, about the unseemliness of an archbishop indulging in such a form as the novel with its mandatory scenes of love. The brother replied in kind.[5] According to the abbé Le Dieu, Bossuet had a similar reaction:

Dès qu'il en eût vu le premier tome, il le jugea d'un style efféminé et poétique; tant de discours amoureux, tant de descriptions galantes, une femme qui ouvre la scéne par une tendresse déclarée et qui soutient ce sentiment jusqu'au bout. . . lui fit dire que cet ouvrage était indigne non seulement d'un évêque mais d'un prêtre et d'un chrétien.[6]

In November, Boileau, in his correspondence, wrote in praise of the work but wished that "la morale fût répandue. . . un peu plus imperceptiblement, et avec plus d'art. . . La vérité est pourtant que le Mentor du *Télémaque* dit de fort bonnes choses, quoique un peu hardies, et enfin M. de Cambrai me paraît beaucoup meilleur poète que théologien."[7] Bayle attributed the novel's enormous popularity mainly to the fact that "l'Auteur y parle selon le goût des peuples, et principalement des peuples qui, comme les Français, ont le plus senti les mauvaises suites de la puissance arbitraire, qu'il a touchées et bien exposées."[8]

The longest and most comprehensive criticism to appear before Gueudeville's was *Six Lettres écrites à un ami, sur le sujet des nouvelles Avantures de Télémaque.* This is a work of 103 pages, without any indication of author, publisher or date of publication. The first letter is dated November 30 1699, and the last is dated February 16 1700. The author discusses all aspects of Fénelon's novel, including the structure, the individual episodes, the characterization, the political content and the style. He particularly deplores the fact that a book announced as the continuation of the fourth book of the *Odyssey* is not, in fact, a logical and coherent development of the Greek epic. He concludes, however, that the work's imperfections "sont des bagatelles où n'a pas cru devoir s'arrêter un homme qui avait l'idée remplie de tout ce que les vertus morales et politiques semblent avoir de plus élevé."[9]

What caused Fénelon's work to be banned, however, was not its literary imperfections or the unseemliness of an archbishop writing a novel, but the political element to which many critics had referred. Indeed, from the moment of its publication the work was widely regarded as a *roman à clef* written for the express purpose of condemning the régime of Louis XIV. According to Saint-Simon, for example:

On avait persuadé au roi qu'Astarbé et Pygmalion dans Tyr était sa peinture et celle de Mme de Maintenon à Versailles. Celle-ci n'y pouvait penser sans frémir de rage, et le nom de M. de Cambrai, la vue même de ses fidèles amis, la lui renouvelait toujours, et cette peinture imprimée dans l'esprit des fils de France par un précepteur donné par le roi pour les instruire, et qui les instruit de la sorte dans leurs thèmes et par conséquent en toute occasion, fut un crime aux yeux de ce prince et une plaie dans son coeur, d'autant plus poignante qu'il n'osait s'en plaindre, ni l'avouer.[10]

It was this aspect of Fénelon's novel that encouraged Gueudeville, some time before April 1700, to publish anonymously, and with a fictitious imprint, the first part of his *Critique générale des Avantures de Télémaque,* which was followed, in the same year, by the *Critique du premier tome des Avantures de Télémaque, Critique de la suite du second tome des Avantures de Télémaque,* and the *Critique de la première et seconde suite du tome second.* In 1702 appeared the sixth and final part: *Le Critique ressuscité ou fin de la Critique des Avantures de Télémaque.* The six parts together contain nearly 1300 pages, and each part went through two or more editions.[11]

Some confusion arose over the authorship of this work. The abbé Faydit, who later brought out his own anonymous assessment of Fénelon's novel, was identified as the author of the *Critique générale.* He was mortified, but what he did not realize, and what no one has pointed out, is that the identification came from Gueudeville himself![12] In the preface to his book Faydit described Gueudeville's critique as "brutale et séditieuse" and as "cet infâme et scandaleux libelle", whereupon Jacques Bernard, who had taken over Bayle's *Nouvelles de la République des Lettres,* sprang to the defense in a review of the first two parts of Gueudeville's critique:

Le public s'est si ouvertement déclaré en faveur de *Télémaque* que c'est être bien hardi que d'entreprendre de critiquer cet ouvrage, et vouloir se hasarder à être accusé de n'avoir ni goût ni esprit. Ce n'est pas qu'il ne paraisse souvent avoir raison, et qu'il n'y ait, peut-être, quelques personnes, dont le jugement n'est pas tout à fait méprisable, qui ont pensé à peu prés ce que pense l'auteur de la Critique; mais moins téméraires, ou peut-être plus vains que lui, ils n'ont eu garde de s'opposer au torrent. Quoi qu'il en soit il nous promet de n'en demeurer pas là, et outre les réflexions générales, et la Critique du premier tome qu'il a déjà publiées... il se prépare à poursuivre sur le même ton, et à nous dire ce qu'il pense du reste de l'ouvrage. Peut-être se trouverait-il plus d'une personne qui l'exhorteraient à tenir parole s'ils ne craignaient de se voir siffler des partisans de Télémaque, gens redoutables et sans quartier... Cette critique, qui a été imprimée dans ces provinces, est fort différente de celle qu'en a fait Mr. l'Abbé Faydit en France, et qui n'a pas eu, dit-on, l'approbation générale.[13]

In his *Critique de la première et seconde suite du tome second des Avantures de Télémaque*, Gueudeville also responded to Faydit's attack.[14] There also appeared, in 1700, an anonymous *Lettre de M. l'abbé de G**** à un de ses amis, sur la Critique générale des Avantures de Télémaque*. This was a forty-page rebuttal which produced a vigorous response from Gueudeville.[15]

In 1701, in the preface to a new edition of *Télémaque*, the abbé de Saint-Rémy took both Gueudeville and Faydit to task:

Je ne prétends pas ici justifier Télémaque contre les dégoûts injustes de quelques censeurs... Ces auteurs se décrient eux-mêmes, en voulant se tirer de l'obscurité où leur peu de mérite les a réduits malgré eux. En effet, leur plume serait à jamais ignorée, s'ils n'avaient eu la hardiesse de se faire un si noble adversaire. Ce sont proprement des pygmées qui attaquent un Hercule (xvii).

Saint-Rémy went on to link Gueudeville's attack on Fénelon to the similar attacks he made on notable personages in *L'Esprit des cours de l'Europe*. He characterized Gueudeville's criticism of *Télémaque* as "un tissu de mauvaises plaisanteries, en quoi il est trés abondant, car il trouve moyen d'en débiter tous les mois contre tout ce qu'il y a de plus grand en Europe. Je trouve M. de Cambrai bien heureux d'être mis en si bonne compagnie, et de n'avoir pas l'approbation d'un si faible écrivain, puisque pour la mériter il faudrait renoncer à celle des personnes de bon goût."[16] In *Le Critique ressuscité* Gueudeville replied by referring to:

... ce sec et ridicule apologiste qui estime le meilleur des humains, je veux dire Monsieur de Cambrai, fort heureux de ce qu'un mauvais plaisant le traite comme il traite chaque mois les princes perfides, oppresseurs, usurpateurs. A qui convient mieux la qualité de mauvais plaisant, au journaliste qui raille l'injustice, ou au faiseur mercenaire de préface qui félicite un très honnête homme d'être raillé comme les rois injustes?... Je sors de la lice... sans autre honneur que celui que peut se faire un pygmée d'avoir osé se mesurer avec un Hercule; c'est la comparaison dont se sert l'apologiste; je vous déclare sans fard qu'elle m'a paru très juste, et pour l'en remercier je le renvoie à la fable de cet animal à longues oreilles et si décrié dans toutes les républiques bestiales, qui demandait fièrement au lion ce qu'il pensait de son exploit *asinin*, et si sa belle voix n'avait pas contribué beaucoup à la victoire (pp. 112–113, 117).

In March 1702, Bayle, although claiming to have read neither *Télémaque* nor the criticisms of it, reported that Gueudeville's critique "a été fort applaudie."[17]

Gueudeville's work was banned in France, as was that of Faydit.[18] The

Chancellor Pontchartrain, who controlled the book trade in France at this time, found that Gueudeville's work "ne mérite aucune attention, et il suffit que vous en empêchiez le débit, ainsi que vous êtes obligé de faire des ouvrages de cette espèce."[19]

Throughout the eighteenth century opinion was divided over the value of Gueudeville's critique. This division of opinion seems to depend largely on whether the writer was favourably or unfavourably disposed towards France and the policies of Louis XIV. Lenglet Dufresnoy found merit in it, and thought that "quoique Gueudeville n'eût pas été capable de faire un ouvrage de la beauté et de la délicatesse du Télémaque, il avait assez d'esprit pour en faire une critique raisonnable."[20] In this opinion he was supported by Prosper Marchand who also felt that the criticisms of both Gueudeville and Faydit "n'ont pas toujours porté à faux, et ont peut-être contribué au redressement de divers endroits du Télémaque dans les éditions qui les ont suivies."[21] But Gachet d'Artigny considered Gueudeville's work "moins une critique qu'une satire brutale et séditieuse, où il paraît que le but principal qu'on s'est proposé n'est pas tant de faire apercevoir des défauts dans le livre de M. de Fénelon, que de le rendre odieux lui-même, et avoir un prétexte de noircir la conduite de Louis XIV."[22] The editors of the *Nouveau Dictionnaire historique portatif*, in evaluating Gueudeville's critique and his monthly periodical, found that both of them "ne méritent guère d'être lues que par ceux qui aiment les écarts d'une imagination sans frein, et de l'emportement sans goût et sans correction."[23]

In the nineteenth century the same division of opinion persists. While the *Biographie universelle* says that "Cette critique est oubliée depuis longtemps; et, en la lisant, on a peine à concevoir qu'elle ait été applaudie,"[24] the abbé Caron echoes the favourable sentiments of some earlier critics in finding that Gueudeville's series of criticisms "contient quelques bonnes observations dont Fénelon peut avoir profité; car il a corrigé depuis, plusieurs endroits que le critique avait censurés." But he goes on to state that the rest of Gueudeville's work is simply "un ramas de mauvaises plaisanteries et de froides déclamations." The worst feature, according to Caron, is that Gueudeville's criticism "est remplie de principes antimonarchiques, et de maximes destructives de toute subordination."[25] It is this antimonarchical element, then, that is clearly of the very essence of the work:

Gueudeville est prolixe jusqu'à la satiété, et son goût n'est pas sûr; mais son livre n'est dépourvu ni d'agrément ni de justesse, ni de vigueur, et, s'il paraît manquer de netteté, c'est à ceux qui n'en voient pas ou feignent de n'en pas voir le véritable objet. *La Critique du Télémaque* appartient au même genre d'ouvrages que l'*Apologie pour Hérédote* ou les *Pensées sur la Comète*: le titre n'en révèle pas le vrai dessein. A plusieurs reprises Gueudeville proteste de son admiration et de son respect pour Fénelon, et ses protestations sont sincères: la critique du *Télémaque* n'est que le prétexte de la publication de Gueudeville; le véritable objet en est la satire, parfois sous la forme d'une apologie ironique, du gouvernement de Louis XIV et de la patience des Français.[26]

The most recent assessment of Gueudeville's work occurred some forty years ago when E. Delval published a fairly lengthy article in which he examined, in detail, four of the six parts of Gueudeville's critique. He was unable to find the *Critique de la première et seconde suite de tome second*. Delval also devoted an article to Faydit's attack on Fénelon.[27] Apart from the fact that Delval omitted two sections of Gueudeville's critique, the manner in which he conducted his study is open to serious objections. His attitude to Fénelon, for example, fell just short of idolatry, so that he resented, in principle, any criticism of the archbishop or his work. Moreover, as a conformist Frenchman, he was upset by attacks on Louis XIV. It was with some reluctance, therefore, that he undertook the studies of Gueudeville and Faydit, since he regretted the brief moment of glory his articles would accord to these men. Nevertheless, he felt that "il serait intéressant de voir les efforts impuissants de ces deux médiocres esprits contre le grand Archevêque de Cambrai. Tirer de l'oubli leurs noms qui mériteraient d'y rester engloutis est certainement leur faire un trop grand honneur, mais la gloire de Fénelon en resplendira davantage, plus éclatante et plus pure encore."[28] He did no research on Gueudeville, and knew nothing about the man except what he found in conventional sources. Even then, he failed to use all the sources available to him and, consequently, made several errors of fact.[29]

But even so partial a critic as Delval was forced to admit, as earlier commentators had done, that there was some justification in the criticisms of Fénelon's style,[30] and that Gueudeville himself:

... avait de la verve... Ses pamphlets successifs et courts sont amusants. Ils n'ont pas la lourde et indigeste érudition de Faydit... Il en évite aussi les longues et interminables phrases qui ajoutent la lourdeur du style à celle de l'exposé. Sa phrase court en général avec facilité... Les attaques de Gueudeville contre le roi et contre Fénelon ne vont pourtant jamais jusqu'à l'insulte, ce qui le différencie de Faydit. On ne trouve pas non plus la mauvaise foi insigne qui poussait ce dernier à falsifier les textes.[31]

Delval's method of dealing with Gueudeville's criticism is quite subtle. He draws attention away from Gueudeville's political attacks by devoting a good deal of space to Gueudeville's literary criticism. Now, while it is true that Gueudeville spent as much time attacking Fénelon's narrative technique as he did reflecting on the régime of Louis XIV, he made it abundantly clear that the political element was the important one, and that the literary criticism, though justified, was to be regarded as a piece of badinage:

Je n'attribue point à Monsieur l'Archevêque de Cambrai d'autre intention que celle de bannir l'injustice de dessus la terre... Il est vrai que je badine sur les moyens dont il s'est servi pour exécuter ce beau et très louable dessein; mais.... le but de ma téméraire critique n'est pas tant de montrer le ridicule de la fiction, que d'exprimer le suc nerveux que celle-ci contient pour la politique et pour la morale (*Critique de la première et seconde suite du tome second* (p. 128).[32]

Since this is the case, one would expect an evaluation of Gueudeville's work to concentrate more on the principal than on the subsidiary elements. But Delval, as I have said, tends to dwell on the latter. Even this could be defended if, while pointing out the fatuousness of much of Gueudeville's literary criticism (and there is no doubt that, to modern readers, much of it seems ridiculous), he also acknowledged that many of Gueudeville's strictures were thoroughly justified. Let us look first, then, at this problem of Fénelon's technique.

It was Gueudeville's opinion that while Fénelon expressed admirable ideas, his manner of expressing them was totally without skill. In short, Fénelon was an archbishop and not a novelist, and he should never have tried a genre at which he was so inept. Because of his ignorance of the exigencies of the novel form, Fénelon made elementary and inexcusable mistakes in every aspect of narrative technique, including structure, characterization, style, *vraisemblance,* and taste:

Jamais il ne fut d'auteur plus inégal, ni qui se soutint moins que celui de Télémaque... Quand [il] donne ses maximes politiques, c'est un oracle qui parle au genre humain... Revient-il à sa narration? c'est un conteur; il n'est propre qu'à éblouir les sots, ou qu'à amuser les enfants (*Critique du second tome*, pp. 244–245)

Elsewhere Gueudeville describes Fénelon's novel as:

Des fictions mal cousues et entassées les unes sur les autres avec une affectation continuelle; un torrent de mots dont la moitié est l'écho de l'autre, et qui rendent le bon sens imperceptible à force de le diviser; des contradictions sans nombre qui jettent dans l'embarras un lecteur attentif. ... un mélange monstrueux ou le sacré est englouti dans le profane, et où le vice est peint des mêmes couleurs que la vertu... enfin, du guindé au naturel et de la poésie en prose. (*Critique de la première et seconde suite du tome second*, p. 7)

Even if Fénelon had been a competent novelist, Gueudeville argues, the novel form itself is quite unsuitable for achieving the author's avowed intention which was to teach the art of kingship to the young duke of Burgundy. Works of fiction lead to depravity. They are full of hyperbole and imagination, and utterly devoid of rational thought. *Télémaque* is written in flowery prose and full of the most extreme *invraisemblances.* Why is it necessary to create an imaginary world to learn how to reign in the real one? Kings, surrounded as they always are by flatterers who lie consistently, have a greater need than any of practical, prosaic wisdom. The scabrous adventures of amorous and jealous goddesses do nothing but titillate the senses, and threaten to corrupt rather than enlighten the pupil. Furthermore, why is it necessary to use paganism to teach Christian morality? The result is that:

cet ouvrage, étant un ambigu de piété et de superstition, d'erreur et de vérité, de figure et de naturel, de vice et de vertu, de bon et de mauvais sens, il favorise la disposition que le jeune prince a au mal, et n'est propre qu'à embarrasser et qu'à confondre ses idées du côté du bien (*Critique générale*, p. 16)

By choosing the novel form, then, Fénelon seems to be writing more to entertain than to instruct. What surprises Gueudeville is that French critics, who flatter themselves they can tell a good work from a bad one, and who claim that the only worthwhile works are those that instruct, are the very ones who worship *Télémaque:*

. . . ces beaux esprits prennent un singulier plaisir à voir le soleil sortir du sein de son amoureuse Thétis, s'arracher d'entre les bras de cette amante, pour monter en carosse, et faire à son aise le tour du monde, tiré par son attelage ignée: l'Aurore leur paraît charmante dans son char de rosée? un char de rosée! Remarquez-le bien, la rosée n'est autre chose que des gouttes d'eau qui tombent, cependant ces gouttes forment un char; que cela est naturel? que cela est beau? Vénus va baiser son Papa mignon, et le conjure en pleurant de trouver bon que Télémaque se laisse débaucher; le bon Papa est attendri et sans le cruel destin qui lui fait la loi, il consentirait de bon coeur, pour l'amour de son aimable fille, que Télémaque devînt le plus grand paillard qui fût sous le ciel. . . comment ne pas se récrier sur une prose si succulente et si fleurie? (*Critique générale*, pp. 30–31)

The above quotation contains examples of two of Gueudeville's main criticisms of *Télémaque* as a novel. He objects to the "prose versifiée," and the constant violation of *vraisemblance.* Most of Gueudeville's literary criticism is based on his prosaic interpretation of Fénelon's poetic conceits. His refusal to accept the author's frequent use of imagery is, to the modern reader, quite unreasonable, puerile and, after the first few objections, extremely tedious. In the *Critique du premier tome,* for example, Calypso looks out to sea and notices, in the distance, an old man and young one, hanging on to part of a mast and tossed about by the waves. The young man looks like Ulysses. No explanation is given, objects Gueudeville, as to how the men got there, or how Calypso can tell, at such a distance, that one of the men is old and the other young, that the younger one looks like Ulysses, especially when the men's faces would have been covered with sand and mud:

Si la nymphe avait de si bons yeux par le privilège de sa divinité, la chose valait bien la peine de nous en avertir; mais si l'on nous propose cela comme n'ayant rien d'extraordinaire et qui soit au-dessus de l'usage humain, de deux choses l'une: ou l'on suppose que la déesse approchait les objets par de bonnes lunettes, ou l'on nous prend pour des enfants qui trouvent tout bon pourvu qu'on conte. (p. 72)

There are many such fatuities in Gueudeville's work, and I do not intend to bore the reader with them. In any case, a lot of them are recorded by Delval to whose study the reader is referred. I should, however, issue a note of caution. It is important to remember that Gueudeville did not intend these observations to be taken entirely seriously. Most of his literary criticism is delivered in a joking, tongue-in-check manner. Now it may well be that the modern reader finds nothing amusing in such trivial and frivolous observations. Gueudeville, however, was writing *not* deathless prose for posterity, but a topical and facile political tract for a particular public. It must be assumed that he knew what that public regarded as humorous, and how much of that type of humour he could get get away with.[33] It is true, as we have seen, that his work was described as "un tissu de mauvaises plaisanteries," and that Gueudeville, himself, although he probably did not mean a word of what he said, was his own severest critic. The number of editions of his work, however, attest to its popularity.[34]

Moreover, not all Gueudeville's accusations of *invraisemblance* were unjustified. In the *Critique du second tome,* for example, we return to Mentor and Telemachus, hanging on for dear life to the broken mast. Mentor uses the occasion for further instruction of his pupil:

Figurez-vous deux hommes posés sur un mât flottant, et qui, toujours emportés par la violence de la vague, tantôt s'élèvent jusqu'aux nues, tantôt ont une montagne d'eau sur la tête, *buvant l'onde amère qui coule de leur bouche, de leurs narines et de leurs oreilles,* le plus souvent précipités de leur siège mobile et agité, et ayant toutes les peines du monde à le rattraper; dans des ténèbres épaisses, et ne pouvant se voir l'un l'autre. . . quoiqu'à tous moments ensevelis dans la vague, Mentor. . . explique à son disciple aussi tranquillement que sur un siège de gazon, le mystère impénétrable de la providence de Dieu sur le sort et sur la vie des hommes (p. 188)

There are many similar instances of lack of *vraisemblance.*[35]

Fénelon is particularly weak in the area of characterization. His characters, for example, often speak and act in contradictory ways. The goddesses behave one moment as if possessed with divine powers, and the next moment as if they were no more powerful or prescient than humans. Minerva who, as Mentor, is supposed to be a shining example of virtue, displays, from time to time, somewhat questionable ethics. Idomeneus has a miraculous transformation from a tyrant to a "saint". Telemachus is more changeable than the chameleon. These inconsistencies of character are not lost on Gueudeville:

Tous les autres faiseurs de romans distribuent à chacun de leurs personnages le rôle qui lui convient, et ils s'appliquent à bien soutenir ce caractère depuis le commencement jusqu'à la fin; mais notre illustre auteur s'est mis au-dessus de cette règle, dictée à la vérité par le bon sens, mais trop commune pour un esprit sublime; il change sans façon de caractère sans changer de personnage, il accommode le naturel de son héros aux idées qui lui viennent, au lieu d'ajuster ses idées au naturel de son héros; a-t-il besoin d'un Télémaque docile, patient, complaisant, sensible, reconnaissant, humain? Télémaque est tout cela. Lui faut-il un Télémaque avare, hautain, méprisant, emporté jusqu'à la fougue, insensé jusqu'à ne plus se souvenir qu'il est un homme? Télémaque est aussi tout cela. Un parterre de comédie serait frappé d'un grand étonnement s'il voyait un acteur changer d'habit tout à coup sans disparaître et sans interrompre sa même déclamation; notre auteur fait un plus grand prodige, puisque sur la même scène son acteur change de naturel comme d'habit, qu'il n'est et n'est plus le même homme, et qu'il porte deux coeurs tout opposés sous une même figure (*Critique de la première et seconde suite du tome second* (pp. 169–170).

To sum up this brief discussion of the value of Gueudeville's literary criticism, I think it is fair to say that Delval was justified in dismissing many of Gueudeville's remarks as trivial and tedious. He did not, however, accept them in the spirit in which they were intended, and he failed to acknowledge that some of Gueudeville's criticism was perceptive and perfectly valid.

Where Delval most failed to appreciate Gueudeville, however, was in the area of political satire, and this element I want to consider now. Although Delval was fully aware of the political satire, and faithfully reproduced some of Gueudeville's attacks on Louis XIV, he did not place these attacks in their proper context. He did not, or would not see that Gueudeville's criticism was but another shot in the pamphlet war that writers in Holland had been waging against France for nearly thirty years.[36] Delval was under the impression that Gueudeville wrote "plus pour gagner de l'argent que par conviction réelle."[37] Although it is certainly true that Gueudeville wrote for money, his hatred of France's political régime was intense, unwavering and utterly sincere.

Many of the ideas in the critique are first outlined in *L'Esprit des cours*. Indeed, Gueudeville's opening shot against *Télémaque* is found in the very first issue of the periodical where he comments on Pope Innocent XII's condemnation, in March 1699, of twenty-three propositions found in Fénelon's quietist tract, *Explication des maximes des saints sur la vie intérieure*, first published in 1697:

... voir la cour du monde la plus éclairée suer sang et eau; en voir une autre où le zèle ferveur marche à côté de la puissance, employer tout son crédit et toute sa et cela, pourquoi? Pour dénoncer à toute la terre qu'il est dangereux de trop aimer Dieu; et qu'un amour divin trop épuré peut conduire à l'erreur et au crime; la chose est assurément rare, et il faut vivre dans un siècle aussi fécond que le nôtre en grands événements pour n'être pas frappé de celui-ci. Si. M. de Cambrai était le continuateur de l'Odyssée d'Homère, comme le public le veut, peut-être à cause de l'esprit et de la délicatesse de l'ouvrage, il serait bien plus censurable que sur l'amour pur, d'avoir imité et habillé, à la française, le fondateur de la théologie grecque et païenne. . . (June 1699, 29–30)

In almost every issue during the first year of its publication Gueudeville's journal defends Fénelon against his attackers. It is not that Gueudeville was especially sympathetic to Fénelon's cause, or even to Fénelon himself. His main interest was in reporting dissension in the church, and he also hoped that the Gallican church and the Paris parlement might accuse the Pope of interfering in a purely internal affair. His hopes were dashed when all parties united to condemn the Archbishop.

Gueudeville's condemnation of Louis XIV for his treatment of French Protestants, which would find expression in his criticisms of *Télémaque,* had already been voiced in his very first publication, and was repeated at length in *L'Esprit des cours.*[38] Similarly, the attack on the absolute monarchy of Louis XIV, on the apathy and gullibility of the people, all these considerations that feature so prominently in Gueudeville's critique, were already prefigured in the early issues of *L'Esprit des cours.* In the very first issue, for example, Gueudeville speaks of the enormous amount of money the Dauphin and the Duke of Burgundy fritter away on pleasure. All this is paid for out of the royal treasury while nothing is done "pour guérir quantité de malades qui gémissent dedans et dehors le royaume" (June 1699, 45). In the same issue he discusses the blindness of despots and tyrants who, because they are always surrounded by sycophants, never get to know the truth about themselves or anyone else.[39] And it is not only the tyrants whom Gueudeville attacks, but also the people, "ces grenouilles de la fable qui ne sont jamais contentes de ce que Jupiter leur envoie, parce qu'elles ne savent ce qu'il leur faut" (October 1699, 490). Finally, Gueudeville uses the occasion of the birth of a son to the Duke and Duchess of Lorraine to make a direct reference to the political implications of Fénelon's novel:

... on ne peut nier de bon sens, et de bonne foi, que les peuples pâtissent de la mauvaise éducation des princes; la véritable école d'un homme destiné au commandement, c'est celle de l'obéissance... Ceux qui sont nés pour faire le bonheur des autres devraient avoir senti la misère... mais comme la chose est moralement impossible... il est d'autres voies de former une tête à la couronne... c'est de trouver un Mentor qui conduise un jeune Télémaque par le droit chemin du trône, qui sache développer les objets, et les montrer au naturel, qui soit entendu à mettre les bons et les mauvais princes dans une juste opposition, qui munisse le coeur de son élève d'un bon antidote contre le poison de la tyrannie, qui... le rende tout de diamant contre la maxime *que les peuples sont pour les rois, et non pas les rois pour les peuples...* Ces Mentors ne sont pas aisés à découvrir; Minerve ne descend pas du ciel pour tout le monde; elle ne prodigue pas ainsi sa divinité sous le dehors d'une avanturière. Cette déesse n'est pas à qui en veut, et parce que tous les rois ne sont pas des Ulysses, elle ne s'empresse pas à former des Télémaques... (October 1699, 506–509)

Gueudeville, knowing the furore created at court by the publication of *Télémaque,* goes on ironically to praise Louis XIV for having so wisely chosen such an excellent teacher for the Dauphin and the grandchildren — "Dieu veuille que son peuple en ressente les heureux effets, et qu'il bénisse un jour la

mèmoire d'un roi qui a travaillé avec application à se donner de bons successeurs."
We can see, therefore, that months before Gueudeville began to publish his
critique of *Télémaque,* he had already outlined his position. His comments on
the novel in the six parts of the critique are simply an elaboration of ideas
adumbrated in the first issues of his journal.

The critics have been perplexed by Gueudeville's attitude towards Fénelon.
Because of Gueudeville's frequent apologies for his criticisms of the archbishop,
and his repeated protestations of admiration for the man and his work, Delval
concluded that Gueudeville "ne pouvait s'empêcher de l'admirer et... il était
au fond, honteux de son rôle."[40] Although Cahen thought that Gueudeville's
expressions of admiration and respect for the archbishop were absolutely
sincere, he was not always sure that Gueudeville's attitude was free from
malice.[41]

Gueudeville's attitude towards Fénelon and his work is best understood by
considering his polemical techniques in *L'Esprit des cours de l'Europe* where
his badinage commonly takes an ironic form. As we have seen, Gueudeville
delighted in reporting and encouraging any form of dissension in the Catholic
religion and in France. If Fénelon's quietism caused trouble, then Fénelon was
a man to be admired, even if the ideas he expressed were utterly worthless.
When the publication of *Télémaque,* therefore, scandalized the French court,
and ruined the archbishop's already damaged reputation, Gueudeville was
absolutely delighted, especially since the political ideas expressed in the book
were so close to his own:

L'illustre auteur que je critique est avec justice dans une vénération singulière
chez tous les honnêtes gens; moi-même qui, à ma manière toujours outrée,
lui fais si peu de grâce, j'estime infiniment sa politique et sa morale; j'ose dire,
sans prétendre me mesurer avec ce grand homme, que ses maximes sur ces
deux genres sont tout à fait les miennes (*Critique de la première et seconde
suite du tome second,* p. 6).[42]

The reason Gueudeville admired Fénelon was that, like many others, he
considered *Télémaque* to be a veiled attack on the person and régime of
Louis XIV. The main purpose of Gueudeville's criticism was to lift this veil:

... ces traits de politique morale excellent trop à mon goût pour les laisser
obscurcis et comme effacés par les ténèbres du roman; il n'y a point de justice
que des vérités si grandes, si belles, si solides, doivent le jour à la chimère, et
qu'elles restent enveloppées dans le mensonge et dans la fiction. Un jour
viendra peut-être que je ramasserai toutes ces perles, et que les tirant de la fable
que je regarde pour elles comme un véritable fumier, je tâcherai d'en bâtir un
système (*Critique de la première et seconde suite du tome second,* p. 92)

Gueudeville did not believe, or did not find it convenient to believe Fénelon's
claim that the work had never been intended for publication, that it had been

written simply to amuse and instruct his pupil in the art of kingship, and that there had never been any thought of applying these general observations on rulers, politics, morality and the like, to any real person or situation. If Fénelon did not intend to attack the France of Louis XIV, says Gueudeville, he must have been a fool, since only a fool could have failed to see the obvious application of his supposedly general remarks to the specific instance:

... oseriez-vous bien soutenir que notre auteur a tiré son coup en l'air et sans réflexion sur aucun prince? Ce serait vous inscrire en faux contre la voix publique, ce serait, j'en suis sûr, étouffer vos propres lumières; je ne sais si monsieur de Cambrai lui-même vous en croirait sur votre parole, du moins est-il certain que vous lui attribueriez une vue bien courte, et que vous feriez passer ce grand homme pour un grand étourdi (*Le Critique ressuscité*, p. 114).

What has confused the critics is that, from time to time, Gueudeville pretended to accept the argument that Fénelon's only aim was to "bannir l'injustice de dessus la terre." But this was part of Gueudeville's amusing badinage. In any case, whether Fénelon intended specific satire or not, the damage had been done, and the reader was now free to make of it what he liked:

J'ai attribué, dit-on, à notre auteur, un certain point de vue que la prudence m'empêche de nommer; je ne me défendrai point d'avoir formé là-dessus quelques conjectures; mais je ne l'ai fait qu'après la voix publique... enfin, qu'a-t-elle de si criant cette vue dont on me fait un crime impardonnable?... Depuis quand est-ce être scélérat que de montrer le désordre présent à travers le voile ingénieux d'un passé figuré? Est-ce calomnier la vertu de dire d'un homme, il a vu l'injustice, il l'a déplorée, il en a gémi tout bas, et n'ayant pu l'attaquer à force ouverte il a employé le mystère comme une arme toute propre à la combattre? (*Critique de la première et seconde suite du tome second*, p. 129)

The main object of Gueudeville's critique, therefore, was to "développer cette satire toute mystique, laquelle on veut que l'auteur répande avec dévotion sur le plus sage et le plus puissant gouvernement qui fût jamais." Gueudeville's method consists principally in making specific Fénelon's general and "veiled" observations, and in constantly finding parallels between the mythological framework and the situation in Europe at the end of the seventeenth century.

Gueudeville presents his critique in the form of a communication supposedly written by a loyal Frenchman who has been asked by a Huguenot friend in Holland to set down his opinion of Fénelon's *Télémaque*. This elementary subterfuge, which is abandoned later on, enables Gueudeville to discuss the situation in France as it appears to a victim of the régime, now living in freedom, and as it appears to someone who is a victim without realizing it.

It is not until well over half way through the *Critique générale* that, after discussing the unsuitability of fiction for instruction, the narrative technique and the style, Gueudeville reaches the heart of the matter. He has been discussing how the French consider themselves the arbiters of good taste in literature, and he ends this discussion by saying that "il n'appartient qu'à eux d'aspirer à la monarchie universelle de l'esprit." With the expression "monarchie universelle" we are plunged immediately into what was the most topical and burning issue of the day, the accusation that Louis XIV intended to emulate the exploits of his illustrious predecessor, Charlemagne. The loyal Frenchman rejects this accusation, but because the Frenchman also happens to be Gueudeville, his defence of Louis XIV only adds fuel to the fire, and ends in an ill-concealed tribute to William III:

... les ennemis de notre incomparable prince ont publié longtemps qu'il projetait de conquérir l'Europe; la calomnie était grossière; on connaît la justice et la modération du roi, et Sa Majesté en a donné des preuves éclatantes, en arrêtant plusieurs fois la rapidité de ses courses victorieuses, et en donnant la paix au monde; ce qu'il y a de vrai c'est que, si Louis le Grand n'a pas cherché à se rendre maître de l'Europe, il a été en passe de le devenir, jusqu'à ce que le Ciel, dont les desseins sont profonds... ait suscité comme de rien un autre prince capable d'abaisser une fière puissance, et de faire échouer les plus vastes projets (p. 31).

The Frenchman then goes on to consider the charge that Fénelon's intention was to attack the régime. If so eminent and religious a man denies the charge then it must be false "car les saints, et surtout les saints mystiques ne sauraient mentir." But there are still malicious people who insist on applying Mentor's general remarks on tyranny to the court of Louis XIV. It is understandable that enemies of France should interpret the work in this way. Nations such as the English or the Poles, "idolâtres de la liberté, ne jettent sur nous que des regards méprisants et dédaigneux"; and the French refugees would naturally adopt such a stance:

... vous vous regardez comme les martyrs de la cause de Dieu et de celle des lois... vous vous croyez les victimes d'une injuste oppression; il n'est pas étonnant que vous preniez un grand goût à tout ce qui peut décrier la conduite de votre persécuteur; enfin je vous pardonne vos commentaires et vos joies sur Télémaque: c'est la moindre grâce qu'on puisse accorder à des innocents malheureux; à plus forte raison n'en ferai-je point de querelle à vos frères qui languissent au milieu de nous: leur disgrâce est encore bien plus grande que la vôtre (p. 37).

But, says the Frenchman, that Catholics and Frenchman should also profess to find in Fénelon's novel a criticism of their own régime is incomprehensible and disgraceful. This, however, is characteristic of the French who, even when they worship their monarch, are delighted to see him criticized. One has only to examine in detail what Mentor says about the qualities necessary in a good king, to see how fortunate we are in Louis XIV, and to see how vapid is the idea that satire was intended.

Mentor says that the fundamental requirement of a good king is that he should live only for his subjects. That is exactly what Louis XIV does. He lives only to reign, and he intends to reign until his death. Mentor says a king should be to his subjects as a tender father is to his children. This is precisely how Louis XIV behaves. He is always looking after the welfare of his subjects. When he came to the throne he found disorder everywhere. By assuming sole control of all the administration he established peace and order so that France is now like a well-run house in which the father, "disposant de tout le bien, retient tout son monde dans l'ordre, dans la dépendance et dans le devoir." You do not hear any more complaints, and there is no more internal conflict — "l'ambition des princes est calmée, les gouverneurs sont soumis, les parlements ouvrent leurs régistres, les peuples n'ont plus qu'à ouvrir leurs bourses, et, le pouvoir absolu influant partout, chacun vit en paix sous son figuier."

The Dutch, of course, regard the French as slaves. It is true that the French are not as well-nourished as the Dutch, and the peasants not as rich, but they live in peace. Besides, the king does not control the nation's wealth for personal gain but to manage the economy wisely. Although France is not at war it still has to raise taxes. What does Louis do, then, with all the millions he gets in revenue?:

Il en fait généreusement part à ceux qui ont l'honneur de le servir, et principale- ment à ces personnes entendues qui manient ses finances; il entretient des armées formidables qui le rendent l'arbitre des lois et la terreur de ses voisins; il agrandit ses palais: il y fait des embellissements qui vont jusqu'au miracle, et réforme la nature en aplanissant le montagnes et en creusant de nouvelles rivières... Combien de villes achetées? Combien d'espions entretenus? Je ne dis rien du fameux commerce de Constantinople lequel, s'il n'a pas été le plus glorieux de tous, a été du moins le plus utile pour la France (pp. 42–43).[43]

Louis looks after not only the temporal state of his people but also their spiritual welfare. He may have taken away the people's money which, in any case, caused them only troubles, but he has given them in exchange peace and glory. He may have ruined French commerce by getting rid of the Protestants, but the French prefer their religion to business. No French peasant would want to change his lot for that of a Dutch burgomaster. Moreover, poverty suits the French, so it is just to ensure that they remain poor. Finally, a proof that the French are happy in their present state is the fact that no one complains. There is not a word of protest in the French gazette, although the Huguenots publish in their gazettes reports of unrest in France.

Mentor speaks against unjust wars. But are there such things? Louis XIV simply behaves in the way that previous conquerors such as Alexander have done. These men have always been regarded as heroes, and the Church still speaks of them with approval. Louis XIV's conquests, then, are beyond reproach, and all initiated for sound reasons.

But suppose, for a moment, that Louis XIV were the very opposite of the good king portrayed by Mentor, is it not the case that no king, in real life, could possibly measure up to such an ideal standard. Is not Mentor's portrait ridiculously utopian?:

Si un roi observait tous ces divins préceptes, il deviendrait la victime de son peuple, et sa condition serait pire que celle d'un particulier. Je souhaite à toutes les nations le prince de Mentor: mais où le trouver? Mentor veut un roi sans faiblesse et sans passions: cela se peut-il! Les rois étant maîtres et hommes tout ensemble, il est impossible qu'ils ne soient sujets à des vices éclatants: un ambitieux ruinera toujours son peuple par la guerre: un voluptueux ne saurait donner bon exemple: un avare sucera toujours le sang de ses sujets: un coeur de fer ne sera touché de rien: un roi fier et absolu voudra dominer sur tout: un prince prévenu d'un faux zèle persécutera jusqu'à la mort: ainsi des autres défauts: c'est au peuple à baisser la tête et à les supporter (pp. 46–47).

The first part of Gueudeville's critique ends with a request to the Dutch correspondent to burn the document, and thus ensure that no Huguenot sees it. Since the Frenchman has a great deal of respect for the tenacity of these refugees, he would prefer not to offend them by his praise of Louis XIV.

All the major elements of Gueudeville's political satire are present in this first part. The remaining parts will serve to make them more specific. In the *Critique du premier tome,* Gueudeville returns to Mentor's portrait of the good king as father of his people, and shows the impossibility of such a relationship. Even if a king did try to behave as a father, would the people know how to behave as children? The French have a father for a king yet their lives are miserable. Whose fault can it be but their own?:

Notre France a un roi sage s'il en fût jamais. . . Son royaume est le mieux policé de l'Europe; sa Majesté règne sur un peuple soumis, fidèle, affectionné. Je puis même soutenir. . . que le roi aime tendrement ses sujets. Cependant l'abondance n'est pas notre partage, les lois fondamentales sont éteintes, la liberté est morte: mais à quoi faut-il s'en prendre? Au roi? Nullement. Ce serait la plus grande injustice du monde. Nous l'avions obtenu du Ciel par nos voeux, par nos prières, et par nos larmes (p. 101).

Mentor paints a picture of the contentment of the Egyptians under a wise king who finds his happiness in virtue, who is loved by his subjects, a king for whom his people would die rather than lose him. All this is utopian nonsense, says the Frenchman. Not a nation in Europe has such a king, except perhaps France where, to some extent, "on y meurt pour l'amour de son roi."

Even if a king were virtuous he would soon be corrupted by those around him. Sesostris, king of Egypt, is an excellent king who has as minister, "un certain Métophis, homme pernicieux, scélérat achevé, qui possède l'esprit de son maître, et qui lui fait accroire tout ce qu'il veut." It is not entirely clear which minister Gueudeville had in mind. According to the author of the 1719 edition of *Télémaque,* Gueudeville was referring here to two men, the duc de Lerme, minister of Philip IV, king of Spain, and Louis' right-hand man, Louvois. Whether these attributions are correct is hard to say, but there is little doubt about the parallel drawn, in the following passage, between the situation of the cruel king Boccoris, successor to Sesostris, and James II of England:

... à peine est-il [Boccoris] sur le trône qu'il veut tout bouleverser. Ses sujets ont recours à une puissance étrangère, et il aurait eu le même sort qu'un prince de notre temps si son courage avait été aussi modéré que celui de ce prince, et s'il avait eu, comme lui, la prudence de chercher deux fois son salut dans une fuite précipitée (p. 109).

Nor is there any difficulty in drawing a parallel between Tyre and Holland, the Phoenicians and the Dutch, since Gueudeville, alias the Frenchman, does it for us, although he says, with evident malice, that Fénelon did not intend such a parallel to be drawn:

Je ne vous dis rien de la description de l'heureuse ville de Tyr, de la sagesse des Phéniciens, de la diligence, du travail, du commerce, de la bonté, de l'hospitalité de ces amiables peuples... je reconnais votre chère Hollande dans ce portrait naïf; et comme j'ai une vénération infinie pour cette incomparable république, sans entrer dans les intentions d'un prélat tout romain, j'ai cru voir vos provinces dans cet endroit, et je m'en suis su fort bon gré. Je dis, sans entrer dans les intentions de l'auteur, car je ne crois point du tout qu'il y ait visé (pp. 116–117).

At this point in Fénelon's novel there is a fairly lengthy discourse on the value of international trade and how best it should be conducted. Tyre is held up as the example to follow. Competition between the French and the Dutch was keen, and the desire to restrict each other's trade led, in 1699, to a tariff war which effectively reduced trade between the two countries. It must be this consideration that is behind the comment of Gueudeville's Frenchman who, in referring to Fénelon's account of the business practices in Tyre, says:

... si l'on avait suivi une politique si ronde et si unie, nos marchands ne crieraient point si fort, et le règlement des tarifs n'aurait point tant traîné. Mais, de bonne foi, Monsieur, cette politique est-elle française? Que le prince donne toute satisfaction aux étrangers, qu'il les laisse faire avec ses marchands, et qu'il ne prenne aucune connaissance du commerce de son royaume! En vérité, cela ne peut sortir que de la plume d'un ecclésiastique qui n'entend rien dans ces matières (pp. 118–119).

At the end of the *Critique du premier tome,* Gueudeville quotes another of Fénelon's portraits of the good king "[qui] peut tout sur les peuples, mais les lois peuvent tout sur lui. Il a une puissance absolue pour faire le bien, et les mains liées dès qu'il veut faire le mal. . ." This gives Gueudeville another opportunity to criticize Fénelon for his hopelessly utopian view of kings and of human nature, and to bring the discussion round again to the situation in France, a situation with which the "loyal" Frenchman is quite satisfied:

Le roi est pour le peuple, il est vrai; mais le peuple est assez bête pour vouloir être gouverné, comme s'il n'était que pour le roi. Au compte de notre auteur, la monarchie française aurait fait le tour, et ne subsisterait plus que par son envers. Cependant, interrogez nos Français: il n'y a pas un de leurs politiques qui ne fasse retentir la justice du roi et le bonheur de la nation. Que Mentor garde donc son fantôme de prince! Nous sommes contents du nôtre, et nous craignons qu'il nous échappe trop tôt (pp. 123–125).

In the *Critique du second tome* Gueudeville discusses Fénelon's presentation of Idomeneus, king of Crete, "le pays de la raison et de l'équité." When Idomeneus ceases to be a good king and behaves as a tyrant, the Cretans revolt, and Idomeneus is driven from the country whence he goes with his friends to found a new kingdom in Salentum. Gueudeville, in characteristic fashion, speculates on why Fénelon included this episode. Surely he cannot have really meant that when a people is governed by a tyrant the people have the right to revolt:

. . . de croire que l'auteur ait voulu insinuer dans cet endroit que les sujets peuvent se faire raison d'un roi violent et qui commet des injustices criantes, c'est donner dans l'entêtement de ces gens qui prennent des fantômes pour des corps, et qui trouvent du fin et du solide dans les plus creuses rêveries de Télémaque; l'auteur est trop éclairé et trop bon sujet pour avoir proposé, sous une enveloppe si mince, un sentiment capable de bouleverser la plus puissante monarchie du monde (p. 138).

The flight of Idomeneus from Crete puts Gueudeville in mind of the more recent departure of James II from England:

C'est un roi rempli de terreur et d'épouvante, à qui l'ombre d'un père supplicié donne des frayeurs bien fondées: qui. . . cède la victoire avant le combat, qui traverse la mer et se réfugie chez ses voisins. . . entraîné par les remords de sa conscience ou par son mauvais destin, il quitta une partie qu'il crut désespéré. . . Personne ne le vit partir, et tout le monde le plaignait, excepté ceux qui connaissaient les justes bornes de l'autorité royale (p. 139).

Having got rid of Idomeneus, the Cretans turned to the question of a successor. Instead of giving the throne to Hippomachus, who claimed it by virtue of family ties, the Cretans resolved to settle future successions by the elective process. Gueudeville clearly has in mind the imminent conflagration over the question of succession to the throne of Spain, and he suggests that "notre auteur avait ses raisons pour donner de nouveaux fondements à la monarchie crétoise" (p. 141).

In order to be a candidate for the Cretan throne it is necessary to distinguish oneself in physical combat, after which one must answer three questions, the first of which asks which man is the freest. This question gives Gueudeville an opportunity to discuss the nature of liberty, to condemn those nations such as the Turks, the Muscovites, the Moroccans and, by implication, the French, all of whom live in a condition of slavery. The only free man, he says ironically, is the absolute monarch who, like God, is omnipotent and answerable to no one. The only difference is that man is not immortal, and even a tyrant is afraid to die. However, the Jesuits can do something about that:

Mais il y a des remèdes contre ces frayeurs. La religion bien ou mal entendue fournit à l'esprit de quoi s'assurer contre les menaces de la mort. On a recours à certaines menues dévotions que les esprits éclairés et solides traitent de bagatelles et de superstition, mais qui sont d'un grand secours à une âme qui a peur. On se flatte de mérites et de couronnes éternelles; on croit les directeurs qui n'ont garde de promettre autre chose, et qui l'assurent avec un air et un ton de prophètes (p. 155).

The second question asks who is the most unfortunate of men. Telemachus thinks it must be a king who finds his only happiness by making others miserable, and who will be punished for his crimes in the next world. Gueudeville finds this answer unsatisfactory. The fact that a tyrant may be punished in the next world in no way prevents him from enjoying himself in this one.

The third question asks who is to be preferred, a gentle and pacific king or an impetuous, warrior king. Telemachus speaks in favour of the former, and shows what miseries are brought about by the policies of a warlike king. Gueudeville suggests that Fénelon, in writing this speech, had someone in mind — "Cela est du dernier malin et n'est pas avancé en l'air" (p. 164). Gueudeville finds this portrait of a pacific king to be pure fantasy. Such a king, nowadays, could never stay in power:

Dans le temps où nous sommes, la principale affaire d'un prince c'est de se bien tenir sur ses gardes; et s'il est assez modéré pour ne pas attaquer, il ne peut prendre trop de précautions pour être toujours en état de se bien défendre. Quand on jette les yeux sur la face de l'Europe, l'on est surpris de la voir toute armée, et que, quoique dans un temps de paix, on y parle beaucoup plus de guerre que du commerce et de la culture des beaux arts; qui fait cela? C'est que la politique ne roulant que sur le droit du plus fort et du meilleur canon, chaque prince craint la surprise et tâche de la prévenir (pp. 166–167).

Gueudeville opts, then, for a warrior king "pourvu qu'il n'abuse point de son courage ni de ses forces, et qu'il ne se serve de l'un et de l'autre que dans une nécessité indispensable." An excess of valour, however, can be a defect in a good king, since he constantly risks his life in the service of his people. This was the case of William III during the war of the League of Augsburg:

On sait les alarmes et les cruelles inquiétudes qu'un héros a données à tout son parti pendant la dernière guerre, lorsqu'il allait au feu comme un lion, et qu'il exposait sa précieuse personne comme si elle n'eût fait que nombre, et que sa tête n'eût pas été le principal appui de la confédération (p. 168).

In Fénelon's novel, the crown of Crete is offered in turn to Telemachus, Mentor and Hazaël who all refuse it because they regard the duties of a king as too onerous. Gueudeville finds this ridiculous. The responsibilities of a king may be heavy, but there are many compensations. No one in real life refuses a crown. On the contrary, in the real world people fight for it. "Les Polonais, par exemple, ayant à se donner un roi sont dans un embarras tout opposé à celui des Crétois. Ceux-ci ne peuvent trouver un homme, et les autres n'en trouvent que trop."[44]

The *Critique du second tome* ends with Gueudeville's comments on Fénelon's account of Boetica, a kind of earthly paradise in which all the inhabitants are free and happy. Gueudeville thinks Fénelon portrayed this ideal society in order to make us aware of the miserable conditions under which we live, but he also thinks this could be a dangerous procedure:

... si tous les adorateurs du Télémaque s'allaient mettre en tête de former en Europe un gouvernement semblable à celui de Bétique n'entendrait-on pas sonner la révolte et l'anarchie de tous côtés; il est permis à nous de déplorer tout bas notre malheur et de balancer en secret notre condition contre la raison et le droit naturel; mais il nous est défendu d'en avertir publiquement les autres; c'est un attentat contre la tranquillité publique, et contre l'autorité du souverain (pp. 249–250).

Fénelon, says Gueudeville, errs in condemning kings whose only ambition seems to be to dominate others, who, through unjust wars, invade and conquer other nations for the sole purpose of enslaving them. Of course, Louis XIV has never been guilty of such acts. All his wars have been just and legitimate instances of self-defence or attack, but not all the nations of Europe share this view, and they must be encouraged in their beliefs when they see so eminent a man as the archbishop, entrusted by Louis XIV with the education of his grandson, inveighing so forcibly against conquerors. He certainly has made it necessary for himself to prove that all Louis XIV's conquests since the Treaty of the Pyrenees have been legitimate.

Fénelon also gets himself into difficulties when he suggests, in his portrait of Boetica, that a monarch who rules people by force is a tyrant. But what else has Louis XIV done with the French Protestants?:

Quand on ramène ces prétendus dévoyes par bandes comme des troupeaux de moutons, qu'on en peuple les prisons, les couvents, les galères, et qu'on les traite avec la dernière cruauté, à la mort près qui leur serait douce, et qu'ils se donneraient eux-mêmes si la religion ne le défendait, n'est-ce point là gouverner des hommes par force. . . ? (p. 254).

Gueudeville also notes that, in describing the perfections of Boetica, Fénelon makes no provision for religion. Gueudeville cannot understand such a signal omission when "il n'y a point de véritable bonheur en ce monde sans la connaissance et sans l'amour de la divinité." The book ends with a discussion of Fénelon's own quietist views which Gueudeville condemns as heretical.

In the *Critique de la suite du second tome,* Mentor and Telemachus visit Idomeneus in Salentum, and Mentor lectures Idomeneus on the art of kingship. The responsibilities of monarchy are so great, says Mentor, that kings wear out, grow old, and suffer more than any man. Gueudeville does not agree. In another patent reference to the Bloodless Revolution and the flight of James II to the protection of Louis XIV, Gueudeville observes:

. . . le plus grand malheur qui puisse arriver à un roi c'est de se brouiller tellement avec la religion et les lois que son peuple, justement irrité contre son génie despotique, et craignant les dangereuses suites d'une tyrannie naissante, appelle à son secours un prince voisin et intéressé à la succession; et, sitôt qu'il paraît, et sans tirer l'épée, oblige ce roi effrayé. . . de prendre la fuite. . . Avec tout cela ne voit-on pas de ces sortes de rois mener après une si affreuse disgrâce, une vie longue et paisible; ne les voit-on pas à la faveur d'une généreuse et magnifique protection partager leur temps entre la piété et les plaisirs, avoir une petite cour qui semble être comme l'ombre ou l'écho de la grande qui la leur donne? (p. 298)

Nor is it true to say that kings wear themselves out in the service of their people. As far as wars are concerned, very few kings take an active part. They prefer to leave the fighting and the dangers to their generals. Moreover, those kings who do participate in person, far from ruining their health, actually thrive on the military life. Gueudeville, without naming him, cites Charles XII of Sweden as an example:

Ce serait à un prince de nos jours que toute l'Europe a vu courir, voler cent fois à la gloire, et toujours pour une juste défense, endosser la cuirasse avec plus de plaisir que ses habits royaux, fournir à tout dans la mêlée, aller de rang en rang, animer le soldat plus par son exemple que par sa parole, se trouver au feu, affronter la mort d'un courage intrépide, forçant les villes prétendues imprenables, ou restant victorieux même dans ses défaites; ce serait à lui qu'on aurait droit de dire que le nombre de campagnes a diminué ses forces et ralenti sa vigueur. Mais dirait-on vrai? Non sans doute, puisque la guerre est l'élément de ce héros, et que jamais il ne jouit d'une santé plus parfaite que quand il a les armes à la main (pp. 300–301).

It is not even true to say that kings wear themselves out with pleasure. Kings are naturally restricted in their pleasures because they are always in the public eye, and must consider their reputations. Moreover, religion requires a king to set a good example. Some kings, however, sacrifice everything to their passions. Louis XIV is not named but the application to him is evident in the following passage:

... quand on nous citerait des princes dont on pourrait compter des maîtresses par le nombre des rares visages qui ont paru dans leur cour, sans parler de leurs secrètes et mystérieuses amours; quand nous en verrions comme le cruel et inhumain Hérode, qui ont débauché la femme d'un autre, et qui ont soutenu plusieurs années à la face du ciel et de la terre un infâme adultère avec une impudence qui a fait horreur à tous les gens de bien, que gagnerait-on par là?... On a vu ces princes emportés et brutaux survivre à toutes leurs débauches amoureuses, profiter de l'épuisement de leurs reins, métamorphoser leur impuissance en chaste vertu, faire pénitence à leur mode, réciter autant de petites prières qu'ils avaient compté de douceurs, passer du feu de Vénus au zèle du sanctuaire, vouloir sauver les âmes après avoir usé les corps, répandre partout les étincelles d'une ardeur divine, travailler à réduire leur royaume en cloître, après l'avoir réduit en hôpital, enfin, mourir dans une profonde vieillesse, et trouver place dans le calendrier. Charlemagne n'est-il pas, à quelque chose près, un fort bon garant de ce que j'avance? (pp. 303–304)[45]

During the course of their discussions Idomeneus confesses that he has been a tyrant and that his tyrannical treatment of the Cretans cost him his throne and his reputation. All tyrants, he concludes, will suffer the same fate. Gueudeville finds that just the contrary happens. Rather than losing by their behaviour tyrants profit by it.

The *Critique de la suite du second tome* draws to a close with comments by Gueudeville on yet another discourse by Mentor on the art of kingship. The enemies of Idomeneus have sued for peace. Mentor advises Idomeneus that a wise king should always seek to live a peace with his neighbours, and to enjoy their trust and friendship. Gueudeville says that some malicious people have suggested that Fénelon wrote this at the beginning of the last war, and it was not Idomeneus he had in mind at the time. But Gueudeville, himself, does not indulge in such malicious remarks! He wishes, however, that kings would follow this laudable but hardly practical advice, especially the king "qui ne donnant point de bornes à sa puissance [entreprend] d'assujettir l'Europe, et [se met] en tête la monarchie universelle" (p. 329).

Mentor cautions Idomeneus against continuing the war. All he has achieved up to now is to alienate his neighbours, make himself hated abroad, and slowly ruin his country internally by the efforts needed to maintain the war. Gueudeville is shocked that Fénelon could have been so foolhardy as to express such an idea during the last war. If Fénelon did not have Louis XIV in mind:

Il devait au moins éviter les soupçons, et ne pas donner occasion aux ennemis de Sa Majesté, qui faisaient en ce temps-là la meilleure partie de l'Europe, de faire des applications injurieuses. Que l'apologiste de Monsieur de Cambrai justifie tant qu'il voudra son poète oratoire, on n'a pas pu lire dans le Télémaque le trait piquant de Mentor dans un temps où le roi ne fait que sortir d'une terrible et redoutable guerre, sans conjecturer qu'Idoménée ne sert que de rideau (pp. 331–332).

The *Critique de la première et seconde suite du tome second* takes up where the previous part left off. Salentum is surrounded by its enemies whom Mentor addresses. He asks them to make peace with Idomeneus despite the justice of their cause. If they do not make peace there will be great devastation. Gueudeville finds this part of Fénelon's novel quite unbelievable. Idomeneus has only just started to build Salentum. He has few forces and, far from being a threat to others, is in imminent danger of being destroyed. If Fénelon wanted to portray Idomeneus as a menace to other nations he should have described him differently, by drawing an analogy with his modern counterpart:

Il fallait nous représenter Idoménée comme un monarque lequel, se voyant bien affermi sur son trône, médite le vaste projet de conquérir toute l'Hespérie. Ce Prince... profitant de l'indolence, de la faiblesse, ou de la bonne foi de ses voisins... se serait jeté sur eux, et les aurait plutôt opprimés que vaincus; trouvant à la fin de son premier ou second effort plus de résistance qu'il n'attendait, il aurait fait la paix à des conditions avantageuses... (pp. 21–22).

Gueudeville continues at length, in this vein, to draw implicit parallels between Idomeneus and Louis XIV, and between the enemies of Idomeneus and the League of Augsburg. Finally, when one of the allies outlines their grievances against Idomeneus, Gueudeville's commentary becomes more explicit:

Un Allemand, un Flamand, un Espagnol, un Suisse n'expliquerait jamais le fait si clairement touchant l'usurpation des passages et la violation des serments... On a eu de nos jours la même matière en grand volume... S'aviserait-on à présent dans une assemblée de plénipotentiaries de vomir de grosses injures contre une nation dont le monarque aurait usurpé sur tous ses voisins et violé plusieurs fois ses serments? (pp. 53–54).

Mentor, however, insists on Idomeneus' desire for peace. Although, if he wished, Idomeneus could force the others to agree to conditions unfavourable to them, he wants only to deal fairly and honourably with his enemies. This time, Gueudeville makes no attempt to conceal the parallel:

Si les illustres ministres dont la France s'est servie pour négocier la Paix de Ryswick (Paix si glorieuse à sa Majesté Très-Chrétienne, et si utile à l'Europe) avaient parlé de ce ton-là aux plénipotentiaires des Alliés, il n'y aurait pas eu le mot à dire (p. 59).

When peace is finally signed, Mentor places a curse on all violators of treaties. Gueudeville speculates on how much misery has been caused by a king who violated a treaty "pendant une rupture de neuf ou dix années." Mentor then speaks of universal brotherhood and describes, once again, a society in which the king's object is the happiness and welfare of his people, and in which the people love their king. Gueudeville, again, praises the sentiments but finds them utterly unrealistic.

Only Adrastus, king of the Daunians, is not a signatory to the peace. He is described by Mentor as a man who considers himself above everyone, above the law, even above God. All he cares about is the domination of others. Gueudeville says that those who look for parallels in Fénelon's novel will not find one here. He cannot think of anyone who might fit this description! Kings always respect religion. In fact, some of them respect it so much they want to force others to respect it too!

In a further discussion of the attributes of kings, Gueudeville points out how despicable it is to attack régimes in print. Those who publish such calumnies must expect to receive the full weight of the law. It is permissible to attack tyranny, injustice, corruption, etc., and a writer is not responsible for the conclusions a malicious reader might draw. On the other hand Gueudeville cannot see what value there is in one country complaining to another about satirical articles in the press. This only draws attention to the satire and does far too much honour to some unknown and impoverished writer.[46] Louis XIV would never expose himself to such an indignity:

Depuis que la France s'est élevé vers le suprême degré où nous la voyons à présent, a-t-on manqué de la déchirer par des satires et par des libelles? On a été jusqu'à l'insolence de calomnier son illustre prince... mais comment l'a-t-il pris?... La vérité même, j'entends cette vérité offensante qui vous peint tel que vous êtes dans l'imagination des hommes, et dont il n'y a que les sots qui se fâchent, cette vérité... n'a jamais porté jusque dans le coeur de ce puissant monarque; sa Majesté n'y a jamais paru sensible (pp. 87–88).

Much of Gueudeville's criticism of Louis XIV is bound up with the continuing discussion of the qualities required by a good king, and the atrocities perpetrated by bad kings. When he argues, for example, that a king who commands his armies in person is, at least, fulfilling some of his duties as a leader, his attack is directed against Louis who directs his campaigns from the court. The ideal warrior king is someone like William III who risked everything for his people, and for whom the people were willing to risk their lives in return.

The speeches of Mentor to Idomeneus give Gueudeville an opportunity to make comparisons between republics and monarchies. A republican prizes liberty above everything. The subjects of an absolute monarch live not only in a condition of slavery but they enjoy it, and would never even dream of revolting:

Ne les a-t-on pas vus ces peuples si foulés et si opprimés, ne les a-t-on pas vus dans la naissance d'un second successeur, dans la guérison d'une maladie, dans des victoires achetées bien cher, dans la mort prétendue d'un ennemi que l'on a plus craint lui seul que tous les autres ensemble, se répandre follement en acclamation, en réjouissance, en dépenses, en fêtes, et cela d'un air d'empressement qui persuadait au prince qu'il était tendrement aimé. . . ce peuple captif voyant ses fers éclairés par les rayons qui partent de la gloire de son roi, il remarque avec tant de plaisir le brillant de sa chaîne qu'il s'en sent plus du tout la pesanteur. Son roi est son soleil. . . (pp. 115–116).

In the *Critique de la seconde suite du tome second* Gueudeville, in his ironic manner, takes issue with Mentor's argument that war brings misery and disorder to a country, and that a king, in destroying others, destroys himself:

Jamais la justice et la police n'ont fleuri en France que pendant la dernière guerre; presque tous les édits qui sortaient en ce temps-là du Conseil, n'étaient que pour étendre la magistrature, et que pour créer de nouveaux surveillants au maintien de l'ordre. . . Qu'on voie tous les ennemis de Louis Quatorze enchaînés comme des esclaves à la place des victoires; n'est-ce pas par là qu'il s'est confirmé le surnom de Grand et qu'il a acquis celui d'Immortel? (p. 137).

Mentor aruges that wars can always be avoided if the parties concerned submit their claims to a mediator. Gueudeville finds this naïve. In real life, each party is convinced that it alone has God and justice on its side. But, whether it has or not, it is ambition, not justice, that starts wars. By the time mediation is thought of or agreed to, war is well under way. One has only to look at the last war to see how useless mediation is:

Que n'a-t-on point fait depuis peu pour tourner à la paix le coeur d'un prince possédé par le génie de la guerre? Les deux principales puissances de l'Europe jointes à la plus saine partie des propres sujets de ce prince l'ont pressé de renoncer à un dessein qui était alors presque échoué, mais dont la réussite même ne peut jamais être honorable; l'a-t-il fait? De quelle manière a-t-il fallu s'y prendre pour arracher les armes à un autre prince? Il les a mises bas lorsque ses forces ne lui permettaient plus de les porter; inflexible trop longtemps aux sollicitations de ses amis, il n'a acquiescé à leurs instances qu'après les avoir forcés de le traiter en ennemi (p. 145).

In *Le Critique ressuscité* Gueudeville deals with Fénelon's account of Telemachus' visit to Tartarus where the bad kings reside, and to the Elysian Fields, home of the good ones. According to Fénelon's description, the least infraction seems to consign a king to Tartarus. Gueudeville finds this an entirely ineffective deterrent since, in real life, kings live only for the present, and have no interest in what may happen to them when they are dead. Moreover, since kings rule by divine right they are agents of God, and thus partake of his perfection. A bad king further protects himself from the idea that he commits crimes for which there will be unpleasant consequences, by surrounding himself with flatterers who conceal the truth, and with clerics who find a way to justify his actions.

After a lengthy discussion about tyrants Gueudeville turns to a consideration of good kings, of whom there are very few. The only ones deserving of paradise, according to Fénelon, are those who manage to resist the temptations of power and the flattery of their courtiers. Gueudeville finds that under these conditions no one would be admitted to paradise. Certainly Louis XIV would not be allowed to enter. But, of course, Fénelon did not have Louis in mind!:

Ce roi n'a pas été inconnu à notre auteur. Disons mieux. Notre auteur est peut-être celui qui a gémi le plus amèrement de cette dure et barbare autorité, parce que personne ne pénètre mieux que lui ce que vaut l'homme... Or pensez-vous que si ce monarque fût mort avant le pélérinage de Télémaque aux enfers, ce jeune prince ne l'eût pas aperçu d'abord avec sa taille éminente et son port majestueux entre les héros des Champs-Elysées... Notre poète n'oserait damner ce grand prince; il n'oserait le destiner à la rage et au désespoir du Tartare... (pp. 70–71).

Gueudeville continues by commenting on the popularity of Fénelon's novel. No king has identified himself with the portraits of tyrants scattered throughout the work. On the contrary, every sovereign has regarded the remarks as general and having no application to his own régime, every sovereign that is, except one, in whose country the work has been banned. Gueudeville finds "rien de plus irrégulier qu'une puissance qui passe elle-même sa condamnation en se trouvant dans le vague et dans le général, et en prenant pour soi ce qui ne s'adresse qu'au vice." (p. 73)

The last part of Le Critique ressuscité deals with the war against Adrastus, and gives Gueudeville an opportunity to attack, once again, those who violate treaties. This time he criticizes those who try to avoid their obligations by making jesuitical distinctions between the spirit and the letter of the agreement:

Pour me rendre plus intelligible, je m'arrête au Traité de Ryswick. N'est-il pas vrai que le véritable esprit de cette fameuse convention c'est le repos et la tranquillité de l'Europe? Supposons qu'un de nos rois, chagrin de voir... que l'Europe... ne sera jamais parfaitement heureuse qu'elle ne soit réunie sous une même domination... se mettant en tête d'exécuter ce grand ouvrage, aveuglât par son or la moitié des souverains, puis se servît d'eux pour faire la guerre aux autres... ce roi serait-il coupable de perfidie et de mauvaise foi? Rien moins que cela... Ne voyez-vous pas que ce bon prince ayant agi pour le but et la fin de ce traité n'aurait cherché qu'à le rendre plus fructueux... Je m'étais engagé avec vous, il est vrai, dira un souverain... d'observer exactement certaines conditions et certains articles... je ne touche point à l'esprit de notre traité, j'en détruis seulement la lettre qui n'est rien (pp. 94–95).

Gueudeville points out that it is this kind of thinking that has led to the destruction of the social contract.

Finally, the Daunians are defeated and the tyrant Adrastus is killed. The Allies decide to divide up the conquered territory. They offer the best parts to Telemachus who refuses, not because he believes that "il n'y a point de fonds à faire sur un Traité de Partage," (p. 110) but because he finds kingship too heavy a burden. The man who wants to be the master of others for his own profit, says Telemachus, is an impious tyrant and the plague of mankind. Gueudeville comments as follows:

Ce n'est pas en Hespérie que Télémaque harangue; il débute sa morale dans un royaume de l'Europe; ce n'est pas à des alliés fabuleux qu'il parle; il s'explique à des hommes de notre temps et de notre goût (p. 112).

This is the penultimate shot at Louis XIV. The last one occurs in Gueudeville's elaboration of Telemachus' remarks:

Un prince est impie lorsqu'il anticipe sur les droits de Dieu, en forçant les consciences, en les contraignant au sacrilège; un prince est tyran lorsqu'il épuise son peuple et qu'il multiplie de plus en plus parmi ses sujets la misère et la mendicité; un prince est le fléau du genre humain lorsqu'il prodigue le sang par des guerres qu'il suscite par ambition, ou qu'il s'attire par mauvaise foi (p. 116).

With a final tribute to Fénelon and his novel, Gueudeville ends his critique.[48]

Gueudeville's attack on Louis XIV is outstanding in its scope and uncompromising nature. Under the guise of a general discussion of Fénelon's *Les Avantures de Télémaque* Gueudeville draws up a bitter indictment of Louis XIV and his régime. Louis is portrayed as a murderous tyrant whose people live in object slavery, a condition to which they have become so accustomed they are no longer aware of it. Not content with enslaving his own people, this monster is secretly plotting to enslave the world. Every treaty he signs gives him breathing space and time to carry out his insane ambitions. This hypocritical behaviour is reflected in his personal life of self-indulgence and debauchery which ceases only when he is no longer physically able to maintain the pace. Then he turns to religion, and is supported in his efforts to appear devout by the corrupt and fawning Jesuits. In order to divert attention from the gross inequities in French society, and to provide a sense of unity and purpose where none exists, he engages in wars of conquest not only abroad but in France itself, against his own subjects. This cruel and cowardly persecution of an innocent minority is simply a reflection of the cruelty and cowardice of Louis himself who sends others to die on the battlefield but never goes to war himself.

This was the idea of Louis XIV's régime that many of Gueudeville's contemporaries held. If he added nothing new he, at least, gave it popular expression at a time when the fears of France were soon to be justified, once again. In 1702, as Gueudeville finished his critique, the War of the Spanish

Succession officially began. It went on for eleven miserable years during which time the end of Holland as a major power was finally confirmed. Gueudeville's critique of *Télémaque* is no longer read today. As a piece of literary criticism it is justly forgotten, but as an evocation of the attitudes of the French refugees, the Dutch and, indeed, of all those allied against Louis XIV, it still merits our attention.

V. DIALOGUES DES MORTS

Gueudeville's third and final anonymous publication appeared in 1709 in The Hague, and was entitled *Dialogues des morts d'un tour nouveau.*[1] As far as I know, no critic has ever attributed this work to Gueudeville but, apart from the internal evidence of style and content, an advertising catalogue put out by the publisher identifies him as the author.[2]

The idea for this publication was borrowed from Lucian, though it is probable that the dialogues of Fontenelle and Fénelon played a part in the genesis of the work.[3] In the preface, Gueudeville paid tribute to his classical model:

Les morts de ce bel esprit étaient les plus agréables du monde; ils avaient tout ce qu'il faut pour plaire, ne disant rien que d'enjoué, que de fin, que de curieux, soutenant bien le rôle qu'ils ont joué pendant leur vie sur le théâtre des mortels; et d'ailleurs, leurs conversations étant fort courtes, elles ne faisaient qu'entretenir le goût ou plutôt l'avidité du lecteur. . .

Je suis bien éloigné de proposer mes ombres sur ce pied-là: sans fausse modestie, je me connais et je sais qu'en travaillant sur cet excellent original, je n'aurais fait que montrer par une mauvaise copie qu'il est inimitable, ou que du moins il faudrait avoir le mérite de ce maître si fameux pour pouvoir retracer fidèlement un de ses tableaux (xi—xii).

In order to distinguish his dialogues from those of Lucian Gueudeville claims to have introduced several innovations. Since the participants are dead they will behave in an appropriate fashion. Having no feelings, they are no longer motivated by bitterness, obstinacy, impulsiveness and the like. They are interested only in justice and truth since they have nothing to gain by lies or hypocrisy in the underworld where there are no punishments or rewards, and where all are equal. In Gueudeville's dialogues, therefore, the dead are not intended to be faithful representations of their former selves. Furthermore, since the dead have no notion of time, these dialogues, unlike those of Lucian, are leisurely and long. If they put the reader to sleep, at least they will have served a useful purpose, and, if sleep is harmful to the reader, all he has to do is stop reading. Gueudeville ends his preface by replying in advance to any possible charge that his portrayal of the after life is blasphemous:

Ces enfers où je place mes interlocuteurs sont ce même lieu chimérique que la superstition païenne croyait de bonne foi sur les fictions, sur les rêveries des anciens poètes; et les ombres que j'introduis sont des êtres imaginaires qui n'ont nul rapport avec les âmes heureuses ou malheureuses dans l'éternité que la Sainte Ecriture nous a révélées. Les bigots et les visionnaires, gens fort ombrageux, pourraient se scandaliser que je ne mets ni récompenses ni peines chez Pluton, produisant même des scélérats qui semblent y jouir d'une grande tranquillité; mais outre que les Champs Elysées et les Tartares n'étaient que des imaginations, à la vérité très utiles dans la politique, mais dont les éclairés se moquaient, je n'aurais pu bâtir sur ce système sans sortir du mien, qui consiste tout entier à opposer les morts aux vivants (xviii).

There are six dialogues of varying length. The first two involve characters from Greek mythology, the third is between a Roman and a Renaissance philosopher, and, of the six personages portrayed in the last three dialogues, five are Roman emperors.[4]

The first dialogue is between Alcinoë and Aegialia, both of whose lives were ruined by an overwhelming passion.[5] It is only natural, therefore, that love should be the main topic of conversation. Aegialia speaks in praise of love, and calls it the most desirable and most attainable of all the ambitions. It is better to suffer the tyranny of love than lead a life without passion. The true lover enjoys overcoming all the obstacles to success, and appreciates that the battle is often more satisfying than the final victory. Woman's role is to set up obstacles, thus prolonging the pleasurable pain of the fight. At this point, Aegialia, who was unjustly punished for her husband's transgression, interrupts her argument in order to criticize the gods, and Gueudeville is back at his favourite game:

Aegialia. ... la plupart des Divinités ne valent pas grand-chose: Pluton tout le premier, chez qui un rapt dans toutes les formes, ne passe que pour une innocente galanterie. Faites-y réflexion: il en est des Dieux comme de leurs ministres: les uns et les autres communément font ce qu'ils défendent et imposent certains fardeaux dont ils savent fort bien se décharger.

Alcinoë. Ajoutez hardiment que les uns et les autres profitent de la sottise et de la prévention: les Dieux pour se faire craindre, et leurs ministres pour se rendre nécessaires.

Aegialia. Les hommes ne renverront-ils jamais toute cette canaille céleste dans le monde fantastique d'où elle est venue? Ne reconnaîtront-ils jamais une Divinité véritable, souverainement pure et souverainement digne de leur culte et de leurs adorations?

Alcinoë. Ce temps de lumière viendra, mais je ne sais si la plupart des sacrificateurs d'alors parleront et agiront de meilleure foi. (pp. 14—15).

After this brief aside the discussion returns to the theme of love and to the story of Aegialia. Soon, however, the subject is, once again, religion. Aegialia explains that when she tried to assassinate Diomedes he took refuge in the temple of Juno. She was frightened to pursue him in this sanctuary, out of fear of the goddess:

Alcinoë. Chez elle la moindre irrévérence contre la religion est un forfait brûlable. Pendant qu'on commerce avec les fourbes et les mauvais coeurs, on fuit comme la peste le censé indévot, et la probité la plus exacte devient un monstre dès qu'elle ne se conforme pas aux superstitions du temps et du lieu.

Aegialia. A ne vous rien déguiser, ce fut par ce principe que je laissai évader mon époux. Junon ne m'inquiétait pas plus que son incestueux mari. Mais le peuple n'eût point souffert la violation d'un refuge sacré; et ce même peuple qui tolérait mes désordres, qui obéissait tranquillement à une abandonnée, à une perdue, m'aurait fait un mauvais parti si j'avais manqué de respect à une de ses Divinités. (p. 24).

From religion the discussion passes to politics, and to how rulers exploit the gullibility of the people who never learn by bitter experience. After this digression the dialogue returns to Aegialia's story but soon reverts to a consideration of Cometes' usurpation of the throne, of the character of all usurpers and of the way people accept them without protest. Since Cometes was a trusted friend of Diomedes the conversation turns to the question of adultery. Alcinoë finds that the man who seduces his friend's wife, far from betraying a trust, does him a favour:

Alcinoë. Ne lui procure-t-on pas de la part de son épouse des complaisances, des caresses, une humeur douce, prévenante, traitable, et toujours égale? Ne décharge-t-on cet ami de la moitié du fardeau? Ce qu'il en coûte à l'amant pour le luxe, pour le jeu, pour tous les autres menus frais, n'est-ce pas autant d'épargne pour le mari qui, d'ailleurs, a le bonheur d'être secouru dans la culture d'un champ dont l'entretien surpasse ses forces?

Aegialia, Vous badinez en morte libertine. Tous ces prétendus services dédommagent-ils l'époux du vol qu'on lui fait du coeur de son épouse?

Alcinoë. Il est bon là. Vous avez assurément perdu l'idée du mariage. Ne vous souvenez-vous donc plus de la manière dont on en use chez les vivants? Les deux partis, avant de contracter, passent les jours et les nuits, et cela avec le plus vif de tous les empressements, à se donner mutuellement le coeur, à s'entre-protester d'une tendresse inviolable, d'un éternel attachement. A peine a-t-on commencé l'exécution du contrat que chacun reprend son coeur: le mari est ordinairement le premier à rompre le marché. Ainsi, quand on lui prend le coeur de sa femme on lui prend un bien sur lequel il n'a plus qu'un droit civil, dont on ne le frustre pas. . . (pp. 34—35).

When Alcinoë tells her story Aegialia is surprised to learn that Minerva, the goddess of wisdom, had inspired her fatal passion. Aegialia had always thought that those who worshipped Minerva were intellectuals and above considerations of the flesh. Now she understands why those who profess to be *savants* find time to involve themselves in affairs of the heart. Indeed, celibacy was never an invention of the gods since it is unnatural. God created man as a perfect being, but man made himself imperfect. Alcinoë objects that such an argument defies reason. If a machine is perfect it cannot render itself imperfect. Aegialia replies that man was created with the freedom to choose his destiny. If he has chosen badly he must blame himself and not his divine author. The theological discussion terminates abruptly, and the dialogue returns to Alcinoë's story with which the conversation ends.

The second dialogue is between Alcmena and Myrrha.[6] The main topic is the decadence of society and the disappearance of fidelity. The dialogue begins, however, with another attack on the gullibility of the populace who worship Alcmena as a divinity because of her association with Jupiter, and on those who capitalize on the people's stupidity. Myrrha points out that people have a natural propensity for being duped:

Myrrha.   Il suffit que les Thébains soient un peuple pour avoir du penchant à diviniser. Vous aurez apparu en songe à quelque visionnaire; un imposteur aura juré vous avoir vu monter au Ciel; ajoutons quelques miracles de votre façon, c'est tout ce qu'il fallait pour votre apothéose. Mais n'ayez pas regret à la dépense qu'on fait pour votre culte: s'il vous est inutile, il est à Thèbes un certain genre d'homme qui sait très bien en profiter.

Alcmena. J'entends qui vous voulez dire. Ne sont-ce pas ces gens qui trouvent si bien leur compte dans la superstition populaire; là ces gens qui, par un pieux savoir faire, tirent d'un fond d'ignorance crasse et ridicule, de bons et copieux revenus?. . .

Myrrha.   . . . Vous n'êtes pas le seul objet craint, vénéré, invoqué, mis en oeuvre, qui ne soit qu'un des sujets du noir Pluton; à combien de menus et de grosses Divinités s'adresse-t-on, qui ne sont rien du tout, et qui ne subsistent que par une tradition qui s'est emparée insensiblement des esprits, et à laquelle il est même quelquefois plus dangereux de toucher qu'à l'existence d'une Divinité reconnue presque par toutes les nations. . . (pp. 49—51).

The conversation then turns to a consideration of jealousy which Alcmena finds has largely disappeared to be replaced by a ridiculous tolerance by the injured parties. Husbands accept being cuckolds, and, on occasion, cuckold each other. This has had a disastrous effect on love which, through lack of obstacles, has lost its vitality. Since women can no longer trust their lovers they now deceive them as they formerly deceived their husbands. This has led to a loss of interest between the sexes, with the result that homosexuality is rife, though concealed under the cloak of marriage.[7]

The discussion of these criminal acts leads Alcmena to a reflection on her situation, and gives Gueudeville the opportunity to make one of his strongest statements against the cruelty and tyranny of religious dogma. Juno was angry with Alcmena for having slept with Jupiter but, as she points out, this was an "erreur involontaire" that the gods ought to forgive. Myrrha replies that this is blasphemy:

Myrrha.   Nos Dieux, il est vrai, n'admettent point pour excuse cette erreur involontaire: ils font plus; ils enveloppent des générations toutes entières dans le crime d'un seul homme, et l'on mérite leur colère avant que de naître. Ils posent des conditions humainement impossibles; ils exigent au delà des forces de la Nature, et veulent qu'on leur demande et qu'on fasse ce qu'ils ont résolu de ne point accorder, et qu'on ne ferait pas. Mais, nonobstant tout cela, gardons-nous bien de dire que nos Dieux punissent l'innocence: la justice ne leur est pas moins chère que la bonté. Ils savent concilier admirablement les droits de ces deux attributs opposés. Les Dieux, sans blesser en rien leur bonté, laissent tomber notre espèce dans des disgrâces morales et physiques qu'il ne tenait qu'à eux d'empêcher; les Dieux, sans blesser en rien leur justice, condamnent, châtient, tourmentent des hommes dont la volonté est tournée vers le bien, dont l'âme est droite, et qui, ne connaissant ni ne pouvant connaître d'autre bonne route que la leur, la suivent avec une conscience pure et assurée. . .

Alcmena.   Je n'entends rien à concilier le oui et le non, et j'y vais plus rondement que vous. . . Ou mon intelligence, ce don le plus beau et le plus précieux que j'aie reçu, la plus noble partie qu'il y ait en moi. . . est d'une nature contradictoirement opposée à l'intelligence des Dieux, ou les Dieux se manifestent bien plus par les effets d'une passion déréglée que par les signes d'une saine et droite raison.

Myrrha.   Vous ni moi ne connaissons la grandeur d'une Divinité. Parce qu'elle connaît tout son prix, qui est de n'en point avoir, elle est jalouse de sa gloire à proportion, et quand cette gloire est flétrie par les hommes, ne fût-ce que par un seul, ce n'est qu'à force de malheurs, de souffrances, de sang, et de mort qu'elle peut se réparer. . . (pp. 69–70).

The implications of these statements are not pursued. Instead, Alcmena begins her story. In commenting on Amphitryon's exploits she finds he was less than heroic, and adds that those whom people consider heroes are usually men who have known how to exploit others and undeservedly get the credit for themselves. The ways of the Gods are certainly mysterious. Myrrha replies that Heaven does everything for the best and we must simply have faith. Alcmena says that this may be so on earth but why, after one is dead, should one still be left in a state of doubt:

Il nous serait pourtant bien doux de ne plus douter. Hélas! notre raison n'a-t-elle donc point assez souffert en l'autre monde? Nous y avons tant cru sans voir. Non, je ne demanderais point aux Dieux d'autre occupation ici que celle de dénouer toutes les contradictions qu'on m'a fait digérer pendant ma vie, et que j'ai été obligée de préférer aux démonstrations les plus évidentes. . . (p. 89).

Alcmena then recounts how Jupiter disguised himself as Amphitryon. This brings forth a typically Gueudevillian piece of humour:

Myrrha. . . . Jupiter est heureux de pouvoir se transformer en époux; si tous les amants avaient le même privilège. . .

Alcmena. Y pensez-vous? L'amant, qui déteste tout ce qui sent l'époux, ne pourrait se souffrir sous la forme de l'époux, et la maîtresse, qui est dans la même disposition, n'aurait aucun plaisir avec la ressemblance du mari.

Only a god, says Alcmena, has the power to look like a husband and act like a lover. The long night with Jupiter, which seemed to her so short, was the greatest in her life. Gueudeville, whose writings, not entirely without cause, were termed scabrous, expatiates:

Alcmena. Ah! Si vous saviez! Il vous dit des choses qui enlèvent, qui enchantent, qui transportent, qui vous mettent tout hors de vous.

Myrrha. Ce ne sont apparemment que ses apostrophes amoureuses qui font couler le temps si rapidement en sa compagnie.

Alcmena. Je ne dis pas cela. Lorsque ce Dieu, très âgé sans être vieux, et nourri d'ambrosie et de nectar, daigne en venir jusqu'à communiquer sa divine essence, il jette l'âme dans un ravissement inexprimable. . .

Myrrha. Ces communications se réitèrent souvent sans doute?

Alcmena. Autant de fois qu'il plaît à son ardent et inépuisable amour.

Myrrha. Et vous me ferez accroire après cela que avez pris de bonne foi Jupiter pour Amphitryon?

Alcmena. A ne vous déguiser rien, ce n'était sans quelque surprise que je voyais ces longs et fréquents transports. Je ne pouvais comprendre qu'une absence assez courte eût pu ranimer si fort un mari. . .

Myrrha. Bien des femmes envieraient un semblable étonnement. . . (pp. 93—94).

There follows a discussion of the way in which kings behave as if they were gods, and are treated as if they were. When Amphitryon discovered he had been cuckolded by Jupiter he considered it an honour rather than a disgrace.

Few husbands, says Alcmena, would not react in the same way. Myrrha, in an obvious reference to the attitude of M. de Montespan towards Louis XIV's appropiation of his wife, points out that there are exceptions:

On en a vu pourtant qui ont soutenu le droit de mari contre des amants courronés; il s'en est trouvé qui, contraints de céder à la force majeure, ont regardé leurs femmes dans le lit monarchal comme dans le tombeau, ont envisagé leur élévation amoureuse comme si elles avaient péri par un naufrage d'honneur, et se sont mis en équipage de veufs (p. 105).

When Alcmena has finished her story the discussion returns to its starting point, the deification of Alcmena by the Thebans. All sorts of rumours started up after her death. It was said that her body had disappeared, and relics of all kinds became objects of worship, to such an extent that it was made a crime not to believe in their authenticity. And so Alcmena's story ends, and with it, the dialogue.

The third dialogue is between Apuleius, the Roman philosopher, rhetorician and novelist, and Henri Cornelius Agrippa, the German Renaissance philosopher.[8] Both men were interested in magic and the occult which are the main topic of the dialogue. The conversation opens, however, with a discussion of a non-magical treatise by Agrippa, in which he attempted to show that all knowledge, other than that found in the holy scriptures, is useless. Apuleius finds this a dangerous argument since it belittles not only scholars of the past but also those of Agrippa's own time. Agrippa defends himself by saying that he did not attack the genuine *savant* but only those who pretend to knowledge they do not have. The truly wise man is one who realizes his own inadequacies. This is such a rare species, however, that most scholars felt affronted by Agrippa's treatise. When Apuleius asks why Agrippa undertook such a project Agrippa replies that his aim was to expose man's duplicity and to bring enlightenment to the common people. Apuleius finds this a foolish and vain enterprise, and is not surprised it led to misfortune.

The discussion then turns to Agrippa's dealings in the occult. Agrippa says he became involved in it when he was young, and, although he realized there was no scientific basis for magic, and that the practice of it was fraudulent, he became so well known as a practitioner of the black arts, that he decided to carry on the deception, in hope of making his fortune. However, for a variety of reasons, not the least being "ma trop grande curiosité, ma plume trop libre, et mon humeur inconstante" (133), he did not achieve material success. Apuleius expresses amazement that so many people were taken in by Agrippa's literary hocus-pocus. He says that no one could get away with such trickery nowadays. To which Agrippa responds:

... de tout temps il y a eu de fameux imposteurs, et il y en aura toujours. Siècle éclairé tant qu'il vous plaira, les clairvoyants ne font qu'une légère exception: la sotte crédulité l'emporte toujours infiniment, et sur quelque matière que ce soit, l'erreur et l'illusion absorbent la vérité (p. 157).

Apuleius then discusses his own experiences with magic, his preoccupation with the mystery religions, and his initiation as a priest in the service of Osiris. His real aim, he says, was to learn the art of deceiving the people. This observation introduces a lengthy and thinly veiled attack on Catholicism, and ends in praise of the Reformation:

Apuleius. J'avais pour but de pénétrer à fond l'art de tromper les hommes: pouvais-je l'apprendre en meilleure école? Je trouvais là, comme dans leur centre et dans leur élément, l'artifice, l'imposture, l'hypocrisie; j'y voyais à découvert tous les ressorts qu'on employait sous le voile de religion, pour faire valoir un gain sordide, pour dominer tyranniquement sur les esprits, pour tourner les hommes à son gré par des promesses trompeuses et par de vaines frayeurs.

Agrippa. Ne découvriez-vous pas aussi, parmi les ministres de vos Dieux, de la sincérité, de la bonne foi, une vénération religieuse pour la Divinité au temple et aux autels de laquelle on s'était consacré?

Apuleius. Assurément. Nous avions dans nos confraternités sacrées des collègues superstitieux par persuasion. Ces bonnes gens ne doutaient nullement que le Dieu ou la Déesse du lieu ne les enivrât d'une fureur poétique lorsqu'il s'agissait de rendre un oracle. Ces prêtres crédules se seraient fait brûler pour la réalité de leur fantôme; pénétrés de la vérité, de la sainteté de leur ministère, ils remplissaient leurs devoirs aussi exactement que la faiblesse humaine peut le permettre, et ils hasardaient les prédictions avec toute l'assurance d'un inspiré.

Agrippa. Quoi? une contradiction formelle dans les principes de leur doctrine, une impureté criante dans leur morale, une bizarrerie dans leurs rites, une grossièreté manifeste dans leur service divin, rien de tout cela n'était capable de leur ouvrir les yeux?

Apuleius. Non, le préjugé de l'enfance et de l'éducation était chez eux le plus fort: la raison avait beau se soulever, elle se brisait toujours contre cet écueil...

Agrippa. ... J'ai vu là-haut tout ce que vous y avez vu en matière d'officiers de culte: des charlatans qui vendent chèrement à leur gloire, à leur profit, et à leur volupté, des drogues qu'ils savent très bien n'avoir nulle vertu...

Apuleius. De quoi a donc servi à l'aimable et infaillible vérité d'établir son culte, si ses ministres sont tels qu'étaient ceux de l'erreur?

Agrippa. Vous n'y êtes pas. Les prêtres de la vérité sont éclairés de sa lumière: elle brille dans leurs paroles et dans leurs actions; sans fard et sans parure ils ne disent que ce qu'ils croient...

Apuleius. Y avait-il dans le monde un grande nombre de ces prêtres-là de votre vivant?

Agrippa. Très peu. Une ignorance crasse et un débordement de vices couvraient alors le sanctuaire: la vérité commençait à dissiper le nuage et la mauvaise odeur, à purifier l'air; comme cette sérénité renouvelée était nuisible aux avantages de la vie j'eus la lâcheté de lui fermer les yeux. . .

Apuleius. . . . Vous avez refusé de participer à la réformation du vrai culte, et moi j'ai refusé de participer à son établissement. (pp. 161—166).

Apuleius tells of his reputation as a magician, and of how the material rewards for serving Osiris were so meagre that he was obliged to turn to law where he was able to put his rhetorical powers to good account. When he married the rich, elderly widow, Pudentilla, he was accused of having bewitched her, but, as Agrippa points out, it takes very little magic to persuade a plain, sex-starved widow to marry a virile young man, even if he is poor! With a brief reference to Apuleius' *The Golden Ass*, the dialogue ends.

The fourth and shortest of the dialogues is between the Roman Emperor Heliogabalus[9] and Diogenes, the cynic. The main purpose of the dialogue is to present two opposing philosophies: the hedonism of Heliogabalus and the detachment of Diogenes. Although, in the preface, Gueudeville portrayed his dead as devoid of all emotion, this dialogue opens with a series of insulting exchanges.[10]

Heliogabalus says his guiding principle was that whatever pleased him must be good for the people. One of his innovations was to set up a senate composed entirely of women to deal with women's affairs. His mother was proclaimed chief magistrate. Those who objected to the formation of this body were put to death since the subjects of a sovereign, he argues, are duty bound to follow his orders without question. In reply Diogenes comments that men can be forced to obey authority but they cannot be forced to believe in it:

Tu poussais donc bien loin ton autorité. C'est tout ce que la Divinité pourrait exiger des hommes: encore ne veut-elle point de leur obéissance s'ils ne se soumettent par persuasion et avec une entière liberté (p. 189).

When Diogenes speaks of his own life, Heliogabalus tries to get him to confess to a lack of sincerity. Diogenes admits there were moments of doubt but denies he ever deviated from his cynical ways. Despite the temptations of comfort and wealth he always clung to his freedom:

. . . La vraie liberté ne consiste-t-elle pas dans l'empire de soi-même? J'étais le maître absolu de Diogène, ou du moins je tâchais de l'être: ainsi la servitude même ne servait qu'à me faire goûter davantage la douceur de ma royauté philosophique (p. 194).

Heliogabalus is unable to see any fundamental difference between his way of life and that of Diogenes. It seems to him that both of them lived according to their own laws, and disregarded the conventional and the acceptable. The dialogue ends with no meeting of minds.

The fifth and longest dialogue is between Julius Caesar and Marcus Junius Brutus. The subject of the discussion, as might be expected, is absolutism versus republicanism. All the attacks on arbitrary power are intended to apply to the régime of Louis XIV. Caesar begins by asking why, after he had been like a father to him, and had pardoned him for siding with Pompey at the battle of Pharsalus, Brutus joined in his assassination:

Caesar.   Tout est permis pour régner. D'ailleurs, le Ciel s'étant déclaré pour moi, j'occupais sans scrupule le premier poste de l'univers; et si j'étais privé de la vraie estime j'avais de quoi m'en dédommager en me faisant craindre. Mais quelque violente que pût être ma situation, la voie que vous prîtes pour m'en tirer n'en est pas moins scélérate. . .

Brutus.   . . . Je vous aimais autant que je devais vous aimer; j'aimais ma patrie de même, et conséquemment elle m'était plus chère que vous. Ainsi quand je vous sacrifiai à cette mère commune dont vous étiez l'oppresseur, je me sacrifiai moi-même. . . (pp. 206–207).

Brutus argues that Caesar had usurped power to which he had no legitimate claim. Caesar replies that he took over at a critical moment and saved the republic from anarchy. He did his duty. Brutus suggests it was not duty but ambition that motivated his actions. Caesar points out the impossibility of defining intention:

. . elle est au-dessus de la portée humaine; il n'y a que les Dieux qui aient droit d'en connaître; et puis, combien trouverez-vous de grands qui agissent par le motif du bien public? Comme Pluton ne vous a point encore assigné de demeure fixe je m'imagine bien qu'il vous placera dans le quartier des princes désintéressés; mais vous serez surpris de voir le peu de terrain qu'ils occupent. . . (p. 211).

Brutus says that even if Caesar had been justified in taking over, he should have done it according to the established laws and not in defiance of them. He should have ruled by the constitution and not by arbitrary power. Caesar replies that the republic was already dead before he assumed supreme authority. Brutus cannot accept this construction. The republic had been in danger before but had always managed to survive. In the cause of truth Caesar admits he enjoyed the feeling of absolute power, and that he was a victim of *amour-propre*. This is why the republic had to become an absolute monarchy:

J'avais tout le solide de la souveraineté, il est vrai: je disposais absolument des armées; la noblesse tremblait sous ma puissance; le peuple m'adorait; ma volonté donnait la force aux lois. Mais les apparences et la fumée du monarchisme me manquaient. Outre que Rome conservait sous ma domination tous les dehors de son gouvernement consulaire, on ne me nommait point roi; je ne me voyais point revêtu des ornements royaux; on ne me rendait point précisément les mêmes honneurs qu'on rend aux rois. Cela seul me faisait trouver un grand vide dans ma fortune, et quoique si élevé au-dessus de tous les hommes, il me semblait que tous les hommes étaient encore mes égaux (p. 227).

Brutus says that this is where Caesar made his mistake. People who are free can easily be overcome and kept in subjection by a powerful enemy, as long as the oppressor is careful to maintain the appearance of liberty. But once the tyrant openly proclaims his tyranny there is a danger of revolution. Caesar, tired of defending himself, turns to the attack. He accuses Brutus himself of having acted not from altruistic motives but out of a desire to emulate and appropriate the glory of his ancestor Lucius Junius Brutus who drove Tarquin from Rome. Brutus denies the charge and, in doing so, recalls the tyranny of Tarquin. This gives rise to a discussion of the advantages and disadvantages of monarchy. Caesar argues that a monarchy unites the people and guarantees their security, while Brutus reasons that a republic is the only legitimate form of government:

Caesar. Puisque les hommes sont mauvais, prévenus, entêtés, puisqu'ils ne savent pas assez se servir de leur raison, pour convenir d'eux-mêmes sur leurs intérêts tant généraux que particuliers, il faut nécessairement une autorité suprême qui les dirige et qui les fixe. Or moins cette autorité est partagée plus elle est supportable, et moins elle a d'inconvénients. N'est-il pas plus doux de n'avoir qu'un maître que d'en avoir plusieurs? Où le gouvernement n'a pour chef qu'un seul homme qui a l'art de se faire obéir, la soumission ne pèse point. Les sujets, accoutumés à vénérer la dignité du prince, à le regarder comme le conservateur de l'ordre, comme le promoteur du bien public, respectent ses volontés et s'y conforment sans opposition et sans répugnance. Où plusieurs têtes sont chargées de la souveraine administration, l'obéissance est plus pénible. Les sujets, ne reconnaissant dans leurs supérieurs et dans leurs conducteurs que comme des espèces d'égaux, ou tout au plus des députés qui les représentent, se donnent ordinairement la liberté d'examiner leurs résolutions et leurs décrets; et pour peu qu'ils les trouvent onéreux, ce n'est pas sans plainte ni sans murmure qu'ils se soumettent; quelquefois même la chose va jusqu'à la mutinerie et jusqu'au soulèvement.

Brutus. ... Toutes les différentes espèces d'états sont sujettes à de grands inconvénients: le gouvernement monarchique a de très fâcheuses suites; le gouvernement républicain en a peut-être encore de plus mauvaises. Mais ce dernier est plus juste et plus équitable que l'autre; c'est sur quoi il faut faire uniquement attention.

74

Caesar. S'il vous fallait prouver cette proposition je vous trouverais fort embarrassé. Tous les gouvernements ne sont-ils pas également légitimes dans leur première institution? N'est-il pas indifféremment permis aux sociétés, ou de se reposer de leur conservation et de leur agrandissement sur les soins d'un seul homme, ou de se gouverner elles-mêmes, en ne cédant point leur droit de souveraineté?

Brutus. Qui saurait de quelle manière se sont formés tant de sortes d'états qui subsistent sur la terre pourrait vous répondre plus à fond. Peut-être vous montrerait-il évidemment que la plupart des monarchies ne sont originairement que des usurpations... Mais sans remonter jusqu'à ces sources toutes couvertes de nuages et de ténèbres, je ne crains point de vous dire que par rapport à la justice, je mets une grosse différence entre la société qui se donne un prince absolu et héréditaire, et la société qui s'érige en république.

Caesar. Oh, oh! Voici un cas de conscience républicaine auquel je ne m'attendais pas. Et la raison s'il vous plaît?

Brutus. La raison; C'est que la première société ôte d'avance aux générations futures l'usage du droit naturel, et les expose aux violences et à la tyrannie des mauvais successeurs; au lieu que la seconde, fondant son établissement sur son propre pouvoir, et n'engageant point sa liberté, ne fait nul tort à ses descendants.

Caesar. Tournons la médaille. Une société qui choisit le monarchisme arbitraire, procure à sa postérité ce bonheur inestimable dont on jouit infailliblement sous un prince éclairé, judicieux, bon, juste et pacifique. Une société qui se charge de sa propre conduite expose ses descendants aux jalousies, aux massacres, et à toutes les suites funestes du gouvernement républicain.

Brutus. Une république dans le désordre peut faire de bonnes lois pour en sortir. Au pis aller elle peut confier pour un temps l'autorité suprême à celui de ses membres qu'elle jugera le plus digne et le plus capable de rétablir l'ordre et le calme. Mais une nation a-t-elle le malheur d'être tombée sous le règne d'un mauvais prince, le mal est sans remède, et le seul parti qu'il y ait à prendre, c'est de souffrir et d'espérer. (pp. 232–236).

In that case, says Caesar, suddenly reverting from the general to the particular, why did you not put up with my reign in the hope that my death would be an occasion for Rome to recover its freedom? The situation was different, replies Brutus. It is not permitted to overthrow a system based on fundamental laws and of long standing. But, in the case of a nascent oppression, every citizen has the right to oppose it. According to your argument, Caesar observes, the life of every conqueror would be legitimately in jeopardy. Brutus does not deny it, as long as the conqueror is motivated solely by personal ambition, and is not acting on behalf of a higher authority.

Caesar then asks Brutus to behave like a lawyer and take the other side. Brutus obliges by condemning rebellion:

... Qu'on se plaigne tant qu'on voudra de ceux qui ont établi cette forme de gouvernement, ou qui l'ont laissée introduire; mais qu'on ne s'écarte jamais du respect dû au monarque, et qu'on lui soit soumis en tout ce qui ne préjudicie point à la gloire de la Divinité. L'intérêt même de l'ordre, et celui de l'humanité, prescrivent cette obéissance aveugle; car supporter la domination d'un tyran est un malheur beaucoup moindre que la rébellion. La tyrannie n'ôte point la tranquillité publique; tant s'en faut, elle contribue ordinairement à la maintenir, et à l'affermir. La tyrannie ne coûte guère de sang aux sujets; il faut qu'un prince soit bien perdu pour faire mourir quantité de particuliers, au moins sans des prétextes très spécieux; il faut qu'un prince en vienne à un terrible excès pour commettre des cruautés dans la seule vue de contenter son barbare et féroce naturel. Mais la révolte entraîne des suites affreuses, et plonge un état dans tous les maux qui peuvent lui arriver... (pp. 242–243).

As the conversation continues it emerges clearly that Brutus is opposed to civil war in an established society, but considers a threat to the republic a justifiable reason for revolt. In the choice between slavery or rebellion the true patriot chooses rebellion. What if the uprising destroys the very system it was supposed to preserve, asks Caesar? Brutus replies that one must judge the rebels by their intentions and not by the outcome.[11] The discussion continues with Caesar on the attack and Brutus defending his position. Caesar returns to his earlier point that the republic had collapsed before he assumed power. In effect, he questions the capability of the Roman constitution to provide the freedom it was intended to provide:

Dites-moi, je vous prie, cette liberté que Rome s'attribuait si fièrement, et dont elle faisait tant de bruit; sur combien de citoyens s'étendait-elle? Il y avait quelques têtes, soit dans le Sénat, ou parmi le peuple, qui entraînaient, chacune ses clients et ses suppôts, et qui partageaient ainsi entre elles tout le pouvoir de la république. Si bien qu'à l'exception d'un petit nombre, ceux qui avaient droit de suffrage, étaient les esclaves de l'éloquence, du crédit, de la fortune, de la crainte. Mais ceux qui avaient droit de suffrage, qu'est-ce que c'était en comparaison de ceux qui ne l'avaient pas? Quand je dirais que ces derniers faisaient mille contre un, dirais-je trop? Sur ce pied-là quelques Sénateurs et quelques bourgeois, sous le nom et sous l'apparence de la liberté, exerçaient réellement dans Rome un empire despotique. Non seulement ils étaient les interprètes et les arbitres des loix, mais ils en étaient aussi les auteurs... (p. 254)[12]

Brutus deals with this analysis by arguing that liberty in a state does not require the equal participation of every individual in the general administration. To have a large society one must have order, and order implies subordination. The different classes of Roman society played different roles and had distinct responsibilities and prerogatives, but the people, the most numerous of the classes, had the final word. Those who rose in the hierarchy did so by merit, and not by usurping power. It was because liberty existed in Rome that some people were persuaded to sell it to the highest bidder. In a monarchy, far from selling their liberty the people are forced to purchase tyranny. This is why Cato said that "un roi est toujours de sa nature un animal vorace, un oiseau de proie." The cost of maintaining royalty, and all its appurtenances, bleeds the people white. And for all the king receives he gives nothing in return. Caesar defends kings on the grounds that their duties are onerous and that, in the last resort, they are responsible for everything. Brutus replies that this would be true if kings took their responsibilities seriously, but they never do.

The discussion returns to the assassination. Caesar says that if he were a usurper it was up to the gods and not to men to punish him. Brutus interjects that killers of tyrants are favoured in the eyes of the gods, but Caesar cannot accept that gods would condone the shedding of blood. Brutus agrees that a divine retribution would have caused less trouble, but would have also prevented the display of patriotism. He takes up again the obligations of a patriot when confronted by a tyrant. He had to kill Caesar to restore liberty, and as an example to others with similar ambitions. Caesar observes that once liberty is lost it can never be regained. Republics have been transformed into monarchies but the reverse has never happened. As for killing a tyrant as an example to others, it often happens that the new monarch is even more tyrannical than his predecessor. He refers Brutus to what a historian[13] had written about the assassination:

Premièrement, qu'une fureur de scélérat s'empara de quelques-uns qui me portaient envie et les poussa à me tuer injustement. En second lieu, qu'encore qu'ils alléguassent le beau prétexte de rétablir la liberté, leur action fut réellement impie, et replongea dans les séditions un état qui commençait à goûter les avantages d'une bonne administration. Il déclare ensuite que la monarchie est préférable au gouvernement démocratique... (p. 301).

Brutus can only repeat that liberty is "le fondement de tous les biens dans la société civile," and that absolute authority is "la source de tous les maux."

In response to Caesar's prompting, Brutus recounts the events after the assassination. He tells how the conspirators were forced to flee, how Cassius and then himself were defeated in successive battles, and how they chose suicide rather than dishonour. When Brutus speaks of his great disillusionment with the outcome of the assassination, Caesar cannot refrain from expressing his satisfaction at the thought that virtue triumphs no more frequently than iniquity. An account of the bravery and heroic death of Brutus' wife, Porcia, brings the dialogue to a close.

The sixth and final dialogue is between Caligula and Nero, and the object of the discussion is to decide who was the greater villain. The dialogue opens with both emperors in agreement that the people are stupid:

Caligula. C'étaient de bonnes gens que nos Romains, n'est-il pas vrai?

Néro. Le meilleur genre d'hommes qui fût sous le soleil. Oh que Jules César notre fondateur les avait bien guéris de la sotte passion de la liberté! Ils devinrent en peu de temps infiniment plus soumis qu'ils n'avaient été libres depuis l'expulsion de Tarquin; et jamais on n'a vu de nation, après avoir été au souverain degré jalouse de l'indépendance... porter le joug de si bonne grâce.

Caligula. Vous lui faites trop d'honneur à cette nation. Nos Romains ne sont pas les seuls qui se soient familiarisés bien vite avec la servitude; et j'ai ouï dire qu'il y a sur la terre des peuples qui se sont piqués longtemps d'être gouvernés en hommes et qu'on prendrait à présent pour des bêtes de charge.

Néro. Il est vrai que le peuple est un animal bien facile à apprivoiser: avec un peu de crainte on en fait tout ce qu'on veut; et ce qu'il y a de plaisant c'est que ce peuple fournit lui-même de son propre fond l'argent, les hommes, et généralement tout ce qu'il faut pour le mettre et pour le tenir à la chaîne.

Caligula. Ce n'est nullement son intention. Le peuple donne de quoi défendre le pays, de quoi s'agrandir, de quoi l'orner, enfin de quoi le rendre heureux; et ceux qui le conduisent, employant ces forces et ces secours à leur contentement personnel, le rendent misérable; c'est un inconvénient qu'il ne peut pas éviter.

Néro. Il l'éviterait aisément s'il voulait ouvrir les yeux sur ses intérêts...
(pp. 338–339)

Caligula begins by cataloguing his crimes, all of which the people received without protest. Among his outrageous acts was his marriage to his sister Drusilla whom, on her death, he forced the populace to worship as a goddess. Nero heartily approves of his method of enslaving the people, and agrees with Caligula that "l'homme n'est pas en société pour consulter sa raison, ni pour s'y conformer dans tout ce qu'elle lui dicte par rapport à lui-même. L'homme n'est en société que pour obéir..." At one point during the narration of Caligula's crimes Nero observes that it must have been very hard for people to believe in a god who would allow men to perpetrate such atrocities. Caligula replies that men's actions are rarely consonant with their beliefs:

Comment la plupart des mortels, très persuadés que Jupiter voit tout, qu'il balance tout, qu'il met tout en ligne de compte, agissent-ils tout de même que si Jupiter ne voyait rien, ne se mêlait en aucune façon de leurs affaires? Demander aux hommes du rapport entre ce qu'ils croient de la Divinité et leur conduite à son égard, ce n'est à la vérité que demander le premier et le plus important usage de leur raison; mais c'est pourtant ce qui se trouve le moins chez eux (p. 383).

There follows a long discussion about superstition, religious hypocrisy, and Caligula's efforts to ridicule and undermine the people's beliefs. Eventually, he became so thoroughly detested that he was assassinated. There was no public outcry, however, when his successor had the assassin put to death.

Nero then tells his story. At the beginning of his reign he was all the people could have wished. But, as soon as he realized how easy it was to enslave them, he gave up the pretence of being benevolent, and revealed his true despotic nature. If only the Romans had revolted immediately they could have thwarted Nero's ambitions. But, as always, they remained passive while Nero assumed absolute authority: "Il est si aisé au prince de jouer les hommes! La politique est bien moins l'art de gouverner que de tromper. . ." At the end of Nero's recitation Caligula pronounces him the winner of the contest:

Ne m'en dites plus, je vous prie: je vous donne gagné; et j'avoue que si j'ai traité les hommes comme des sots, vous les avez menés en vraies bêtes. Séparons-nous, et allons chacun de notre côté nous moquer de nos ombres romaines qui, étant mortels, se piquaient de raison et avaient pourtant la folie inconcevable de nous obéir. . . (p. 469)

The *Dialogues des morts* is, in a sense, Gueudeville's only piece of creative literature. That is to say, his other works come under such classifications as journalism, literary criticism, commentaries, documentation and translation. On the other hand, the style and content of the *Dialogues* are, as we have seen, indistinguishable from many sections of *L'Esprit des cours de l'Europe* and the critique of *Télémaque*. Only the form is different. But even here, the difference is more apparent than real. In the critique of *Télémaque,* for example, there is an implicit dialogue between the Frenchman and his Dutch correspondent, and, in his periodical, Gueudeville keeps up a constant dialogue with an imaginary reader to whom he attributes questions which he then proceeds to answer,[14] and sometimes he invents dialogues between himself and a non-European.[15] But the *Dialogues des morts* is the only work in which he employs one form exclusively, and it is for this reason, I think, that we are entitled to use this work as a means of assessing Gueudeville's creative abilities.

My general conclusion is that he had no great artistic ability. The characters in the dialogues, although they are dead, would benefit from a little lively individuality. They all tend to speak with one voice, that of Gueudeville himself, for whom they are merely mouthpieces. For Gueudeville was essentially a polemical writer, and, in this field, as we have already seen, he was undoubtedly talented. The ideas in the dialogues, as elsewhere, are expressed with force, clarity, verve and humour. And these ideas benefit from the dialogue form which allows Gueudeville legitimately to digress, to lengthen or shorten the exchanges as he sees fit, and to range over a wide variety of topics according to the interests of the participants. As a purveyor of ideas, then, Gueudeville commands our respect, but, as a creator of deathless prose, whether his creations are alive or dead, he lacks certain qualities that are hard to define but often easy to recognize.

VI. COLLABORATIVE WORKS

(i) *Atlas historique* (1705–1720)[1]

Once the great voyages of discovery had opened up the New World to soldiers, merchants and missionaries, and led to the establishment of colonies, there was an increasing demand for knowledge about these exotic places. Apart from those who had a genuine need for information, ordinary people were curious to know where these places were, what sort of men inhabited them, and how they lived. Publishers were not slow to realize that the production of atlases, geographical and historical works, and travel reports, both real and imaginary, could be a very profitable enterprise. As a consequence, the market was flooded with such publications of which many were quite inaccurate. It was no doubt with the hope of benefiting from the popular demand that François L'Honoré and company, i.e., the Châtelain family of Amsterdam, undertook their production of the *Atlas historique* of which the first volume appeared in Amsterdam towards the end of 1704.[2]

It is not absolutely clear with whom the idea originated or who was mainly responsible for this venture, since, on the title-page, the work is attributed to a Mr. C***. All that is certain is that this was not Henri Châtelain, the person to whom it is ascribed in the standard biographies and the major libraries.[3]

The *Atlas historique* was published in folio in seven volumes, and in several editions, from 1705 to 1739.[4] Originally it had been intended to publish simply an atlas, but it was found necessary to provide so much other supporting information that the work became a collaborative undertaking. Mr. C*** looked after the organization of the material and compiled the maps; J.G. von Imhof and F.A.D. Bresler supplied the genealogical tables, and Gueudeville, later assisted by H.P. de Limiers, wrote the *Dissertations,* i.e., the historical and geographical commentaries based on the works of ancient and modern authorities in the field.[5] Gueudeville had no hand in the *Supplément* or seventh volume for which Limiers alone wrote the *Dissertations.* The work became so ambitious and so comprehensive that, after the publication of the third volume, one reviewer described it as "un travail immense et énorme, et capable d'épouvanter l'auteur le plus laborieux."[6]

The aim of the work was frankly popular, as Gueudeville explained in the preface to the first edition. The story of history, he said, is of vital importance for one's education, and a great source of moral teaching. But it is also full of difficulties, obscurities and complications, and sometimes dull. The intention of the *Atlas historique* is to make the study of history agreeable and accessible to all ages. For this reason the author has also included geographical and chronological information which is inseparable from the study of history. We have to know not only what happened, but also where and when it happened. The originality and great value of the *Atlas historique* is that, for the first time, it brings all this material together in such a way that it is immediately available to the reader, in a well laid out and digestible form. In addition there are many visual aids in the form of maps, chronological and genealogical charts, and portraits, that allow the reader to visualize and memorize the events, people and places referred to. For those who prefer simply to read, there are dissertations, separated from the explanations of the maps and other material. These dissertations give a general introduction to and idea of all the regions covered in the work.

In the preliminary *Discours sur cet Atlas historique,* Gueudeville goes on to discuss the great difficulties involved in establishing precise chronologies when there is so much disagreement among respected scholars, and so much contradiction in ancient sources. Similar problems arise in the study of ancient history and geography. All one can do is present the evidence objectively and impartially, and leave the conclusions to the reader. This, he says, will be his aim in the dissertations.

In the opening *Dissertation sur l'histoire universelle,* Gueudeville speaks again of the importance of a knowledge of history, and of the difficulty in discovering our past because of the ignorance or the unreliability of ancient writers, and the destruction of documents due to the ravages of time. While modern history is largely free of these defects it has others:

Combien de faussetés et de mensonges ne la souillent-elles pas? Le oui-dire étant l'un de ses fondements, et tracée, comme elle est fort souvent, par des plumes vendues, il ne se peut qu'elle soit très brouillée avec la sincérité.

N'oublions pas le préjugé, la passion, la crainte, et la prudence de l'historien, autant d'obstacles invincibles à la vérité de l'histoire . . .

But it is because of this obscurity and uncertainty of history that we must make an effort to find out about our past, since we are all part of the family of man. We must not be deterred by poor historians who neither seek out the facts nor, when they do possess them, have any idea how to present them in a clear, interesting and impartial manner. Gueudeville ends this dissertation with his portrait of the ideal historian:

C'est un homme qui pense solidement, et qui écrit de même. Son style est plein, moelleux, succulent, épuré de toute affection et de faux brillant. Avare pour l'ornement, pour la figure, et n'en donnant qu'autant qu'il en faut pour soulager l'attention du lecteur. Ni trop concis, ni trop diffus, et marchant dans son chemin d'un pas réglé, grave et majestueux . . . Exact et familier pour le détail, mais sans bassesse; grand, sublime, élevé quand il le faut; n'évitant jamais le difficile, travaillant d'un fond universel et inépuisable pour tout éclaircir.

Affranchi de la prévention et maître de ses sentiments . . . De nul culte, de nul gouvernement dans son ouvrage; sans famille, sans amis, sans soi-même, mais l'homme de la vérité . . .

The model for this portrait was, I think, Pierre Bayle.

Apart from the general preliminary dissertations, Gueudeville composed seven others in the first volume, dealing with Greece, ancient Rome, modern Rome, Italy, France, Spain and the United Provinces. All of them contain typically Gueudevillian observations, written in that inimitable style, which readers of *L'Esprit des cours de l'Europe* and the various parts of the *Critique générale des Avantures de Télémaque* had come to enjoy or detest. In fact, it would be no exaggeration to say that, in Gueudeville's hands the *Atlas historique* becomes another tract, another opportunity to inveigh against Louis XIV, the Pope, and against man's inhumanity to man. Let me give some examples.

The first dissertation begins by praising Greek civilisation. Before the Greeks "les hommes n'étaient animés que d'un courage brutal et féroce; l'anarchie couvrait encore la face de la terre, et toutes les lois aboutissaient à la raison du plus fort." The Greeks were the first to realize that man cannot live by instincts alone. They invented the first republics in that golden age when happiness and mutual respect were the principles of society, when all men were equal and ignorant of "cette inégalité monstrueuse qui bigarre et qui défigure nos sociétés d'à présent." The Greeks, who valued their liberty, were prepared to defend it to the death. Later on they became apathetic and, as a consequence, the golden age passed away. But their contribution to politics, to the arts and sciences was enormous. As for their ethics, "Je crois pouvoir le dire sans profanation: la morale de plusieurs philosophes n'en cède point, quant à la matière, à la divine morale de l'Evangile."

Discussing heroes and heroines of Greek history or mythology Gueudeville finds the supposed cause of the Trojan war beyond belief:

. . . ces princes risquaient beaucoup pour la fidélité conjugale, et . . . ils s'exposaient à essuyer chez eux le même affront qu'ils allaient venger si loin. Agamemnon eût fait bien plus sagement de garder sa Clytemnestre que de courir après Hélène; ce monarque n'aurait pas perdu l'honneur et la vie; et je ne sais si le vagabond Ulysse trouva sa Pénélope aussi chaste qu'il l'avait laissée, et qu'elle faisait semblant de l'être. Toujours est-il certain que Messire Cocuage, quelque noble qu'il fût, n'exciterait point tant de bruit dans notre siècle. Nos contemporains se sont apprivoisés sur cette chimérique matière, et tel honnête homme saurait sa femme entre les bras de son voisin, qui ne ferait point un pas pour l'en arracher (p. 4).

Gueudeville also uses the occasion to minimise the exploits and stature of Alexander with whom, in the critique of *Télémaque,* he had compared Louis XIV. Alexander was little more than a cruel tyrant whose aim was to conquer the world. Wherever he went he caused misery and devastation, in the vain belief that, in this way, he would somehow achieve immortality: "Triste, mais solide matière à réflexion pour ces monarques qui ne bornent point leurs désirs, chez qui l'ambition s'accroît avec l'âge, et qui se repaissant d'une douce chimère, se figurent qu'ils mourraient en repos, si l'univers en les perdant perdait un maître." Alexander was not only a tyrant but also a drunkard and a lecher. This is the sort of man people regarded and still regard as a hero. Gueudeville gives his own portrait of the ideal hero and suggests there are few nowadays who approach this ideal.

Although Gueudeville opens his dissertation on modern Rome by promising to treat the subject "en homme parfaitement désintéressé," he immediately breaks his promise by describing the Pope as "un monarque qui prétend dominer sur toute la terre, et qui croit que son autorité n'a point d'autres bornes que celles de notre globe." After this "auspicious" beginning he takes up his well-tried and familiar catalogue of grievances against the Catholic Church. The popes foment trouble between people and nations in order to divide and conquer. The Church has turned the peaceful teachings of Christ into a militant, political doctrine that enslaves the masses, and the threat of excommunication is used to terrify and hold them in abject submission. When one looks at the lives and characters of popes throughout the ages one finds hardly a crime in which they have not excelled. And so on until the end when, in an attempt to disarm the reader, Gueudeville writes:

On ne manquera pas de me reprocher que je suis un mauvais prometteur, et que, contre ma parole, j'ai pris parti. Oui, celui de la raison; et si la passion n'a dicté rien de tout ce que j'ai dit, je supplie mon lecteur de me plaindre, et de tâcher à me guérir. (p. 34).

The dissertation on France gives Gueudeville an opportunity to compare the French monarchy with the English, to the detriment of the former, to dwell on the St. Bartholomew massacres and their continuation in his own day, and to attack the tyranny of Louis XIV and the gullibility of the French people. In short, to continue the same war he was simultaneously waging in *L'Esprit des cours.*

Similarly, in the dissertation on Spain, in the guise of giving a history of that country, Gueudeville keeps returning to the present situation:

Notre Ferdinand, néanmoins, n'usa de sa supériorité qu'avec une espèce de cruelle modération. Il ne lâcha point sur les Mores de dogues furieux et affamés; il n'abandonna point ces pauvres vaincus à une soldatesque déchaînée, et à qui l'on n'ordonne d'épargner le sang qu'afin de mettre les persécutés dans un plus grand désespoir. Il ne réduisit point les Mores à la barbare alternative d'embrasser sa foi, de croire comme lui, ou de perdre leurs biens, leurs enfants et leur liberté. Enfin il ne les força point à rester dans ses états pour y

mener une vie sacrilège, et pour souffrir par les remords d'une conscience violen-
tée, ce qu'en matière de peines d'esprit, l'on ne peut concevoir de plus affreux
(p. 72).

In the opening to his dissertation on the United Provinces, Gueudeville
again promises to control his prejudices. Faced with the prospect of writing
about his adopted country, he has to restrain his desire to praise it to excess:

Je ne m'engage point à suivre infailliblement le chemin de la vérité. Je suis tout
Hollandais d'inclination; je fais gloire de la déclarer; et cela suffit, je l'avoue,
pour me rendre suspect. Mais je promets de veiller soigneusement sur le préjugé;
je tâcherai qu'il ne me séduise point; et comme je n'attends de mes maîtres
d'autre fortune que celle de me laisser vivre jusqu'à la fin sous la douceur de ce
gouvernement, je n'ai aucun sujet de me tenir sur mes gardes contre les impressions de l'intérêt. (p. 75).

He goes on to praise the system of government, the freedom of worship and the
courage of the Dutch in facing up to Louis XIV, and ends by saying that never
has the republic enjoyed greater glory than it does today when, internally, it
enjoys liberty and peace, and, together with its allies, "elle fait tête au dehors
à une puissance énorme, pour sa propre sûreté, et pour l'équilibre de l'Europe."
This first volume of the *Atlas historique* was favourably reviewed by Henri
Basnage de Beauval and Jacques Bernard.[7] Although the former thought the
project somewhat overambitious and, therefore, susceptible to imprecision and
errors, he felt, nevertheless, that "les fautes qu'on y remarque n'empêchent
pas que l'ouvrage ne soit d'une grande utilité, et d'une grande commodité."
As for the dissertations, he found that "Mr. Gueudeville s'exprime . . . avec
beaucoup de feu. Dans tout ce qu'il écrit il y a beaucoup de brillant et de vivacité." He added, however, "On peut dire même qu'il aurait plus d'esprit s'il
en avait un peu moins." The review by Jacques Bernard restricted itself mainly
to a description of the work, but emphasized its usefulness and originality of
organization. In order to give some idea of the dissertations, the reviewer cited,
without comment, the following passage from the end of the article on modern
Rome:

La guerre étant allumée de tous côtés, et la religion chrétienne se réformant
par le sang, comme elle s'est établie par le sang, on cria au Concile. Ce seul
mot fait trembler la cour de Rome, et certains princes ne craindraient pas plus
chez eux la convocation des Etats-Généraux. Il fallut pourtant en venir là.
Mais ce fut avec tant de précaution, que le Pape, ayant éludé la proposition
d'assembler un corps libre, et d'ailleurs envoyant à Trente son S. Esprit par
des courriers, il sortit glorieusement de ce dangereux pas. Depuis ce péril, le
S. Siège conserve soigneusement ce qui lui reste de son ancienne puissance.
On n'y élève ordinairement que des personnes incapables, à cause de la vieillesse, de donner des scandales grossiers, mais capables, par une longue expéri-

ence, de s'intriguer avec les princes, et de ménager l'autorité pontificale, sans la commettre.

In 1708 the *Atlas historique* was reissued as volume one, and the first edition of volume two was published. This was divided into two parts of which the second would later be renumbered volume three.[8] The first part of volume two contained dissertations on the Empire, including the Roman Empire, Germany, Prussia, Hungary and Bohemia. Part two of the second volume dealt with Great Britain, Ireland, Switzerland, Savoy, Lorraine and Venice.

Encouraged by the favourable reviews, Gueudeville, in the two new volumes, returned to the attack. His aim, he said, was to write "non en historien ni en chronologue, mais en m'arrêtant superficiellement à tout ce qui me paraîtra dans mon chemin de plus fameux et de plus conforme au but de cet ouvrage" (p. 1). He lingered lovingly over the atrocities perpetrated by various Roman emperors, in the sure knowledge that tales of sex and violence always have popular appeal, and he seasoned the dissertations with doses of burlesque style à la Scarron, such as: "ce beau feu le pressait lorsque sa Philis à face argentine découvrait toute la moitié de son orbe, ou, si ce galimatias vous choque, lorsque la lune était pleine." He also used the occasion to mount an attack on the exploits, character and reputation of Charlemagne, as he had done in the case of Alexander. After portraying Charlemagne as a licentious and tyrannical megalomaniac Gueudeville ends by noting that he had been canonized. Gueudeville thinks this must have been because all the atrocities he committed, and all the blood he shed, were in the service of Christianity which teaches that people must be forced to convert, "en un mot il contraignait d'entrer." This reminder of the famous treatise by Bayle, recalls also Bayle's unflattering portrait of David in the *Dictionnaire historique*. In case we do not take the allusion, Gueudeville terminates his portrait of Charlemagne by observing that "nous devons le croire dans le paradis entre David et Salomon."

In discussing the disputes between Charlemagne's son, Louis, and the Church, Gueudeville takes the opportunity of indulging in one of his anti-clerical asides:

Louis apparemment n'avait jamais réfléchi sur l'esprit de l'Eglise, et il jugeait des ministres de l'autel par ce qu'ils devraient être et nullement par ce qu'ils sont. Fermer la porte de l'ambition à l'espèce d'hommes (je parle de ce temps-là et non pas du nôtre au moins) . . . la plus inquiète et la plus intrigante? Interdire le luxe à des gens qui ne respirent que les cours et que le grand monde? Il ne manquait plus qu'à les exclure de l'avarice ou de la mollesse et de la volupté (p. 22).

Although Gueudeville claims not to be referring to the situation in his own day, all his comments are written in the light of his own prejudices and experiences of the world around him. Most of the comparisons are implicit, and it is left to the reader to make the connection. But, since they are hardly subtle, the reader is rarely in doubt as to what conclusions he is supposed to draw.

Occasionally the comparisons are quite explicit as, for example, in one of the dissertations on Germany where he gives an account of the battle of Nordlingen (1634):

J'ai transcrit, et j'insère la narration de cet événement, parce qu'il a du rapport avec ceux de nos jours. Je compare la victoire de Nordlingen avec celle d'Hochstet, et je reconnais dans l'une et dans l'autre le sort de la Sérénissime maison d'Autriche qui, lorsque sa fortune est chancelante, se relève avec avantage et avec éclat. On ne peut encore dire quelle utilité cette puissante maison tirera des grands coups que le Ciel a frappé depuis peu en sa faveur; la pièce n'est pas finie, nous en ignorons le dénouement . . . (p. 41).

In the dissertation on Prussia and Brandebourg, Gueudeville embarks on one of his frequent digressions. On this occasion he compares the supposedly uncivilised barbarian of old with modern man. He finds them both equally bestial except that the savage was more charitable and compassionate than his modern counterpart. This leads him into a discussion of the advantages of polygamy over monogamy. He notes, among other drawbacks of monogamy, that "l'obligation de s'en tenir à une seule femme est trop souvent la cause innocente des écarts criminels qu'on fait en amour; et cette loi rigoureuse empêche aussi que le nombre des compatriotes ne soit aussi grand qu'il pourrait être." The only real disadvantage of polygamy is that it tends to assign women an inferior role in society whereas, "généralement parlant, les femmes ne sont point inférieures aux hommes en aucunes qualités du corps et de l'esprit." In case it is inferred from this that Gueudeville was the founder of the movement for the liberation of women, the reader should be reminded that he was not always so generous to the opposite sex.[9]

The preface to the second part of volume two contains a plan of the volume and a reply to those who criticized the *Atlas* for its orthographical inconsistencies. It is pointed out that, apart from typographical errors that occur in all works, there is no agreement as to how names of people and places should be spelled. Many examples are given of the wide diversity in the spelling of names by noted authorities. In any case, although there is much in the *Atlas* that is valuable for scholars, the work is essentially popular, and its main purpose is to lead the reader "par un chemin court, clair, divertissant et agréable, en lui donnant le précis de l'histoire, et ce qu'il peut retenir pour en faire usage . . . On délasse sa vue de temps en temps par des objets agréables qui le frappent, et qui font entrer par les yeux . . . ce que l'on a en vue de lui faire comprendre et retenir."

These two new volumes were favourably reviewed by Basnage de Beauval.[10] Referring to Gueudeville's dissertations he wrote, "On ne s'ennuyera pas à les lire; car, outre la brièveté, il y fait venir des réflexions qui semblent naître incidemment du sujet." As an example, he summarizes the dissertation on Switzerland in which Gueudeville questions the morality of Swiss neutrality.

The reviewer also praises the project as a whole, the extensive research behind the genealogical information, the accuracy of the maps and the general organization of the material; even scholars, he says, can use it as ready reference.

Volume four appeared in 1714, and contained dissertations on Denmark, Sweden, Lapland, Poland, Moscow, and Turkey. The preface was again devoted to answering those who had criticized the work, and to defining its contents, organization and utility. The dissertations contain Gueudeville's customary comments on religion and monarchy, with the added observation that satire is the only thing worth living for: "Oui je le confesse avec toute la franchise d'un philosophe contraint à cacher ses sentiments, avec toute la contrition du stoïcisme, hors le plaisir de satiriser le ridicule des mortels . . . je mourrais d'impatience pour le paradis."

Volume four was reviewed in the *Journal des savants* and the *Journal de Trévoux*.[11] The former compared the contributions of Mr. C*** with those of Gueudeville, to the detriment of Gueudeville:

M. C.*** et M. Gueudeville paraissent de caractères fort différents. Les dissertations dont le dernier est l'auteur peuvent sans doute plaire à une sorte de lecteurs que nous ne croyons pas devoir désigner autrement. Il sera aisé aux autres de séparer ces pièces du reste du recueil. Elles ne sont pas fort instructives pour le fonds, et l'auteur y mêle des plaisanteries et des expressions prétendues facétieuses qui ne peuvent faire rire que ceux qui pensent comme lui, qui ont les mêmes préjugés, et le même tour d'esprit.

The review continues with a long extract from the dissertation on Sweden,[12] and concludes: "Ces échantillons épargnent peut-être la peine à bien des gens de lire ce qu'il y a de la façon de M. Gueudeville dans ce grand recueil qui, d'ailleurs, peut avoir son utilité." The *Journal de Trévoux* found the work excellently organized but unoriginal, since it only copied earlier works by Blaeu and Janson who had treated the subject more extensively and in greater detail. The reviewer also found Mr. C.***'s efforts much superior to those of Gueudeville whose dissertations:

. . . ne servent qu'à prouver le mauvais goût des libraires; il n'y a point en France de garçon imprimeur qui n'eût senti le ridicule de ces dissertations, dignes à peine d'être mises dans la bibliothèque bleue, et vendues dans les foires.

The fifth and sixth volumes were published in 1719. The dissertations in these volumes were the work of both Gueudeville and Limiers. According to the preface to volume five, "On reconnaîtra M. Gueudeville à ses saillies vives et brillantes, et à son style enjoué. Mais la méthode, l'arrangement, les réflexions plus sérieuses, sont du partage de M. de Limiers qui a pris sur lui le soin de fondre le tout ensemble." It is not clear why Limiers was brought in at this stage. Perhaps the publishers were finally persuaded that the tone of the dissertations detracted from the more sober aspect of the maps and tables. On the other hand, by 1719, as we shall see, Gueudeville's works were much in demand. It is more likely that his health began to fail around this period which was an extremely productive one.

Volume five had dissertations on the principal regions of Asia, and volume six dealt with Africa and America. It is not difficult to distinguish Gueudeville's contributions from those of Limiers. A characteristic sample of the former occurs in the account of the birth of Mahomet, in the dissertation on Turkey:

La mère de l'homme céleste, étant grosse de lui, le porta neuf mois en toute joie et en pleine santé: accoucher sans douleur, c'était bien la moindre grâce qu'elle pouvait se promettre; je ne sais même si ce fruit béni ne passa point, pour naître, à travers le corps maternel, comme le rayon pénètre le verre. Toujours passe-t-il pour un fait incontestable, et malheur qui en doute! que le petit Messie naquit d'une manière très édifiante, et qui déclara l'infaillibilité de sa mission. Dès que l'enfant qui, à ce qu'on doit présumer, épiait le moment, vit qu'il était temps d'apparaître, il ne fit qu'un saut de sa prison à terre où, prosterné dans les formes, il entra par un acte d'adoration dans la carrière d'une vie qui devait être si importante à l'univers. La dévotion fut courte et bonne: l'enfant se mettant pour la première fois sur ses pieds, car il avait sauté la tête la première, fit sa confession de foi, et annonça sa venue: "Il n'y a qu'un seul Dieu," s'écria-t-il, "et je viens au monde de sa part." Dieu, pour épargner à son envoyé la douleur de l'opération sacramentale, le fit naître circoncis; si bien que le Mahométisme n'a point chez soi la relique du saint prépuce (pp. 31–32).

Volume six is of great interest for its portrayals of "primitive" societies and noble savages. Gueudeville, here, draws on travel reports to emphasize those aspects favourable to a critique of European society. He also adds comments of his own. In his remarks on Africa, for example, he used the accounts given by such writers as Mocquet and Dapper,[13] but the following digression on population was almost certainly his own invention:

Y a-t-il un pays généralement plus fertile que la France? Cependant, il s'en faut bien que les femmes y fassent autant d'enfants qu'en Suisse, qui est un pays rude et ingrat, et qu'en Hollande ou la terre ne produit presque rien. Cela me ferait croire que cette diversité de tempérament vient de l'air et du climat, aussi bien que de la nourriture et de la qualité des aliments. J'ajouterai que la liberté des républiques, où chacun possède son héritage sans trouble et sans inquiétude, contribue encore, à ce que je crois, à rendre les mariages plus féconds. Cette liberté met les familles dans une certaine aisance qui, donnant de la vigueur et de la santé aux corps, les met aussi en état d'exercer leurs fonctions naturelles avec plus de succès. Les hommes et les femmes y sont plus robustes, et y ont généralement, jusque parmi les gens de campagne, un air de prospérité qu'on ne voit pas régner ailleurs si communément. Au lieu que la misère, inséparable de la servitude des monarchies, rend les esprits tristes et mornes; et cette tristesse faisant impression sur les corps, qui se ressentent nécessairement de tous les mouvements de l'âme, les fait devenir secs et languissants et, par conséquent, mal propres à la propagation de l'espèce. Les sucs nécessaires pour cette propagation sont rares dans des corps exténués de fatigue et travaillés par les inquiétudes du lendemain (p. 2).

As far as I know, this is the first time that the psychological relationship between political systems and fertility was discussed.

In considering the way in which the white man has cruelly and indiscriminately massacred the black, Gueudeville anticipates Rousseau's discussion of pity in the *Second Discourse,* except that Gueudeville finds pity to be a quality innate only in animals, while *amour-propre* seems to be man's dominant instinct:

La Nature ne nous a point donné de plus forte impression que l'amour de notre être personnel. Mais quoi! cette mère si sage et si bonne ne nous aurait-elle donc rien imprimé en faveur de nos semblables? Elle a pourtant usé de cette précaution chez les bêtes, et elle l'a fait pour la conservation des espèces. Un cheval vivant ne voit point un cheval mort sans une espèce d'horreur. L'homme seul aime à se soûler du sang de son espèce. Quel monstrueux animal! (p. 3).

All these atrocities, says Gueudeville, are committed in the name of Christianity which is supposed to be based on charity and brotherly love. But, of course, there is another side to Christianity:

Je ne suis point venu pour la paix, mais pour l'épée. C'est ce que notre législateur homme-Dieu a déclaré de sa propre bouche, et c'est assurément ce qui s'est le mieux vérifié de sa divine mission. Comment concilier cela avec l'aimable titre de Sauveur? Rien de plus áisé: Dieu a ses raisons, et les raisons du Toutpuissant sont aussi impénétrables qu'elles sont justes (p. 4).

Despite all their efforts, the missionaries, whether they be Catholic or Calvinist, made little headway in converting the savages of Africa to their beliefs. Gueudeville regards this failure as a proof of the dictum of Pierre Bayle that atheists may behave as virtuously as Christians: "Car, enfin, il n'est pas rare de voir chez ces misérables ... n'ayant ni foi ni loi ... plus de droiture, plus de probité, plus d'honnêteté et, surtout, plus d'humanité que chez la plupart des meilleurs croyants." (p. 5) And as for those tribes that do worship idols and fetishes, Gueudeville sees very little difference between their religion and the one practised by Catholics:

[ceux-ci] prient les saints, ils font des offrandes à des reliques, ils adressent des prières à des images, ils les parent, ils les ornent, et consacrent des fêtes à leur honneur, ils les portent solennellement dans les nécessités publiques, ils leur dressent des autels, ils brûlent devant elles de l'encens ... Tous honneurs qui ne sont dûs qu'à la Divinité, et qu'il n'est pas plus permis de rendre à la créature pour honorer le Créateur qu'il n'est permis aux nègres de servir leurs fétiches et de leur adresser des voeux (pp. 54—55).

Gueudeville ends his dissertation on Africa with a discussion of the Hottentots whom he describes as "philosophes sans le savoir" (p. 73). They lead a simple, primitive existence, and seem to have no religion other than a kind of celebration held when the new moon appears. This consists of dancing and singing all night long. Gueudeville comments:

> Si c'est là toute la religion des Hottentots, on doit convenir que leur culte est bien agréable; exempts de ces frayeurs qui tourmentent pour cette vie-ci, et encore terriblement pour l'éternité, ils adorent une déesse cornue qui ne leur inspire que de la joie; mais ces pauvres aveugles auront bien à déchanter dans l'autre monde (p. 74).

The characteristic feature of the Hottentots is their laziness. They live in a fertile country but are poor because they are too lazy to till the ground. This puts Gueudeville in mind of a European country which he does not name but which is obviously France, and which reminds us of Voltaire's comparison, in the *Lettres philosophiques*, between the industry of the English aristocracy and the idleness of the French: "Quant aux Hottentots, ils sont grands partisans de la paresse; leur plus agréable occupation est de ne rien faire; et, sans connaître la plaisante maxime d'une certaine nation de l'Europe, qui croit l'agriculture au-dessous de sa noblesse et de sa réputation, les Hottentots imitent assez bien cette nation-là."

But if the white man, through his greed, had despoiled Asia and Africa, he had done even worse in America of which the discovery had utterly destroyed the native civilisations:

> ... on leur a ôté ... le plus précieux de tous les biens, je veux dire la liberté: pillés, dépouillés, on a exercé contre eux des cruautés horribles; enfin ces pauvres mortels, dont tout le crime était d'être nés, sans le savoir, les dépositaires des trésors de la nature, éprouvèrent les effets les plus funestes, les plus criants, de l'injustice, de la violence; et, pendant qu'on faisait sonner bien haut le zèle évangélique pour travailler au salut éternel de ces nations, on les traitait d'une manière anti-chrétienne, et tout opposée à la morale de l'Evangile; et cela pourquoi? Parce qu'ils employaient les moyens légitimes pour défendre leurs droits naturels (p. 75).

For the dissertation on Canada or New France, Gueudeville claimed to be basing his account on the reports of Lahontan, but it is from the 1705 edition of Lahontan, extensively modified by Gueudeville himself, that this section is derived.[14] There are many attacks on the missionaries, and many comparisons between Canada and France, not present in the original. Gueudeville, however, has little to add to Lahontan's description of a utopian society of Indians who know nothing of money, private property, government or religion, and who live in perfect peace and harmony, or did so until the white man came. What Gueudeville does is reinforce the comparison between this natural and primitive society and the present state of European civilisation:

Est-ce pour être maîtrisés par d'autres hommes que les habitants de la terre se sont mis en société? Leur première intention en s'unissant a-t-elle été de laisser usurper tout aux uns, et de laisser manquer de tout les autres? . . . Les sauvages dont nous parlons ne vivent point seuls, ennemis de leur nation, et de tout ce qui s'appelle hommes. Mais contents du commerce des hommes qui leur ressemblent, ils n'en veulent point avec ceux qui regardent les autres hommes comme inférieurs à eux . . . ils sont indignés de la lâcheté avec laquelle des créatures raisonnables sacrifient leur raison et leur liberté, et, dans leur profonde ignorance des coutumes qui ont établi une domination injuste, ils sont heureux d'ignorer en même temps les suites fâcheuses de cette domination. Qu'importe, après tout, qu'il y ait des royaumes si florissants et si riches, si leurs richesses ne servent qu'à exciter l'envie des voisins, et qu'à attirer des guerres cruelles dans le sein de ces états? . . . Ne vaudrait-il pas mieux que l'or et l'argent fussent encore dans les entrailles de la terre, que d'en avoir été tirés pour corrompre ceux qu'ils ont éblouis par leur éclat? . . . Et n'était-ce pas assez de dépouiller la terre des fruits que son sein nous donne libéralement, sans aller encore fouiller dans ses entrailles pour y chercher, à grands frais, la source de tous nos maux? (p. 89).

One could go on giving examples of the way in which Gueudeville exploits the reports of travellers to ram home the doctrines that would be so much a part of the faith of the *philosophes* as the century progressed. There is, for instance, the utopian description of Virginia before the arrival of the English (pp. 95 et seq.), the description of Montezuma as an early Louis XIV (p. 105), the observation that black is beautiful (p. 148), and that we have something to learn from the marriage customs of others, especially in Madagascar:

Un jeune homme qui veut se marier n'a nulle inquiétude sur le pucelage de sa future, une fille étant maîtresse de son corps, et pouvant en disposer à son plaisir. Que cet usage-là, fondé en nature néanmoins, accommoderait bien de jeunes Chrétiennes, surtout dans cette fâcheuse enflure qui ne paraît, et dont on ne guérit, que par la perte de l'honneur! Un Insulaire . . . qui vise au mariage, s'adresse aux parents de la belle et . . . leur fait présent de bétail, de menilles d'or et d'argent . . . mais ce prétendant ne fait ces libéralités qu'à condition que si son épouse, peu contente de la fonction maritale, ou pour quelque autre raison, s'avise de la quitter, le tout lui sera exactement rendu. Cette loi-là serait admirable pour ces vilains et indignes mortels qui, de peur de toucher au coffre-fort, laissent languir leurs filles dans les peines secrètes et dangereuses de la virginité (p. 149).

But enough examples have been given to show how, by popularizing and embellishing the accounts of "ideal" societies furnished by travellers and explorers, and by using these accounts for satirical purposes, Gueudeville helped to promote some of the ideas that would contribute to the eventual, but only temporary overthrow of those political and religious institutions designed to deprive mankind of freedom of action, of expression, and even of thought.

Volumes five and six were reviewed in the *Journal des savants.*[15] Once again the review was complimentary to the work in general but unfavourable to Gueudeville, especially to his attempts at humour "qui font tant de plaisir en Hollande." The reviewer provided some samples of this humour, taken from the dissertation on Egypt. Gueudeville made no contributions to the seventh and final volume for which the dissertations were done by Limiers. Again, it is hard to know why he was dropped from the project. The most probable explanation is that he was not well, although he continued with his translations during this period. Perhaps there was some disagreement over money. It is impossible to say.

The *Atlas historique,* judging by the number of editions, was a great success, and Gueudeville's dissertations formed a not inconsiderable portion of the work. However unfavourably they were received in the scholarly world they were obviously greeted with approval by the less well educated who shared his views on France and the Pope, and enjoyed his manner of expressing them. The editors wanted the *Atlas historique* to be a popular aid to knowledge. When they chose Gueudeville as a collaborator they were assured that no one would mistake their intentions, and that readers would know, from previous experience, what to expect. By the time volumes five and six were published, the name of Gueudeville was almost a household word. This is why the reviewer in the *Journal des savants* (1719) could begin his comments with, "On n'ignore pas dans la République des Lettres quel est le caractère de M. Gueudeville." And this is why, even though Limiers was equally if not more responsible than Gueudeville for the dissertations in volumes five and six, it was Gueudeville's name alone that appeared on the title-pages, for, by this time, the very appearance of his name was enough to generate an interest in the product.

(ii) *Le Nouveau Théâtre du monde* (1713)[16]

In 1713, Pierre van der Aa, the Leiden publisher who had made his name partly through publishing "spectacular" atlases of all kinds, especially for the popular market,[17] invited Gueudeville and a Mr. Ferrarius, whom I have been unable to identify, to collaborate with him in the publication of a new venture, *Le Nouveau Théâtre du monde.* This was a single-volume, folio production. The part for which Gueudeville provided the text was devoted to a description of places in Europe; the descriptions of Asia, Africa and America were handled by Ferrarius.[18] This association between Gueudeville and van der Aa that began in 1713 was to prove, as we shall see, a very important one for both of them.

Gueudeville's contribution to the atlas was in his usual style. Although in the preface he disclaimed any expertise in the field, and said that Van der Aa could not have chosen anyone less competent for the task, he undertook to compensate for his deficiencies by drawing on well-known authorities in the field.

This laudable awareness of his limitations did not, however, prevent him from enlivening the descriptions, from time to time, with his characteristic brand of humour.

In his opening description of the earth in general, Gueudeville ridiculed the ignorant Church authorities who had condemned the discoveries of Copernicus and Galileo. In spite of the edicts of Pope Urban VIII:

. . . la terre a obtenu permission de tourner, et il n'y a plus que l'ignorance, que l'entêtement, que le mauvais scrupule qui tiennent encore pour la vieille opinion . . . Au reste, le mouvement de la terre est si vraisemblable que, pour en douter, il faut être d'une intelligence bien courte ou d'une crédulité religieuse à l'excès (p. 1).

In the introduction to the section on Europe he speaks of two kinds of travellers, those who wander the earth observing and reflecting on what they see, and those who derive nothing from their travels. We should strive to emulate the former, and be interested in our fellow men everywhere because we are all fundamentally the same species, and we should all feel that common bond of humanity that ought to unite us, but that, "depuis que l'intérêt, depuis que *le mien* et *le tien* règnent dans le monde, est devenu le plus faible et le plus fragile de tous les liens."[19] The avarice of man has led him to explore unknown lands where he has robbed, pillaged and destroyed the simple civilisations of innocent people so that he could pursue a life of luxury and waste. This, he says, is the situation today.

When Gueudeville comes to the description of specific regions his observations are predictable. Spain, for example, is underpopulated because her women are generally sterile, because of the expulsion of the Moors, and because many of her men are involved in affairs overseas. As for the Spaniards themselves, they are like most people, a mixture of good and bad:

Zélés jusqu'à une superstition ridicule et souvent même scandaleuse pour l'extérieur de la religion; n'en voulant absolument point tolérer, et ne concevant point de crime plus odieux, ni plus punissable, que de s'écarter tant soit peu de leur créance, qui presque toujours n'aboutit qu'à un pur bigotisme (p. 12).

In the section on Portugal, Goa is described as a city of particular interest. It has "un Archevêque et cinq maisons de Jésuites, quelle bénédiction!" From the section on France, Gueudeville's account of the kings from Louis XI to Louis XIV reads more like a rogues' gallery than a history of monarchy. Louis XI was "soupçonneux et cruel . . . fondateur du pouvoir arbitraire pour les subsides . . . aimant pourtant l'ordre et la justice." Charles VIII had good intentions but died at the age of 27. Louis XII carried on the war against Italy but was unsuccessful because of his avarice and, above all, because of his alliance with Alexander VI, "méchant pape et père d'un fils tout à fait scélérat.

Louis XII récompensait mal, mais il aimait ses sujets, et on l'appela le père du peuple." François I was unlucky in his dealings with Charles V. Henri II reigned through his old mistress, Diane de Poitiers, and the Connétable de Montmorency, his favourite. He died "en jouant à la lance, et cette mort ne fit guère d'honneur à sa mémoire." François II died prematurely, and Charles IX, "emporté, dissimulé, fourbe et sanguinaire . . . mourut à 24 ans, non sans soupçon d'avoir été empoisonné par sa mère." Henri III "avilit la majesté royale par un entier dévouement à ses mignons . . . il mourut de la main d'un moine dominicain." Henry IV was an excellent king, and so would his successor, Louis XIII, have been "s'il avait fait par lui-même ce qu'il exécuta par le ministère de Richelieu, qu'il craignait comme son maître." Louis XIV, the reigning monarch "a poussé au dedans et au dehors la puissance monarchique aussi loin qu'elle puisse aller; toujours heureux soit à vaincre, soit à réparer ses pertes."

Of all the European monarchies Gueudeville most admired England and its people. But, even here, his admiration was hedged with reservations:

Cette heureuse nation est, que je sache, la seule au monde qui jouisse de la liberté dans une monarchie; mais que ce précieux trésor lui coûte de repos et de sang! Avec tout cela, quand les Anglais trouvent un maître ils deviennent esclaves tout comme les autres; et toujours divisés entre eux ils forgent leur chaîne en travaillant pour la liberté qu'ils perdront apparemment un jour (p. 38).[20]

And so Gueudeville proceeds throughout the section on Europe, interspersing facts and figures with personal comments. By contrast, the parts dealt with by Ferrarius are of an admirable objectivity, and rather dull.

I am not able to say if the work sold well. There are not many copies still to be found in major libraries,[21] although this is not a very reliable guide as to how many were printed. Because the texts by Gueudeville and Ferrarius were unoriginal and consisted mainly of information culled from well-known sources, the work would most likely have attracted attention because of its numerous maps. But since these were also sold separately it is probable that the work as a whole was not a profitable venture.[22]

(iii) *Maximes politiques du Pape Paul III* (1716)[23]

Gueudeville's final collaborative effort brought him into contact with the equally notorious Jean Aymon[24] for whose *Maximes politiques* Gueudeville was invited to supply commentaries and other material. The work consists of extracts of thirty-seven letters written by Dom Diego Hurtado de Mendoza, amabssador of Charles V at the Council of Trent.[25] The letters were written between May 15 1547 and April 17 1549, and their purpose was to keep Charles informed of the political manoeuvering of Pope Paul,[26] especially with regard to the removal of the Council from Trent to Bologna, a move to which Charles strenuously objected.

According to the preface, these letters were found in one of the libraries of the Escurial:

. . . mais pour ne confondre pas les différentes matières et les affaires d'état qu'elles contiennent, on ne donne maintenant, ici, que les extraits de celles qui sont propres à démasquer ce souverain pontife romain, et à faire son véritable portrait dans lequel on voit ses opinions bizarres, ses fanfaronnades comiques, ses tergiversations rusées, ses intrigues secrètes, ses entreprises étonnantes, ses dévotions affectées . . .

In the preface, Aymon provides his own portrait of Pope Paul whom he describes as a lecherous hypocrite who employed poisoners and assassins to gain his nefarious ends. By contrast, ambassador Mendoza is presented as a sober, thoroughly scrupulous individual whose judgements are invariably sound and utterly reliable.

The extracts are preceded by a document, dated October 18 1542, in which Charles V appoints Mendoza as plenipotentiary at the forthcoming Council of Trent. Each extract is printed in two columns, Spanish on the left and the French translation on the right, and is followed by a "reflexion" written by Gueudeville. At the end of the extracts there is a letter, dated September 5 1548, in which Antoine Filholi, archbishop of Aix, asks Henry II to punish all those who failed to support the Pope. This letter is also supplied with a "réflexion." Finally, there is an essay in which Gueudeville compares the present Pope, Clement XI, with Paul III.

Except for the rather longer letter XXVII, the extracts are all very short, varying from one to about six sentences. The "réflexions," by contrast, occupy three or more pages. One example is more than sufficient to illustrate the form and content:

Extract — Certainement le Pape est un homme qui fera de grandes extravagances et folies s'il vient à perdre la crainte qu'il a de la Réformation.

Réflexion — Ce pauvre Saint Père me fait pitié. Il ne demanderait qu'à suivre son naturel impétueux, et il faut qu'il se retienne. Son état est bien violent, au moins: fi! fi de la tiare à ce prix-là! Paul III mourait d'envie de se faire craindre. Il aurait bien voulu lancer la foudre! Les bras lui démangeaient d'une grande force, mais pas moyen de se contenter. Parlait-il de faire le mauvais? On vous lui mettait devant les yeux une grosse bête à gueule béante nommée REFORMATION. Le pontife tremblait devant ce monstre, et se tenait coi.

Effectivement c'était un méchant animal que cette Réformation: sans parler du ravage qu'il eût fait sur les terres de la foi, il aurait abîmé le faste, le luxe, la grandeur, la mollesse, les voluptés bacchiques et amoureuses; enfin il aurait desséché ces fontaines sucrées qui arrosent le pays délicieux de la gent cléricale et tondue, et alors, quelle ruine pour l'empire papal!

D'ailleurs, un pape introduit le moindre changement dans la croyance des fidèles et dans les moeurs de la cour? Oh! la chose n'était pas faisable; il y allait trop de l'honneur et de la Vice-Déité. Le Souverain Pontife n'est-il pas infaillible en doctrine, en morale, en droit, en tout? Or, si notre PAUL avait consenti à une Réformation, quelle qu'elle fût, il se serait confessé sujet à l'erreur et à l'abus, au quel cas tomberait cette infaillibilité divine qui est la prérogative essentielle du monarchisme de Saint Pierre.

PAUL III avait donc un puissant intérêt à ne permettre ni innovation ni changement. Sur ce pied-là, à quoi bon le concile? Le bon Saint Père ne demandait pas mieux que de l'éviter, et à ce que je crois, s'il avait été aussi absolu dans son empire papal que certains monarques, parvenus heureusement au despotisme, sont arbitraires dans leurs états, il aurait aboli chez eux la convocation des trois ordres du royaume.

En effet, cet assemblage de prélats et de théologiens est incommode et dangereux pour le Père Béatisime et Sanctissime. Le Concile s'arroge la souveraineté, tout au moins spirituelle, et prétend que, pendant sa tenue, le pontife participe en membre à l'autorité du corps, et n'a pas plus de pouvoir qu'un autre évêque. Il y a eu même tel concile qui a détrôné deux saints pères à la fois pour en faire un nouveau qui se tint dûment, canoniquement, divinement élu. Jugeons de là si ces assemblées qui se nomment oecuméniques ne doivent pas être un horrible épouvantail aux portants-tiare, aux lieutenants de la couronne divine.

Il est donc presque hors de doute que notre PAUL employait volontiers toutes les machines de la politique papale pour rompre le concile; mais, ne pouvant venir à bout, il se réduit à traverser la Réformation, et y réussit. Les évangélistes nouveaux, les apôtres modernes avaient beau crier, invectiver, demander revision de catéchisme et de culte, il leur fut répondu de prouver leur mission par des miracles; et comme il ne plaisait pas au Saint Esprit de leur infuser ce don-là qui, aussi, était à la vieille mode, on les condamnait comme hérétiques aux fagots de ce monde-ci et de l'autre où ils durent longtemps.

Du reste, la superstition triompha de tout, et la cour papalement sacrée ne déchut d'aucune prétention. Les chapeaux rouges houppés d'or, les éminences couvertes de pourpre, coururent pourtant grand risque.

Un archevêque portugais dit hautement en plein concile que les illustrissimes cardinaux avaient besoin d'une illustrissime réformation. Mais l'orage fut conjuré; ces princes de l'église élevés ensuite à l'éminence, ne reçurent point d'échec. Pour notre PAUL il en fut quitte pour la peur; et on se contenta de lui épargner charitablement les "extravagances et les folies" (pp. 56–60).

In his *Parallèle des Papes Paul III et Clément XI* Gueudeville begins by noting that both men had an interest in science and literature. Pope Paul studied astrology and was reputed to have dabbled in magic, a most suitable aid to infallibility. He was an accomplished writer of letters and of poetry. Clément XI spent his youth studying literature and philosophy, and spent little time on the study of theology. He corresponded with the queen of Sweden about astronomy, and if he no longer indulges in poetry, "l'art de bien mentir, au moins l'honore-t-il toujours de son estime et de sa protection."

Paul III always managed to appear neutral, whether in the struggles between the Emperor and the king of France, or between the Guelphs and the Ghibellines. Clément behaved in the same way. Although they both gave the appearance of being neutral their policies favoured the French. Both popes were always active and energetic from their youth, but they pretended to be sickly so that they would be elected to office. Young, healthy men are not normally elevated to the papacy since it is feared they might hold office too long. Paul practised nepotism, and the present pope does the same. The former instituted the Inquisition in Rome, and the latter ensures its continued implementation. The Jesuits owe their existence to the encouragement of Paul, and Clément is their most zealous protector. Both men were afraid to speak out against the horrors perpetrated in the name of religion, and both found themselves powerless to keep war away from their own territories. Although they claimed to be concerned solely with the spiritual they both played an active role in fomenting hostilities. Pope Paul encouraged and facilitated the extermination of Protestants while Pope Clément supplies money for the suppression of the Protestant cantons in Switzerland. Paul managed to arrange a truce between Charles V and François I, and some claim it was Clément who negotiated the Treaty of Radstadt between Prince Eugène and Marshal Villars. Paul was very jealous of his office and would not suffer the slightest affront to the papacy which he strove incessantly to make supreme. Like his predecessor, Clément will do anything to encourage the spread of Catholicism, and foster its growth in Protestant countries. Both men threatened excommunication for those derelict in their obligations to the Church. The schism in the Church that began with the Reformation has its counterpart in the modern split between the various Catholic sects, Jansenists, Thomists, Molinists, Semi-Pelagians, over the question of predestination and grace. Neither Pope was able to cope successfully with these controversies. Paul's only solution was to use brute force to suppress dissension and to create new converts. Clément does not have that power and has to depend on France to stamp out heterodoxy. Neither of them succeeded in their policies of fear, and Paul died a disappointed man. Perhaps, now that Louis XIV is dead, there will be an opportunity for reason and justice to prevail. Gueudeville ends his comparison by noting that Paul was pope for fifteen years from 1534 to 1549, when he died, and that Clément, who became pope in 1700, had also been in office for fifteen years. He ought to do the decent thing and imitate his predecessor.[27]

For someone of Gueudeville's temperament and beliefs it must have been enjoyable to collaborate on this publication. Perhaps this is why, as one critic observed, Gueudeville let himself go:

Nous ne dirons rien . . . de ces Réflexions; on sait assez par les exemples qu'en ont donné depuis peu les autres journalistes, quelle est aujourd'hui la manière d'écrire de M. de Gueudeville, et l'on peut dire qu'il s'est surpassé lui-même dans cette nouvelle production.

On trouve ensuite . . . le parallèle des Papes Paul III et Clément XI. Il est de M. de Gueudeville et par conséquent de même caractère que ses Réflexions. La matière était susceptible de quelque chose de plus ingénieux, et c'est dommage qu'il ne se soit trouvé en état de la traiter comme il traitait autrefois ses matières dans ses premiers *Esprit des Cours*.[28]

One would have thought that the combined efforts of so notorious a pair as Aymon and Gueudeville would have resulted in a literary sensation, but perhaps, by this time, the fickle public had become inured to their anti-Catholic diatribes, and was looking, as always, for something new. After all, the war was over, Louis XIV was dead, it was time for a change. Whatever the explanation, the *Maximes politiques* seems to have caused no stir, and passed, as would its authors, into obscurity.

VII. THE TRANSLATIONS

In 1713, Gueudeville embarked on a new career, that of translator of Renaissance and classical texts. Apart from his contributions to the *Maximes politiques* and the *Atlas historique,* all his writings from 1713 were in the form of translations, some of which were brought out after his death.

(i) *L'Eloge de la folie* (1713)

Of all the French translations of Erasmus' *Moriae Encomium* (1511)[1] none has been more popular and more frequently re-published than the one by Gueudeville which was first published by Pierre Van der Aa in Leiden, under the title *L'Eloge de la folie.* Between 1713 and 1777 there were twenty-one editions of which two were re-issued three times. The fact that several of these editions were piracies is added testimony to the popularity of the author and his translation. It is even more remarkable that this translation was considered still worthy of a new edition as late as 1936.[2]

The choice of a new French translation of Erasmus was particularly opportune for both the publisher and translator. Van der Aa had already made his name in the field by publishing Le Clerc's edition of the *Opera Omnia,* and the works of Erasmus, as Margaret Mann Phillips has pointed out, were particularly favoured by the proponents of a reasonable Christianity who professed to find in the Renaissance scholar a precursor of the Enlightenment:

In the seventeenth century, it is. . . his sharp critical eye which gains him friends. The great standard edition of his works was published at Leyden from 1702 to 1706. . . by Jean Leclerc, himself a Socinian. Pierre Bayle fed the current of scepticism from his solitary room in Rotterdam, and put an engraving of the statue of Erasmus on the title page of his *Nouvelles de la République des Lettres.* Richard Simon translated and commented the text of Scripture, from a supposedly orthodox standpoint, but more ruthlessly rationalistic than any earlier editor's had been. He was condemned by Rome, and Boussuet. . . associated him with Erasmus under the same accusation of impertinence.[3]

Gueudeville, therefore, naturally admired Erasmus in whom he found all those qualities he possessed himself. Erasmus, like Gueudeville, was a "censeur du genre humain" and a master of the subtle art of *badinage*:

Badinant sur tous les ridicules qu'il rencontre en son chemin, ses railleries sont si bien assaisonnées de grâce et de délicatesse, de bon sens et de modération, qu'on ne saurait décider si l'agréable y domine sur l'utile, ou si l'utile l'emporte sur l'agréable.[4]

Other important affinities with Erasmus are revealed in the account of his life that Gueudeville provided in the preface to his translation of the *Colloquia*. Just as, by entering the Benedictine order, Gueudeville had found that "le premier usage que je fis de ma liberté, ce fut de me l'interdire pour toujours," with the result that he became "dégoûté de la moinerie,"[5] so Erasmus:

... fit le grand et téméraire sacrifice de la liberté... il eut bonne envie de se délivrer avant la fin du noviciat... l'émission de ses voeux fut beaucoup moins un acte de sa volonté que l'effet d'une timidité de tempérament, qui l'empêchait de faire triompher ses lumières et son inclination de toutes les différentes machines dont on étourdissait son esprit: mais enfin il subit le joug; et peut-être que ce qu'il y eut d'involontaire et de forcé dans son engagement, ne contribua pas peu à lui faire concevoir cette aversion invincible qu'il marque si souvent, pour l'état monacal, et pour les dérèglements des moines.[6]

As soon as *L'Eloge de la folie* appeared in 1713 Gueudeville was criticized, not altogether unfavourably, for the liberties he had taken with the original text. The first reviewer found the translation so free "qu'on pourrait dire qu'en quelques endroits Erasme n'a fait que fournir le fonds et que Mr. de Gueudeville l'a brodé à sa manière."[7] Jean Le Clerc, in 1717, described it as "plutôt une paraphrase burlesque qu'une version." But he went on to add, in favour of the translation, that "comme c'est la Folie qui parle, et non Erasme, sous sa propre personne, le style burlesque, et quelque fois tabarinique, ne lui convient pas mal."[8] La Barre de Beaumarchais, in 1732, welcomed a new edition of the translation.[9] But, as time went by, judgements of the translation became more severe. By 1751, the attack was no longer confined to the text but extended to Gueudeville himself:

Les agréments de l'original, si capables de se faire sentir dans la plus défectueuse copie, ont donné du cours à une version que Gueudeville, avec plus de goût, moins de licence et un meilleur style, aurait pu rendre plus exacte. Ces défauts ne sont pas les seuls qu'on ait à lui reprocher... Ses méchantes plaisanteries ou plutôt ses quolibets perpétuels, ses allusions forcées et conformes à ses préjugés de religion, et ses hardiesses d'expressions, tous ses faux ornements, si propres d'ailleurs à piquer les gens d'un goût faux, ont déplu aux gens raisonnables qui ne veulent point qu'on aperçoive dans un ouvrage de pur agrément, la religion ni la profession de l'auteur.[10]

In 1780, because of the inadequacies of Gueudeville's translation, La Veaux was inspired to try his hand. His version was followed by others. In 1826, C.B.

de Panalbe produced his own translation because "l'amplification de Gueudeville, la version inélégante de J. de Laveaux... laissaient trop à désirer." And so it went on.

The translation of *Moriae Encomium* seems to have presented insurmountable problems from the very beginning. Pierre de Nolhac's optimistic belief that one could adequately translate Erasmus if one were able to "retrouver la langue d'un Français du siècle d'Erasme,"[11] does not seem to be borne out by the reception given to the first French translation, produced by Georges Haloin, contemporary of Erasmus, in 1520. On reading this version, Erasmus complained that "Haloin made such additions, excisions, and changes in his translation that he actually wrote a different book."[12]

Every translator has to decide, in advance, what principles to adopt. The translators of *Moriae Encomium* before Gueudeville opted for freedom in preference to fidelity. Theodore Maire, in his 1642 edition, warned the reader that "je ne me suis pas attaché en esclave à rendre mot pour mot. Il m'a suffi de bien exprimer mon auteur, le traduisant comme lui-même l'eût écrit si notre langue eût été l'interprète de sa pensée." In 1760, M. Petit de Pontau de Mer adopted a similar stance by declaring that "étant né libre je n'ai pu me résoudre à devenir esclave en écrivant; je me suis contenté de ne point perdre de vue mon auteur, sans vouloir le suivre pas à pas." Gueudeville, then, was simply following the example of his predecessors when he embarked on his own version of the work:

Quant à ma traduction, j'ai suivi le chemin du milieu, c'est-à-dire, autant que je m'y connais, le plus raisonnable, ne m'étant pas borné scrupuleusement à l'idée de mon auteur, mais aussi n'ayant rien ajouté que de conforme à son sens.

J'avertis aussi que, si on trouve dans mon style une trop grande abondance de mots, on doit me le pardonner: je me suis accommodé en cela à la diction de mon auteur, et je n'aurais pu, sans l'affaiblir, serrer mes expressions; outre que des redites passent à la chaleur d'une déclamation. (Préface du traducteur).

This principle of freedom was one that Gueudeville would follow consistently in all his translations.

It would be both otiose and impractical to go systematically through the texts pointing out the ways in which Gueudeville is unfaithful to the original. In any case, his method is uniform throughout the translation. Gueudeville's object was to popularize the text, to make the thought and spirit of Erasmus accessible to those who knew little or no Latin. In order to do this he "clarified" the original. Where Erasmus was subtle or allusive Gueudeville was blatant. The result is that the French version is much longer, much more wordy, and much more direct than the Latin. The following example provides a good illustration of Gueudeville's method:

Verum ipsum Deum pater atque   ... lui qui est le père et le monarque
hominum rex, qui totum nutu treme-   absolu de tous les hommes, lui qui

factat Olympum, fulmen illud tri-
fulcum ponat oportet, et vultum illum
Titanicum, quo, com lubet, Deos
omneis territat, planeque histrionum
more, aliena fumenda misero persona,
si quando velit id facere, quod
nunquam non facit, hoc est
παισᾶπιειγ.

d'un coup d'oeil fait trembler le Ciel,
il faut pourtant, le maître sire, ne lui
en déplaise, qu'il mette bas tout
doucement sa foudre à trois pointes
et que, quittant cet air affreux par
lequel, quand bon lui semble, il fait
transir de peur toute la cour céleste,
il descende du sommet de sa puissance,
qu'il s'adoucisse, qu'il se familiarise,
qu'il se *dédivinise* en quelque manière;
et quand cela? Je n'oserais presque
le dire; lors qu'il est en amour, lorsqu'il
veut faire des *Jupineaux,* envie qui le
prend souvent chez lui, et ailleurs:
alors le pauvre Dieu est obligé de se
masquer comme un harlequin pour
jouer, et pour faire un tout autre
personnage que celui qu'il fait sur son
trône.

Most of the second half of the French passage is not found in the Latin. The
triad of verbs, "s'adoucisse," "se familiarise," and the neologism "se dédivinise,"
is stylistically effective, especially as it comes so close to the reference to the
"foudre à trois pointes," but it is an invention of Gueudeville designed to entertain the reader. Similarly, the Gueudeville invention "Jupineaux" (little Jupiters)
derived from "Jupin," a popular form of Jupiter, is provided for humorous
purposes. Instead of the allusive nod that Erasmus attributed to Jupiter and that
reminds us of Homer, Gueudeville supplied "un coup d'oeil" which robs the
original of its subtlety. Instead of Olympus we have the vague "Ciel," instead of
the "histrio" the "harlequin." Nevertheless, if one is not pedantic, it is fair to
say, when one looks at the passage as a whole, that Gueudeville has undoubtedly
captured the thought and the spirit of the original. If we compare Gueudeville's
comic version with the sober attempts of Th. Maire in 1642 and Pierre de Nolhac
in 1927 we can see why his translation enjoyed such popularity:

1642
... ce grand monarque, qui ébranle le
ciel d'un clin de ses yeux, quitte son
tonnerre et change le visage terrible
dont il étonne les immortels, et
comme un homme de théâtre prend
une autre apparence quand il veut
faire, ce qu'il fait toujours, ce sont des
enfants.

1927
Le père des divinités et le maître des
humains, qui fait trembler tout
l'Olympe d'un signe de tête, est bien
obligé de remiser sa foudre à triple
pointe et ce visage titanique qui
terrifie les Dieux, pour emprunter un
pauvre masque, comme un acteur de
comédie, chaque fois qu'il veut faire,
ce qu'il fait souvent, un enfant.

I think the final judgement on Gueudeville's translation should be the one already cited: "comme c'est la Folie qui parle, et non Erasme sous sa propre personne, le style burlesque, et quelquefois tabarinique, ne lui convient pas mal."

(ii) *L'Utopie* (1715)

Doubtless encouraged by the reception of their first joint venture in the field of translation, Gueudeville next produced a translation of More's *Utopia* which was published by Van der Aa in 1715, reissued in 1717, and brought out in a new edition in 1730.[13] Although it was stated, in Van der Aa's dedication to Jacques Emmeri, that this was the first time More's work had been translated into French, there had been three earlier translations. It seems incredible that apparently neither Van der Aa nor Gueudeville had heard of them, especially the one by Samuel Sorbière, published in Amsterdam in 1643.[14]

Parts of the dedication read as if they were written by Gueudeville himself: "Les loix, les usages, les moeurs qu'on attribue ici à ces peuples imaginaires fortunés ne sont point au-dessus de la raison humaine. C'est le mauvais usage que font les hommes de leur raison qui est le véritable obstacle à la fondation d'un gouvernement utopien."[15] Certainly the preface is Gueudeville's. Here he praises More's ideas, and says how much he enjoyed translating them despite the difficulties involved. One can appreciate how delighted he must have been to have this opportunity of popularizing the work of someone whose ideas he shared so completely: the glorification of reason, the attacks on corruption in the monarchy and the Church, the condemnation of luxury and extravagance, the criticisms of France whose ambitions and claims in More's day were little different from those of Louis XIV. More, says Gueudeville, identified and destroyed the evils that afflict mankind: "La propriété, l'avarice, l'ambition, ces trois pestes de la société civile, ces trois monstres qui ravagent le genre humain, ne se trouvent pas en Utopie." The Utopian society is so organized that each individual finds his greatest happiness in the happiness of the community. By contrast with the real world one does not find in Utopia "cette quantité prodigieuse d'infortunés qui, bien loin de goûter les douceurs de la vie, trouvent à peine de quoi mourir. Triste effet de la dureté, de l'inhumanité, de la barbarie des riches." But Utopia exists only in the imagination, and the chances of its realization are infinitesimal.

The translation, itself, was, as one might anticipate, not entirely faithful to the letter:

... on ne doit pas s'attendre ici à une traduction exacte, et qui ne fasse que rendre précisément le sens de l'auteur. J'avertis d'avance que je ne me suis point arrêté à ce scrupule-là; j'ai souvent étendu l'idée; je lui ai donné le peu d'enjouement dont je suis capable; enfin, sans aller contre l'intention de l'original, je n'ai pas laissé, quelquefois, de le commenter. C'est donc une paraphrase, direz-vous: pardonnez-moi, c'est une traduction libre; et si vous n'aimez que les versions scrupuleuses, je ne vous conseille pas de lire celle-ci.

... l'Utopie française m'a coûté beaucoup de peine et de travail, soit l'affectation du latin qui, selon moi, n'est rien moins que Cicéronien, soit mon ignorance; j'ai trouvé dans mon chemin des endroits qui m'ont tenu longtemps. Je me suis débarrassé de ces broussailles le mieux que j'ai pu, mais je n'oserais répondre que j'ai attrapé partout la pensée de mon auteur; je crains d'avoir quelquefois deviné; c'est au lecteur habile et curieux à s'en éclaircir. (Préface du traducteur).

Gueudeville indulged in his usual elaborations of the original, adding jokes and comments, inventing new words, modernizing the situations, but never betraying the author's ideas which, as we have noted, he shared. A characteristic sample of his method can be found in his translation of the section on marriage in Utopia:

Foemina non ante annum duodevicesimum nubit; mas non nisi expletis quatuor etiam amplius. Ante conjugium mas aut foemina si convicatur furtivae libidinis, graviter in eum eamve adnimadvertitur, conjugioque illis in totum interdicitur, nisi venia principis noxam remiserit: sed et pater et mater-familias, cuius in domo admissum flagitium est, tanquam suas partes parum diligenter tutati, magnae objacent infamiae. Id facinus ideo tam severe vindicant, quod futurum prospiciunt, ut rari in conjugalem amorem coalescerent, in quo aetatem omnem cum uno videant exigendam, et perferendas insuper, quas ea res affert, molestias, nisi a vago concubitu diligenter arceantur. Porro in deligendis conjugibus, ineptissimum ritum (uti nobis visum est) adprimeque ridiculum illi serio ac severe observant. Mulierem enim, seu virgo seu vidua sit, gravis et honesta matrona proco nudam eshibet, ac probus aliques vir vicissim nudum puellae procum sistit. Hunc morem quum velut ineptum ridentes improbaremus.

Il n'est point permis d'entrer dans le lieu de la génération, autrement d'épouser, qu'à dix-huit ans pour la fille et qu'à vingt-deux pour le garçon. Si les accordés, par un transport de tendresse mutuelle, ont succombé à l'impatience amoureuse, et ont prévenu l'action conjugale, on leur fait une rude censure: on leur défend même, absolument de se marier; et ces pauvres amants n'oseraient le faire; ils brûlent à petit feu, chacun de leur côté, à moins que le prince ne fasse grâce et ne dispense de la loi. Mais le père et la mère de famille chez qui le délit, la fornication, le larcin amoureux a été commis, ont à essuyer une grande infamie, pour n'avoir pas veillé assez exactement sur l'honneur de la fille ou du garçon, et sur le leur propre. Pourquoi, à votre avis, punissent-ils si sévèrement une chose, un écart qui ne passe chez nous que pour une légère faiblesse, que pour une peccadille? Voici sur quoi ils se fondent. Le mariage, disent-ils, est un étrange et bizarre engagement: il faut y passer ses jours avec une prétendue moitié qui, trop souvent, est un terrible antagoniste; il faut souffrir et partager ensemble tous les chagrins, toutes les traverses qui surviennent dans le ménage. On ne saurait, donc, prendre trop de précautions pour empêcher que l'amour nuptial ne ralentisse et ne s'éteigne; surtout ce flambeau brûlant ordinairement d'une flamme de paille. Or, quelle meilleure mesure pour obvier à cet inconvénient-là que d'éloigner, autant que cela se peut, les sourdes et secrètes pratiques de Vénus, que d'interdire tout commerce génératif, excepté celui d'une conjonction légitime?

Au reste, voyez un peu comment l'opinion fait tout chez les mortels. Quand il est question d'épouser, les Utopiens ont une coutume qui passerait chez nous pour déraisonnable, pour ridicule, pour malhonnête; et laquelle, néanmoins, ils observent avec beaucoup de sérieux et de gravité. Nos insulaires ne savent ce que c'est de se marier au hasard quant au corps. Une prude et vénérable matrone fait voir à l'amant sa maîtresse, en pure nature, c'est-à-dire toute nue; et réciproquement, un homme de bonnes moeurs, un homme de probité, montre à la fille, ou à la veuve, l'étalage viril. Il lui ôte la chemise, et le lui présente à contempler, à examiner depuis la tête jusqu'aux pieds. Nous ne pouvions garder notre sérieux en apprenant ce beau spectacle du paradis terrestre avant l'inconcevable chute d'Adam; nous ne pûmes même nous empêcher de leur dire que cet usage-là était sot et impertinent. (pp. 222–226).

The translation is, as usual, twice as long as the original, and contains much that is entirely of Gueudeville's own invention. Where More speaks of illegal pre-marital relations as "furtivae libidinis" Gueudeville expands this into "un transport de tendresse mutuelle" and "l'impatience amoureuse." There is nothing in the Latin to suggest that the lovers "brûlent à petit feu, chacun de leur côté" while awaiting royal dispensation. The illicit act is referred to by More as a "flagitium" which, in French, becomes "le délit, la fornication, le larcin amoureux." The best example of Gueudeville's expansion for purposes of comedy occurs towards the end of the passage where More's description of the man being shown naked to his intended: "ac probus aliquis vir vicissim nudum puellae procum sistit. Hunc morem quum velut ineptum ridentes improbaremus," becomes "un homme de bonnes moeurs, un homme de probité, montre... l'étalage viril. Il lui ôte la chemise, et le lui présente à contempler, à examiner depuis la tête jusqu'aux pieds. Nous ne pouvions garder notre sérieux en apprenant ce beau spectacle du paradis terrestre avant l'inconcevable chute d'Adam."[16]

Judging by the fact that it was reissued in 1717 and re-edited in 1730, one can assume the book to have been a popular success, aided no doubt by the success of *L'Eloge de la folie*. The critical reception, as one might expect, was not so favourable, although the first review, in the *Journal des savants*, was relatively innocuous, if one had not read the earlier review referred to:

La vie de Thomas Morus et son utopie sont si connues que nous n'avons point d'analyse à donner de cet ouvrage. La traduction de M. Gueudeville est, comme il le dit lui-même, une paraphrase ou traduction libre dans laquelle, sans s'arrêter à suivre scrupuleusement son auteur, il tâche de lui donner "de l'enjouement." Le public, qui connaît M. Gueudeville par ce que nous avons rapporté de lui sur un autre ouvrage, peut juger par le génie du traducteur s'il a embelli l'original.[17]

The earlier review referred to is the one on the *Atlas historique*. It should be noted that this reviewer ignores the distinction Gueudeville made in his preface between a "paraphrase" and a "traduction libre." In his review, Jean Le Clerc preferred the earlier translation by Sorbière, and found the new one:

... plutôt une paraphrase, où Mr. Gueudeville parle en style burlesque... Ceux qui veulent qu'il y ait partout de la plaisanterie s'accommoderont de celle-ci... Il est vrai que Morus était naturellement plaisant, et qu'il ne put même s'empêcher de plaisanter sur l'échafaud. Mais ses plaisanteries ne consistent pas à fabriquer de nouveaux mots, et ne régnaient pas dans tout ce qu'il écrivait. On en voit très peu dans l'Utopie où le traducteur en a mis à pleines mains.[18]

The reviewer in the *Journal de Trévoux* was much harsher, disliking not only the translation but also the original. He described Gueudeville's style as "ce fade et misérable jargon... un mélange d'expressions triviales et de mauvaises plaisanteries; de mots hasardés qui choquent, et des pensées froides, insipides qui glacent le lecteur," and ended his review as follows:

Nous laissons aux lecteurs à faire les réflexions convenables sur ce système politique, également repréhensible dans plusieurs maximes, et impossible dans la pratique, que l'auteur semble avoir composé dans l'ivresse, si j'ose ainsi parler, d'une espèce de débauche philosophique, et que le traducteur a gâté par son affectation à joindre aux idées du philosophe toutes les badineries d'un mauvais plaisant.[19]

The only favourable review I have found occurs, significantly, much later in the century, in the *Bibliothèque universelle des romans*,[20] a work destined for popular and not scholarly consumption. Nevertheless, if people wanted to read the *Utopia* in French, and the popularity of voyage literature, both real and imaginary, indicates that they did, Gueudeville's translation was, for some time, the only one available.[21]

(iii) *Les Comédies de Plaute* (1719)[22]

Having successfully marketed the works of two Renaissance authors, Gueudeville and Van der Aa turned their attention to the classics, and produced a ten-volume translation of the plays of Plautus whose works, when compared with those of Terence, were almost unknown in French.

In the sixteenth century there were no French translations of Plautus, although there was a verse play, *Le Brave,* closely based on *Miles Gloriosus,* performed in Paris in 1567.[23] In the seventeenth century, playwrights such as Rotrou, Mareschal and Molière drew heavily on Plautus for the material of several of their plays.[24] The first attempt at a translation appeared in 1656 when Claude Nicole published *Le Fantôme,* a verse translation of *Mostellaria.* This was followed, in 1658, by Michel de Marolles' translation of all the plays with which he also published the Latin text, a life of Plautus, comments on the plays, and fragments of lost plays. In 1666 there appeared Thomas Guyot's prose translation of *Captivi,* followed, in 1683, by prose versions of *Amphitruo, Rudens* and *Epidicus,* by Mlle Le Fèvre, later to become Mme Dacier, the celebrated translator of Terence, Aristophanes and Homer. Her translations also included the Latin text, comments on the plays, and notes.

Three features of Plautus seem to have deterred translators in the French classical period. First, the style itself, with its enormous vocabulary, its obscurities and puns, presented insurmountable problems. Second, the violation of the unities of time, place and action, with the consequent lack of *vraisemblance,* offended French taste. Third, the obscenities offended French taste even more. Even though Mme Dacier did her best to defend Plautus against the last two charges, her arguments do not seem to have encouraged further attempts at translation in the seventeenth century.

In 1706, Jean-François Regnard's verse adaptation of *Menaechmi* was performed in Paris,[25] and, in 1716, Pierre Coste published, in Amsterdam, a new prose translation of *Captivi* which, because Coste maintained the play in no way violated the unities, occasioned a considerable amount of discussion and disagreement in the columns of French periodicals published in Holland.[26]

Perhaps it was as a result of all this interest in Plautus that Gueudeville decided to try his hand at a new translation. Curiously enough, Philippe de Limiers, with whom Gueudeville was collaborating on the *Atlas historique,* also decided to bring out a version of his own. He translated sixteen of the plays, two of them *Stichus* and *Trinummus,* in verse, and published them together with the translations of Mme Dacier and Pierre Coste. He also included the Latin text, a life of Plautus, and comments on the plays. The translations of Limiers and Gueudeville were both published about the same time in 1719.[27]

Both authors were conscious of the objections raised against Plautus, and both dealt with them in different ways. Limiers followed the practice of his predecessors. He tried to conform as closely as possible to the original text, without offending the sensibilities of the reader. In the preface to his work he said that the obscenities in Plautus almost dissuaded him from the enterprise. He felt, however, that no one would blame the translator for imperfections in Plautus, and he did his best, by using French euphemisms, to retain the spirit of the original without giving offence. As for the puns and other linguistic features peculiar to Latin, he tried to find equivalents. In short, his aim was to produce a kind of language "comme aurait parlé Plaute en français, s'il eût vécu de notre temps."

Gueudeville's theory and practice of translation were somewhat different. For him, as we have seen, translation consisted of following the spirit but not the letter of the original. Fidelity to the text, therefore, plays little or no part in his translation of Plautus, and no Latin text is included for comparison with his version. Even the spirit of the original sometimes requires "improvement," perhaps by the addition of a speech or two, an extra joke here and there, and so on. In the preface to his translation Gueudeville says he knows he will be accused, as in the past, of displaying a frivolous approach to a serious undertaking, and of distorting the original by an excess of Gallicisms. His answer to such criticisms is that those who make them produce translations that succeed only in sending the reader to sleep. If they stick closely to the original it is simply because their knowledge of French does not extend beyond conventional terminology. Gueudeville, by contrast, enriches the language with his inventiveness, to such an extent that foreigners, by reading his translation, will acquire a greater understanding and a practical knowledge of the French language. For these reasons, therefore:

Ma traduction est fort libre : je ne me suis gêné que par le sens de mon auteur : encore est-il vrai qu'il y a tels endroits où à cause de l'épaisse obscurité du texte, je ne sais pas trop moi-même ce que je dis. Du reste, je n'ai rien omis pour habiller ce vieux comique à la française et à la mode. J'étends, sans façon, ses pensées : je tâche de ne lui faire rien dire qui ne soit de son génie, et qu'il aurait peut-être dit, s'il avait vécu dans notre génération. Je n'ignore pas qu'une telle liberté formalise nos critiques rigides, et qu'ils la condamnent comme une licence impardonnable. Mettre du sien à un célèbre auteur? C'est, selon ces Messieurs, le corrompre, le défigurer; c'est lui ôter tout son prix. Mais enfin, est-il juste qu'un traducteur tienne en esclavage son imagination? J'ai suivi mon penchant et je me flatte que les lecteurs du vrai goût, petit troupeau!, me sauront gré d'avoir voulu contribuer à les mieux divertir.[28]

There is no doubt that Gueudeville believed his translations improved on the originals. Much as he admired Plautus with whom he felt, as he did with Erasmus, certain affinities in the comic art and in the satirizing of human foibles,[29] he disliked the playwright's excessive moralizing. He also had little patience for the obscure allusions, the puns and, above all, Plautus' uneconomical style, especially his fondness for repetition. He also professed an objection to the obscenities. In fact, he included, at the end of his work, a list indicating where all the obscenities could be found, so that the sensitive reader could avoid them! As one reviewer pointed out, "Il est vrai que [Gueudeville] dit que c'est afin que ceux qui veulent les éviter sachent où elles sont. Mais la corruption de quelques lecteurs en fait un tout autre usage, et c'est un prompt moyen de commencer par là la lecture."[30] In any case, Gueudeville's objection to the obscenities is somewhat weakened by the fact that he supplied some of his own.

Finally, he criticizes the playwright for his lack of *vraisemblance*. Plautus, he charges, sacrifices the unity of time to exigencies of the action. There frequently occur, between scenes, events that could not possibly have taken place in so short a time. Equally improbable is the manner in which bearers of news (of whom there are so many), so anxious to deliver their messages that they arrive all out of breath, always seem to have the time to protest, to an empty stage, that no one should try to stop them, and to dissert at length on the human condition. It was with these objections in mind that Gueudeville undertook his translation. Since it would be tedious to go systematically through all the plays to demonstrate how Gueudeville put his ideas into practice, examples from one or two plays, and comparisons with other translations will be used to demonstrate the individuality of his approach.

One of Gueudeville's favourite devices for rendering Plautus more "amusing" for eighteenth-century readers is the employment of a burlesque style by which he juxtaposes different levels of language and uses them in an appropriate manner. In the last two lines of *Amphitruo*, for example, Amphitruo says:

. . . . missum facio Teresiam senem.
Nunc, spectatores, Iovis summi causa clare plaudite.

Gueudeville's rendition of these lines is as follows:

Je n'ai plus besoin de faire venir les vieux Druïdes; qu'ils aillent en faire accroire à leurs dupes et à leurs sots; ils ont assez à qui parler. Pour vous, Messieurs les spectateurs, applaudissez bien fort à l'honneur et à la gloire de sa Majesté Jupine, et ensuite reprenez, s'il vous plaît, le chemin du chez-soi.

Now since the term "senex" is not pejorative, Gueudeville, by translating "Teresiam senem" as "les vieux Druïdes" changes the tone of the line, especially when he continues by using the inappropriate reference to Druids as an opportunity for an attack on religion. The suggestion is that the Druids, i.e. priests, delude (faire accroire) people who are fools and dupes for believing in them. The abrupt transition from speaking of "dupes" and "sots" to addressing the spectators, also has humorous if insulting implications. The style, however, is formal and elevated, and involves such terms as "honneur", "gloire" and "Majesté", after which the level suddenly drops with the use of the word "Jupine", a vulgar form of Jupiter. This example displays not only the way in which Gueudeville alters the tone and level of the language of Plautus, but also his fondness for expanding the text.

In Act II, Scene 2 of *Aulularia*, for example, Euclion, thinking his servant has told Megadorus about his treasure, says:

Anus hercle huic indicium fecit de auro: perspicue palam est.
Cui ego iam linguam praecidam atque oculos effodiam domi. (188–189)

which Gueudeville translates quite faithfully, except that he adds the words italicized:

Ah! il n'en faut point douter; la vieille *sorcière* l'aura instruit du trésor; la chose est parlante. *Ah! puante charogne,* laisse-moi entrer seulement; si je ne te coupe la langue, si je ne t'arrache les yeux. . . tu verras.

His justification for these insertions is that they add movement and energy to the dialogue. One would have thought Plautus had already provided more than enough!

If it were simply a question of the addition of one or two words or phrases to the original text, one would hesitate to complain. But when, to conform to Gueudeville's notions of wit and vitality, translation becomes paraphrase as, for example, in the following exchange between Sosia and Amphitruo in Act II, Scene 1 of *Amphitruo*:

S. Merito maledicas mihi si non id ita factum est.
   Verum haud mentior, resque uti facta dico.
A. Homo hic ebrius est, ut opinor. (572–574)

S. Je consens de bon coeur à être maudit, roué de coups, si j'ai la moindre pensée de ce que vous m'imputez. Mais, mon noble et vaillantissime maître, une bonne fois pour toutes, faites-moi la grâce d'ajouter foi à ce que je vous ai dit; que je tombe mort à vos pieds si j'ai exagéré d'une syllabe. Croyez donc votre pauvre Sosie, c'est un bon diable; ô si vous aviez l'honneur de le connaître à fond!
A. Je ne désespère pas de l'avoir quelque jour. Certainement je crois qu'il a bu, et que sa tête bien conditionnée extravague dans les espaces imaginaires de la bouteille.[31]

and when one finds whole passages of which hardly a word appears in Plautus,[32] one begins to share the impatience of the critics.

It would be untrue to say that Gueudeville never follows the text faithfully and never translates literally, but when he does so it is usually because he has not understood the Latin or because the Plautine play on words is untranslatable. In the following lines from Act II, Scene 1 of *Aulularia,* for example, I have the impression he has missed the meaning:

Megadorus.   Quid est id, soror?
Eunomia.   Quod tibi sempiternum
             Salutare sit, liberis procreandis. . . . . (147–148)

The expression used by Eunomia is correctly understood by Megadorus as a suggestion that he should get married. Gueudeville who, on this occasion, would be justified in translating freely, adheres closely to the Latin, and gives Eunomia's response as, "Puisse mon souhait s'accomplir, et vous être toujours salutaire pour la génération." Similarly, when Megadorus protests, and his sister asks him why, he says:

Quia mihi misero cerebrum excutiunt
Tua dicta, soror, lapides loqueris (151–152)

Gueudeville, instead of developing the image of the stones, takes the lines quite literally:

Je veux dire, ma soeur, que votre proposition me fend la tête, et que vos paroles sont de grosses pierres.

When it comes to puns such as the one in Act I, Scene 1 of *Amphitruo* where Plautus plays on the words "promptaria cella" and "depromar" by describing the prison as a larder from which the "promus" supplies provisions:

Sosia. Quid faciam, nunc si tresviri me in carcerem compegerint?
      Inde cras quasi e promptaria cella depromar ad flagrum (155–156)

Gueudeville's solution is simply to ignore the problem (if indeed he was aware of it) and translate literally:

Que ferais-je à présent si le triumvirat de notre magistrature m'honorant des beaux titres de vagabond et de voleur, allait se saisir de ma petite personne, et me faisait jeter dans le fond d'un cachot? On m'en tirerait demain à peu près comme d'un garde-manger, pour m'étriller d'importance.

When Gueudeville's translation is compared with that of Limiers, the results are not always unfavourable to the former. In Act I, Scene 1 of *Asinaria,* for example, Libanus, speaking of a grain mill that servants, as a punishment, were required to operate by hand, says:

Num me illuc ducis, ubi lapis lapidem terit? (31)

Limiers translates this as, "De bonne foi ne m'allez pas mener, là où une pierre en broie une autre." But this is incorrect since the stones pulverize the grain, not each other. Gueudeville has it more logically as ". . . où une pierre en frotte une autre." In Act III, Scene 3 of the same play, Argyrippus, trying to get some sense out of a servant, says:

Quin ad hunc, Philaenium, adgredimur,
Virum quidem pol opitmum et non similem furis huius? (680—681)

Limiers translates this as "Adressons-nous à celui-ci, ma chère, il est bon enfant, et bien différent de cet autre voleur." This distorts the sense of the situation by having Argyrippus call both servants thieves when only one of them is being insulted. Gueudeville translates the last part correctly as ". . . et qui ne ressemble point à ce voleur-ci."

But since Limiers' translation fared no better with the critics than Gueudeville's it is much more revealing of Gueudeville's methods to compare his work with that of Mme Dacier whose translation was generally favourably received. In rare cases Gueudeville's version is shorter and more accurate than that of Mme Dacier, as, for example, in the prologue to *Amphitruo*:

Mercurius.　　Humana matre natus, humano patre,
　　　　　　　Mirari non est aequum, sibi si praetimet (28—29)

Dacier—　　　Car, au reste, ce Jupiter dont je vous parle appréhende tout autant que vous de s'attirer des affaires; et vous ne devez pas vous en étonner, puisqu'il est né de père et de mère mortels.

Gueudeville—　Etant né de race humaine, et se souvenant toujours d'avoir détrôné son père, il ne faut pas s'étonner s'il a peur de sa peau.

Mme Dacier's translation of "sibi praetimet" as "s'attirer des affaires" (to get into trouble) is not nearly as precise as Gueudeville's "il a peur de sa peau." In most instances, however, the Gueudeville translation is both longer and freer. This can be seen best by comparing the two versions of the well-known speech by Sosia in Act I, Scene 1 of *Amphitruo*. The differences of approach are so striking that I offer them without comment:

Certe edepol, quom illum contemplo et formam cognosco meam, | Quem ad modum egosum — saepe in speculum inspexi —, nimis similest mei. | Itidem habet petasum ac vestitum; tam consilimest atque ego. | Sura, pes, statura, tonsus, oculi, nasum vel labra, | Malae, mentum, barba, collus, totus. Quid verbis opust? | Si tergum cicatricosum, nihil hoc similist similius. | Sed quom cogito, equidem certo idem sum qui semper fui. | Novi erum, novi aedis nostras; sane sapio et sentio. | Non ego illi optempero quod loquitur; pultabo foris. (441—449)

Dacier — En vérité quand je le considère, il me semble voir mon visage, comme il me souvient de l'avoir vu souvent dans le miroir. Il me ressemble en toutes choses; il n'y a pas jusqu'à son chapeau et à son habit qui ne soient pareils aux miens. Enfin, deux gouttes d'eau ne se ressemblent pas mieux. La jambe, le pied, les cheveux, les yeux, le nez, les dents, les lèvres, les joues, le menton, la barbe, l'encolure, bref, sans tant de discours, tout; et s'il a le dos cicatrisé de coups de fouet, il n'y a rien au monde de si semblable. Mais avec tout cela, quand j'y fais réflexion, je suis le même que j'ai toujours été; je connais mon maître, je reconnais notre maison. Quoiqu'il puisse dire, je suis en mon bon sens. Je suis résolu de ne lui point obéir et d'aller heurter à notre porte.

Gueudeville — Après tout, je ne sais plus qu'en juger; et vrai comme Pollux m'entend, je me perds, je m'abîme dans cette aventure-là. Plus je regarde et j'examine mon homme, plus je me reconnais en lui. Je me vois assez souvent dans le miroir, et jamais je ne me suis planté devant une glace que je ne bénisse la Nature, que je ne la remercie de son beau travail. J'ai donc mon image toujours présent dans l'esprit. Mais, en vérité, ce personnage qui est devant moi quel qu'il soit, est pour ma personne un miroir vivant; il imite, il représente, il copie mon corps dans la dernière perfection. La jambe, le pied, la taille, les cheveux, les yeux, le nez, les lèvres, les joues, le menton, la barbe, le cou; enfin il me ressemble tout à fait bien, c'est un autre moi-même. Il n'y a plus qu'un point à examiner: s'il a aussi le dos enluminé par les marques et les cicatrices des coups de verge, le voilà Sosie accompli: deux gouttes d'eau, deux gouttes de lait ne se ressemblent pas mieux. D'un autre côté, j'y fais bien réflexion, je ne puis pas être et n'être pas moi. Quel changement serait-il arrivé en ma personne? Ne suis-je pas le même que j'ai toujours été? D'ailleurs, je connais mon maître, il y a assez longtemps que je mange de son pain, Dieu merci; je sais de science certaine, que c'est là notre maison; je suis sûr que je ne dors point, que je ne rêve point; car enfin je me tâte, je me retâte; et je ne trouve que moi. On ne me reprochera pas non plus, j'espère, que j'ai perdu la tramontane, les Sosies ne sont nullement gens à cela; le Ciel a paîtri d'une trop bonne cervelle. On ne s'avisera pas de dire que je ne suis point dans mon bon sens. J'y suis, oui je le soutiens hardiment, j'y suis autant qu'un Sosie y peut être. Je ne suis pas fou, une fois; et nous nous connaissons un peu à ce qu'on porte dans la tête. Qu'ai-je donc à faire de m'amuser à ce causeur, à ce babillard-là? Je le laisserai jaser tout son soûl, et je vais à bon compte, frapper à notre porte.

In his "réflexions" on the plays Gueudeville discusses the question of *vraisemblance,* mainly in its application to the characters and the plot. But he also uses the occasion to make his own observations on the follies of mankind. Once again, he cannot resist the temptation to introduce his lifelong obsessions. In his remarks on the *Amphitruo,* for example, he finds the action of Jupiter, who lengthens the night so he can spend more time with Alcmena, typical of "ces Dieux terrestres, ces princes tyranniques qui, pour contenter leurs passions dominantes, plongent tout un grand peuple dans les ténèbres d'une disette

affreuse, et lui font souffrir tous les mauvais effets de l'indigence." His observations on the *Miles Gloriosus* naturally lead him to reflect on the power of
praise, and this reminds him, even more naturally, of the late, but not lamented
Louis XIV:

N'a-t-on pas vu un des plus puissants et des plus fameux monarques qui ait
jamais manié le sceptre; oui, ne l'a-t-on pas vu si affamé de cette exhalaison
enivrante, qu'il l'a savouré avec délices pendant tout son long, et peut-être trop
long passage sur le trône; et cela sans se soucier que l'encens fût vrai ou faux,
légitime ou bâtard.

In his reflection on *Captivi* Gueudeville praises the Roman practice of dis-
tinguishing beliefs from behaviour. While the Romans permitted the veneration
of all kinds of gods whose characters and reputations left much to be desired,
they also instituted strict civil and criminal laws to regulate the conduct of men
in their daily life:"Heureux ces temps où la religion n'influait point en mal.
Depuis que le culte s'est épuré, depuis qu'il n'exige qu'un acquiescement d'esprit,
et qu'une observation exacte des devoirs naturels, n'est-il pas chez les humains
la cause innocente d'une infinité de malheurs?" As in the critique of *Télémaque*,
then, literary criticism is mingled with political and religious satire.

As far as we know, the principles of Gueudeville's method that worked so
well for him in his translations of Erasmus and More, were not so successful
when applied to Plautus. Certainly there was no second edition or even a reissue,
and no other publisher thought the work worthy of pirating.[33] It may simply be
that a work in ten volumes is less likely to be a commercial success than a one-
volume publication. The critics, as usual, were hostile. The reviewer in *L'Europe
savante* considered the translations nothing more than a series of bad jokes. The
editor of the *Journal Littéraire,* although finding Gueudeville's translation
superior to that of Limiers, considered it inferior to that of Mme Dacier. The
abbé Goujet, in 1744, wrote that Gueudeville's work was "Plaute travesti plutôt
que traduit." He deplored what he viewed as Gueudeville's bad taste, his dis-
gusting humour, and his ignorance of Latin. As for Gueudeville's claim that his
translation would help foreigners acquire a better knowledge of French the abbé
stated:

... rien n'était plus propre à donner une mauvaise idée de notre langue aux
étrangers. . . que de leur offrir un ouvrage plein de redites, de phrases et de
termes inutiles, de répétitions de mots qui signifient la même chose, d'expressions
nouvelles qui ne présentent rien de plus que les fruits bizarres d'une imagination
qui extravague, ou qui ne sont en usage que chez la populace la moins retenue
dans ses discours.

In 1831, J. Naudet ended the preface to his translation of Plautus by stating:
"Quand je l'ai entreprise, on convenait généralement que Plaute n'avait point
encore été traduit."[34] It was not that he was unaware of the earlier attempts,
but that he simply discounted them.

It is only in the twentieth century, with an established text, that it has been possible to contemplate an "accurate" translation of Plautus. And still the same old problems remain, at least if we are to judge by a recent attempt at a translation of *Aulularia*:

Voici une traduction nouvelle, et qui se veut fidèle, de la fameuse "Comédie à la marmite" de Plaute. Quand je dis "fidèle", j'entends une traduction qui respecte le texte, certes, mais avec ses nuances, sa saveur, ses impondérables, autant qu'il est possible: traduire, sans trop trahir...

Cette pièce a été écrite... par un homme pour des hommes, par un être vivant pour des êtres vivants qui ont ri, applaudi... Une traduction fidèle visera donc à rendre ce ton familier, cette verdeur de langage qui n'appartient qu'au petit peuple.

J'ai donc essayé d'une part de suivre de très près le texte latin pour être "à couvert" du côté de latinistes légitimement pointilleux; d'autre part de donner à la traduction une allure populaire, facile, moderne, qui ne sente pas l'huile, qui ne "pue" pas à plein nez la version latine, mais qui puisse donner, autant que possible, à un lecteur non latiniste, l'impression d'un texte original.[35]

It would appear that things have not changed all that much since Gueudeville's day, and if Gueudeville, during his sojourn in the Elysian Fields (or elsewhere), should come across the above, we must forgive him if he enjoys a moment of malicious laughter.

(iv) *Les Colloques d'Erasme* (1720)[36]

The final publication with Van der Aa,[37] and the last to appear in Gueudeville's lifetime, saw a return to the works of Erasmus. The *Colloquia* were originally written about 1498, but were not published until 1518, apparently without their author's knowledge. The colloquies were so well received that Erasmus decided to rework and to supplement them. The definitive edition appeared in 1533.

The *Colloquia*, originally intended for Erasmus' students, are a series of dialogues or conversations about religion and morals, written in the bold, critical, sometimes scabrous spirit of the Renaissance. The topics discussed include concerns of everyday life, such as marriage, children, travelling, and the like. The aim of the work is didactic. On its first appearance the work had been condemned by the authorities who, according to Gueudeville, probably helped to double the sales.

In his preface Gueudeville presents the customary disclaimers and statement of principles:

Pour rendre compte, à présent, de cette traduction, je dois avertir qu'elle n'est point littérale, ne m'étant attaché qu'au sens de mon auteur. J'y ai donné, autant que la matière le permettait, le même tour qu'à l'ELOGE DE LA FOLIE; et

comme cette dernière traduction n'a pas été mal reçue, j'ai quelque sujet
d'espérer que celle-ci ne déplaira point.

He goes on to explain that his original intention was to translate only those parts
of the works that would be of interest to the general public, and leave out the
sections concerned with the teaching of Latin, the education of children, and
some of the dialogues that are not easily rendered into French. However, the
publisher, whose aim has always been to cater to all tastes, requested a translation of all the work, and Gueudeville complied on condition that the less
interesting sections would be printed at the end. The colloquies, he says, are
arranged according to their subject matter.[38]
    Gueudeville's translation of the colloquies was received, in the scholarly
world, in a predictable manner. Perhaps the criticism is best summed up in
Victor Develay's 1875 translation of the *Colloquia*:

Peu de livres, parmi les oeuvres importantes que nous a laissées le XVIe siècle,
sont plus connus de nom que les *Colloques d'Erasme,* et le sont moins de fait.
L'oubli relatif dans lequel est tombé ce curieux ouvrage est dû en partie à
l'absence d'une traduction française, car l'on ne peut appeler ·de ce nom l'essai
informe donné par Gueudeville, et dont Quérard, dans sa *France littéraire,* dit
que "c'est plutôt un travestissement qu'une traduction."

However, Professor Halkin, in the preface to his recent translation,[39] finds all
the translators, including Develay, guilty of excessive freedom and *longueurs,*
although Gueudeville is judged to be the worst offender by far. A brief comparison of the opening of Professor Halkin's translation of the dialogue of
Pamphilus and Maria with that of Gueudeville, demonstrates, once again, the
latter's characteristic method of elaboration for comic effect:

P. Salue crudelis, salue ferrea, salue adamantina.

P. Bonjour fille cruelle. Bonjour, fille impitoyable. Bonjour, fille au coeur plus dur que le diamant.

M. Salue tandem et tu, Pamphile, quoties et quantum voles, et quocunque libet nomine. Sed interim mihi videris oblitus nominis mei, Maria vocor.

M. Bonjour, Pamphile, aussi souvent et autant que tu le veux et par n'importe quel nom qui te plaise. Mais il semble que tu as oublié mon nom : Je m'appelle Marie.

P. At Martiam dici oportuit.

P. Il eût mieux valu t'appeler Martiale.

M. Quid ita, quaeso? Quid mihi cum Marte?

M. Pourquoi, je t'en prie. Qu'ai-je donc à faire avec Mars?

P. Quia quemadmodum illi deo pro ludo est homines interficere, ita et tibi. Nisi quod tu Marte crudelior occidis etiam amantem.[40]

P. Comme Mars, tu frappes les hommes par jeu. Voilà comme tu es. En outre, tu es plus cruelle que Mars: tu assassines même ton amoureux.

Gueudeville's translation reads as follows:

P.   Bonjour cruelle, bonjour âme de fer, bonjour coeur de diamant!

M.   Je vous renvoie aussi trois saluts, Monsieur Pamphile. Je vous en donnerai tant qu'il vous plaira; et je vous saluerai sous quels titres que vous voudrez. Cependant je crois que vous avez oublié mon nom. Pour vous en rafraîchir la mémoire, vous voulez bien que je vous dise qu'au baptême je reçus de mon parrain ou de ma marraine, car je ne me souviens pas de si loin, je reçus dis-je, le beau nom de Marie.

P.   On ne prévoyait guère ce que vous seriez un jour, Mademoiselle, quand on vous donna ce nom-là; on vous aurait sans doute appelé Martie.

M.   Oh, oh! et pourquoi cela, je vous prie? Trouvez-vous quelque rapport entre le Dieu de la Guerre et ma petite personne?

P.   Fort grand; car comme cette Divinité barbare se divertit à tuer des hommes, de même ce n'est qu'un jeu pour vous de les faire brûler à petit feu. Il est vrai qu'il y a une grande différence entre Mars et vous; car enfin, ce Dieu meurtrier n'extermine que ses ennemis, au lieu que vous consumez mortellement les gens qui vous adorent, qui vous aiment; mais en cela même, n'êtes-vous pas cent fois plus dure et plus impitoyable que le Maître des Armées?

Again, we have no information about the success of Gueudeville's translation in his own day. There was only one edition and no re-issues, but we cannot tell if this was because Van der Aa printed a great quantity of copies or because there was no demand for the work. Until evidence is forthcoming, therefore, we must suspend judgement on the matter.

(v) *Sur la noblesse et excellence du sexe féminin...* (1726)

With the translations of two works by Agrippa, the sixteenth-century cabbalistic philosopher, we embark on a consideration of the first of Gueudeville's works, published after his death, and the question as to when these posthumous publications were actually written, and why they did not appear in his lifetime.

As far as the translation of Agrippa is concerned, we know that Gueudeville was interested in him as early as 1709 when he was included in the *Dialogues des morts d'un tour nouveau,* in a conversation with Apuleius (see Chapter five). So it is possible that he did the translation at that time, or began it then but did not complete it until much later. As to why this, or the other works to be considered, were published after his death, it is difficult to say. It could simply be that the publishers he offered them to were not interested in them, or that they intended to publish them eventually, or that the works were among Gueudeville's papers when he died, and were found by or bequeathed to someone who arranged for their publication. There are many possible explanations but there is no evidence to support any one of them.

The two works of Agrippa that Gueudeville translated were *De incertitudine et vanitate scientiarum* and *De nobilitate et praecellentia foeminei,* which were published, in 1726, in a three-volume edition entitled, *Sur la noblesse et excellence du sexe féminin. . . avec le traité sur l'incertitude, aussi bien que la vanité des sciences et des arts.*[41]

Although Agrippa's writings were not highly regarded in the scholarly world[42] they had enjoyed a certain popularity from the beginning, and appeared in several editions, including some clandestine ones, throughout the sixteenth, seventeenth and eighteenth centuries. Towards the end of the seventeenth century they were placed on the Index.[43] There had also been several French translations before that of Gueudeville, one as recently as 1713.[44] The two works that Gueudeville translated are both, like *L'Eloge de la folie,* in the rhetorical tradition of the paradoxical discourse. In the first, written for Marguerite d'Autriche, Agrippa argues that women are superior to men (the paradoxical nature of this contention would not be understood today), and in the second, that there is nothing more pernicious or dangerous to the life of man and the salvation of his soul than the arts and sciences. Both works display all the characteristic features of Renaissance erudition and wit.

In the "Préface du traducteur" Gueudeville praises Agrippa for the boldness of his thesis that all books, except the Bible, should be burned, but he suspects Agrippa's real intention was to chastize man for his vanity and his obsession with worldly fame. As for the idea that women are superior to men Gueudeville rejects it out of hand. For him, men and women "sont également capables de tout bien et de tout mal." With regard to the translation, he takes the usual liberties:

. . . pour rendre compte, en peu de mots, de ma traduction, j'avoue ingénument que je plaisante mon auteur, et que je fais de mon mieux pour le tourner en ridicule. Deux raisons m'ont porté à prendre ce parti-là: l'une, la nature du sujet, si absurde et si risible en soi-même que je me serais condamné d'impertinence si je l'avais tourné sérieusement. L'autre raison, la voici: mon original étant d'un style sec, aride, diffus, dépourvu de tout agrément, et surtout plein de redites, une traduction littérale, sérieuse, et faite dans l'intention du moins apparente de l'auteur, eût été, à ce que je crois, quelque chose de bien dégoûtant et de bien ennuyeux. J'ai donc tâché d'égayer ma matière, et sans perdre de vue le déclamateur, je le fais parler avec le plus d'enjouement qu'il m'est possible. Peut-être me trouvera-t-on quelquefois trop libre dans les idées et dans les expressions; mais outre qu'un écrivain doit, autant que cela se peut, se conformer à tous les goûts, ce n'est qu'au fond un badinage de plume, faisant ici une déclaration sincère que le coeur et le sentiment n'y ont nulle part. Je dois aussi avertir qu'ayant eu à travailler sur une édition extrêmement défectueuse, la correction n'est pas ce qui m'a donné le moins de peine, ni ce qui m'a emporté le moins de temps! Il y a peu de pages où je n'aie été obligé de deviner; et je n'oserais me flatter que j'aie toujours rencontré juste.

The comparison of a few lines from the opening of the treatise on the excellence of women will suffice to show that Gueudeville remained true to his practice of translating freely:

Principio itaque;vt rem ipsam ingrediar: Mulier tanto viro excellentior facta est, quanto excellentius prae illo nomen accepit: Nam Adam terra sonat, Eua autem vita interpretatur. At vita ipsa quam terra est excellentior, tam viro ipso mulier est praeferenda. Neque; est quod dicatur debile hoc argumentum esse ex nominibus de rebus ipsis iudicium ferre. Scimus enim summum illum rerum ac nominum artificem prius cognouisse res quam nominasse, qui cum decipi non potuit, eatenus nomina fabricauit, quatenus rei naturam, proprietatem et vsus exprimeret.

Premièrement donc, et pour entrer en matière, *Femme* est un nom incomparablement plus excellent que le nom d'Homme; en voici une preuve décisive: Comment Dieu, qui fut en même temps, le père et le parrain des deux premiers individus de l'espèce humain les nomma-t-il? N'est-il pas vrai qu'il appela l'homme, Adam, et la femme, Eve? Or, prenez bien garde à ceci, qui que vous soyez qui avez l'honneur de me lire, le mot, *Adam,* signifie *Terre*; et *Eve* est un terme qui veut dire la *Vie.* Sur cette révélation *scientifiquement* étymologique je bâtis ce puissant raisonnement: la Vie est tout d'un autre prix que la Terre: ergo la Femme excelle autant par-dessus l'Homme; elle lui est autant préférable que la vie est plus précieuse que la terre. Cette seule botte suffirait pour atterrer le plus fier ennemi du beau Sexe. C'est là pourtant, direz-vous, tirer en l'air; l'enthymème ne vaut rien: car du nom à la chose la conséquence est nulle, Et moi je réponds que vous ne tenez rien par là, vous allez voir.

Nous savons que l'Artisan suprême des choses et des noms a connu les êtres ou les choses avant de les nommer; et comme il est plus infaillible que notre Saint Père le Pape, lorsque Dieu a fait les noms il les a fait propres pour exprimer la nature, la propriété, et les usages de la chose.

It will be seen from the above translation that Gueudeville has more or less faithfully retained the ideas of Agrippa but has expressed them in his own style and added a few of his own humorous touches. For example, the first sentence in the Latin, which states that woman has been made more excellent than man to the extent that she has received a more excellent name than he, for Adam sounds of the earth whereas Eve means life, is expanded in the translation to include references to God, to the author and the reader, not present in the original. Similarly, towards the end of the passage, Gueudeville manages to incorporate a gratuitous but entirely typical allusion to the pope. It will also be noted that the translation is, as usual, about twice as long as the original.

Agrippa's *De incertitudine et vanitate scientiarum* was once thought to have been the basis for Rousseau's *Discours sur les sciences et les arts,* which contains many similar arguments. But it has since been established that it was not until 1751, after he had published the discourse, that Rousseau borrowed, from the Bibliothèque du roi, a Latin edition of Agrippa's treatises on the vanity of science and the excellence of women.[45] It is not known if he also read the Gueudeville translation. The author of a recent article hopes he did not:

On se félicitera qu'il n'en ait rien fait quand on saura que celle-ci n'est qu'une "infidèle", et qui se veut telle. Gueudeville ne fait d'ailleurs pas mystère de ses intentions, "j'avoue ingénument, écrit-il, que je plaisante mon Auteur, et que je fais de mon mieux pour le tourner en ridicule". Mais sa préface retiendra malgré tout l'attention du comparatiste: les arguments, et jusqu'aux sarcasmes qu'on y trouve sont tels que, n'était le nom d'Agrippa, on les croirait dirigés contre le *Ier Discours* et son auteur.[46]

The above comment seems to me to be based on a misunderstanding. While Rousseau genuinely believed the arts and sciences were inimical to man's happiness, it is not clear that Agrippa shared these sentiments, or that he was indulging in anything more than a rhetorical exercise. Certainly Gueudeville doubted the seriousness of Agrippa's intentions, and this is why he decided to liven up the arguments with his badinage.[47] The works Gueudeville chose to translate all lent themselves to humorous treatment although perhaps not always to the particular treatment he provided.

(vi) *L'Eloge de la fièvre quarte* (1728)[48]

In 1728, Theodore Haak of Leiden who, two years earlier, had published the translation of Agrippa, brought out Gueudeville's version of another Renaissance encomium in the manner of Erasmus. This was the *Encomium febris quartanae...,* written by Insulanus Menapius, and first published in 1542.[49] Gueudeville's translation was bound with a similar work, *L'Eloge de la goutte,* by Etienne Coulet, which will be discussed in the next chapter. In 1743, there was a new edition of Gueudeville's translation and of the work by Coulet. They were published in one volume under the general title of *Amusement philosophique...*[50]

Gueudeville introduces his translation with some modesty, and says, as he did in the preface to the *Dialogues des morts,* that if the work serves only to put the reader to sleep it will have been of some use. Anyone seeing the title will know he is going to read a "jeu d'esprit." At least, that is what Gueudeville expected when he first saw the title of Menapius' treatise and decided to translate it. In fact, he was so confident that he translated the work first and read it afterwards! It was only then that he discovered his error:

Ayant eu l'imprudence inexcusable de ne pas lire *L'Eloge* avant de le franciser, je croyais de bonne foi que la composition serait aussi réjouissante que le titre, et que tout roulerait sur le badinage et sur l'enjouement. Je ne pouvais pas plus me mécompter. Au lieu de trouver un rieur divertissant et propre à échauffer, par d'agréables et fines saillies, l'imagination d'un traducteur, je trouve, au contraire, un médecin qui prêche l'excellence, les prérogatives de la fièvre quarte... avec toute la gravité annexée au doctorat. Un sérieux, si à contre-temps, ne me détourna point de mon dessein; mais je résolus de me venger à la fois de mon étourderie et de Guillaume Ménape... Je me suis puni de mon étourderie en laissant courir une traduction dont je ne suis rien moins que content, et je châtie le sérieux mal placé en donnant à Monsieur le docteur des airs de plaisanterie qui ne lui conviennent point (pp. 10–11)

Menapius' treatise, although somewhat jocular in tone, is a well-documented account of early descriptions and treatments of quartan fever. There are quotations from and references to such authorities as Hippocrates, Galen, Avicenna, and the like. The work opens with a discussion of how difficult it is for an author to get the public to accept a paradox. He must be both a *savant* and a talented writer. Although this author considers himself neither of these he has reflected a lot on the matter and he trusts that readers will appreciate his efforts. He then goes on to define and describe quartan fever, which is distinguished from other fevers by the regularity of its onsets and periods of remission, by its lack of severity, and by the fact that it eventually goes away by itself if one leads a life of moderation. It is, in fact, a very generous fever in that it provides a smooth and steady transition from illness to health. Because of its regularity, quartan fever never takes the sufferer by surprise, never upsets his stomach, and requires no special dietary restrictions. Doctors have only to let the fever take its course to be assured of a successful treatment. Because patients know they are going to recover in due course they are good-tempered and easy to treat. Quartan fever rarely attacks children but prefers those of a maturer age who are robust and well able to withstand some discomfort. It usually appears in autumn, and disappears by spring, thus sparing us in the heat of summer when we are weakest. Once it has gone it leaves the sufferer more healthy and robust than he was before, since the fever has destroyed all other bodily ailments. It is not contagious. In conclusion, therefore, one ought to welcome quartan fever as being the mildest, most dependable and most generous of all fevers that, by virtue of some intermittent discomfort, cleanses and fortifies the body. Appended to the treatise is a selection of passages by eminent authorities on the treatment of quartan fever.

Gueudeville's translation, as he intimated, is very free. Indeed, the liberties he takes with the original are comparable only with those he indulged in when translating Plautus. That is to say, he embellishes the text with long digressions of his own invention that have little to do with the subject under discussion. A characteristic example is found near the end of the work:

Fuerit fortassis superuacuum hic repetere superius dicta, quod quartana etiam liberet hominem a maleficis illis febribus quae alias erraticae, alias mutuatione a Graecis accepta, planeticae dicuntur. Redigitur saltem mentio in memoriam, ut intelligatur, quae illic dicta sunt, huc quoque referri commode posse. Postremo liberat quoque interdum ab abscessu, penitus autem, si interim sanguis abunde de naribus fluxerit: autore Hippocrate libro sexte Epidemiorum.

Il serait peut-être inutile de répéter ici ce que j'ai déjà dit plus d'une fois. Mais si vous saviez Monsieur le Lecteur! Il est si doux de rechanter ce qu'on aime. Cela ne fait qu'irriter l'appétit. Je l'avoue sans fard: la *Fièvre Quarte* m'est fort chère; je l'aime à la folie: il est vrai que j'ai bien du sujet de la chérir; je serais un ingrat *fieffé* si elle m'était indifférente: elle remplit ma poche, voyez-vous! Je n'ai qu'une plainte à faire de ma bienfaitrice; c'est qu'elle s'en va trop tôt, et ne revient jamais à la même auberge. Je tombe donc hardiment dans la redite; pourquoi les écrivains et les orateurs n'auraient-ils pas le privilège de rebattre souvent la même chose? Les poètes ont bien la prérogative de mentir; et ceux de cette gent rimante qui trahissent le plus pompeusement la vérité, sont même les plus estimés.

J'ai donc déjà dit, qu'il vous en souvienne, que la *Fièvre Quarte* délivre son homme de ces fièvres scélérates que les uns appellent vagabondes, et que les autres, par une allégorie tirée des Grecs, nomment *Fièvres Planétiques*. Il ne sera pas inutile de vous rappeler cela dans la mémoire: vous y trouverez du moins l'avantage de reconnaître que tout ce que j'ai dit en d'autres endroits de cet *Eloge* peut fort bien se rapporter ici. Enfin, dans la *Fièvre Quarte*, il n'y a point d'abcès à craindre, et principalement quand le *Quarténiste* saigne beaucoup du nez. Je voudrais bien voir un peu que quelque abcès fût venu par plaisir à notre malade après qu'Hippocrate l'a expressément, formellement défendu; et où? au sixième livre des *Epidèmes*; vous pouvez prendre la peine d'y aller voir.

There seems little need to comment on the above example of Gueudeville's technique in which, for the purpose of amusing the reader, he introduces such irrelevant items as the profit to be made from writings such treatises, the necessity to repeat oneself, and the advantage of poetic licence. This last demonstration of Gueudeville's principles of translation simply confirms what we have noted in all his other efforts. His main aim was to entertain a non-scholarly public. To do this he took liberties with the text which were considered inexcusable by the *savants,* but which he justified on the grounds that if one wants to make learned works accessible to a general audience it is necessary to endow them with elements calculated to appeal to more "simple" minds. If some accuracy is lost in the process, so much the worse. The important thing is to retain the ideas and spirit of the original. As we have seen, Gueudeville succeeded in his attempts to popularize certain important works, and, even if some of his translations seem not to have enjoyed much success, I think the effort was, nonetheless, worthwhile.

VIII. WORKS ATTRIBUTED TO GUEUDEVILLE

A number of works have been attributed to Gueudeville. Among these are the *Voyages* of the baron de Lahontan, a historical publication entitled *Le Grand Théâtre historique,* a periodical in the style of the *Spectator,* called *Le Censeur,* the treatise, *L'Eloge de la goutte,* referred to in the previous chapter, and a novel entitled *Histoire . . . du chevalier de la plume noire.*[1]

Since, in most cases, there is little or no external evidence available, my arguments for or against the correctness of these attributions are based largely on questions of style. This kind of internal evidence is notoriously deceptive but, in the case of a writer with so distinctive a style as Gueudeville's, one is less liable to errors of attribution. It is acknowledged from the outset, however, that some of the arguments in this chapter are more speculative than substantive.

(i) The *Voyages* of Lahontan (1703)

About the middle of 1702 there was published by the brothers L'Honoré of The Hague a work in two volumes of which the first was entitled, *Nouveaux Voyages de Mr. le Baron de La Hontan dans l'Amérique septentrionale,* and the second, *Mémoires de l'Amérique septentrionale ou la Suite des Voyages de Mr. le Baron de La Hontan.* Both title-pages bear the date 1703. In September 1703 there appeared a third volume entitled, *Supplément aux Voyages du Baron de La Hontan où l'on trouve des dialogues curieux entre l'auteur et un sauvage de bon sens qui a voyagé.*[2]

Louis-Armand de Lom d'Arce, baron de Lahontan (1666–1715?) was born in the Basses-Pyrénées. When his father died, in 1674, Louis-Armand inherited an estate saddled with debts and litigation. By 1683, the family was ruined and, in that year, Lahontan is reputed to have sailed for Canada where he spent ten years as an officer in the French army involved in the consolidation and promotion of the French colony. During this period he came to know and respect the Indians and their way of life. He also carried out explorations and claimed to have discovered areas previously unknown. In 1693, having been transferred to Placentia, Newfoundland, he incurred the displeasure of the Governor, and fled to Europe in order to avoid arrest. Little is known of him after this. He seems to have spent time in Portugal, Holland, Germany, France, England, and Denmark, and probably died at the court of the Elector of Hanover. While Lahontan was in Canada he kept diaries in which he recorded in great detail his experiences and impressions of the New World, and he later used these diaries as the basis for the three volumes "which were to make him, next to Louis Hennepin, the most widely read author on North America in the first half of the 18th century."[3]

The *Nouveaux Voyages,* consisting of twenty-five letters addressed to a relative in France, trace the development of the French colony, the campaigns against the English and the Iroquois, and provide many descriptions of people and places, notably those encountered in Lahontan's exploration of a region he claimed to be the site of the Long River. The *Mémoires* deal, in greater detail than the first volume, with the flora and fauna of the country, and with the social, cultural and religious life of the Indians. This second volume also contains a "dictionary" of the Algonkian language. The *Supplément* reproduces a series of dialogues, supposedly held between Lahontan and an Indian chief named Adario, on such subjects as religion, law, happiness, medicine and marriage, and ends with some observations made by Lahontan during his travels through various European countries.

The work was an immediate success, not only because readers of the day were fascinated by all kinds of travel literature both real and imaginary, but because its publication coincided with the beginning of the War of the Spanish Succession. This meant that the attacks on the French administration in Canada, and the criticisms of Louis XIV and his régime, with which Lahontan's writings are replete, had a distinct appeal for the enemies of France.

But the element of Lahontan's work that attracted most attention, if one is to judge by the reviews, was the condemnation of Christianity and European civilization, through the idealization of the Indian, the noble savage who lived a peaceful, happy, "communistic" existence, according to natural law, and who worshipped a Spinozist deity, indistinguishable from Nature.

In June 1705 the brothers L'Honoré brought out a second edition "avec des changements considérables."[4] This edition, in two volumes, made no changes to the *Mémoires,* but did make considerable changes to the *Nouveaux Voyages* and *Dialogues,* replacing a whole section of the latter with mainly new material, and omitting entirely the part dealing with Lahontan's European travels. The reasons for these revisions were explained in the preface:

Quelques personnes d'esprit ayant représenté que l'autre édition péchait dans le style, qu'on y trouvait des phrases basses, des expressions vulgaires, des railleries froides, et de l'embarras dans la narration, l'on a tâché de remédier à tout cela. On a presque refondu toutes les lettres, et l'on croit que le style en paraîtra plus pur, plus net, plus dégagé, et avec un peu plus de finesse dans l'enjouement. On a conservé le sens de l'auteur, mais on a donné un nouveau tour à la meilleure partie de son ouvrage: comme il était rempli de transpositions qui gâtaient absolument le bon ordre du récit . . . on a eu soin de les ôter, et de donner à chaque chose l'étendue et la liaison naturelle qu'elle devait avoir dans un narré . . .

Il faut encore avertir que cette édition est augmentée des *Dialogues de l'Auteur avec un Sauvage.* On aurait pu les donner ici tels qu'ils ont déjà paru; mais comme d'habiles gens les ont trouvés pauvres, et remplis d'un long et ennuyeux galimatias, on en a tiré le meilleur, et on l'a ajusté au nouveau style des Voyages, en observant d'entrer toujours dans la pensée et dans le sentiment des interlocuteurs. Au reste, on a jugé qu'il n'était pas à propos de charger cette édition des *Voyages de Portugal et Danemarc* . . . Le Baron de Lahontan n'est pas assez nécessaire pour fatiguer les hommes de ce qui le concerne personnellement dans ces deux relations, et quant à ce qu'elles contiennent de plus, il n'y a rien de mieux connu . . .

While it is true that some of the changes made to the letters do clarify the context and improve the narrative technique, many of them are entirely gratuitous and are introduced as an excuse for the editor to indulge in his own brand of humour, usually of the burlesque variety, and to intensify the criticism of France, of Catholicism, and of Christianity in general. This is particularly the case in the *Dialogues* where the original, fairly innocuous discussions of medicine and marriage, are largely replaced by attacks on Christianity, on private property, on monarchy, and by a call to the people to unite and throw off the yoke of oppression.[5]

Two of his contemporaries said that Gueudeville was the one responsible for these drastic revisions. In 1715, Jean-Frédéric Bernard, in making this attribution, described Gueudeville as "un homme dont le caractère est suspect à tous égards, et qui, même, ne s'en cache pas, puisqu'il affecte de semer le libertinage dans ses ouvrages, ce qui, sans doute fait tort au crédit du baron." According to Bernard, Gueudeville was not simply the editor of Lahontan's works, he was also the author of the dialogues: "Il est bon d'apprendre au public que le sauvage Adario est un moine défroqué et libertin, auteur de quelques ouvrages dans lesquels on ne trouve qu'un grossier burlesque et beaucoup d'irréligion."[6] In 1724, Jean Le Clerc repeated the charge: "le baron de Lahontan n'est proprement l'auteur que de la première édition qui porte son nom: les Dialogues ajoutés ensuite en une autre, sont d'un nommé Gueudeville, et le baron de Lahontan s'est assez plaint du tour qu'on lui avait fait."[7] In Germany, some critics went so far as to state that Gueudeville was not the editor but the real author of the works of Lahontan who never existed and whose name had been invented by Gueudeville as a *nom de plume.*[8]

Although there is no incontrovertible evidence that Gueudeville did the 1705 revisions, modern authorities have accepted the idea that he was the one responsible, mainly because Bernard and Leclerc said so, but also because he was in the right place at the right time to have done so, because he expressed similar ideas in his periodical and his critique of *Télémaque,* and because his dissertation on Canada, in volume six of the *Atlas historique* (1719), was based on the text of the 1705 edition.

It could be argued, of course, that this evidence is largely circumstantial, that the ideas expressed by Gueudeville and Lahontan did not originate with them, and that any number of French refugees could have made the revisions. The fact that Gueudeville used the 1705 text as a basis for his article on Canada, could be explained on the grounds that this was the only edition available to him at the time. Therefore, if we want to be certain that Gueudeville did the revisions we need further evidence of his interest in the subject, and indications of a more than coincidental similarity between the style of the revisions and Gueudeville's own style. My purpose is to offer evidence of this type that has not previously been considered.[9]

Before Lahontan published his work Gueudeville had shown an interest in the New World, and in the possibilities of using the noble savage for purposes of satire.[10] He did not use the dialogue form, however, until early 1702. It is possible that, at this time, Lahontan's manuscript was in the hands of the brothers L'Honoré, and that Gueudeville had an opportunity to read it. Perhaps he was even involved in the publication from the beginning. On the other hand, the *Dialogues* came out first in England, in translation, possibly before the manuscript was seen in Holland.[11] In which case Gueudeville anticipated the work of Lahontan. Whatever the explanation, in the February 1702 issue of his periodical Gueudeville invented a brief dialogue to condemn the Catholic preparations for Lent:

Introduisons un Indien sensé dans un de ces lieux où rien ne manque à la célébration de la longue et délicieuse fête, appelée Carnaval . . . Cet Asiatique ou Américain, n'importe lequel des deux . . . est enchanté . . . Que signifie cet épanchement énorme de volupté, me demande-t-il, en fronçant le sourcil? . . . Ces gens ont-ils oublié leur condition humaine? Sont-ils assurés contre la révolution? Ont-ils trouvé le secret de ne point mourir? Je souris à ces propositions; elles m'embarrassent, et voici la réponse que la vérité me met dans l'esprit. La pénitence est le mobile de cette agitation toute sensuelle, le principe de cet excès et de ce dérangement qui vous étonnent; c'est que ceux qui s'y plongent vont entrer dans un temps de sanctification . . . c'est pour se disposer à cette sainte quarantaine qu'ils donnent dans toutes sortes de voluptés . . . Mais ces gens-là sont-ils dans leur bon sens, réplique le judicieux habitant du nouveau monde? Pourquoi non? Les hommes raisonnent très juste, mais ils ne sont pas esclaves de leurs conséquences . . . Il n'y a pas jusqu'à ceux qui se disent les guides et les flambeaux des autres chez qui la pratique est souvent l'antipode de la spéculation . . . (127–130).

What is particularly interesting about this dialogue is that the European finds himself embarrassed by the questions of the savage, and is finally obliged to make concessions. This is precisely the role played by Lahontan in his conversations with Adario,[12] and by the "loyal" Frenchman in the critique of *Télémaque*.

In August 1702, speculating on the purpose of the visit of the ambassador of the king of Naples to the Pope, Gueudeville writes:

Imaginons-nous un de ces Américains qu'on vous dit être pourvus de bon sens, et juger des choses par les pures lumières de la raison. Je pose cet étranger sur le passage du prince Borghese faisant son entrée publique et marchant superbement à l'adoration du Pape. Mon sauvage, étonné d'un spectacle si magnifique . . . demande à quoi tend ce bel étalage, et quel est le but de tout ce fracas? (118)

The following year, describing the ceremony in which the doge of Venice "marries" the sea, Gueudeville comments, "qu'on apprenne ce fait à un Siamois ou à quelque autre Indien qui n'en ait jamais ouï parler, je suis sûr qu'il prendra la nouvelle pour une fable, et qu'il aura peine à tenir son sérieux en l'écoutant" (June 1703, 605–606).[13] In 1705 there are similar allusions,[14] one of which is particularly noteworthy for its use of certain expressions found in the 1705 edition of the *Dialogues* but not in the original. Both passages make reference to the injustice of the salt tax, and both describe the mineral in the same way:

Esprit des cours (March 1705)
Que quelques gouttes d'eau condensée . . . soit mise au prix des choses rares et précieuses, . . . et qu'on force le pauvre aussi bien que le riche . . . à la payer . . . c'est ce qu'un Indien aurait peine à croire sur le témoignage même de ses propres yeux (325).

Dialogues (1705)
. . . n'ai-je pas eu plus d'une fois occasion de m'instruire . . . par le témoignage de mes propres yeux . . . je rencontrai un homme condamné aux galères pour avoir . . . pris secrètement un peu d'eau de mer condensée (p. 256).

In April 1706, Gueudeville entertains his readers with a dialogue on the War of the Spanish Succession, and draws some pointed conclusions about the advantages of using a noble savage to express one's ideas:

Faisons venir ici du Nouveau Monde un de ces hommes qui suivent le pur instinct de la nature, et lesquels, s'ils ne jouissent pas des douceurs de la société, n'en connaissent pas aussi les amertumes et les désagréments. Mettons ce bon sauvage de terre inconnue, mettons-le au milieu de cette société tumultueuse et embrasée. Quelle boucherie! s'écrie-t-il; hé, quelle peut donc être la cause d'un désordre si affreux, d'une si copieuse effusion de sang? Il faut sans doute que ces gens-là se haïssent mortellement. Pardonnez-moi, judicieux sauvage, vous êtes bien loin du fait; au contraire, ces gens-là se tuent parce qu'ils sont amis, et qu'ils craignent que le noeud de leur amitié ne soit coupé. A cette réponse il me semble voir mon étranger ouvrir de grands yeux et me dire, vous n'êtes donc pas vous autres des hommes de notre espèce; il faut assurément que votre raison diffère essentiellement d'avec le nôtre: vous ne me ferez jamais comprendre qu'on se tue par bonne volonté; la philosophie que nous apprenons dans notre école de la Nature, et de la propre voix de cette divine maîtresse, nous fait regarder cela comme une contradiction manifeste. Je lui réplique: je ne vous avance pourtant rien que de fort vrai. Ces hommes qui vous paraissent si acharnés, les uns sur les autres, n'ont point d'autre but que de se procurer un bonheur commun; ils ne disputent que pour la personne qui doit être le premier mobile de ce bonheur . . .

Note sauvage sourit et, tirant sa conséquence sur le champ: ergo, dit-il, vous êtes des extravagants ou nous sommes des insensés. Nous autres en votre place ne nous aviserions jamais d'en venir aux armes civiles pour la félicité publique; renonçant à toutes les vues personnelles nous nous rapporterions de nos différends d'état à un petit nombre de sages tirés de l'élite de la nation . . . Ce sauvage commence à m'embarrasser avec sa politique; je prévois qu'il me mènerait loin; de peur de tomber en chemin il vaut mieux le laisser là. C'est un fâcheux disputeur qu'un sauvage; il faudrait avec lui soutenir la négative par de bonnes preuves, et l'on n'en a pas toujours à lui donner; il est en droit et en possession de dire tout ce qu'il pense, au lieu que nous autres confrères de société nous disons souvent ce que nous ne pensons pas. Combien d'écrivains changeraient de style si leurs plumes étaient aussi libres que la langue d'un sauvage . . . Encore un coup donc, faisons taire notre sauvage: qu'il aille prêcher sa morale et sa politique dans ses cabanes; ne serait-ce point là où la vérité naturelle bannie de notre monde se serait retirée? (350—353)

The last sentence of the above is very reminiscent of a line in the 1705 edition of the *Nouveaux Voyages*: "il semble que la liberté, presque bannie de toute la terre, ait choisi sa retraite et son style chez eux" (p. 35).

I think we are entitled to conclude from the foregoing that Gueudeville had more than a passing interest in Lahontan's noble savage.[15] What is more revealing, however, of Gueudeville's involvement in the work of Lahontan is the style of the revisions. It is, as I have said, a hasardous enterprise to draw conclusions on the basis of style, but fortunately, our study of Gueudeville's principles and practices of translation enables us to proceed with caution but confidence.

As we saw in the previous chapter, the one feature that emerges consistently and forcefully from all Gueudeville's efforts at translation is his desire to render the original more humorous. He prided himself on his badinage, and looked for every opportunity to enliven his translations with his own brand of burlesque humour, anecdotes, digressions, neologisms and the like.

Now, when one compares the 1705 edition with the original, especially the *Nouveaux Voyages,* one discovers that the principle governing the various attempts to clarify the text, improve the narrative technique, and intensify the anti-clerical and anti-French elements, is humour. In short, whoever was responsible for the revisions in the 1705 edition, used all the devices that Gueudeville would later use in his translations. Indeed the preface to the 1705 edition embodies the same justification with which, as we have seen, Gueudeville would preface all his translations: "On a conservé le sens de l'auteur, mais on a donné un nouveau tour à la meilleure partie de son ouvrage." As a consequence of this liberty Gueudeville accorded himself, his translations were invariably much longer than the originals. The same phenomenon is seen in the revised version of the *Nouveaux Voyages,* most notably in letter sixteen, which was originally about fifty pages in length, and is almost double that length in the 1705 edition. A comparison of passages taken from this letter will undoubtedly recall to the reader Gueudeville's techniques of translation and his inimitable style:

1703

. . . dix soldats amenèrent les quatre esclaves Essanapés. J'étais actuellement avec cette espèce de roi, lorsque ceux-ci passèrent une demi-heure à se prosterner plusieurs fois devant lui. Je lui fis présent de tabac . . . Sa Cabane est bâtie vers la côte du lac, dans un quartier séparé, mais environnée de cinquante autres où logent tous ses parents. Quand il marche, on sème des feuilles d'arbres dans le chemin. Il est ordinairement porté par six esclaves; son habit royal n'est pas plus magnifique que celui du chef des Okoros; on le voit tout nu, excepté les parties inférieures, qui sont couvertes devant et derrière d'une grande écharpe de toile d'écorce d'arbre (pp. 155—157).

1705

. . . dix de mes soldats, en exécution de mon ordre, se rendirent auprès de nous avec les quatre prisonniers Essanapés; j'en fis ma cour à cette figure de prince, et je les lui présentai: je remarquai qu'il prenait goût à l'offrande. Pour les quatre esclaves je crus qu'ils ne finiraient point leurs prostrations: ils ne cessaient de se jeter à terre devant le Grand Chef et de se relever; sans exagération cette cérémonie dura une bonne demi-heure. Le bon homme de sauvage tenait alors une contenance grave, et l'on aurait dit qu'il sentait tout le plaisir mystérieux de l'adoration. Vous jugez bien, Monsieur, que je ne me présentai pas les mains vides devant ce Dieu Pan. Tant s'en faut je me surpassai avec lui en magnificence. Je lui donnai un bon gros morceau de tabac, c'était le meilleur encens que je pusse offrir à cette rustique et champêtre divinité . . . son Louvre, son château, son Versailles en un mot, consiste en un trou de cabane bâtie vers la côte du lac; ce palais brille au milieu de cinquante autres moins magnifiques où demeurent les parents du Prince, en sorte que l'on peut nommer ce quartier qui est séparé du reste de l'habitation, le quartier du Sang Royal. Au reste Sa Majesté Sauvage ne marche jamais qu'en pompe, et on lui fait l'honneur de joncher son chemin de feuilles d'arbre; ses habits royaux sont sa peau, et une écharpe de toile d'écorce qui lui cache sa virilité. Cette idole ne fait pas grand usage de ses pieds, car il est ordinairement porté par six esclaves (pp. 209—212)[16]

A prominent characteristic of Gueudeville's style that we noted in the translations, and that is not displayed in the above illustration of burlesque humour, is his fondness for neologisms. However, he finds opportunities elsewhere in the *Nouveaux Voyages* to invent such expressions as "la troupe festinante," "Sa Majesté Essanapienne," "Son Altesse Sauvageonne," and, in the *Dialogues,* "Huronnage," "Déhuronnisé," and "Huronnoise." A favourite word of Gueudeville is "galimatias," a term he uses extensively, especially to ridicule religious beliefs and practices. This word occurs six times in the 1705 edition of the *Dialogues,* and not at all in the original.

These arguments in favour of Gueudeville's participation in the work of Lahontan are, of course, like the earlier ones, circumstantial. Perhaps it is purely coincidental that in the July 1704 issue of *L'Esprit des cours* Gueudeville likened a woman to a place under siege:

Il en est d'une ville faible comme une femme qui combat entre l'amour et l'honneur . . . souhaitez pour elle que l'assiégeant modère son transport et s'en tienne là; car la place est faible, peut-être tombera-t-elle au premier assaut (19)

and that the same image occurs in the 1705 edition of the *Dialogues:*

En vérité, Adario, nos dames te sont bien redevables; tu as assez bonne opinion d'elles pour les croire des places fortifiées: ce n'est pourtant pas leur ordinaire de résister longtemps, et communément elles capitulent avant même qu'il y ait brèche. Celles de ces forteresses vivantes qui sont le mieux revêtues tombent assez souvent le plus tôt . . . (p. 293)

But when one puts all these indications together, and adds them to the evidence already collected, there no longer seems much doubt that it was Gueudeville who was responsible for the rewriting of Lahontan.

The above discussion has raised several questions and left them unanswered. Since the first edition was so successful, why was it revised? When it was revised, why were the *Mémoires* left unaltered? Did Gueudeville have a hand in the project from the very beginning? Before these problems can be solved we need much more information about the genesis and publication of the work. Until such information becomes available we can only speculate, and since this chapter will necessarily contain more than enough speculation, perhaps it would be better to bring this discussion to an end.

(ii) *Le Grand Théâtre historique* (1703)[17]

There is no mention, either on the title-page or in the preface, of the name of the author of the above work, but in the standard biographies and library catalogues it is said to be a free translation by Gueudeville of the first five volumes of a work written in German by A.L. von Imhof.[18] The fact that, as far as we know, Gueudeville knew no German does not seem to have been an obstacle to this attribution. Perhaps the work was first translated into Latin and then adapted by Gueudeville. If so, it is curious that he did not avail himself, as he did on all other occasions, of the perfect opportunity for introducing his own version of history, and his ideas on religion and politics.

The only reason I can think of that this work has been attributed to Gueudeville is that his name was associated with geographical and historical works, and, more particularly, with Van der Aa who published this work and with whom he later collaborated on the *Nouveau Théâtre du monde.* It is significant, however, that, in his advertising catalogues, Van der Aa never mentions Gueudeville's name in connection with *Le Grand Théâtre historique,* but advertises it as being by Imhof.[19] It is also worth remembering that Gueudeville's association with Van der Aa did not begin until 1713. Fortunately, we have some indication as to who was responsible for this work. In the *Journal de Trévoux* (March 1705)[20] it is described as being "assez dur à la vente," and the author is referred to as "un notaire de La Haye" whose *Les Délices de l'Italie* is also being published by Van der Aa. Now, one of the authors of this latter work was a certain Rogissart,[21] probably Pierre de Rogissart, who negotiated the formation and dissolution of the partnership between Jonas L'Honoré and Thomas Johnson (see Appendices B and C), and whose son, Alexandre, and daughters, Charlotte and Susanna, were later involved in book publishing in The Hague.[22] Whether or not he knew German I am unable to say. What I can say with a reasonable degree of confidence is that Gueudeville had nothing to do with the project.

(iii) *Le Censeur* (1715)

The enormous success of Addison and Steele's *Spectator* inspired many imitations throughout the eighteenth century. The first one in French, *Le Misantrope,* was published anonymously in 1711 in The Hague where it appeared every Monday until the end of 1712.[23] When it ceased publication the issues were bound together and sold in two volumes. A contemporary critic accurately described *Le Misantrope* as "un ouvrage de critique. Les vertus, les vices, les modes, les goûts, les bons, les mauvais auteurs, l'histoire, la fable, tout servait, selon la fantaisie de l'auteur, de sujet à ses réflexions."[24]

In 1714, two more imitations appeared, *Le Censeur*[25] and *L'Inquisiteur.* The former, which is our present interest, appeared, like *Le Misantrope,* on Mondays, beginning on March 12 1714, and continuing for forty-four weeks until December 31 when the issues were bound in one volume. Like *Le Misantrope, Le Censeur* was published anonymously but the author, referred to on the title-page as Mr. de G***, has been identified as Gueudeville.[26]

Although the author takes great pains to hide his identity[27] it is not surprising that he has been thought to be Gueudeville. Nearly all the topics dealt with were treated by him at some time or another, notably in *L'Esprit des cours de l'Europe*. There are articles dealing with marriage, fashion, love and jealousy, gambling and other vices, attacks on religion, especially Catholicism, anecdotes about misers, hypocrites, lecherous monks, references to Lahontan, the noble savage, the curse of private property, criticisms of *savants*, both male and female, quotations from classical, Renaissance and modern writers.[28] There is even a dialogue between Bayle and Jurieu, that would not be out of place in Gueudeville's *Dialogues des morts*. In short, there is nothing in *Le Censeur* that is out of tune with the ideas we know he possessed, and very little he had not already discussed.[29] It seems perverse, therefore, to question his authorship of the work. Nonetheless, I am hesitant to accept this attribution for several reasons.

In the first place, the author makes one or two references to himself that do not fit with what we know of Gueudeville. He talks, for example, of "les différents pays où j'ai voyagé" (44), when, as far as we know, at the time of writing Gueudeville had seen only France and Holland. On another occasion he speaks of his incompetence to discuss marriage because he is not "engagé sous les lois d'Hyménée" (121), a situation not applicable to Gueudeville. It could be objected that these remarks are introduced to help him disguise his identity and play his assumed role as critic of mankind, and it is hard to refute this objection. There are, however, other considerations.

Although the content of *Le Censeur* is in keeping with Gueudeville's preoccupations, the style is not typically Gueudeville's. This, of course, is a very subjective impression, but I do not find in *Le Censeur* those *tics* that are so characteristic: the neologisms, the burlesque humour, the extravagance in length and expression. On the whole, the style of *Le Censeur* is economical, and the humour lacks variety. It could be argued, of course, that since each issue was restricted to eight pages, economy was of the essence, that Gueudeville adopted a style suitable to this type of periodical, and that he disguised his style to protect his anonymity. Again it is difficult to answer these arguments except by noting how hard it is to sustain completely over a long period, a deliberate change of style.

Finally, there is some dubious external evidence that speaks against Gueudeville's authorship. In his *Lettres sérieuses et badines*, begun in 1729, La Barre de Beaumarchais, who had collaborated with Jean Rousset on the monthly political periodical, *Mercure historique et politique*, and had subsequently quarrelled with him, attacks him without naming him. The reason we know Rousset is intended is that La Barre de Beaumarchais refers to him as the author of the periodical, the *Quintessence*, in which Rousset was involved after 1712. Now, as we have noted, Gueudeville was also, some time before 1712, temporarily involved in the *Quintessence*, and this, I think, is where the confusion has arisen. Among the writings La Barre de Beaumarchais attributes to the author of the *Quintessence* is a *Censeur*, "premier ouvrage de l'auteur de la

Quintessence, ouvrage malin s'il en fut jamais, et qui ne fut pourtant pas goûté, parce qu'il était aussi sot que malin."[30] The expression, "premier ouvrage", could hardly apply to Gueudeville who, by 1715, had an impressive list of publications to his credit, and who, in any case, was dead when the comment was made. Jean Rousset, on the other hand, was still very much alive, and *Le Censeur* could have been his first publication.

Jean Rousset de Missy (1686–1762) was a Huguenot whose family was ruined by persecution. His parents are reputed to have died at the hands of the French "inquisition." At the age of eighteen he enlisted on the Dutch side against France, and, like Gueudeville, carried on the war through his journalism and other writings. Indeed, La Barre de Beaumarchais' attack on Rousset simply echoes similar ones against Gueudeville:

Qu'y a-t-il de plus inutile au monde, de plus abject, de plus méprisable que toi! Qu'on t'ôte les bouffonneries grossières contre l'Eglise romaine, les satires impertinentes contre les puissances, les traits piquants et outrés contre toute sorte de personnes . . . que te restera-t-il?"[31]

After his military service Rousset settled in The Hague, in 1709, and, like Gueudeville, supported himself by teaching. Perhaps it was during this period that he published *Le Censeur* and, if so, this would have been his "premier ouvrage", although, according to the biographies, his literary career did not begin until 1724.[32] It is not absolutely certain, of course, that the *Censeur* referred to by La Barre de Beaumarchais is the one under discussion, but I know no other with that title at the time.[33] If Rousset were the author this would explain the reference to travelling in different countries, which he did during the course of his military service, and it would also account for the statement that he was not married.

It would be helpful to be so immersed in Rousset's style that one could point to certain features in *Le Censeur* that are found in his other writings. Unfortunately, my knowledge of Rousset's work is too slight to be of help here, but we can certainly see from the above discussion that the content of *Le Censeur* would be just as much in keeping with his preoccupations as with Gueudeville's.

To sum up, *Le Censeur* could have been written by either man, separately or in collaboration. It is more likely, however, that it was written by only one of them. The style does not seem to me to be characteristic of Gueudeville's usual way of writing, but this is a subjective impression. There is some external evidence that favours Rousset as the author, although it is not certain that the *Censeur* he is said to have written is the one published in The Hague in 1715. Nor, it should be added, is it clear why he should have chosen G*** for his identity. On the whole, however, despite these unsolved problems, the evidence seems to be against Gueudeville's authorship and in favour of Rousset's.

(iv) *L'Eloge de la goutte* (1728)[34]

It was noted in the previous chapter that when Theodore Haak published Gueudeville's translation of Menapius, *L'Eloge de la fièvre quarte,* he bound it together with another work, *L'Eloge de la goutte* by Etienne Coulet. An examination of this latter work reveals a style and an approach remarkably reminiscent
of those employed by Gueudeville.

The treatise opens dramatically with the writer in the very throes of an
attack of gout:

Oh! oh! un moment Mrs . . . Madame la Goutte ma souveraine est irritée, je ne
sais pourquoi; mais elle me fait bien sentir à ce moment tout le poids de sa
colère. Arrêtez, Madame la Goutte, arrêtez donc, s'il vous plaît. Oh! Miséricorde! Un ton plus fort! Hélas! Que vous ai-je fait? Ai-je bu du vin contre vos
ordres? Ai-je été autre part qu'ailleurs . . . Mais non. Oh! non. Plus j'examine . . .
oh! ma conscience; oh! . . . la peste étouffe; non, non, je me reprends; la goutte,
la goutte, puisse prendre à celui qui . . . quoi? . . . qui fera votre éloge? . . .
(pp. 1–2)

When the attack has passed the writer takes up his pen in a hurry so he can
finish the praise of gout before he is overcome by another paroxysm. There
is no time to worry about style and presentation, but he will deal with the
subject under four headings. He will show (a) that gout is very old and illustrious; (b) that it has special properties that ought to command our respect and
love; (c) that its force is irresistible; (d) that it endows the sufferer with certain
advantages.

One writer has suggested gout is as old as Adam, and that the reason Adam
did not prevent Cain from killing Abel was that he was, at the time, suffering
a spasm of gout and could not get up. It can certainly be traced back to Nimrod.
Gout is hereditary so that every attack reminds us of our beloved parents. It
is also something we cause ourselves by overindulgence in food and drink, i.e.,
gout is a product of our free will and of the bounteous gifts of nature. Since
it rarely afflicts women it must originate with men, and is probably the result
of ejaculations of semen which deprive our bodies of the fluids necessary to the
lubrication of the joints. Thus, the act of producing children causes gout which
is, therefore, not only hereditary but caused by our posterity. Idleness is also
a cause of gout which lodges most easily where there is little activity. It is,
however, glorious to live in indolence while others wait on you.

Gout comes slowly and when we are old. It is like a general distributing and
establishing his troops in enemy territory. The moves are planned in such a way
as to take the victim by surprise in the middle of the night. Once one foot has
been captured the attack moves to the other one:

C'est l'autre pied que notre héroïne attaque donc maintenant; c'est là qu'elle
emploie les mêmes ruses de la guerre, qu'elle fait bruire ses fuseaux, ses canons
j'ai pensé dire . . .

Enfin le temps vient que la goutte, sûre qu'elle croit être que sa conquête ne lui échappera pas, la quitte pour voler à d'autres, se contentant d'y laisser une bonne garnison, avec ordre, cependant, de ne commettre aucune hostilité, mais de vivre en paix et en fraternité avec tous les habitants . . . Mais, ma foi, il est grand temps de quitter le style allégorique; je ne le puis plus soutenir; il me fatigue, il me chagrine; et rien n'est plus contraire à la gaîté et à la liberté de mon humeur; parlons donc naturellement (pp. 56–58)

The force of gout is irresistible because, although man can dominate the elements, he cannot tame the power of gout. There is no way of preventing its arrival and no way of causing its departure. Doctors are powerless to control it, and they merely add to the patient's suffering. It does, however, confer certain benefits. In the first place it provides a topic for authors to write about, and thus gives them a chance to make a name for themselves, and for publishers to make money. It also makes money for those who claim to have treatments and cures. Those who are afflicted with the disease command not only the respect due to their age and wealth, but sympathy because of their condition. People with gout are normally immune to other diseases, and, since the progress of the illness is slow, they have plenty of time to prepare for death. Meanwhile, those relatives and friends who hope to profit by this death are very attentive to the invalid, who is thus able to control and exploit them. The conclusion is that:

Vous devez la regarder comme un joyau précieux qui vaut seul des empires, et qui même leur est préférable. Vous ne devez vous laisser aller à aucune impatience, à aucune expression emportée, ou qui marque peu ces respects et cette estime dont vous devez être remplis . . . Enfin votre patience et votre résignation à ses ordres doivent être entières, dans l'attente qu'elle accomplira ses promesses, et que, voyant votre douceur et votre soumission, elle vous traitera plus tendrement, plus amiablement . . . (pp. 140–141)

Apart from the obvious similarities in style there is another indication that Gueudeville had a hand in this work by Coulet. On the title-page of the 1743 edition the treatise is described as having been "mis au jour" by Gueudeville.[35] The question arises, then, as to what Coulet originally wrote, and what is meant by "mis au jour?"

The problem is complicated by the fact that almost nothing is known about Etienne Coulet. According to the standard biographies he was a medical doctor whose family fled to Holland after the Revocation of the Edict of Nantes. Since he was unable to support himself as a doctor, he did what Gueudeville and many others did, and tried to live by writing. He published medical treatises which he passed off as original but which were discovered to be free translations of works originally written in Latin by the noted Italian doctor, Ramazzini. He had theories about the reformation of the French language, and claimed to have written a French grammar, but no trace of it has been found. He also invented a new system of orthography, and used his method in the translation of a history of medicine by the English doctor Freind. The spelling was apparently so bizarre that the work was unreadable. It is not known when Coulet died but he is thought to have been still alive in 1729 or 1730.[36] If this is so, the problem is even more complex. If Gueudeville, who died about 1721, was responsible for bringing Coulet's work to light, then Coulet must have completed it before that time, even though it was not published until 1728. As to Gueudeville's role in the affair we can only speculate. Presumably the work was originally written in French so there can be no question here of a translation. Perhaps he "edited" Coulet's treatise in the way he did the voyages and dialogues of Lahontan. Or perhaps Coulet originally wrote the work in his bizarre orthography, and Gueudeville was invited to rewrite it in a more acceptable and accessible form. The possibilities are numerous. It could be, for example, that Gueudeville wrote the entire treatise himself, and that Coulet lent his name to the publication. Certainly the style would lend support to this view.

As if the mystery were not deep enough the introductory pages addressed to the reader introduce a third name as author of the treatise. Here, the reader is asked to pay homage to:

Maître *Nicolas Farnabe,* ou à quelque autre qui se cache sous son nom . . . Ne serait-ce pas dommage qu'un *Gouteux* de si bonne humeur eût jamais lieu de se plaindre de l'ingratitude de son siècle? Faut-il donc, que de si beaux talents que les siens restent ensevelis dans l'obscurité d'un cabinet, et qu'après avoir sué sang et eau pour mettre au jour l'Eloge de la *Goutte,* il n'en recueille pour tout fruit que le mérite d'une charité à la *Turque* . . .

Needless to say, I have been unable to identify Nicolas Farnabe, for it seems that whoever was initially responsible for this work was determined to conceal his identity. My own impression, as I have suggested, is that this was an elaborate hoax by Gueudeville himself. Why publication was delayed until 1728,[37] and why Gueudeville's connection with the treatise was not revealed until 1743, I am unable to say. One can only hope that the discovery of new information will one day lead to a solution of this enigma.

(v) *Histoire abrégée . . . du chevalier de la plume noire* (1744)[38]

The last work to be attributed to Gueudeville was published anonymously in Amsterdam in 1744. The attribution is found at the end of the preface which states: "On attribue cet ouvrage au fameux GUEUDEVILLE." In 1750 it appeared in a German translation.[39]

The *Histoire . . . du chevalier de la plume noire* is a picaresque novel in which an illegitimate and low-born scoundrel travels through various European countries in the hope of making his fortune as an expert in horsemanship.

He is alternately the trickster and the tricked, usually managing to dupe men but almost invariably being duped by women. He is utterly devoid of scruples, and changes his religion whenever it is convenient to do so.

As a piece of literature the novel is of little worth. The hero is a wooden figure with no semblance of reality, the episodes are repeated with little variation, without proper motivation or satisfactory resolution. The décor is vague. In short, the work is boring. There are passages, however, that are reminiscent of Gueudeville's style, so that we are obliged to consider what little evidence there is that he could have written it.

We saw, in the discussion of the *Dialogues des morts*, that Gueudeville was not a creative artist, so that the inferior technique in this novel would certainly be consistent with his lack of abilities. Furthermore, although the work appears not to have been published until 1744, the events of the novel take place between 1690 and 1712. Finally, and most puzzling, among the minor characters there is mentioned a Monsieur Masclary, écuyer du duc d'Ormond. Now Masclary was the name of the family who befriended Gueudeville's wife when she first came to Holland.[40] The mention of this name could be purely coincidental, and is certainly not sufficient, by itself, to link the novel with Gueudeville. There are, however, other minor characters, whom I have been unable to identify, who seemed to be named and introduced quite gratuitously. There is, for example, a M. Clignet, maître de postes à Utrecht, or a certain La Roche, marchand de vin sur le Spui, who seem to be mentioned simply because of their names. As a result, one begins to wonder if the author was enjoying some joke at the expense or for the entertainment of his friends, much as Tyssot de Patot did in his *Voyage de Groenland*.[41] I have been unable, however, to establish a connection between these people and Gueudeville.

Against Gueudeville's authorship is the long delay in publishing the work. It rather looks as if the publisher wanted to profit from the name Gueudeville had made for himself through *L'Eloge de la folie* which was being brought out again in several editions in the late thirties and early forties. Also, there is a good deal of material to do with horsemanship in the novel, a subject not known to be of interest to Gueudeville. The style, as I have indicated, is sometimes reminiscent of Gueudeville's but is not uniformly characteristic, although I must confess this is a highly subjective impression that I am unable to substantiate.

In summary, then, the evidence is inconclusive. Gueudeville could have written the novel and failed to have it published in his lifetime. Or the publisher could simply have been capitalizing on his reputation. Until more information is available we can do no better than suspend our judgement.

CONCLUSION

It is clear from the foregoing that this study cannot be described as definitive. There is much still to be discovered about Gueudeville's life, and many questions about his work must, for the moment, remain unanswered. On the other hand, this is the first time any attempt has been made to document his career, and to identify and consider systematically everything he wrote. The results have been rewarding.

The chance discovery of what appears to be the only surviving copy of his first publication, *Les Motifs de la conversion*, a work hitherto unknown, has filled in some of the gaps in his early years in France and his arrival in Holland. Archival material has thrown light on his family and friends, and detailed bibliographical investigation has revealed the previously unsuspected degree of popularity of his polemical writings and translations. Some success has been achieved in identifying which works he wrote and which were incorrectly attributed to him. One of these works, the *Dialogues des morts d'un tour nouveau*, not previously recognized as being by Gueudeville, has been shown to be from his pen, and it is now fairly conclusive that he was responsible for the 1705 edition of the works of Lahontan, and that he had nothing to do with the publication of *Le Grand Théâtre historique*.

Through the examination of his monthly political periodical, *L'Esprit des cours de l'Europe*, we have gained an insight into the principles and practice of journalism in Holland and France at the turn of the century, and seen how typical Gueudeville was of his colleagues in the field. Similarly, in analysing the various parts of the critique of Fénelon's *Télémaque*, we have noted that Gueudeville's views were representative of the attitudes adopted by the French refugees and the Dutch towards the exploits and ambitions of Louis XIV.

Apart from his notoriety as a polemicist Gueudeville was best known as a translator of classical and Renaissance works. Although not all his translations were equally successful it can be fairly said that he was largely responsible for the popularity enjoyed by Erasmus in the eighteenth century, and that he made More's ideas accessible at a time when such ideas were beginning to have revolutionary significance.

What emerges so clearly from this study of Gueudeville's life and work is the underlying unity of his thought. Whether he was writing explicitly polemical tracts, or simply translating the works of others, whether he was dealing with history or geography, past or present, his main and consistent aim was to attack arbitrary and tyrannical power in politics and in religion. His main battle was with France and the Catholic Church, but he sought out the enemy everywhere, even in his own camp. For Gueudeville, although of necessity hypocritical in his early encounters with the Walloon Churches, was a man of deep conviction on the subject of liberty in all its forms. He was not fundamentally a revolutionary, but he did recognize that, in certain circumstances, revolution was the only way out. Nor was he a socialist, in the modern sense of the word, but he was what might be termed a progressive *moraliste* and an early advocate of the rights of man.

During the course of this study we have met other refugees and *moines défroqués* such as Aymon, Gabillon, La Barre de Beaumarchais and Rousset who, like Gueudeville, were all engaged in the business of satire and polemics, and all dependent for their livelihood on the power of their pens. These men were not great writers but their style was forceful, energetic, and often passionate. Gueudeville was a master of this kind of writing. He knew how to present his ideas in a form that would earn him the plaudits of the populace and the scorn of the scholar.

I have tried to convey some of Gueudeville's personality, energy and popular appeal, by quoting extensively from the texts themselves, many of which are not readily available. It may be that some will wish to delve further into his writings but, if not, the reader will have had more than a cursory acquaintance with them. Much more needs to be done in the way of analysis, the identification of references and sources, and placing the works more specifically in the period. To do this, however, it would be necessary to know considerably more about Gueudeville's life. It would be interesting to know, for example, what his arrangements were with the publishers, if he worked under contract, how much he earned and how he was paid. It would, perhaps, solve some bibliographical mysteries if we knew precisely when and where he died. But, until such information is discovered, we must be content with this partial picture of the relationship between his work and his daily life.

Gueudeville, as we have seen, offended the scholars, both by his personality and by his work. And, since it is mainly scholars who are responsible for preserving the past, they have taken their vengeance by allowing his name to fall into obscurity. The object of this study has been to show that this obscurity is unjustified, and that Gueudeville should still be of interest to us because, although he was not a great man, he was truly a man of his time.

APPENDIX A
(see chapter three, note 18)

Op den XIX^{en} Octobris a^0 XVII^c en drie compareerden voor my Henrick Weydwaert, openbaar Notaris, by den Hove van Holland geadmitteerd, in 's-Gravenhage residerende, en voor de nagenoemde getuigen Monsieur Etienne Foulque, Boekverkoper wonende alhier, ten ene, en Messieurs Jonas en François l'Honoré, mede Boekverkopers, alhier woonachtig, ten andere zijde, de welke verklaarden met malkanderen overeengekomen en verdragen te zijn, ter zake en in maniere hiernavolgende, namelijk dat de eerste comparant zal rederen en overgeven, zo alshijredeert en overgeeft bij dezen, aan en ten behoeve van de tweede comparanten het recht van copie, en de gedrukte exemplaren van zeker boekje, geintituleerd l'csprit des Cours, of nouvelles des Cours de l'Europe.

Waartegen de tweede comparanten zullen op zich nemen, gelijk zij op haar nemen bij dozen de Prestatie en nakoming van het contract, 'twelk de eerste en tweede comparanten met de Auteur van het voorz. boekje gemaakt hebben, en dienaangaande de eerste comparant afhouden alle moeilijkheden en kosten, die hem daarover zouden mogen worden aangedaan; En daarenboven aan de eerste comparant beloven te betalen twee hondered en vijftig Caroli guldens voor het recht van de copie van het voorz. Boekje, mitsgaders zes honderd en dertig gelijke guldens voor acht duizend vierhonderd gedrukte exemplaren van hetzelve boekje, zijnde een stuiver en een half van elk separaat stuk van iedère maand, tezamen makende achthonderd and tachtig Caroli guldens, in deze voege, te weten in geld, met termijnen van vijftig Caroli guldens alle drie maanden precies, waarvan de eerste drie maanden vervallen zullen wezen de eerste Januari XVII^c en vier naastkomende, en zo voort van drie maanden tot drie maanden gelijke som tot de effectuele voldoening toe.

Bijaldien aan de eerste comparant enige exemplaren van 't voorz. Boekje zouden mogen wederom gezonden worden na het passeren van deze contracten, zo zal het aan de eerste comparant vrijstaan de zelve wederom gezonden exemplaren over te leveren aan de tweede comparanten, die gehouden zullen wezen dezelve met de eerste comparant tot zijn contentment te changeren en verwisselen en dat boekje tegen boekje; wel verstaande nochtans dat de voorz. wederomgezonden exemplaren zullen zijn gedrukt op de naam van de eerste comparant, en anders niet.

In geval een van de tweede comparanten deze contracten niet zou kunnen of in gebreke blijven na te komen en voldoen, door zijn overlijden of andenszins, zo zal de andere tweede comparant geobligeerd zijn alleen deze contracten te presteren en te voldoen.

Compareerden mede voor mij Notaris en de nagenoemde getuigen Juffrouwen Philippine de Lo--- huisvrouw van Monsr. Jonas l'Honoré, en Marthe Chastelain huisvrouw van mons^r. François l'Honoré, als ten deze door dezelve hare mans gequalificeerd, de welke verklaarden haar te stellen borgen elk als principaal, onder behoorlijke communicatie van de beneficien ordinis excussionis, divisionis, senatus consulti vellejani, et authentica signa mulier, ten effect van dien onderricht, voor de voorz. hare mans, ten behoeve van de voorz. Monsr. Foulque, en dat voor de voldoening van de voorz. som van acht hunderd en tachtig guldens in voege als boven.

Tot naderkoming van 't geen voorz. staat verbinden alle de comparanten hare respective personen en goederen, geen uitgezonderd, stellende dezelve ten bedwang van alle rechten en rechteren, en specialijk den Hove van Holland; te vreden zijnde om haarlieden in de inhouden dezes vrijwilliglijk tot hare kosten te laten condemneren bij den gemelde Hove van Holland, of den gerechte dezer Stede, constituerende tot dien einde onwederroepelijk Matthaeus Stipel, Henrick van de Wijver, en Willem Coelemeij, procureurs voor den meergemelden Hove, mitsgaders Adriaen van der Heijde, Pieter van Aerden, en Gabriel Valette, procureurs voor den voorz. Gerechte, tezamen en ieder van hen bijzonder, zo om de voorz. condemnatie te verzoeken, als daar in te consenteren respectief; belovende van waarde te zullen houden 't gene bij de voorz. Procureurs daarin zal worden gedaan en verricht, onder verband als boven. Aldus gedaan en gepasseerd in 's-Gravenhage, ter presentie van Monsr Matthaeus Rogguet, Burger alhier, en Joannes Vroom de jonge, klerk mijn's Notaris, als getuigen hiertoe verzocht.

Philipe de lo	F. Foulque
Marta Chatelain	J. L'Honoré
Matthaeus Rogguets	F. L'Honoré
	J. P. Vroom
	1703
	Henri Wegewaert Nots. Publ.
	a^0 1703 com
	10 m
	19 d

APPENDIX B
(see chapter three, note 20)

Aujourd'hui trente-unième jour de Décembre mil sept cent quatre comparurent par devant moi Pierre de Rogissart, Notaire public admis par la Cour de Hollande résidant ici à La Haye, en présence des témoins sousnommés, les Sieurs Jonas L'Honoré Bourgeois Marchand Libraire de cette ville d'une part, et Thomas Jonson demeurant au dit lieu de La Haye d'autre part, lesquels ont reconnu et confessé avoir fait ensemble le contrat de Société et de compagnie aux clauses et conditions suivantes; c'est à savoir.

Que la dite Société sera et demeurera ferme entre les dites parties pour deux années consécutives, à commencer le premier jour de Janvier de l'année prochaine *1705* et expirant le dernier jour de Décembre *1706* inclusivement, sans que pour quelque raison ou prétexte que ce puisse être, la dite Société puisse être dissoute pendant le dit temps; les dites parties consentant au contraire que leur présente association continue dans la suite, comme ils le trouveront à propos; chacun étant tenu et promettant de travailler de tout son pouvoir, pour le bien et l'avancement de leur intérêt commun; la dite association n'étant faite au reste que pour les choses qui s'imprimeront ou qui s'achèteront à frais communs depuis le dit premier jour de janvier *1705* jusqu'à l'expiration du terme du dit contrat, ainsi qu'il sera spécifié plus bas.

Et afin qu'il ne puisse y avoir d'abus ni de confusion dans les affaires qui concerneront la dite Société, il sera fait fidèle et exact inventaire de tous les livres, papiers, ustensiles, etc. qui appartiennent au dit Sr. Jonas L'Honoré, et qui sont actuellement ou dans sa boutique, ou dans son magasin, avec leur prix et valeur, duquel inventaire vérification sera faite article par article, par le dit Sr. Thomas Jonson, laquelle vérification sera aussi signée du dit Thom. Jonson, afin d'y pouvoir avoir recours en temps et lieu.

Tous les dits livres, papiers, ustensiles et autres effets ainsi inventoriés et approuvés, seront et demeureront toujours en pleine et entière propriété au dit Sr. Jonas L'Honoré, sans que le dit Sr. Thomas Jonson doive ou puisse y rien prétendre. En sorte que quand il se vendra ou débitera quelque chose des effets propres du dit Jon. L'Honoré, la Société en tiendra compte au fonds du dit Jonas L'Honoré.

Et comme le dit Sr. Thomas Jonson ne peut et ne doit en aucune façon prétendre aucun profit sur les dits livres, papiers et autres effets du dit Sr. Jonas L'Honoré vendus pendant le cours de leur dite présente Société, aussi ne sera-t-il tenu à aucune perte ou dommage que le dit Jonas L'Honoré pourrait faire dessus. Le dit Sr. Thomas Jonson n'étant point tenu des dettes, si aucunes il y en a, contractées par le dit Jonas L'Honoré à ce sujet ou à tous autres faites et créées avant la dite Société, et le dit Jonas L'Honoré promettant et s'engageant de garantir de toutes poursuites à cet égard comme aussi de tous dépens, dommages et intérêts.

Et en cas qu'aucuns des dits livres, papiers ou autres appartenant à la présente Société viennent à être vendus ou échangés, après le dit premier jour de janvier *1705* et pendant tout le temps de l'Association, soit pour acquitter les dettes contractées par le dit Jonas L'Honoré, si aucunes il y en a, soit pour liquider avec d'autres Libraires, le dit Jonas L'Honoré sera tenu de rembourser incessamment à la Société la valeur des dits livres, papiers ou autres, et ce sur ce qu'il aura de plus liquide.

Tout ce qui s'imprimera, négociera, ou achètera depuis le dit premier jour de janvier *1705,* le paiement de copies, de papiers, d'impression, de correction, ports de lettres et de paquets, et généralement tout ce qui regarde le fonds de la Société, sera payé du fonds de la dite Société; et quant à ce qui regarde les autres dépenses qui concernent également le fonds en particulier du dit Jonas L'Honoré, et celui de la dite Société, telles que sont le loyer de la boutique et du magasin, et les gages des garçons, chacun des dits fonds y contribuera à proportion de la vente qui se trouvera avoir été faite au bout de l'année.

On tiendra registre exact et correct de tout ce qui sera vendu, acheté, reçu et payé pour le compte de la dite Société, et ce dans de bons journaux et livres de comptes tenus dans la méthode la meilleure et la plus claire que les associés pourront trouver, sans qu'il soit loisible à l'un ou à l'autre d'en excepter la moindre chose. Lesquels dits registres seront tenus alternativement par les dits associés de semaine en semaine, ou de mois en mois, de la manière qu'ils conviendront; étant en outre arrêté, que celui qui sera chargé de la tenue des dits registres sera aussi chargé en même temps de la recette et du débours de l'argent; l'un et l'autre étant tenu de liquider sa caisse tous les samedis; pour lequel effet, comme aussi afin d'éviter la confusion, il y aura un registre séparé. De plus, il se fera à la fin de chaque année, un bilan ou inventaire général de tous les effets, dettes, et crédits de la Société, afin de voir clairement l'état des affaires communes, et de connaître l'augmentation ou la diminution qui sera arrivée pendant le cours de l'année.

Arrivant que les deux associés vinssent à se séparer après l'expiration du temps porté dans ce présent contrat, ou que l'un ou l'autre vînt à mourir pendant la dite association, la Société venant par ce moyen à être dissoute tous les effets communs à la dite Société, comme aussi les dettes et les crédits seront séparés en deux portions égales, s'il est possible, et le sort décidera de la portion d'un chacun; les effets qui seront trouvés restants de ceux qui auront été portés dans le susdit inventaire approuvé et signé, aussi bien que les dettes et crédits qui en dépendront, demeurants toujours en toute propriété au dit

Sieur Jonas L'Honoré ou aux siens. Que si pendant la dite association un tiers connu des deux parties, offrait d'entrer dans leur présente association, les deux contractants consentent à l'y recevoir aux conditions dont ils pourront convenir.

Que si durant le cours, ou à la fin de cette présente association il survenait quelque difficulté ou différend entre les dits associés, ils s'engagent et promettent réciproquement pour éviter tous procès, de nommer chacun de sa part un arbitre raisonnable, judicieux et modéré, pour terminer le dit différend à l'amiable, et en cas que les dits arbitres ne puissent convenir et s'accorder ensemble, les dits associés consentent et veulent qu'ils puissent prendre et nommer un surarbitre pour décider, à la pluralité des voix, du dit différend, absolument et définitivement, promettant l'un et l'autre de se soumettre à leur sentence arbitrale, à peine de tous dépens, dommages et intérêts, et voulants en outre que cette présente clause ait lieu, même en cas de mort de l'un d'eux.

Ainsi fait et passé à La Haye en l'étude de moi, Notaire, jour que dessus, en présence de Gerrit van Hedikhuysen et Paul Romyn, témoins.

Gerrit van Hedijkhuisen
Paul Romyn

Jonas L'Honoré
Tho. Johnson
P. Rogissart
1704

APPENDIX C
(see chapter three, note 21)

Aujourd'hui dix-neuvième mai mil sept cent six, comparurent par devant moi Pierre de Rogissart, notaire public admis par la Cour de Hollande résidant ice à La Haye en présence des témoins sousnommés Messieurs Jean Neaulme, Daniel Servaes, et Louis Chastelain, tous trois habitants de ce lieu de La Haye, en qualité de curateurs des biens et effets de Jonas L'Honoré, ci-devant marchand libraire de ce lieu, en faveur des créanciers du dit Jonas L'Honoré, comme tels établis par la noble et Vénérable Justice de La Haye en date du [   ] de cette présente année 1706 d'une part, et le Sieur Thomas Johnson Bourgeois marchand libraire de ce lieu, d'autre part; lesquels pour prévenir et empêcher les poursuites et procès qui pourraient survenir entre eux au sujet de la liquidation des comptes de la Société de librairie qui aurait été faite entre les dits Jonas L'Honoré d'une part, et Thomas Johnson d'autre, en date du 31 décembre *1704*. Laquelle Société aurait été rompue du commun consentement des parties le 9 octobre *1705*. Pour lesquelles choses aurait déjà été intenté action devant la dite Justice de La Haye; ont déclaré que pour lever toutes difficultés qui pourraient être au sujet que dessus, et éviter les frais qui pourraient consumer une grande partie de leurs prétentions, ils ont convenue et accordé ensemble d'en sortir à l'amiable par voie d'arbitré, pour examiner, régler et solder les dits comptes, et juger et terminer les dits différends, procès et contestations. Et pour cet effet les dits Jean Neaulme, Daniel Servaes et Louis Chastelain en leur dite qualité de curateurs, ont choisi et nommé pour arbitre Monsieur et Mre Jean van der Burgh, avocat devant la Noble Cour de Hollande, et le dit Thomas Johnson, Monsieur et Mre Ytel Auguste van Middelgeest, aussi avocat devant la dite Cour, auxquels ils ont donné respectivement plein pouvoir de régler, juger et terminer tous et un chacun les différends* et cela sur les pièces, papiers, livres, et documents que les parties promettent réciproquement de leur mettre incessamment entre les mains afin que dans [   ] au plus tard, les dits Sieurs arbitres puissent rendre leur jugement arbitral; que si les dits Sieurs arbitres ne pouvaient pas s'accorder entre eux à rendre le dit jugement arbitral dans le dit temps, ils pourront élire et assumer tel surarbitre, qu'ils jugeront à propos, pour conjointement rendre la dite sentence, à laquelle les parties promettent respectivement d'acquiescer à peine par le contrevenant ou les contrevenants de [   ].

Obligeant pour l'exécution des présentes leurs personnes et leurs biens, lesquels ils soumettent à la contrainte de toutes Cours, Juges et Justices et spécialement de la Cour de Hollande, et consentant en outre à une condamnation volontaire en conséquence de la dite sentence arbitrale tant devant la Noble et Vénérable Justice de celui de La Haye, que devant la Noble Cour de Hollande, constituant à cet effet Barent Vos Charles van Belle, procureurs devant la Justice de La Haye, et Matthieu Hipel et Joach Huyssens, procureurs devant la dite Cour, les uns pour demander la dite procuration, et les autres pour y consentir.

Fait et passé à La Haye en présence de Jean Jenes et Antoine de Coeur, témoins dignes de foi.

*to replace two lines crossed out after "différends" — qui peuvent être entre les dits comparants au sujet que dessus en leur dite qualité. Approuvé la rature ci-dessus.

Jan Jenes	jean neaulme
Anthoine de Coeur	Daniel Servas
1706	
P. Rogissart	
L. Chastelain	
T. Johnson	

APPENDIX D.

A Provisional Check-list of Editions of the Critique of *Telemaque.*

In offering this check-list I should point out that because I was unable to examine enough copies I cannot vouch for the complete accuracy of the collations. The main advantage of what follows is that there is presented, for the first time, an indicator of how many editions of Gueudeville's critique were produced.

1. CRITIQUE / GENERALE / DES / AVANTURES / DE / TELEMAQUE. / [vignette of armillary sphere] / A COLOGNE, / Chez les Heritiers de PIERRE / MARTEAU. 1700.

Formula
12° A–C^{12}D^8
pp. [4] 5–87   Page numbers in curved brackets at top centre. 22 lines per page except in D gathering which has 26 lines per page and smaller type.

Contents
A1, title; A2-A2v, Avis au lecteur; A3-D8, text. A1v and D8v are blank.

Signatures
$7 signed centrally. In the last gathering the first five leaves are signed.

Catchwords
On every page

Running-title
None

Watermarks
None visible

Plates, etc.
Headpieces of type ornament at A2 and A3, and decorated initials L and E at A2 and A3.

Comments
The alteration of type size in the last gathering is characteristic of the miscalculation that occurs in casting off from a manuscript. For this reason I believe this

147

edition to be the first. It is also significant that when this work was reviewed, in May 1700, it was described as having 88 pages; a feature peculiar to this edition. In his preface to the 1701 edition, the abbé de Saint-Rémy says the *Critique générale* was published in Holland. The abbé Caron, art. cit., thought the publisher was probably Moetjens, although he offered no evidence for this. It is just as likely the publisher was François L'Honoré, with whom Gueudeville was associated at this time.

This first edition was published before April 1700 since, in the April 1700 issue of *L'Esprit des cours,* there is a reference to Faydit's authorship of it.

Locations
Paris (Ma, So); Schenectady (UnC); Tours (U)

2. CRITIQUE / GENERALE / DES / AVANTURES / DE / TELEMAQUE. / [vignette of armillary sphere] / A COLOGNE, / Chez les Heritiers de PIERRE / MARTEAU. 1700.

Formula
12° A–C^{12}D^{10}
pp. [4] 5–92 Page numbers in curved brackets at top centre. 22 lines per page.

Contents
A1, title; A2–A2v, Avis au lecteur; A3–D10v, text. A1v is blank

Signatures
$7 signed centrally

Catchwords
On every page

Running title
None

Watermarks
Not examined

Plates, etc.
Headpieces of type ornament and decorated initials L and E at A2 and A3.

Comments
I have no special reason for considering this edition the next to appear after the first, except that this edition, like the first, contains no frontispiece (at least in the few copies I have seen), whereas some subsequent editions do. This could be a piracy of Dutch origin.

Locations
Halle (U); The Hague (R); Princeton (U)

3. CRITIQUE / GENERALE / DES / AVANTURES / DE / TELEMAQUE / [Vignette of armillary sphere] / A COLOGNE, / Chez les Heritiers de PIERRE / MARTEAV. 1700.

Formula
6° A–G^{6}H^4
pp. [4] 5–92 63 and 87 misnumbered 64 and 77. Page numbers in curved brackets at top centre except for pp. 9, 15, 16, 19, 23, 27, 35, 37, 40, 43, 50, 55, 59, 61, 68, 71, 73, 74, 82, 85, 91 where the numbers are in square brackets. 22 lines per page.

Contents
A1, title; A2–A2v, Avis au lecteur; A3–H4v, text. A1v is blank

Signatures
$4 signed centrally. F2 not signed. H–H3 are signed.

Catchwords
On every page

Running-title
None

Watermarks
Fleur de lis, SAUVADE?

Plates, etc.
Headpieces of type ornament at A2 and A3. Decorated initial E at A3.

Comments
This is a piracy, perhaps of French origin. The watermark seems to contain the name of a French papermaker. The type is very worn, and the whole edition has the appearance of being carelessly and hurriedly produced.

Locations
Aix (Me); Brussels (R); Chicago (Ne)

4. CRITIQUE / GENERALE / DES / AVANTURES / DE / TELEMAQUE. / [vignette of armillary sphere] / A COLOGNE, / Chez les Heretiers de Pierre / Marteau. 1700.

Formula
12° A^8 (± A1, A2; –A8) B–G$^{4/8}$ H^2
pp. [2] 5–92 Page numbers in curved brackets at top centre

Contents
A1, frontispiece; A2, title; A3–H2v, text. A2v is blank.

Signatures
Irregularly signed in a mixture of roman and arabic numerals as follows:
arabic numerals are found at A5, C3, C4, C6, E3, E6. C5 and E5 are unsigned.
The rest are in roman numerals with F2, G2, G4 missigned L2, L4, G3, and G5,
G6, H1 unsigned.

Catchwords
Between gatherings

Running-title
None

Watermarks
Not examined

Plates, etc.
There is an engraved front., unsigned, showing a satyr brandishing a club and
uttering the words "NON SAPIO MENDACIA." Headpiece of type ornament
and decorated initial E at A3.

Comments
This is another piracy that seems to have involved more than one compositor.
The use of quire catchwords suggests French origins. The make-up of the first
gathering is unusual. In the copy at Geneva, the frontispiece, which is of
different paper, is tacked on to A6; the title-page, which seems to be a
cancel, is tacked on to A5; A3 and A4 are conjugate. A7 appears to be a loose
leaf. I am unable to explain the purpose of this composition, but it must have
something to do with the absence of the Avis au lecteur found in the other
editions. I have not seen a copy that contains the Avis au lecteur but I
assume one exists.

Of the first four editions of the *Critique générale* this is the one most
frequently found.

Locations
Besançon (M); Bonn (U); Cambridge (U); Geneva (U); Lyon (M); Madrid (BN);
Mannheim (U); Marseille (M); Nice (U); Oxford (TI); Rouen (M); Tours (U);
Troyes (M)

5. CRITIQUE / GENERALE / DES AVANTURES / DE / TELEMAQUE. /
Seconde Edition. / [vignette of bowl of flowers] / A COLOGNE, / Chez les
Heritiers de PIERRE / MARTEAU. / [rule] / M. DCC.

Formula
12° A–B^{12}
pp [6] 7–47   Page numbers in curved brackets at top centre. 31 lines per page.

Contents
A1, front.; A2, title; A3—A3v, Avis au lecteur; A4—B12, text. A1v, A2v and B12v are blank

Signatures
$6 signed centrally

Catchwords
On every page

Watermarks
A cross surmounted by a crown with a lion or eagle on each side. Two adjacent circles, one of which contains the letter T.

Plates, etc.
Engraved front. Woodcut headpiece and headpiece of type ornament at A3 and A4. I have not found a second edition with a sphere as the title-page vignette. This edition, with the bowl of flowers and small type, also contains: CRITIQUE/ DU / PREMIER TOME / DES / AVANTURES / DE / TELEMAQUE. / *Seconde Edition.* / [vignette of bowl of flowers] / A COLOGNE, / Chez les Heritiers de PIERRE / MARTEAU. / [rule] / M. DCC.

Formula
$C–E^{12} F^4 (–F4)$
pp. [2] 51—125

Contents
C1, title; C2—C2v, Avis au lecteur; C3—F3, text. C1v and F3v are blank.

Plates, etc.
Woodcut headpiece at C2; headpiece of type ornament at C3. Tailpieces at C2v and F3. Decorated initials L and A at C2 and C3.
CRITIQUE/DU/SECOND TOME/DES/AVANTURES/DE/TELEMAQUE./*Seconde Edition.*/[vignette of bowl of flowers]/A COLOGNE,/Chez les Heritiers de PIERRE/MARTEAU./[rule]/M. D C C.

Formula
$F^{12} (–F1, F2, F3) G–L^{12} M^2$
pp. [2] 129—268   131 and 211 misnumbered 13 and 111.

Contents
F4, title; F5—M2, text; F4v is blank

Plates, etc.
Headpiece of type ornament and decorated initial P at F5; tailpiece at M2v.
CRITIQUE / DE LA SUITE / DU SECOND TOME / DES / AVANTURES / DE/ TELEMAQUE. / *Seconde Edition.* / [vignette of bowl of flowers] / A COLOGNE, / Chez les Heritiers de PIERRE / MARTEAU. / [rule] / M. / D C C.

152

Formula
$\pi1M^{12}$ (−M1, M2, M3) N−O^{12} (−012)
pp. [2] 271−334

Contents
$\pi1$, title; M4−011, text. $\pi1v$ is blank

Comments
The same publisher also brought out the last parts of Gueudeville's critique: *Critique de la première et seconde suite du tome second* (1701) and *Le Critique ressuscité* (1704), which are described later. It is from this second edition that the quotations in chapter four are taken.

Locations
Albi (Ro); Chicago (Ne); Edinburgh (U); Lausanne (U); Leipzig (KM); Lille (M); Namur (U); Nancy (U); Ottawa (U); Oxford (TI); Périgueux (M); Princeton (U); Schenectady (UnC); Sherbrooke (U); Toulouse (U); Wolfenbüttel (HA)

6. CRITIQUE / GENERALE / DES / AVANTURES / DE / TELEMAQUE. / Troisiéme Edition. / [Vignette of armillary sphere] / A COLOGNE, / Chez les Heritiers de PIERRE / MARTEAU. 1700.

Formula
12° A−C^{12} D^8
pp. [4] 5−87 Page numbers in curved brackets at top centre. 22 lines per page except in D gathering which has 26 lines per page and smaller type.

Contents
A1, title; A2−A2v, Avis au lecteur; A3−D8, text; A1v and D8v are blank.

Signatures
$7 signed centrally. In the last gathering the first five leaves are signed.

Catchwords
On every page

Running-title
None

Watermarks
None visible

Plates, etc.
Headpieces of type ornament at A2 and A3; decorated initials L and E at A2 and A3

Comments
Although this edition is closely modelled on the first edition a comparison of the two reveals that the type has been completely reset.

Locations
Göttingen (U); Illinois (U); Oslo (U); Paris (BN, So)

7. CRITIQUE / GENERALE / DES / AVANTURES / DE / TELEMAQUE /
Quatriéme Edition. / [vignette of armillary sphere] / A COLOGNE, / Chez les
Héritiers de PIERRE / MARTEAU. / [rule] / M. DCCI.

Formula
12° A–C¹²
pp. [4] 5–70 26 lines per page except from pp. 62–70 which have 30 lines
per page and smaller type. p. 7 has a comma instead of a number

Contents
A1, title; A2–A2v, Avis au lecteur; A3–C12, text. A1v is blank.

Signatures
$6 signed centrally

Catchwords
On every page

Running-title
CRITIQUE / GENERALE

Watermarks
Very large design containing a cross and the initials EB

Plates, etc.
Engraved front. Headpiece of type ornament at A2 and A3. Tailpiece of basket
of flowers at A2v. Decorated initials L and E at A2 and A3.

Comments
The engraved front. is very similar but not identical to either engraving found
in nos. 4 and 5.

Locations
Chicago (U); Grenoble (U); The Hague (R); Harvard (U); Leiden (U); Namur (U);
Paris (BN); Saskatoon (U); Tubingen (U); Uppsala (U)

1. CRITIQUE / DU / PREMIER TOME / DES / AVANTURES / DE / TELE-MAQUE. / [vignette of armillary sphere] / A COLOGNE, / Chez les Heritiers de PIERRE / MARTEAU. 1700.

Formula

12^6 $\pi 1 A^{12}$ ($-A12$) $B-F^{12} G^8$

pp. [2] 3–118 117–154 (= 156) [2]

> Page numbers in curved brackets at top centre. The left bracket is reversed on 18, and the right one is absent from 47. 22 lines per page up to and including 145, then 26 lines per page and smaller type to the end.

Contents

$\pi 1$, front.; A1, title; A2–A2v, Avis au lecteur; A3–G7v, text; G8, Errata. $\pi 1$v, A1v and G8v are blank

Signatures

$7 signed centrally

Catchwords

On every page

Running-title

None

Watermarks

Design of two circles within which are such initials as CC, GAB, and II. Some circles show a cross.

Plates, etc.

Engraved front. Headpieces of type ornament at A2 and A3; decorated initials L and A at A2 and A3.

Comments

The use of small type at the end, and the existence of an errata page suggests a first edition.

The errata page lists:

> p. 11. l. 1. suposer, lisez suporter
>
> p. 11. l. 11. hétérdooxie, lisez héterodoxie
>
> p. 22. ligne dernière, privé, lisez privée

The engraved front. is very similar but not identical to any of those previously noted.

Locations

Amsterdam (U); Darmstadt (L); Iowa (U); London (UC); Paris (So); Schenectady (UnC)

2. CRITIQUE / DU / PREMIER TOME / DES / AVANTURES / DE / TELE-MAQUE. / [vignette of armillary sphere] / A COLOGNE, / Par les seuls Heritiers Universels de / PIERRE MARTEAU, Juré. 1700.

Formula
12° A^8 $(-A8)$ $B-L^{4/8}$ $M^4 N^4 O^2$
pp. [2] 3–118, 117–151 (= 153) [1]

> 122 is misnumbered 112. Numbers are in curved or square brackets at top centre. No brackets on 125, 126, 138, 139, 140. Right bracket absent from 68. 22 lines per page up to and including 140, then 26 lines and smaller type to the end.

Contents
A1, title; A2-A2v, Avis au lecteur; A3–O2, text. A1v and O2v are blank

Signatures
In principle, half the leaves of each gathering are signed, but there are many irregularities: A4 and D2 are not signed; C2, C4 and C6 are missigned B2, B4, B6; E5, E6 and G5 are signed, and L2, L3, L4 and M2 are signed in roman numerals.

Catchwords
Between gatherings except between L and M.

Running-title
None

Watermarks
Grapes, crown, (A[♡]R)

Plates, etc.
Identical headpieces of type ornament at A2 and A3.

Comments
The appearance of roman numerals in the L and M gathering suggests the work of two compositors. The use of quire catchwords is suggestive of French origins. The similarity of the composition of this edition and no. 4 of the *Critique générale* leads one to conclude they may have been printed at the same time. The Avis au lecteur is absent from the copies at Oxford, Cambridge and Lyon, but is present in the copy at Toronto.

Locations
Cambridge (U); Lyon (M); Neuchâtel (P); Oxford (TI); Rouen (M); Toronto (VC)

3. CRITIQUE / DU / PREMIER TOME / DES / AVANTURES / DE / TELE-MAQUE. / *Seconde Edition.* / [vignette of armillary sphere] / A COLOGNE, / Chez les Heritiers de PIERRE / MARTEAU. 1700.

Formula

$12° \pi 1 A^{12}$ $(-A12)$ $B-F^{12}G^8$ $(-G8)$

pp. [2] 3–118 117–154 (= 156)

> Page numbers in curved brackets at top centre. 22 lines per page up to and including 145, then 26 lines per page and smaller type to the end.

Contents

$\pi 1$, front; A1, title; A2–A2v, Avis au lecteur; A3–G7v, text. $\pi 1$v and A1v are blank.

Signatures

$7 signed centrally

Catchwords

On every page

Running-title

None

Watermarks

Not examined

Plates, etc.

Engraved front. Headpieces of type ornament and decorated initials L and A at A2 and A3

Comments

The engraved front. is the same as that found in the first edition of this part. Although this edition is closely modelled on the first, the errata noted in the first edition have been corrected and the type has been reset.

Locations

Geneva (U); Göttingen (U); Stockholm (R); Tubingen (U)

4. CRITIQUE/DU/PREMIER TOME/DES/AVANTURES/DE/TELEMAQUE./
Troisiéme Edition./[vignette of armillary sphere]/A COLOGNE,/Chez les
Héritiers de PIERRE/MARTEAU./[rule]/M. DCCI

Formula
$12° \pi1 A^{12} (-A12) B-E^{12} F^4$
pp. [4] 7–127 [1]   26 lines per page. Digit 8 missing from 80

Contents
$\pi1$, front.; A1, title; A2–A2v, Avis au lecteur; A3–F3, text. $\pi1v$, A1v and
F4v are blank.

Signatures
$6 signed centrally

Catchwords
On every page

Running-title
CRITIQUE DU / PREMIER TOME.

Watermarks
Circles containing the initials TN and EB

Plates, etc.
Engraved front; headpieces of type ornament and decorated initials L and A at
A2 and A3

Comments
The engraved front is the same as that found in no. 7 of the *Critique générale.*

Locations
Chicago (U); Grenoble (M); Leiden (U); Paris, (BN, So)

1. CRITIQUE / DU / SECOND TOME / DES / AVANTURES / DE / TELE-MAQUE. / [vignette of armillary sphere] / A COLOGNE, / Chez les Heritiers de PIERRE / MARTEAU. 1700.

Formula
$12° \pi 1A^{12}$ $(-A12)$ $B-M^{12}N^8$
pp. [2] 3–22, 25–303 (= 301)

23 lines per page except for N gathering which has 26 and smaller type. Page numbers in curved brackets at top centre.

Contents
$\pi 1$, front.; A1, title; A2–N8, text. $\pi 1v$, A1v and N8v are blank.

Signatures
$7 signed centrally Sig. K2 is on the same level as the text.

Catchwords
On every page. Catchword at K2 on same level as text.

Running-title
None

Watermarks
Not examined

Plates, etc.
Engraved front; headpiece of type ornament and decorated initial P at A2.

Comments
This edition must have been published after May 1700 since it contains a quotation from the review in the *Nouvelles de la république des lettres* (see chapter four, note 13).

The engraving is the same as the one found in nos. 1 and 3 of the *Critique du premier tome*.

This edition also includes:

CRITIQUE / DE LA SUITE DU / SECOND TOME / DES AVANTURES / DE / TELEMAQUE. / [vignette of armillary sphere] / A COLOGNE, / Chez les Heritiers de PIERRE / MARTEAU. 1700.

Formula
12° $\pi1O^{12}$ (−O12) P−T^{12}
pp. [2] 305−444   323 misnumbered 233. Page numbers in curved brackets at
                     top centre. 23 lines per page.

Contents
π1, front.; O1, title; O2−T12, text. π1v and O1v are blank.

Plates, etc.
Engraved front.; headpiece of type ornament and decorated initial V at O2.

Comments
The engraved front. is the same as the one found in no. 7 of the *Critique générale* and no. 4 of the *Critique du premier tome.*

Locations
Brussels (R); Chicago (U); Coburg (L); Columbia (U); Grenoble (M); Paris (Ar, BN, Ma, So); Princeton (U); Schenectady (UnC); Tubingen (U); Uppsala (U); Wolfenbüttel (HA)

2. CRITIQUE / DU / SECOND TOME / DES / AVANTURES / DE / TELE-MAQUE. / *Troisiéme Edition* / [Vignette of armillary sphere] / A COLOGNE, / Chez les Héritiers de PIERRE / MARTEAU. / [rule] / M. DCC. II.

Formula
12° π1A^{12} (−A12) B−K^{12}L^4
pp. [2] 3−22, 25−248 (= 246)   25 lines per page.

Contents
π1, front.; A1, title; A2-L4, text. π1v and A1v are blank.

Signatures
$7 signed centrally. C7 not signed.

Catchwords
On every page

Running-title
CRITIQUE DU / SECOND TOME.

Watermarks
None visible

Plates, etc.
Engraved front.; headpiece of type ornament and decorated initial P at A2.

Comments

The engraved front. is the same as the one found in the first edition of this part. The fact that this edition contains the same errors in pagination suggests that it was modelled on the latter.

Locations

Chicago (U); Grenoble (M); Paris (So); Tours (U); Uppsala (U)

---

1. CRITIQUE / DE LA PREMIERE ET / SECONDE SUITE DU / TOME SECOND / DES / AVANTURES / DE / TELEMAQUE. / [vignette of armillary sphere] / A COLOGNE, / Chez les Heritiers de PIERRE / MARTEAU. 1700.

Formula

$12° \pi 1A^{12}$ $(-A12)$ $B-R^{12}$

pp. [2] 3–406   Page numbers in curved brackets at top centre. 22 lines per page except in last gathering which has 26 and smaller type

Contents

$\pi 1$, front.; A1, title; A2–L12v, text of *Critique de la première suite*; M1–R12v, text of *Critique de la seconde suite.* $\pi 1$v and A1v are blank.

Signatures

$7 signed centrally

Catchwords

On every page

Running-title

None

Watermarks

Not examined

Plates, etc.

Engraved front.; identical headpieces of type ornament at A2 and M1; decorated initials J and M at A2 and M1

Comments

The engraved front. is the same as the one found in nos. 1 and 2 of the *Critique du second tome.*

Locations

Brussels (R); Chicago (U); Coburg (L); Darmstadt (L); Geneva (U); Grenoble (M); Illinois (U); Leiden (U); Liège (U); Paris (Ma, So); Schenectady (UnC); Stockholm (R); Tours (U); Tubingen (U); Uppsala (U); Wolfenbüttel (HA)

2. CRITIQUE / DE LA PREMIERE ET / SECONDE SUITE / DU TOME
SECOND / DES / AVANTURES / DE / TELEMAQUE. / *Seconde Edition.* /
[vignette of armillary sphere] / A COLOGNE, / Chez les Heritiers de PIERRE /
MARTEAU. / [rule] / M. DCCI.

Formula
12° A–H^{12} I^2
pp. [2] 5–196   Page numbers in curved brackets at top centre. 31 lines per
page. The right bracket at 50 is reversed.

Contents
A1, front.; A2, title; A3–F3, text of *Critique de la première suite;* F3v–I2v, text
of *Critique de la seconde suite.* A1v and A2v are blank.

Signatures
$6 signed centrally

Catchwords
On every page

Running-title
None

Watermarks
Not examined

Plates, etc.
Engraved front. Woodcut headpiece at A3 and F3v; decorated initials J and M
at A3 and F3v; tailpieces at F3 and I2v

Comments
Apart from the substitution of a sphere for a bowl of flowers on the title-page,
this edition betrays the same compositorial practices as in the parts listed in no.
5 of the *Critique générale.* The engraved front is also the same as the one found
in this edition.

Locations
Edinburgh (U); Lausanne (U); Leipzig (KM); Lille (M); Namur (U); Ottawa (U);
Périgueux (M); Sherbrooke (U); Toulouse (U); Wolfenbüttel (HA)

---

1. LE CRITIQUE / RESSUSCITE' / OU / Fin de la Critique / DES / AVAN-
TURES / DE / TELEMAQUE, / Où l'on voit le véritable Portrait / des bons &
des mauvais Rois. / [vignette of bowl of fruit?] / A COLOGNE, / Chez les
Héritiers de PIERRE / MARTEAU. / [rule] / M. DCC. II.

Formula
12° π1A^{12} (–A12) B–H^{12}I^4
pp. [2] 5–200.   144 misnumbered 44. 25 lines per page

Contents
π1, front. A1, title; A1v, Avertissement; A2-I4v, text, π1v is blank

Signatures
$7 signed centrally. I1−I4 signed

Catchwords
On every page

Running-title
LE CRITIQUE / RESSUSCITE'.

Watermarks
Two circles

Plates, etc.
Engraved front.; decorated initial I at A2

Comments
The engraved front. is the same as the one found in the *Critique générale*, no. 7.

Locations
Chicago (U); Coburg (L); Grenoble (M); Halle (U); Liège (U); Paris (BN, So); Sachsen-Anhalt (U); Uppsala (U); Wolfenbüttel (HA)

2. LE CRITIQUE / RESSUSCITE' / Ou fin de la Critique / DES / AVANTURES / DE / TELEMAQUE, / *Où l'on voit le véritable Portrait des* / *bons & des mauvais Rois.* / SECONDE EDITION. / [vignette of bowl of flowers] / A COLOGNE, / Chez les Heritiers de PIERRE / MARTEAU. / [rule] M. DCC. IV.

Formula
12° A−E¹² (−E12)
pp. [2] 3−117. 31 lines per page. Page numbers in curved brackets at top centre.

Contents
A1, title; A1v, Avertissement; A2−E11, text. E11v is blank.

Signatures
$6 signed centrally

Catchwords
On every page

Running-title
None

Watermarks
Very large design with crown and two crosses − X, X, OH9 or bOH.

Plates, etc.
Headpiece and decorated initial J at A2

Comments

The last two words of the 1702 edition, "Je suis", are omitted. This edition conforms to the same compositorial practices as in the parts listed in no. 5 of the *Critique générale* and the second edition of the *Critique de la première et seconde suite du tome second* with which it is bound.

Locations

Lausanne (U); Namur (U); Paris (Ar, BN); Sherbrooke (U); Toulouse (U); Wolfenbüttel (HA).

APPENDIX E
Atlas Historique

According to Dr. Ir. C. Koeman, *Atlantes Neerlandici,* Amsterdam 1967, vol.II, pp. 33–37, the various editions of the *Atlas historique* may be summarized as follows:

Vol.	1st ed.	2nd ed.	3rd ed.	Final ed.
I	1705		1721	1739
II	1708	1720	1737	
III	1708	1720	1737	
IV	1714		1735	
V	1719	1732		
VI	1719	1732		
VII	1720	1732		

1720: nouvelle éd.; 1732: seconde éd.; 1735: nouvelle éd.

As far as I can tell, Dr. Koeman was not able to collate all the editions to find out the extent to which they were different, and neither was I. Judging by title-pages alone, however, the problem seems more complicated than it appears in his schema. My own investigations have produced the following analysis:

Vol.	1st ed.	2nd ed.	No ed. cited	Nouvelle ed.	3rd ed.	Nouvelle ed.	Final ed.
I	1705, 1708	1713		1718	1721		1739
II (pt. 1)	1708	1713	1718	1720		1737	
II (pt. 2)	1708	1713					
III			1718	1720		1737	
IV	1714		1718			1735	
V	1719	1732					
VI	1719	1732					
VII	1720	1732					

The publisher's name on the 1705 title-page is François L'Honoré et Compagnie. From 1708 to 1714 title-pages bear the name Les Frères Châtelain, and from 1718 to 1721, L'Honoré et Châtelain. All the title pages after 1721 bear the name Zacharie Châtelain and appear in reverse order: volumes five, six and seven in 1732, volume four in 1735, volumes two and three in 1737, and volume one in 1739.

In each volume the maps, plates and tables are numbered consecutively, the text is numbered separately except in volumes I (1705) and IV (1714) where each dissertation has its own numbering. The dissertations together occupy about 850 pages. A list and description of the maps is given by Dr. Koeman.

SELECTED LOCATIONS

Vol. I

1705 — Amsterdam (U), Brussels (R), Cambridge (U), Chicago (Ne), Copenhagen (R), Greifswald (U), The Hague (R), Halle (U), Jena (U), Namur (U), Nancy (U), Utrecht (U), Zurich (ETH)

1708 — Chicago (Ne), Liverpool (U), Mainz (U), Orleans (M), Wolfenbüttel (HA)

1713 — Aix (Me), Avignon (Ca), Cambridge (U), Erlangen (U), Freiburg (U), Louvain (U), Michigan (WLC)

1718 — Carpentras (I), Groningen (U), Paris (Ma), Namur (U), Rouen (M), Yale (B)

1721 — Aix-Marseille (U), Amiens (M), Bordeaux (U), Copenhagen (R), Detroit (P), Erlangen (U), Leiden (U), Nancy (U), Paris (So), Pennsylvania (U), Stockholm (R), Utrecht (U)

1739 — Boston (P), Grenoble (M), Halle (U), Kentucky (U), Namur (U), Madrid (U), Neuchâtel (P), Paris (BI)

Vol. II (pt. 1)

1708 — Brussels (R), Erlangen (U), Jena (U), Michigan (WLC), Namur (U), Zurich (ETH)

1713 — Erlangen (U)?

1718 — Namur (U)

1720 — Aix-Marseille (U), Erlangen (U), Grenoble (M), Leiden (U), Namur (U), Pennsylvania (U), Utrecht (U), Yale (B)

1737 — Madrid (U)

Vol. II (pt. 2)

1708 — Brussels (R), Erlangen (U), Jena (U), Michigan (WLC), Namur (U), Zurich (ETH)

1713 — Erlangen (U)?

Vol. III

1718 — Namur (U)

1720 — Aix-Marseille (U), Erlangen (U), Leiden (U), Namur (U), Pennsylvania (U), Utrecht (U), Wurzburg (U), Yale (B)

1737 — Aix-Marseille (U), Madrid (U)

Vol. IV

1714 — Brussels (R), Erlangen (U), Leiden (U), Michigan (WLC), Utrecht (U), Zurich (ETH)

1718 — Namur (U), Yale (B)
1735 — Aix-Marseille (U), Grenoble (M), Namur (U)

Vol. V
1719 — Brussels (R), Erlangen (U), Leiden (U), Michigan (WLC), Namur (U), Utrecht (U), Wurzburg (U)
1732 — Aix-Marseille (U), Boston (P), Grenoble (M), Madrid (U), Namur (U), Pennsylvania (U), Yale (B)

Vol. VI
1719 — Brussels (R), Carpentras (I), Erlangen (U), Iowa (U), Leiden (U), Liverpool (U), Michigan (WLC), Namur (U), Utrecht (U), Wurzburg (U)
1732 — Aix-Marseille (U), Boston (P), Grenoble (M), Namur (U), Madrid (U), Pennsylvania (U), Yale (B)

Vol. VII
1720 — Aix-Marseille (U), Brussels (R), Erlangen (U), Leiden (U), Michigan (WLC), Namur (U), Utrecht (U)
1732 — Boston (P), Grenoble (M), Madrid (U), Namur (U), Yale (B)

APPENDIX F.
L'Eloge de la folie

A NOTE ON THE EDITIONS

Gueudeville's translation is based on the 1676 edition of *Moriae Encomium,* published in Bâle by Charles Patin, which contained not only the notes supplied by Gerard Lijster for the 1515 edition, but also the marginal illustrations of Holbein.[1] Gueudeville's publisher, Pierre Van de Aa, was a man who adorned his publications with illustrations at the slightest provocation, and the publication of *L'Eloge de la folie* gave him an excuse to ornament the text with six engraved folding plates, and 75 half-page engravings, based on the Holbein illustrations. He also added an engraved half-title and an engraving containing the portraits of Erasmus, More, and Holbein. These engravings, although judged by some to be of inferior quality and of little relevance to the text, probably contributed to the demand for the book. At least, this was Van der Aa's expectation when he announced, in the dedicatory preface, that:

ce petit ouvrage s'est remontré plusieurs fois, et en plusieurs langues; mais jusqu'à présent il n'avait point encore paru détaché de la masse des oeuvres de l'auteur, en français avec les figures. (Dédicace à Jean de Bye).

As for the notes of Lijster, Gueudeville was somewhat less enthusiastic:

Les notes sont de Gerard Listre, savant médecin qui, ayant demeuré quelques mois avec Erasme, avait lié avec lui une étroite amitié. Comme il m'a semblé que des remarques de littérature ne conviennent point à une traduction qui n'est proprement que pour ceux qui n'entendent pas l'original, je me suis cru obligé de les omettre, m'étant contenté d'insérer celles que j'ai jugé conformes à la curiosité d'un lecteur qui ne se soucie ni d'hébreu ni de grec. (Préface du traducteur).

The book was dedicated by Van de Aa to Jean de Bye, burgomaster of Leiden, and Gueudeville supplied a preface in which he drew heavily on the Charles Patin introduction. Gueudeville also translated Erasmus' dedication to Thomas More.

The first edition was published in Leiden in 1713, some time before July.[2] Whether Van der Aa miscalculated and failed to print enough copies, or whether he was undercut and outsold by one or both of the piracies that appeared almost immediately, it is not possible to say. What is clear is that Van der Aa deemed it worthwhile to bring out another edition in the same year. This time, he apparently printed so many copies that, two years later, to dispose of his surplus stock, he reissued the work under the guise of a "Dernière édition, revue, corrigée et augmentée de nouveau, avec une Table des matières fort ample et très exacte." In fact, the only difference between the reissue and the first edition is the addition of an Avis du libraire and a Table des matières.[3] There is, however, one feature of the 1715 reissue that is worthy of comment since it represents a minor but noteworthy landmark in the history of publishing in The Netherlands.

In France, at this time, book publishing was rigidly controlled by the government, and if one wished to publish a book in a legal manner it was necessary to apply for permission and obtain a *privilège*. Violations of these regulations could and did lead to imprisonment. In The Netherlands, no such form of control existed, and the only protection Dutch publishers had against piracies was a mutual agreement to respect each other's activities and to handle competitors' products at an agreed price. In cases of violation of this agreement an aggrieved publisher was entitled to apply to the courts and, if his case were successful, to receive compensation of 300 guilders. In a copy of such an agreement, drawn up in 1710, and signed by the major publishers of the day, Van der Aa's name is conspicuously absent. There is evidence to suggest that there was a good deal of animosity between Van der Aa and the other publishers, and that he was not prepared to sign any agreements. Indeed, the presence of the words "Avec Privilège" on the title-pages of his two 1713 editions and one of the 1715 reissues when, as far as one can tell, no such *privilège* existed, is perhaps one reason for the animosity.

What particularly distressed the publishers was the inadequacy of the compensation. It cost so much more than 300 guilders to identify, arrest and successfully prosecute a pirate that it was not worth while to proceed. The booksellers wanted the compensation raised to 3,000 guilders and they wanted Van der Aa, who seems to have been on very good terms with the authorities, to use his influence on their behalf. Van der Aa, however, was apparently unwilling to intercede. Whether or not he finally realized that he, too, would benefit from increased compensation, especially since he was himself a regular victim of pirates, it is not possible to say. But, in 1715, he applied for a *privilège* for his edition of *L'Eloge de la folie* and, on May 17 of that year, was granted the higher indemnity. This increased compensation is announced on the title-page of one of the reissues as "Avec Privilège sous peine de 3000 florins d'amende & c. contre les *Contrefacteurs*."[4]

At an auction held on August 17 1716, Van der Aa sold his stocks and *privilège* of *l'Eloge de la folie* to R. and G. Wetstein of Amsterdam who reissued the text, with a new title-page, in 1717. The Wetsteins then sold the rights to François L'Honoré of Amsterdam who, in 1728, published a new, revised edition which was pirated in the same year. In 1731, L'Honoré brought out another edition, further revised, which was again pirated in the same year. 1735 saw the publication of another piracy, and 1738 produced another, without illustrations. In 1741 there was another piracy, and two more in 1745.

In 1751 the text was modified again, and the format drastically revised. A duodecimo edition and quarto issue were published in that year. The duodecimo edition was reissued in 1752 and 1753. In 1757 there appeared another edition closely modelled on that of 1751. This was pirated in the same year, in 1761 1766 and 1771. Another two editions, based on the text of the 1731 edition, were brought out in 1761 and 1777. The 1936 edition reproduces the text of 1777.

NOTES TO APPENDIX F.

1. For details of the Lijster notes and the Holbein illustrations, see J.A. Gavin and T.W. Walsh "The *Praise of Folly* in Context: The Commentary of Girardius Listrius" *Renaissance Quarterly,* XXIV (1971), 193–209, and Betty Radice "Holbein's marginal illustrations to the *Praise of Folly*" *Erasmus in English,* VII (1975), 9–17.

2. It was reviewed in the July/August issue of the *Journal Littéraire* of that year.

3. That this was a common publishing practice is noted by Bayle (April 14 1695) in reference to one practitioner who:

   ... quoiqu'il assure de la manière du monde la plus positive, dans le titre, que c'est une "Nouvelle Edition, augmentée de beaucoup dans tout le Corps de l'Ouvrage, sur des Mémoires très curieux", c'est cependant, en tout et par tout, la même "Edition" que la précédente, si l'on en excepte les deux "nouveaux Frontispices", et un misérable "Avertissement" qui ne dit absolument rien.

4. For information about Van der Aa and the problem of the *privilèges,* see pp. 179–191, *De Amsterdamse Boekhandel,* vol. V, 1978. The warning of a three thousand guilder fine also appears on Van der Aa's editions of Gueudeville's *Les Comédies de Plaute* and *Les Colloques d'Erasme.*

CHECK-LIST OF EDITIONS

1. [red and black]/L'ELOGE / DE / LA FOLIE, / Composé en forme de Declamation / Par / ERASME DE ROTTERDAM: / Avec quelques Notes de LISTRIUS, / & les belles figures de HOLBE- / NIUS: le tout sur l'Original /

de l'Academie de Bâle. / *Piéce qui, representant au naturel* l'HOMME / *tout defiguré par la* SOTISE, *lui* / *aprend agreablement à rentrer dans* / *le bon Sens & dans la Raison*: / Traduite nouvellement en François / par Mr. GUEUDEVILLE. / [vignette of a vase of flowers] / A LEIDE, / Chez PIERRE VANDER Aa, 1713. / [rule, 42 mm.] / Avec Privilege.
In red: L'ELOGE / LA FOLIE, / ERASME DE ROTTERDAM: / Par Mr. GUEUDEVILLE. / PIERRE VANDER Aa,

Formula
12°: $*^{12}$ (− *1 and *12) $**^6$ A–N^{12} or π^2 (= *1 and *12) $*^{12}$ (− *1 and *12) etc. pp. [*32*] 1–312. 274 misnumbered 374.

Contents
*2, title; *3–*5v, Dédicace à Jean de Bye; *6–**1, Préface du traducteur; **1v–**6, Préface d'Erasme dated 10 Juin, 1508; A1–N4v. Text; N5–N8, Catalogue des livres. . . ; N8v–N12v, Nouvel Atlas ou Table des nouvelles cartes. . .
*2v and **6v are blank

Signatures
$7 signed to the right except in the second gathering of the preliminaries where **1–**4 are signed. Where footnotes are present the signatures appear above the notes. A typical page without notes contains 29 lines.

Catchwords
On every page. At *5 the catchword "la" is misprinted "le".

Running-title
L'ELOGE / DE LA FOLIE.

Watermarks
None visible

Plates, etc.
Two engraved frontispieces, six engraved folding plates and 75 half-page engravings distributed throughout the text. The dedication to Jean de Bye has an engraved headpiece of his coat of arms. Other ornaments include decorated initials J, E, R and O at *3, *6, **1v and A1, a tailpiece of a bowl of fruit and flowers at **1, and a headpiece at A1. The first front. shows portraits of Erasmus, More, and Holbein, and is Signed "F. Bleiswyck fecit." This is the only signed engraving. The other front. is a half-title above and to the side of which three females display, amongst other features, a list of human vices.
The six folding plates show:
A5/A6 − a fool unwittingly stepping into a tray of loaves
B8/B9 − two satyrs and a dancing, one-eyed, satyr-like creature
C9/C10 − two horses representing La Force and L'Esprit
E7/E8 − a hunting scene

I9/I10 — Apollo killing the children of Niobe
N4/N5 — Folly at the end of her discourse to an audience of fools
The 75 half-page engravings show:

A1v — La Folie qui parle
A2   — L'ancien Sophiste
A6   — Un Midas en pourpre
A10 — Jupiter nourri par une chèvre
A10v — Le Stoïcien près d'une femme charmante
B2   — La peine de nourrir et d'élever un enfant
B4v — Un vieux sujet de La Folie bien nourri
B6v — Bacchus
B11v — Divertissement amoureux
C3   — Le cocu
C4v — L'amour propre
C8   — Socrate
C10 — La grande et grosse bête nommée, le Vulgaire
D2   — Un méchant Prince
D6   — Un vieux fou galant
D7   — Une vieille amoureuse
D10v — Un médecin
D11v — Le Légiste
E3   — Un amateur des fous
E5   — Une femme et un bouffon
E10 — Les joueurs de profession
E11v — Dévotion avant l'image de St. Christophe
F1v — St. Bernard et le Diable
F4   — Un gentilhomme
F5   — Un fou qui règle sa pompe funèbre
F6   — Un fou infatué de sa noble race
F8   — Un fou qui fait profession de la littérature
F10 — Deux sots qui se donnent de l'encens
F12 — Un mauvais et pitoyable tableau
G2   — Jupiter en courroux contre l'humanité
G4   — L'adorateur des tableaux et des statues
G6   — L'amateur de dormir et de ne rien faire
G7v — Le pélerin fou qui abandonne sa famille
G8v — Un grammairien ou maître d'école
G11 — Un orateur
H2v — Un jurisconsulte ou chicaneur
H3v — Un sophiste ou philosophe
H4   — Un astrologue
H5   — Le théologien Scot
H6   — Un prétendu savant en théologie
H10 — Ouvrage sans fin ou la toile de Pénélope

H11v — Les ergoteurs s'imaginant être Atlas
I1v — Vulcain et Jupiter accouchant de Pallas
I2v — Un théologien ergoteur
I3v — Un moine mendiant
I4v — Un moine ne touchant l'argent qu'avec deux doigts
I5v — Un Bernardin
I7 — Enée appaisant Cerbère
I10v — Le monstre chimère
I12 — L'âne de la fable
K3 — La vie d'un roi
K3v — Un grand de la cour
K5v — La vie des évêques
K7 — L'image d'un cardinal
K8 — Le souverain pontife
K9v — Une âme délivrée à tous les diables par les papes
K11v — Un prêtre armé par le dîme
L1v — La Fortune et Timothé, duc d'Athènes
L2v — Erasme
L3v — Le prince glorieux
L4v — Horace ou le pourceau épicurien
L6 — L'esprit de Scot traîtant la matière
L6v — L'ecclésiaste
L8 — Salomon parlant des fous
L10v — Nicolas de Lyre
L12 — L'âne à la lyre, interprétant Saint Luc
M2 — Un apôtre armé de pied à cap
M3 — L'image d'une dispute de théologie
M5 — Néron le meurtrier de Sénèque
M6v — St. Jean Baptiste sous le nom d'agneau
M8 — David reconnaissant sa folie
M9 — Le vieillard fou livré à la piété chrétienne
M11v — Le mondain et le pieux
M12v — St. Bernard buvant de l'huile pour du vin
N3 — Un saint vivant hors de lui-même

Comments

This is almost certainly the first edition. At **1 there is an erratum note
about the misprint "Puienssance" for "puissance", p. 18, 1. 29. This error is
corrected in subsequent editions. The first gathering of the preliminaries is
unusual in that it has only ten leaves but is signed as if it had twelve. It is
possible that the publisher intended to include two leaves for the *Privilège*
which is announced on the title-page but which was not granted until
May 17, 1715, or the two frontispieces could be part of the gathering, as I
have suggested in the alternative formula.

As is noted in the *Bibliotheca Belgica* (E 899), the engravings based on Holbein bear only moderate resemblance to the originals.

Locations
Amsterdam (U), Baltimore (JH), Copenhagen (R), Ghent (U), Greifswald (U), The Hague (R), Iowa (U), La Rochelle (M), Leiden (U), Rostock (U), Rotterdam (M), Stockholm (R), Sydney (U), Toronto (RC), Troyes (M)

2. [red and black] / L'ELOGE / DE / LA FOLIE, / Composé en forme de Declamation / Par / ERASME DE ROTTERDAM. / *Avec quelques Notes de* LISTRIUS, / & les belles figures de HOLBE- / NIUS: le tout sur l'Original / de l'Academie de Bâle. / *Piéce qui representant au naturel* l'HOMME / *tout défiguré par la* SOTISE, *lui aprend* / *agreablement à rentrer dans le* / *bon* / *Sens & dans la Raison.* / Traduite nouvellement en François / Par Monsieur GUEUDEVILLE. / [vignette of branches with leaves and flowers] / A LEIDE, / Chez PIERRE VANDER AA, 1713. / [rule] / Avec Privilege.
In red: L'ELOGE / LA FOLIE, / ERASME DE ROTTERDAM. / Par Monsieur GUEUDEVILLE. / PIERRE VANDER AA,

Formula
12° *^{12}(− *1 and *12)**^{6} A–N^{12}
pp. [32] 1–312. 36, 76, 96 misnumbered 38, 75, 90. 111 printed 11 à

Contents
*2, title; *3–*5, Dédicace à Jean de Bye; *6–**1, Préface du traducteur; **1v–**6v, Préface d'Erasme; A1–N4v, text; N5–N8, Catalogue des livres...;
N8v–N12v, Nouvel Atlas ou Table des nouvelles cartes... *2v is blank

Signatures
$7 signed to the right. *7, **2, **4 not signed. Signatures above the notes. 29 lines per page without notes.

Catchwords
On every page

Running-title
L'ELOGE / DE LA FOLIE. except at N4v which has L'ELOGE DE LA FOLIE. L'ELOGE is misprinted L'ELGOE at D7v, E12v, G11v, H8v, and K7v. At B7v it appears as L'EEOGE, and as L'ELOG at I7v. At M2 the D is missing from DE.

Watermarks
I ♡ DUVAL

Plates, etc.
Two engraved fronts, six engraved folding plates and 75 half-page engravings. An engraved headpiece at *3. Other ornaments include decorated

initials J, E, R and O at *3, *6, **1v and A1, a tailpiece at **1, and a headpiece at A1.

Comments

This is a counterfeit of the first edition. The engravings are poor copies of
those found in the first edition. In the Avis du libraire of the 1715 reissue
of the second Van der Aa edition, Van der Aa describes this counterfeit as:

> . . . imprimée à Paris, en grand douze, avec figures; et celui qui l'a imprimée,
> pour mieux couvrir son jeu, donner plus de crédit à son impression, et
> tromper plus facilement le monde, a eu l'imprudence de mettre mon nom
> sur le titre, et de l'imprimer avec ma dédicace, et à la fin le catalogue des
> livres, cartes géographiques, et estampes nouvellement imprimées chez moi. En
> quoi j'ai d'autant plus sujet de me plaindre de lui, que par une injustice tout
> à fait criante, il ne me prive pas seulement du fruit de mon impression, mais
> qu'il met encore sur mon compte tout ce qu'il y a de fautif et de défectueux
> dans son édition. . . elle est imprimée avec un vieux caractère tout barbouillé
> et tout usé, qu'elle se trouve toute défigurée, par une infinité de fautes
> d'impression, jusque là qu'on y trouve non seulement des mots mais même
> des lignes tout entières de manque; on y trouve plusieurs renvois à des
> figures qui ne s'y trouvent pas, et qui devraient s'y trouver, comme
> entr'autres aux pages 10. 40. 66. 111. 210. 296. On en voit d'autres qui sont
> placées tout de travers, comme entr'autres celle de la page 196 qui devrait
> être à la page 112, et celle de la page 112 qui devrait être à la page 196. On
> en trouve d'autres qui au lieu d'être représentées vers la main droite comme
> elles le sont dans mon Edition, y sont mises vers la main gauche dans la
> sienne, comme entr'autres aux pages 129. 288. etc. Il y en a d'autres qui
> ne sont représentées qu'à demi et où l'on a oublié ce qu'il y avait d'essentiel,
> comme entr'autres à celle de la page 276 où l'on a oublié L'*Agnus Dei*; et à
> l'égard de toutes les figures en général, on peut dire que ce n'est qu'un vrai
> barbouillage en comparaison des miennes.'

Despite the fact that no copy I have seen displays all the errors described by
Van der Aa I am inclined to believe he was referring to this edition. It is
possible that he saw a copy containing an unusual number of uncorrected
gatherings. In the copy at Cornell, for example, at *3v, 1.2, the words
"pas inconnue" are misspaced and printed "pasi connue". This error of
spacing is not present in the copy at Montpellier. In the copies I have seen
the type certainly corresponds to Van der Aa's characterization as "un vieux
caractère tout barbouillé et tout usé". There are examples of carelessness
throughout. Apart from errors in pagination, individual digits are displaced
as, for example, in the copy at Nantes where, on p. 143, the last digit is
displaced downwards; on p. 196, the first digit is similarly displaced; on
p. 194, the first digit is displaced upwards. G9v, 11.1–2 has triom-que for
triom-phe; G10v, 1.20 has conseilleres for conseillers; the folding plate at
p. 40 (B8/B9) is inscribed "Fig. 8, p. 21". The lamb is missing from the

engraving of p. 276 (M6v). The ornaments are different from those in the first edition. Van der Aa claims that this counterfeit was published in Paris, and perhaps the name DUVAL, the French paper maker, found in the watermark, lends support to this claim, although it should be remembered that many Dutch printers used French paper.

This counterfeit edition is not described in the *Bibliotheca Belgica* but it does appear in the *National Union Catalog Pre-1956 Imprints,* vol. 161, p.158.

For examples of French pirates using Dutch compositorial practices see my article "The *Voyages et avantures de Jaques Massé* and the problem of the first edition" *Australian Journal of French Studies,* VII No. 3 (1970), 271–288, and, in the same issue, D.W. Smith "Helvétius, Voltaire and a French Pirate: Michelin of Provins", 290–291.

Locations
Cornell (U), Limoges (M), London (BL), Montpellier (M), Nantes (M), Paris (Ma), Toronto (TF)

3. L'ELOGE / DE / LA FOLIE, / Composé en forme de Declamation / Par / ERASME DE ROTTERDAM: / Avec quelques Notes de LISTRIUS, / *Piéce qui, representant au naturel l'* HOM- / ME *tout defiguré par la* SOTISE, *lui* / *aprend agreablement à rentrer dans* / *le bon Sens & dans la Raison*: / Traduite nouvellement en François / Par Mr. GUEUDEVILLE. / [vignette of bowl of fruit and flowers] / A NANTES, / Chez JACOB COURTOIS, / Ruë du Pont. / [rule] / M D C XIII.

Formula
12° *¹² A–L¹² M⁸
pp. [*24*] 1–279. 145 misnumbered 125.

Contents
*1, title; *2–*5v, Préface du traducteur; *6–*12, Préface d'Erasme; A1–M8, text. &1v, *12v and M8v are blank.

Signatures
$7 signed to the right. Signatures above notes. 27 lines per page without notes.

Catchwords
On every page

Running-title
L'ELOGE / DE LA FOLIE.

Watermarks
None legible

Plates, etc.
No plates. A headpiece and decorated initial O at A1.

Comments
In the 1715 reissues of his second edition (see No. 4), Van der Aa, in the Avis du libraire, describes this edition as:

"Sans figures, en petit douze, imprimée à Amsterdam, chez un nommé. . . qui ne m'est pas inconnu, mais qui pour mieux couvrir sa fourberie et se mettre à couvert des peines qu'il mériterait qu'on lui infligeât, a mis sur le titre A NANTES, chez JACOB COURTOIS, *Ruë du Pont.* M D CC XIII. . . l'Edition du prétendu Jacob Courtois est telle, et pour le papier, et le caractère, et la correction, qu'elle ne mérite pas d'être montrée aux honnêtes gens."

We are dealing here with a piracy which, since Van der Aa was in a position to know, must have been published in Amsterdam. This is another example of the animosity between Van der Aa and the other publishers that I referred to earlier.

Locations
Rotterdam (M), Toronto (RC)

4(a) [red and black] / L'ELOGE / DE LA FOLIE, / Composé en forme de Declamation / Par / ERASME DE ROTTERDAM: / Avec quelques Notes de LISTRIUS, / & les belles figures de HOLBE- / NIUS: / le tout sur l'Original / de l'Academie de Bâle. / *Piéce qui, representant au naturel* l'HOMME / *tout defiguré par la* SOTISE, *lui* / *aprend agreablement à rentrer dans* / *le bon Sens & dans la Raison*: / Traduite nouvellement en François / Par Mr. GUEUDEVILLE. / [vignette of a vase of flowers] / A LEIDE, / Chez PIERRE VANDER Aa, 1713. / [rule, 26 mm] / Avec Privilége.
In red: L'ELOGE / LA FOLIE, / ERASME DE ROTTERDAM: / Par Mr. GUEUDEVILLE / PIERRE VANDER Aa,

Formula
$12°$ $*^{12}(-*1$ and $*12)$ $**^4$ $A-M^{12}N^8$
pp. [*28*] 1–304

Contents
*2, title; *3–*5v, Dédicace à Jean de Bye; *6–**1, Préface du traducteur; **1–**4v, Préface d'Erasme; A1–N4v, text; N5–N6, Catalogue des livres. . . ; N6v–N8v, Nouvel Atlas ou Table des nouvelles cartes. . . *2v is blank

Signatures
$7 signed to the right and placed above the notes. **1–**3 are signed. 29 lines per page without notes.

Catchwords
On every page

Running-title
L'ELOGE / DE LA FOLIE, except at N4v which reads, L'ELOGE DE LA FOLIE.

Watermarks
None visible

Plates, etc.
Two engraved fronts, six engraved folding plates and 75 half-page engravings. There is also an engraved headpiece at *3. Other ornaments include decorated initials J, E, R, and O at *3, *6, **1v and A1, and a headpiece at A1.

Comments
This is the second edition by Van der Aa. Except for the absence of a tailpiece at **1, the engravings and ornaments are identical to those found in the first edition.
This second Van der Aa edition is not described in the *Bibliotheca Belgica*. It is this edition, and not the first, that was reissued in 1715 and 1717.

Locations
Valenciennes (M), Wurzburg (U)

4(b) L'ELOGE / DE / LA FOLIE, / Composé en forme de Declamation, / *Par* / ERASME DE ROTTERDAM: Avec quelques Notes de LISTRIUS, / & les belles figures de HOLBENIUS: / le tout sur l'Original de / l'Academie de Bâle. / *Piéce qui, representant au naturel* l'HOMME / *tout defiguré par la* SOTISE, *lui aprend* / *agreablement à rentrer dans le bon Sens* / *& dans la* Raison: / Traduite nouvellement en François / Par Mr. GUEUDEVILLE. / *Derniere Edition, revûë, corrigée et augmentée de nouveau,* / *avec une* Table des matieres fort ample & tres-exacte. / [vignette of fruit and flowers suspended from a cross-beam, with a pendant on either side] / *A LEIDE,* / Chez PIERRE VANDER Aa, / *Marchand Libraire, demeurant dans l'Academie,* / [rule, 35 mm.] / M D C C X V. / Avec Privilége.
N.B. In some copies the rule has been placed after / Avec Privilége / and is followed by: / *Se vend aussi à* PARIS, *chez ETIENNE GANEAV,* / *Marchand Libraire.*

Comments
This is a reissue of 4(a) with a new title-page and additional preliminary materials. These occupy a new gathering ***^{10} (pp. 29–48) of which the first six leaves are signed. This new gathering contains: ***1–***2, Avis du libraire; ***3–***10, Table des matieres. ***2v and ***10v are blank.

It is at the end of the Avis du libraire that Van der Aa describes the two 1713 piracies already referred to. The rest of the Avis is as follows:

Ayant vendu la première impression de cet ouvrage, et jugé à propos de l'imprimer de nouveau, j'ai pris soin de rendre cette édition aussi exacte et aussi complète qu'il m'a été possible, en corrigeant plusieurs fautes qui s'étaient glissées dans l'édition précédente, et en y ajoutant une table alphabétique des matières contenues dans cet ouvrage; et pour cet effet je n'ai épargné ni peine ni dépense, ni travail, comme j'ai toujours fait à l'égard de tous les ouvrages qui sont sortis de dessous ma presse depuis l'espace de plus de 33 années que je fais le négoce de la librairie, et cela d'un côté, dans l'intention de faire plaisir aux savants et aux curieux, et de l'autre dans l'espérance de tirer quelque fruit de mes peines et mon travail.

Mais j'ai trouvé par une fâcheuse expérience qu'il y a dans le monde que trop de ces âmes envieuses qui, poussées par une basse et indigne jalousie, ne se font aucun scrupule de chercher tous les moyens imaginables pour frustrer par une injustice criante le possesseur légitime du fruit de ses veilles et de ses sueurs, et qui, pourvu qu'ils satisfassent leur désir insatiable de gagner, ne se font aucune peine d'agir contre toutes les règles de l'équité et de la justice, de fouler à leurs pieds la majesté des lois et du souverain, et d'arrêter en tant qu'en eux est, la naissance et la production des ouvrages agréables et utiles, dont personne n'entreprendrait jamais l'impression, s'il n'était assuré de jouir du fruit de la dépense qu'il a faite et de la peine qu'il a prise pour cela. C'est ce que j'avais déjà éprouvé autrefois dans plus d'une occasion, et entre autres, lorsque je publiai *Les Délices de L'Italie,* et l'*Introduction à l'Histoire par Puffendorf,* livres dont on m'a voulu enlever le droit de copie, en contrefaisant l'impression que j'en avais faite. Mais c'est ce que je n'ai jamais mieux éprouvé que dans ces derniers temps, où j'ai publié *L'Eloge de la Folie,* car l'édition de ce livre n'eût pas plutôt paru en public qu'on la contrefit dans deux endroits à la fois et dans deux formes différentes.

Van der Aa then goes on to describe the two piracies and finishes as follows:

Je ne crois pas qu'on puisse employer une meilleure précaution contre tant de mauvaise foi que de mettre sa signature à chaque nouvelle édition, c'est le remède que j'oppose à celle-ci. J'attends ici le *contrefacteur:* osera-t-il imiter aussi le paraphe? Ce serait se hasarder à encourir les peines ordonnées par les lois contre les falsificateurs de seing, et contre les faussaires.

In all the 1715 reissues I have seen Van der Aa has appended his autograph. It should be remembered that although the returns on high quality books could be diminished because of piracies, in a book such as the Gueudeville translation it is just as likely that the public's curiosity and desire to purchase would be stimulated by the knowledge that the book was in such demand that it had been pirated not only in The Netherlands but in France. In a sense, therefore, this Avis du libraire is also an advertisement for the book.

The title-page bearing the name Etienne Ganeau is not noted in the *Bibliotheca Belgica*. On p. 68 of the catalogue in A.M. Lottin, *Catalogue chronologique des libraires et des libraires-imprimeurs de Paris,* Paris 1789, Etienne Ganeau, who was in business from 1695–173?, is identified as the son of N. Ganeau, Huissier-Audiencier au Châtelet de Paris. Etienne Ganeau, who published the Jesuit *Journal de Trévoux,* had the title of Directeur de l'Imprimerie de Son Altesse Sérénissime Monseigneur Prince Souverain de Dombes. It is somewhat ironic that Ganeau should publish a journal in which Gueudeville would be severely attacked (see review of *L'Utopie,* vol. XVIII (April 1718) 81–108.

Locations
Brussels (R), Orléans (BC)

4(c) L'ELOGE / DE / LA FOLIE, / Composé en forme de Declamation, / *Par* / ERASME DE ROTTERDAM : / Avec quelques Notes de LISTRIUS, / & les belles figures de HOLBENIUS : / le tout sur l'Original de / l'Academie de Bâle. / *Piéce qui, representant au naturel* l'HOMME / *tout defiguré par la* SOTISE, *lui aprend* / *agreablement à rentrer dans le bon Sens* / *& dans la Raison :* / Traduite nouvellement en François / Par Mr. GUEUDEVILLE. / *Derniere Edition, revûë, corrigée & augmentée* / *de nouveau, avec une Table des matieres* / *fort ample & tres-exacte.* / [vignette of fruit and flowers suspended from a crossbeam, with a pendant on either side] / *A LEIDE,* / Chez PIERRE VANDER Aa, / *Marchand Libraire, Imprimeur Ordinaire* / *de l'Academie & de la Ville,* / *demeurant dans l'Academie.* / [rule] / M D C C X V. / Avec Privilége sous peine de 3000 florins d'amende & c. / contre les *Contrefacteurs.*

Formula
$12°\ \pi^2\ *^{12}(-\ *1, *2, *12)**^4\ ***^{10}\ A–M^{12}N^8$
pp. [*50*] 1–304.

Contents
π1, title; π1v–π2, Privilegie; *3–*5v, Dédicace à Jean de Bye; *6–**1, Préface du traducteur; **1–**4v, Préface d'Erasme; ***1–***2v, Avis du libraire; ***3–***10, Table des matières; A1–N4v, text; N5–N6, Catalogue des livres...; N6v–N8v, Nouvel Atlas ou Table des nouvelles cartes...; ***10v is blank.

Signatures
$7 signed to the right and placed above the notes. π2 missigned *2. **1–**3, ***1–***6 are signed.

Comments
This is a reissue of 4(b) that, for the first time, includes the *privilège* which is dated May 17 1715. The *privilège* is printed in Dutch under the heading

Privilegie. In order to accommodate this new material and still maintain the integrity of the other preliminaries, Van der Aa printed the title-page and *privilège* on conjugate leaves. A stub of what must have been *2 is seen between π2 and *3. This may be related to the cancel referred to in the description in the *Bibliotheca Belgica* of the 1717 reissue (E902).
A fleur de lis is discernible in the following plate at A5/A6.

Locations
Amiens (M), Boston (A), Geneva (U), Grenoble (M), Munich (S), Philadelphia (RF), Rotterdam (M), Stockholm (R), Strasbourg (U), Toronto (RC)

4(d) [red and black] / L'ELOGE / DE / LA FOLIE, / Composé en forme de Declamation, / *Par* / ERASME DE ROTTERDAM : / Avec quelques Notes de LISTRIUS, & les / belles figures de HOLBENIUS: & tout sur / l'Original de l'Academie de Bâle. / *Pièce qui, representant au naturel* / L'HOMME tout defiguré pas la SOTISE, / *Lui aprend agreablement à rentrer dans le bon* / *Sens & dans la Raison:* / Traduite nouvellement en François / Par Mr. GUEUDEVILLE. / *Derniere Edition, revûë, corrigée et augmentée* / *de nouveau, avec une Table des matieres* / *fort ample et tres-exacte.* / [vignette of monogram of publisher] / A AMSTERDAM, / Chez R. & G. WETSTEIN. 1717.
In red: L'ELOGE / LA FOLIE, / ERASME DE ROTTERDAM: / L'HOMME tout defiguré par la SOTISE, / Par Mr. GUEUDEVILLE. / Chez R. &. G. WETSTEIN. 1717.

Comments
Apart from the different title-page and the slightly longer *privilège,* occasioned by the transfer of the rights from Van der Aa to Wetstein, this is a reissue of 4(b). I have not seen a copy with the cancelled page of the *privilège* referred to in the *Bibliotheca Belgica* (E 902).

I have accepted the *Bibliotheca Belgica* classification of the title-page vignette as the monogram of Wetstein since this vignette does contain the initials RGW and it is associated with Wetstein publications. It should be remembered, however, that other publishers with whom the Wetsteins were associated also used this design. Pierre Mortier, for example also used this vignette (see the section on Amsterdam in vol. I of Van der Haeghen, *Marques typographiques. . . des Pays-Bas,* Gand, 1894) and David Mortier used it on the title-pages of the *Bibliothèque ancienne et moderne.*

Locations
Amsterdam (U), Illinois (U), Newark (P) Rotterdam (M)

5. [red and black] / L'ELOGE / DE LA / FOLIE, / Composé en forme de Déclamation, par / ERASME, / Et traduit par Mr. / GUEUDEVILLE. / Avec les Notes de GERARD LISTRE, / les belles Figures de HOLBEIN : / Le tout sur l'Original de l'Académie de Basle. / NOUVELLE EDITION, /

Revue avec soin, & mise dans un meilleur ordre. | [engraved vignette of Minerva surrounded by *putti* engaged in various activities. Signed *B. Picart direxit*) | *A AMSTERDAM,* | Chez FRANÇOIS L'HONORE'. | [rule] | M. DCC. XXVIII. | *Avec Privilege.*
In red: L'ELOGE | ERASME, | GUEUDEVILLE. | NOUVELLE EDITION, | Chez FRANÇOIS L'HONORE'.

Formula
8° *⁸ (− *8) **⁶ (− **6) A–P⁸ Q⁴ R²
pp. [*24*] [1] 2–234 [*18*].

Contents
*1, title; *2–*3, Privilegie; *3v, Avertissement sur cette nouvelle édition; *4–**1v, Préface du traducteur; **2– **5v, Préface d'Erasme; A1–P5v, text; P6–R2v, Table des matières. *1v is blank.

Signatures
$5 signed centrally. **1–**5 are signed. The signatures are above the notes except at B1 and B5 where they are level with them. 31 lines per page without notes.

Catchwords
On every page.

Running-title
L'ELOGE | DE LA FOLIE., except at P5v which reads L'ELOGE DE LA FOLIE.

Watermarks
Not sufficiently clear to be identified.

Plants, etc.
Two engraved fronts., six engraved folding plates and 75 half-page engravings. The six folding plates are found at A4/A5, B8/C1, D2/D3, F3/F4, L2/L3, P5/P6. The 75 half-page engravings are found at A1v, A2, A5, A7v, B1v, B3, B5v, B7, C2v, C5, C6v, D1v, D3, D6, E1, E2, E4v, E5, E8, F1v, F5, F6, F7v, G2, G2v, G3v, G5, G6v, G8, H2, H3v, H5, H6, H7, I1, I3v, I4v, I5v, I6, I6v, I7v, K2v, K4v, K5v, K6, K7, K7v, L1, L4, L5, L7v, L8, M1, M2, M3, M4v, M6v, M8, M8v, N1v, N2v, N3v, N4, N5, N7, N8v, O2, O3, O4v, O5v, O6v, O7v, P1v, P2v, P4v. There are decorated initials E, R, and O at *4, **2 and A1 respectively. There is an ornamental headpiece at A1.

Comments
The *privilège* to this edition reveals that the publication rights have once again been transferred, this time from Wetstein to L'Honoré. On this occasion the rights have been used to produce an edition that is not only different from earlier editions in composition but makes modifications to

the text. The basis for these modifications is set out in the *Avertissement sur cette nouvelle édition*:

Le public a rendu justice à la traduction que Mr. Gueudeville a faite de L'ELOGE DE LA FOLIE. Il y a reconnu ce génie né pour la fine plaisanterie et pour la satire: mais il s'est plaint de l'inexactitude du style. On a tâché de remédier à ce défaut, dans cette édition. Pour peu qu'on veuille se donner la peine de la comparer avec les éditions précédentes, on y trouvera des changements considérables. Ce n'est pas qu'on prétende avoir corrigé toutes les façons de parler vicieuses; il en échappe toujours quelqu'une: mais on croit avoir remédié au plus essentiel. D'ailleurs, si l'on avait fait de plus grands changements, ce n'aurait plus été Mr. Gueudeville: et c'est Mr. Gueudeville que le public demande. Voilà pourquoi l'on a eu grand soin de n'effacer aucun de ces traits qui le caractérisent: expressions figurées, hardies, mots hasardés, on lui a tout laissé: on ne lui a ôté que ce qui le défigurait. On se flatte que, si le livre a plu tel qu'il était, il plaira davantage encore après les corrections qu'on y a faites.

Sample modifications of text of earlier editions:

1728 – p. 6, 11.20–21	je ne puis assez admirer le procédé des hommes. . .
Earlier editions	je ne puis assez admirer les hommes. . .
1728 – p. 7, 1.7	Je suis donc réduite à me louer moi-même. . .
Earlier editions	Je suis dont réduite à me priser moi-même. . .
1728 – p. 10, 1.4	de nos jours
Earlier editions	dans cette partie de notre temps
1728 – p. 12, 1.25	ce boiteux de Vulcain
Earlier editions	ce boiteux et forgeron de Vulcain
1728 – p. 12, 1.27	Je suis fille de plaisir
Earlier editions	Je suis une fille de plaisir
1728 – p. 17, 11.28–29	Mais pourquoi ne pas dire tout? Aussi bien c'est ma manière de parler librement.
Earlier editions	Et pourquoi, selon ma manière, ne parlerai-je pas plus franchement?
1728 – p. 24, 11.8–9	Mais, par un effet de ma bonté, libre de tout chagrin, de toute inquiétude. . .
Earlier editions	Mais, hors de tout chagrin, de toute inquiétude par ma bonté. . .
1728 – p. 24, 1.25	je n'y trouve qu'une différence
Earlier editions	je n'y trouve qu'une exception
1728 – pp. 24–25, 11.31–1	tout se ressemble dans ces deux âges
Earlier editions	tout convient entre ces deux âges
1728 – p. 25, 11.6–7	et qu'on mette dans la balance
Earlier editions	et qu'il compare ce bon office que je rends aux hommes

1728 — p. 25, 11.17—18	je fais rentrer l'homme dans le meilleur et dans le plus heureux âge de la vie
Earlier editions	je rétablis l'homme dans les meilleurs, et dans les plus heureux jours de sa vie
1728 — p. 27, 11.1—2	un proverbe fameux
Earlier editions	un proverbe renommé
1728 — p. 27, 11.4—5	la fâcheuse vieillesse
Earlier editions	la mauvaise vieillesse
1728 — p. 30, 1.24	Laissons là les Divinités amies de la joie
Earlier editions	Laissons là les Divinités de joie
1728 — p. 32, 1.5	Silène, ce vieux fou amoureux
Earlier editions	ce vieux fou et amoureux Silène
1728 — p. 32, 11.10—11	ils écoutent de toutes leurs oreilles
Earlier editions	ils sont attentifs de toutes leurs oreilles
1728 — p. 33, 11.21—22	voilà jusqu'où s'étend son pouvoir
Earlier editions	c'est tout ce qui est en son pouvoir
1728 — p. 34, 11.21—22	il multiplie ses vices, il double ses défauts
Earlier editions	il multiplie son vice, il double son défaut
1728 — p. 35, 11.1—2	si elles veulent peser les choses à la balance de l'équité
Earlier editions	si elles veulent peser le fait à la juste balance
1728 — p. 335, 1.11	des marques prématurées de vieillesse
Earlier editions	des marques avancées de la vieillesse

It will be seen from the above examples that, while some of the modifications are substantial, most of them are of a minor stylistic nature. After page 35 the changes become less frequent and the text closely follows that of the earlier editions.

In most copies the engravings appear to be identical to those found in the first edition. In some copies a few of the engravings appear to have been retouched. In all copies I have seen the engraved fronts. have fancy borders. In some copies the plate with the engraved portraits of Erasmus, More and Holbein, appears not as a front. but later in the preliminaries.

Locations
Besançon (M), Brussels (R), Cambridge (U), Grenoble (M), Heidelberg (U), Leiden (U), London (BL), Paris (BN), Pennsylvania (U), Rochester (U), Rotterdam (M), Rouen (M), Strasbourg (U), Toronto (SMC), Valenciennes (M), Yale (B)

6. [black and red] / L'ELOGE / DE LA FOLIE, / Composé en forme de Déclamation, par / ERASME, / Et traduit par Mr. / GUEUDEVILLE. / Avec les Notes de GERARD LISTRE, / & les belles Figures de HOLBEIN: / Le tout sur l'Original de l'Académie de Bâle. / *Pièce qui representant au naturel* l'HOMME *tout* / *défiguré par la* SOTISE, *lui aprend agréablement* /

à rentrer dans le bon Sens & dans la Raison. | NOUVELLE EDITION. | *Revûë avec soin & mise dans un meilleur ordre.* | [woodcut vignette of Minerva surrounded by *putti* engaged in various activities] | *A AMSTERDAM* | Chez FRANÇOIS L'HONORE'. | [rule broken into four parts] | M.DCC.XXVIII.
In red: DE LA FOLIE, | ERASME, | GUEUDEVILLE. | NOUVELLE EDITION. | Chez FRANÇOIS L'HONORE'.

Formula
12° A–2I⁴/⁸ 2K² (–2K2)

pp. [*26*] 1–340 [*20*]. 222 and 223 misnumbered 121 and 123.

Contents
A1, title; A2–A2v, Privilegie; A3–A3v, Avertissement sur cette nouvelle édition; A4–B5v, Préface du traducteur; B6–C1v, Préface d'Erasme; C2–2H3v, text; 2H4–2K1v, Table des matières. A1v is blank

Signatures
Half the leaves of each gathering are signed to the right. In the preliminaries A3 is missigned *3. 2I3 is not signed. The signatures appear above the notes. There are 26 lines per page without notes.

Catchwords
Between gatherings

Running-title
L'ELOGE / DE LA FOLIE.

Watermarks
JACQUES DUVAL

Plates, etc.
Two fronts., six folding plates and 75 half plates. The fronts. and folding plates are engravings. The 75 half plates were woodcuts of which 29 are unsigned and the remainder signed P.L.S. or some variant such as P.S., L.S., or P.L.S.F. Other ornaments include headpieces at A3, A4, B6, C2; tail-pieces at A3v, B5v; decorated initials, L, E, R, O, at A3, A4, B6 C2. There is a fancy rule at C2.

Comments
This edition reproduces the revised text of edition 5. Although the name and address of L'Honoré appear on the title-page, it was probably published in France. The unsigned woodcut vignette is a copy of the Picart engraving, the watermark is of a French papermaker, and the initials P.L.S. stand for the well-known French engraver Pierre Le Sueur (le jeune), 1669–1750 (see E. Bénézit, *Dictionnaire critique et documentaire des peintres...*, Paris 1924, vol. III, p. 112.
According to the *National Union Catalog Pre-1956 Imprints,* vol. 161,

p. 158, this edition was printed in Rouen, but no explanation is given for the identification of this location.

The engravings and woodcuts are poor copies of the originals. In some copies the plate with the portraits of Erasmus, More, and Holbein is found opposite C2.

This edition is not described in the *Bibliotheca Belgica*.

Locations
Amiens (M), Dallas (SMU), Rotterdam (M), Stockholm (R)

7. [red and black] / L'ELOGE / DE LA / FOLIE, / Composé en forme de Déclamation, par / ERASME, / Et traduit par Mr. / GUEUDEVILLE. / Avec les Notes de GERARD LISTRE, / Et les belles Figures de HOLBEIN. / *Le tout sur l'Original de l'Académie de Basle*. / NOUVELLE EDITION, / *Revue, augmentée, & mise dans un meilleur ordre*. / [engraved vignette of Minerva surrounded by *putti* engaged in various activities. Signed *B. Picart direxit*] / *A AMSTERDAM,* / Chez FRANÇOIS L. HONORÉ. / M.DCC.XXXI.
In red: L'ELOGE / FOLIE, / ERASME, / GUEUDEVILLE. / NOUVELLE EDITION, / Chez FRANÇOIS L'HONORÉ.

Formula
$8°$ $*^6$ $**^6(-**6)$ A$-$P^8 Q^{4}R^2
pp. [*22*] [1] 2$-$234 [*18*]

Contents
*1, title; *2$-$*2v, Avertissement sur cette nouvelle édition; *3$-$**1v, Préface du traducteur; **2$-$**5v, Préface d'Erasme; A1$-$P5v, text; P6$-$R2, Table des matières. *1v and R2v are blank

Signatures
·$5 signed centrally. *2$-$*4, **1$-$**5 and Q1$-$Q4 are signed. Signatures are above the notes except at A1, A2, A3, A4, where they are below, and at F1 where the signature is level with the note. 31 lines per page without notes.

Catchwords
On every page

Running-title
L'ELOGE / DE LA FOLIE. except at P5v which reads L'ELOGE DE LA FOLIE.

Watermarks
Not sufficiently clear to be identified. There is some animal which could be a lion or an eagle and which has claws or talons. There are also letters that look like I ♡ LEGR

Plates, etc.

Two engraved fronts., six engraved folding plates, 75 half page engravings. There is a headpiece at A1, signed *Papillon fecit*; tailpieces at *2v, **2v, **5v, P5v, R2, and decorated initials E, R, J, at *3, **2, A1.

Comments

This is the second edition of L'Honoré and is based on his first edition of 1728. This second edition provides further modifications of the text. The justification for these additional modifications is explained in the *Avertissement sur cette nouvelle édition*:

Le succès qu'ont eu les ouvrages de Mr. *Gueudeville*, et en particulier sa traduction de l'ELOGE DE LA FOLIE, doit être uniquement attribué au talent qu'il avait de badiner agréablement sur toutes sortes de sujets, et au tour original de ses pensées et de ses expressions. L'élégance et la pureté du style n'est point ce qu'on y doit chercher. On avait commencé de remédier à ce défaut dans l'édition de 1728: mais, comme on en convient dans l'Avertissement, il restait encore bien des façons de parler vicieuses, qui échappent toujours dans une première révision. Celle-ci a été faite avec beaucoup plus de soin. Outre plusieurs *Additions* qu'on a cru nécessaires, on a tâché de n'y rien laisser de choquant; et l'on croit enfin avoir mis l'ouvrage dans l'état où le public aurait souhaité de la voir dès la première édition.

Sample modifications of text of 1728

The most important change occurs in the opening sentence which the 1728 edition had left unaltered and which read:

Ordinairement ma réputation est déchirée par la médisance; et il n'y a pas jusqu'à mes favoris, qui ne parlent mal de moi: c'est de quoi je suis bien informée.

This is now replaced by two new sentences:

J'entreprends aujourd'hui de repousser les traits empoisonnés de la Médisance, qui se plaît à m'attaquer. Je sais jusqu'où va son acharnement contre moi; et que Favoris-mêmes ne rougissent point de me déchirer.

The other major change is the insertion of a completely new paragraph at F5v. This section, which must be one of the "additions" referred to in the *Avertissement*, seems to derive neither from Erasmus nor Gueudeville, and reads:

Que dirai-je de ceux qui, après avoir
. . . . commencé par être dupes,
Finissent par être fripons?

Les rangerai-je parmi mes Sujets. Pourquoi non? N'est-ce pas une folie, que de perdre son argent en dupe? et n'en est-ce pas aussi, que d'espérer de jouir en paix de ce qu'on a acquis par la fourberie?

Another "addition" appears in the form of a footnote at D5. Minor modifications include:
the substitution of "et" for "enfin" (p. 2, 1.7), and the elimination of "dans vos places" (p. 3, 1.4). On p. 4:
Caverne becomes Antre
tout prend une nouvelle couleur becomes tout prend une face nouvelle
sur vos personnes becomes sur vous
vous-mêmes becomes les mêmes
On p. 29 la vieille Comédie becomes l'ancienne Comédie (this change also appears in the note)
Minor changes of this nature occur up to F8 after which the text appears to follow exactly that of 1728. The engravings in this edition are the same as those found in the 1728 edition except that the title-page vignette is slightly different. The plate with the engraved portraits is usually found later in the preliminaries and frequently at A1. The designer of the headpiece at A1 was probably Jean-Michel Papillon (1698—1776) of the famous family of engravers (see Bénézit, *op. cit.,* p. 423). This edition was reviewed in 1732 by La Barre de Beaumarchais, *Lettres sérieuses et badines,* vol. 6, p. 209:

On a redonné au public la traduction française de *L'Eloge de la Folie (A Amsterdam,* chez François l'Honoré et se trouve à La Haye, chez Jean van Duren, 1731 in 8, 234 p. sans les pièces préliminaires et la Table) et j'en suis bien aise... Je voudrais seulement qu'on eût retranché de cette édition-ci les notes puériles et triviales de *Listre* et les planches mal-gravées d'après les desseins d'*Holbein.* Cet attirail ne sert qu'à la renchérir.

Locations
Amsterdam (U), Carpentras (I), Chicago (U), The Hague (R), Heidelberg (U), Illinois (U), Leiden (U), London (BL), Michigan (U), Paris (Ma), Princeton (U), Rotterdam (M), Stockholm (R), Utrecht (U)

8. [red and black] / L'ELOGE / DE / LA FOLIE, / *COMPOSÉ* / En forme de Declamation / PAR ERASME, / *ET TRADUIT* / PAR Mr. GUEUDEVILLE. / Avec les Notes de GERARD LISTRE, / & les belles Figures de HOLBEIN. / Le tout sur l'Original de l'Académie de Basle. / NOUVELLE EDITION; / *Revûë avec soin, & mise dans un meilleur ordre.* / [vignette of a bowl of fruit and flowers] / *A AMSTERDAM,* / Chez FRANÇOIS L'HONORE'. / [rule] / M. DCC. XXXI.
In red: L'ELOGE / LA FOLIE, / *COMPOSÉ* / PAR ERASME, / *ET TRADUIT* / PAR Mr. GUEUDEVILLE. / NOUVELLE EDITION; / FRANÇOIS L'HONORE'.

Formula
$12° \, \pi^2 \, *^8 \, **^4 \, \text{A}–2\text{C}^{8/4} \, 2\text{D}^4$
pp. [*28*] [1] 2–230

Contents
$\pi 1$, half title; $\pi 2$, title; *1–*6v, Préface du traduction; *7–**4, Préface d'Erasme; **4v, Avertissement sur cette nouvelle édition; A1–2B4v, text; 2B5–2D4v, Table des matières. $\pi 1$v and $\pi 2$v are blank

Signatures
Half the leaves of each gathering are signed to the right. Signatures are above the notes. 29 lines per page without notes.

Catchwords
On every page

Running title
L'ELOGE / DE LA FOLIE.

Watermarks
Grapes, fleur de lis P ♡ G

Plates
Two engraved plates, six engraved folding plates, 75 half-page engravings. Ornaments include a headpiece at A1, a tailpiece at *6, and decorated initials E, R, O, at *1, *7 and A1.

Comments
This edition is probably a piracy with a false imprint. If it had really been published by L'Honoré it would be hard to explain why this edition follows the text of the 1728 instead of the 1731 L'Honoré edition. The title-page vignette is not one associated with L'Honoré. According to the *National Union Catalog Pre-1956 Imprints,* this is a "counterfeit edition, with fictitious imprint, printed at Paris". No explanation is offered. The initials in the watermark have been identified by E. Heawood, *Watermarks, mainly of the 17th and 18th centuries,* Hilversum, 1950 (no. 2980), as of Parisian origin. The engravings are copies of the originals.

In H. Cohen, *Guide de l'amateur de livres à gravures du XVIIIe siècle,* 6ème édition, Paris, 1912, p. 348, there is confusion between the two 1731 editions. There is cited a 1731 edition with a title-page vignette by B. Picart, but described as a duodecimo with 320 pages. This could be explained only if the title-page of the piracy had been replaced by that of the genuine L'Honoré edition of 1731.

This 1731 piracy is not described in the *Bibliotheca Belgica.* A copy at the Enoch Pratt Free Library, Baltimore, has the frontispiece, half-title, title and preliminaries of this edition, but is then made up of gatherings from this edition (A1–C8, N1–V4) and edition no. 9 (G1–Q8, 2C4–2I8).

To complicate matters further, gatherings 2E, 2F and 2G are bound incorrectly in the order 2G, 2F, 2E. The bizarre pagination that results from the above is as follows: [1] 2–40, 47–166, 145–240, 277–294, 319–334, 311–318, 295–310, 335–340. I am grateful to Mrs. Lyn Hart of the Enoch Pratt Free Library for allowing me to examine this unusual copy.

Locations
Baltimore (JH), Brussels (R), Paris (BN), Rotterdam (M), Tours (M)

9. [black and red] / L'ELOGE / DE LA FOLIE, / Composé en forme de Déclamation, par / ERASME, / Et traduit par Mr. / GUEUDEVILLE. / Avec les Notes de GERARD LISTRE, / & les belles figures de HOLBEIN: / Le tout sur l'Original de l'Académie de Bâle. / *Pièce qui represente au naturel* l'HOMME *tout* / *défiguré par la* SOTISE, *lui aprend agreablement* / *à rentrer dans le bon Sens & dans la Raison.* / NOUVELLE EDITION. / *Revûë avec soin, & mise dans un meilleur ordre* / [woodcut vignette emblematic of the printing industry and surmounted by the device – PRESSA RESURGET] / *A AMSTERDAM,* / Chez FRANÇOIS L'HONORE'. / [broken rule] / M.DCC.XXXV.
In red: DE LA FOLIE, / ERASME, / GUEUDEVILLE. / NOUVELLE EDITION. / Chez FRANÇOIS L'HONORE'.

Formula
12° A–2I$^{4/8}$
pp. [*26*] 1–340 [*18*]

Contents
A1, half-title; A2 title. A3–A3v, Avertissement sur cette nouvelle édition; A4–B5v, Préface du traducteur; B6–C1v, Préface d'Erasme; C2–2H3v, text; 2H4–2I8v, Table des matières. A1v and A2v are blank.

Signatures
Half the leaves of each gathering are signed to the right. A3 is missigned *3. 26 lines per page without notes.

Catchwords
Between gatherings

Running-title
L'ELOGE / DE LA FOLIE.

Watermarks
JACQUES DUVAL DE ROUEN

Plates, etc.
Two engraved fronts., six engraved folding plates, and 75 half-page woodcuts. There are headpieces at A4, B6, C2; tailpieces at A3v, B5v; decorated initials L, R, O at A3, B6, C2.

Comments

This edition appears to be another one with a false imprint. It is modelled very closely on the 1728 edition (no. 6). The compositorial and ortho-graphical practices, the engravings and woodcuts are those found in the earlier edition. The paper bears the same watermark with the added location of the papermaker. The text follows that of the 1728 revisions and not the 1731 revisions. The text of the title-page follows that of editions before 1728. There are strong indications, therefore, that it is another piracy produced in France, perhaps in Rouen.

According to the *Bibliotheca Belgica* (E905) this edition could well be a Dutch piracy made to look like a French one. The reason given is that the title-page vignette with the device, PRESSA RESURGET, is associated with the Rotterdam publishers Fritsch and Böhm whose monogram F B is, apparently, discernible in the vignette.

The *Bibliotheca Belgica* lists only 74 woodcuts and questions the presence of the designer, Pierre Le Sueur, in The Netherlands at that time, by casting doubt on the reliability of the dates 1699–1750, usually ascribed to his life. A similar doubt exists about the dates of L'Honoré himself who was born in 1673/74 but whose date of death is unknown. I.H. van Eeghen points out that publications under his name appeared from 1703–1748 but there is no evidence that he was alive up to that time (see *De Amsterdamse Boekhandel*, vol. III, pp. 208–211)

Locations

Amsterdam (U), Geneva (U), Paris (BN), Rotterdam (M)

10. L'ELOGE / DE LA / FOLIE, / Composé en forme de Déclamation, / Par ERASME. / *ET TRADUIT* / Par Monsieur GUEUDEVILLE. / Avec les Notes de GERARD LISTRE. / *Le tout sur l'Original de l'Académie de Basle.* / NOUVELLE EDITION. / *Revûë & Augmentée.* / [vignette of an angle blowing a horn and carrying a fool's stick] / *A AMSTERDAM,* / Chez JEAN-PIERRE LUCAS. / M. DCC. XXXVIII.

Formula

$12°$ $\pi1$ $*^{10}$ A–H^{12} I^6 $*^6$ $**^8$ $(-**8)$
pp. [*22*] [1] 2–204 [*26*]

Contents

$\pi1$, title. $*1–*1v$, Avertissement sur cette nouvelle édition; $*2–*5$, Préface du traducteur; $*6–*10$, Préface d'Erasme; A1–I6v, text; 2$*–**7$, Table des matières; $\pi1v$, $*5v$, $*10v$, $**7v$ are blank.

Signatures

$6 signed to the right. A7 is missigned B7. C6 and E6 not signed. $*2–*4$ are signed. 31 lines per page without notes.

Catchwords
On every page

Watermarks
None visible

Plates, etc.
No plates. Headpiece at A1; tailpiece at *5; decorated initials E, R, J, at *2, *6, A1.

Comments
Like the 1713 edition with a false imprint (see no. 3) this is another piracy without illustrations. The imprint of Amsterdam, Jean-Pierre Lucas, is clearly false, since no such publisher existed. There was, however, an Etienne Lucas whose imprint was frequently used in pirated editions (see I.H. van Eeghen, *De Amsterdamse Boekhandel*, vol. III, p. 227. The real origins of this edition cannot be determined with certainty since the paper, ornament and compositorial practices offer no useful clues.
The text is based on that of the 1731 L'Honoré edition.

Locations
Berne (BN), Leeds (U), New York (UTS), Paris (BN), Rotterdam (M)

11. [black and red] / L'ELOGE / DE LA FOLIE, / Composé en forme de Déclamation par / ERASME, / Et traduit par Mr / GUEUDEVILLE, / Avec les Notes de GERARD LISTRE, / & les belles figures de HOLBEIN; / Le tout sur l'Original de l'Académie de Bâle. / *Piéce qui represente au naturel* l'HOMME *tout* / *défiguré par la* SOTISE, *lui aprend agréablement* / *à rentrer dans le bon Sens & dans la Raison.* / NOUVELLE EDITION. / *Revûë avec soin, & mise dans un meilleur ordre.* / [vignette of type ornament] / *A AMSTERDAM,* /Chez FRANÇOIS L'HONORE'. / M. DCC. XLI.
In red: DE LA FOLIE, / ERASME, / GUEUDEVILLE, / NOUVELLE EDITION. / Chez FRANÇOIS L'HONORE'.

Formula
12° A–2I$^{4/8}$
pp. [*26*] [1] 2–340 [*18*] 133 and 145 misnumbered 153 and 155. The first digit of 144 is displaced upwards.

Contents
A1, half-title; A2, title; A3–A3v, Avertissement sur cette nouvelle édition; A4–B5v, Préface du traducteur; B6–C1v, Préface d'Erasme; C2–2H3v, text; 2H4–2I8v, Table des matières. A1v and A2v are blank.

Signatures
Half the leaves of each gathering signed to the right. 2E3 is missigned 2E4. 26 lines per page without notes.

Catchwords
Between gatherings

Watermarks
Grapes; J ♡ⁱDUVAL FIN

Plates, etc.
Two engraved fronts., six engraved folding plates and 75 half-page woodcuts. Headpieces at A3, A4, B6, C2; tailpieces at A3v, B5v; decorated initials L, R, O, at A3, B6, C2.

Comments
The same compositorial practices as those of the 1728 piracy, and the same engravings and woodcuts are used. This is probably, therefore, another piracy. The only striking difference between this edition and the two earlier piracies is found in the orthographical practices of which a few samples are offered below:

1728 and 1735	*1741*
p. 4, 1.1 enivrez	enyvrez
p. 6, 1.16 Panegirique	Panégyrique
p. 8, 1.21 meilleure amie	meilleur amie (incorrect)
p. 9, 1.8 Réduite	réduit (incorrect)
p. 10, 1.2 méthode	métode
p. 267, 1.17 mysterieux	misterieux
p. 276, 1.5 renvoient	renvoyent
p. 277, 1.14 infatigables	infatiguables

Locations
Berkeley (UCa), Gouda (Li), Illinois (U), Rotterdam (M), Trier (S)

12. [red and black] / L'ELOGE / DE LA / FOLIE, / Composé en forme de Déclamation par / ERASME, / Et traduit par Monsieur / GUEUDEVILLE, / Avec les Notes de GERARD LISTRE, / & les belles Figures de HOLBEIN; / Le tout sur l'Original de l'Académie de Bâle. / Piéce qui represente au naturel L'HOMME tout / défiguré par la SOTISE, lui aprend agréablement à / rentrer dans le bon Sens & dans la Raison. / Nouvelle Edition, revûë avec soin, & mise / dans un meilleur ordre. / [vignette of type ornament] / A AMSTERDAM, / Chez FRANÇOIS L'HONORE', 1745.
In red: L'ELOGE / FOLIE, / ERASME, / GUEUDEVILLE, / Le tout sur l'Original de l'Académie de Bâle. / Nouvelle Edition, revûë avec soin, & mise / dans un meilleur ordre. / A AMSTERDAM, / FRANÇOIS L'HONORE'.

Formula
12° *⁸ **⁴ A–2G⁸/⁴
pp. [*24*] 1–340 [*20*] 145 misnumbered 155

Contents
*1, title; *2–*2v, Avertissement sur cette nouvelle édition; *3–*8v, Préface
du traducteur; **1–**4v, Préface d'Erasme; A1–2F2v, text; 2F3–2G4v,
Table des matières. *1v is blank.

Signatures
Half the leaves of each gathering signed to the right. 2F3 missigned 2F2.
26 lines per page

Catchwords
Between gatherings

Running-title
L'ELOGE / DE LA FOLIE, except at 2F2v which reads L'ELOGE, & c.

Watermarks
Grapes, FIN, Name not clear – 1745

Plates, etc.
Six engraved folding plates at A6/A7, B1/B2, D3/D4, L4/L5, X1/X2,
2F2/2F3. 75 half-page woodcuts. Headpieces at *2, *3, **1 and A1. Tailpieces at *2v and *8v. Decorated initials L, E, R, O, at *2, *3, **1 and A1.

Comments
This is another piracy modelled on the piracies of 1728, 1735 and 1741 and
having the same engravings and woodcuts. This edition follows, for the most
part, the orthographical practices of the 1741 rather than the 1735 edition.
It is also noticeable that the same misnumbering of 145 as 155 occurs in
1745 and 1741. It is probable, therefore, that the 1741 edition was used as
the model for this one. Both the *Bibliotheca Belgica* and *National Union
Catalog Pre-1956 Imprints* describe a 1745 edition but neither recognizes
the existence of two quite distinct editions dated 1745 (see no. 13),
although both editions are found in the locations they give. The *National
Union Catalog* describes its edition as having an engraved title-page vignette
but, as far as I can tell, both editions have title-page vignettes of type
ornament. There are 75 woodcuts, not 74, as described in the *Bibliotheca
Belgica*.

Locations
Davis (UCa), Grenoble (M), Montpellier (M)

13. [red and black] / L'ELOGE / DE LA / FOLIE, / Composé en forme de
Déclamation par / ERASME, / Et traduit par Monsieur / GUEUDEVILLE, /
Avec les Notes de GERARD LISTRE, / & les belles Figures de HOLBEIN; /
Le tout sur l'Original de l'Academie de Bâle. / Piéce qui représente au
naturel L'HOMME tout / defiguré par la SOTISE, lui aprend agréablement
à / rentrer dans le bon Sens & dans la Raison. / Nouvelle Edition, revûë

avec soin, & mise / dans un meilleur ordre / [vignette of type ornament] / A AMSTERDAM, / Chez FRANÇOIS L'HONORE', 1745.

In red: L'ELOGE, / FOLIE, / ERASME, / GUEUDEVILLE, / Le tout sur l'Original de l'Academie de Bâle. / Nouvelle Edition, revûë avec soin, & mise dans un meilleur ordre / A AMSTERDAM, / FRANÇOIS L'HONORE'.

Formula

12° *⁸ **⁴ A–2G⁸ᐟ⁴

pp. [24] 1–340 [20] Page 20 misnumbered 0

Contents

*1, title; *2–*2v, Avertissement sur cette nouvelle édition; *3–*8v, Préface du traducteur; **1–**4v, Préface d'Erasme; A1–2F2v, text; 2F3–2G4v, Table des matières. *1v is blank

Signatures

Half the leaves of each gathering signed to the right.

Catchwords

Between gatherings

Running-title

L'ELOGE / DE LA FOLIE. except at 2F2v which reads L'ELOGE, & c.

Watermarks

Grapes, FIN, G ♡ DE ROEUN [*sic*], 1748

Plates, etc.

One engraved front., six folding plates and 75 half-page woodcuts. Head-pieces at *2, *3, **1 and A1. Tailpiece at *2v and *8v. Decorated initials L, E, R, O, at *2, *3, **1 and A1.

Comments

This edition is a counterfeit of no. 12, having a different type-setting. The presence of the date 1748 in the watermark (see, for example, the Rotterdam copy) suggests that this edition was not printed before that date and, thus, that it is chronologically later than no. 12. Besides having a different type ornament in the vignette, the title-page of this edition omits the accents on "Academie" and "defiguré".

Locations

Berlin (H), Ghent (U), Limoges (M), Rotterdam (M), Toulouse (U), Yale (B)

14

(a) [red and black] / L'ELOGE / DE / LA FOLIE, / TRADUIT DU LATIN D'ERASME / *Par M.* GUEUDEVILLE. / Nouvelle Edition revûë & corrigée sur le Texte / de l'Edition de Bâle. / ET ORNE'E DE NOUVELLES FIGURES. / *AVEC DES NOTES.* / [Engraved vignette of naked Truth playing with a naked child, surmounted by the device — LUDENDO VERUM. The engraving is signed *Ch. Eisen inv. N. Le Mire Sculp.*] / [unequal rules, thick-thin] / M. DCC. LI.

In red: L'ELOGE / LA FOLIE, / GUEUDEVILLE. / ET ORNE'E DE NOUVELLES FIGURES. / double rule.

Formula

12° π1 2π² a⁸ b⁴ A–S⁸ᐟ⁴ T⁴

pp. [6] [xxiv] [1] 2–222 [2] xv misnumbered v

Contents

π1, title; π1v, quotation from Erasmus; 2π 1–2π2v, Explication des figures and Avis Intéressant; a1–b1, Préface de l'éditeur; b1v–b4v, Préface d'Erasme; A1–T3v, text; T4–T4v, Tables des matières.

Signatures

Half the leaves of each gathering are signed to the right. Signatures are in roman numerals. The signature at b1 is displaced laterally. C4 and F2 are missigned B4 and F1. 28 lines per page without notes.

Catchwords

Between gatherings

Running-title

L'ELOGE / DE LA FOLIE. except at T3v which reads L'ELOGE DE LA FOLIE.

Watermarks

Grapes, AUVERGNE, 1749 or possibly 1742. Fleur de lis. J ♡ DUVAL FIN. The name DUVAL is not clear and could be VIMAL. There is also a name that looks like ARTAUD.

Plates, etc.

One engraved front. and thirteen other engraved plates distributed throughout the text. All the engravings were designed by Charles Eisen and executed by the following — N. Lemire (front. and plates facing pp. 44, 91, 120); J.J. Pasquier (facing p. 1); De Lafosse (facing pp. 20, 68). P.F. Tardieu (facing pp. 89, 92, 104, 135, 167); L. Le Grand (facing p. 90). In some copies the plate facing p. 35 is either unsigned or the signature is not legible. In other copies it is signed Beauvais. The plate facing p. 120 was retouched by A. Pincio. The engraved headpiece on p. 1 and engraved tailpiece on p. 222 were designed by Eisen and executed by J. Flipart maj. and J. Aliamet respectively. The tailpiece bears the device — LA PAZZIA REGINA DEL MONDO. Other ornaments include a woodcut headpiece with the initial N at bottom right at a1, and a headpiece of type ornament at b1v. There is a tailpiece with the initial P. at bottom left at b1, and another tailpiece with the initial D. at b4v. There are decorated initials

L and O at a1 and A1. The fourteen plates show:

Front. Momus présentant une marotte à Minerve

p. 1   La Folie et son public
p. 20   La folie de l'enfance et de la vieillesse
p. 35   La folie de la table
p. 44   La folie des combats
p. 68   Les folies amoureuses
p. 89   La passion de la chasse
p. 90   La folie des batiments
p. 91   Les souffleurs
p. 92   La folie du jeu
p. 104   La folie de l'amour-propre
p. 120   La folie de l'avarice
p. 134   La folie des sciences
p. 167   La folie des cours

The engraved headpiece on p. 1 shows La Folie environnée d'enfants badins, and the tailpiece on p. 222 shows La Folie appuyée sur le globe du monde.

Comments

According to Barbier, *Dictionnaire des ouvrages anonymes,* 3rd ed., vol. II, p. 72, this edition was published in Paris by Hochereau and edited by Anne-Gabriel Meusnier de Querlon. However, in d'Hémery's *Journal de la libraire* (Ms. fr. 22156, fol. 46), under "Livres nouveaux" for 18/3/51, we find this edition attributed to Meusnier de Querlon as editor and author of the preface, but the publishers are identified as "Grangé, Mérigot, Robustel et Le Loup [i.e. Jean-Noel]." Meusnier de Querlon (1702–1780) was well known for his editing and "improving" the style of others (see Michaud, *Biographie universelle,* 1854 (a), vol. 34, pp. 629–630). These characteristics are clearly displayed in this edition and in the preface where one of the justifications offered for the new edition is the necessity to correct Gueudeville's tasteless translation:

Quelques éloges que son travail ait eus en Hollande, on nous permettra de le dire, ce n'est point là qu'il pouvait être justement apprécié... C'est en France qu'il faut juger des écrits français. La véritable urbanité ne se trouve guère hors d'un pays où elle est en quelque façon concentrée dans la capitale, comme l'*Atticisme* l'était à Athènes.

On further reflection, however, the editor decides not to attempt a wholesale revision of the text since it is the Gueudeville translation, with all its faults, that has made the book so popular. Moreover, there was the danger that "une version faite par un écrivain moins connu par sa liberté de penser, quelque fidèle qu'il pût être, ne fût suspecte à bien des lecteurs". The editor, therefore, is content "de rectifier le sens... d'annoblir l'expression... de substituer le terme propre à l'impropre, d'élaguer les superfluités et les redondances. . ." Now that Gueudeville is dead, the editor feels free to make any changes necessary. For this reason he eliminates many of the notes by Listre (this was recommended by La Barre de Beaumarchais in his review of the 1731 revision), substitutes his own explanatory notes, and adds marginal summaries to help the reader follow the arguments. He also eliminates the Holbein engravings on the grounds that they have little relevance to the text (a point made by the *Journal littéraire* on the appearance of the first edition in 1713, and repeated by La Barre de Beaumarchais in his review). In eliminating the Holbein material, the editor saw no need to retain the references to Holbein in the Préface du traducteur and, since this was to be an entirely new edition there was no purpose in keeping the Préface du traducteur. This was replaced by the Préface de l'éditeur.

The text is based on that of the first edition, and although there are many minor modifications of style throughout, there are no major departures from the original.

The Avis Intéressant at the end of the Explication des figures was probably composed by the editor and is certainly in the spirit of Gueudeville:

Ceux qui croiront se reconnaître dans quelques uns de ces différents portraits, en se représentant aux libraires, et en justifiant de la ressemblance, auront sur le prix de chaque exemplaire, une remise honnête et proportionnée à la conformité qui se trouvera entre la copie et l'original.

Locations
Amsterdam (U), Ghent (U), Paris (Ar, BI), Rotterdam (M), Tours (RC), Troyes (M)

14
(b) [red and black] / L'ELOGE / DE / LA FOLIE, / *TRADUIT* / DU LATIN D'ERASME / *Par M. GUEUDEVILLE.* / NOUVELLE EDITION REVÛE ET CORRIGÉE / SUR LE TEXTE DE L'EDITION DE BASLE. / ORNÉE DE NOUVELLES FIGURES. / *AVEC DES NOTES.* / [engraved vignette of naked truth playing with a naked child, surmounted by the device- LUDENDO VERUM. The engraving is signed *Ch. Eisen inv. N. Le Mire Sculp.*] / [unequal rules, thick − thin] / M. DCC LI.
In red: L'ELOGE / LA FOLIE, / DU LATIN D'ERASME / NOUVELLE EDITION REVÛE ET CORRIGÉE / ORNÉE DE NOUVELLES FIGURES. / double rule

Formula
$4°$ π^2 $2\pi^2$ a−c^4 A−2E^4
pp. [*8*] [xxiv] [1] 2−222 [*2*]

Contents
π1, half-title; π2, title; π2v, quotation from Erasmus: 2π 1−2π 2v, Expli-

cation des figures and Avis Intéressant; a1–c1, Préface de l'éditeur; c1v–c4v, Préface d'Erasme; A1–2E3v, text; 2E4–2E4v, Table des matières. π1v is blank.

Signatures

$3 signed to the right in roman numerals. 2A3 missigned 2A2; b3 printed B3 in some copies.

Catchwords

Between gatherings

Running-title

L'ELOGE / DE LA FOLIE. except at 2E3v which reads L'ELOGE DE LA FOLIE.

Watermarks

AUVERGNE 1742 and ?1749. J♡PARIVAL FIN. J♡BERGER. P♡CUSSON FIN. I♡MARGIVAL

Plates, etc.

One engraved frontispiece and thirteen other engraved plates distributed throughout the text. All the engravings were designed by Eisen and executed by – N. Lemire, J.J. Pasquier, De Lafosse, P.F. Tardieu, L. Le Grand, and Beauvais. The plate facing p. 120 was retouched by A. Pincio. The Frontispiece has a fancy border signed *Ch. Eisen inv. et fec.* and *Gravé sous la direction de Mr. Le Bas par P.F. Martinasie.* The engraved headpiece on p. 1 and engraved tailpiece on p. 222, were designed by Eisen and executed by J. Flipart maj. and J. Aliamet respectively. Other ornaments include a wood cut headpiece with the initial N. at bottom right at a1, and a headpiece of type ornament at c1v. There is a tailpiece with the initial P. at bottom left at c1, and another tailpiece with the initial D. at C4v. There are decorated initials L and O at a1 and A1.

Comments

This edition was issued in both duodecimo (14a) and quarto, the latter with a new title-page and with a half-title. Its text is almost dwarfed by the wide margins and spaces above and below. The quarto issue soon became a collector's item because of the fine bindings and the fine quality of the engravings which, in some copies, were all provided with fancy borders. In some copies the engravings were done in one or more colours. Details of this quarto issue are found in the *Bibliotheca Belgica* (E 909) and in H. Cohen, *Guide de l'amateur de livres à gravures du XVIIIe siècle,* 6e édition, Paris, 1912, pp. 348–349.

It is not possible to say whether the duodecimo or quarto was printed first, and I have arbitrarily assigned priority to the duodecimo.

Locations

Aberystwyth (BN), Besançon (M), Brussels (R), Cambridge (U), The Hague (R), Illinois (U), Leipzig (KM), London (BL), Lyon (M), Montpellier (M), Nancy (U), Paris (BN), Toulouse (U), Troyes (M), Valenciennes (M)

14

(c) [red and black] / L'ELOGE / DE / LA FOLIE, / TRADUIT DU LATIN D'ERASME / *Par M.* GUEUDEVILLE. / Nouvelle Edition revûe et corrigée sur le Texte / de l'Edition de Bâle, / ET ORNE'E DE NOUVELLES FIGURES. / *AVEC DES NOTES.* / [engraved vignette of naked Truth playing with a naked child, surmounted by the device – LUDENDO VERUM. The engraving is signed *Ch. Eisen inv. N. Le Mire Sculp.*] / [unequal rules thick-thin] / M.DCC.LII.

In red: L'ELOGE / LA FOLIE, / GUEUDEVILLE. / ET ORNE'E DE NOUVELLES FIGURES. / double rule

Formula

$12°$ $\pi 1$ $2\pi^2$ a^8 b^4 $A-S^{8/4}$ T^4

pp. [*6*] [xxiv] [1] 2–222 [*2*] xv misnumbered v

Comments

This is a reissue of the 1751 edition and, apart from the change of date on the title-page, is identical to it in all respects. The paper bears the same watermarks as those found in the quarto issue. In the copy of Rotterdam there is an extra engraving between b1v and b2. This is a portrait of Erasmus after Holbein and signed "S:Gränicher f." In the copy of Liège, F2 is correctly signed. The copy at Rotterdam has no Table des matières, and the copy at Ghent has the "Explication des figures"at the end of the text.

Locations

Ghent (U), Liège (U), Montpellier (M), Rotterdam (M)

14

(d) [red and black] / L'ELOGE / DE / LA FOLIE, / TRADUIT DU LATIN D'ERASME / *Par. M.* GUEUDEVILLE. / Nouvelle Edition revûe et corrigée sur le Texte / de l'Edition de Bâle, / ET ORNE'E DE NOUVELLES FIGURES. / *AVEC DES NOTES.* / [engraved vignette of naked Truth playing with a naked child, surmounted by the device – LUDENDO VERUM. The engraving is signed *Ch. Eisen inv. N. Le Mire Sculp.*] / [unequal rules thick-thin] / M.DCC.LIII.

In red: L'ELOGE / LA FOLIE, / GUEUDEVILLE. / ET ORNE'E DE NOUVELLES FIGURES. / double rule.

Formula

$12°$ $\pi 1$ a^8 b^4 $A-S^{8/4}$ T^6

pp. [*2*] [xxiv] [1] 2–222 [*6*] xv misnumbered v

Comments

This is another reissue of the 1751 edition and, apart from the change of date on the title-page, is identical to it in all respects. The Explication des figures and Table des matières now seem to be more regularly placed after the text. In the copy at Cambridge University, F3 is not signed. In the copy at Vassar College, I3 is signed I2. The paper bears the same watermarks as those found in the quarto issue.

Locations
Boston (P), Cambridge (U), Ghent (U), Lausanne (U), New York (V), Paris (BN), Rotterdam (M), Rouen (M), Tours (M)

15. [red and black] / L'ELOGE / DE / LA FOLIE, / TRADUIT DU LATIN D'ERASME / *Par M.* GUEUDEVILLE. / Nouvelle Édition revûe & corrigée sur le / Texte de l'Édition de Bâle, / ET ORNE'E DE NOUVELLES FIGURES, / *AVEC DES NOTES.* / [engraved vignette of naked Truth playing with a naked child, and surmounted by the device-LUDENDO VERUM. The engraving is signed *Ch. Eisen inv. N. Le Mire Sculp.*] / [equal rules thick-thin] / M.DCC.LVII.
In red: L'ELOGE / LA FOLIE, / GUEUDEVILLE. / ET ORNE'E DE NOUVELLES FIGURES, / double rule

Formula
$12°$ $\pi 1$ $2\pi^2$ a^8 b^4 A–S$^{8/4}$ T4 (– T4)
pp. [6] [xxiv] [1] 2–222 63 misnumbered 33

Contents
$\pi 1$, title; $\pi 1$v, quotation from Erasmus; $2\pi 1 - 2\pi 2$v, Explication des figures and Avis Intéressant; a1–b1, Préface de l'éditeur; b1v–b4v, Préface d'Erasmus; A1–T3v, text.

Signatures
Half the leaves of each gathering are signed to the right. Signatures are in roman numerals. T3 is signed. 28 lines per page without notes.

Catchwords
Between gatherings

Running-title
L'ELOGE / DE LA FOLIE., except at T3v which reads L'ELOGE DE LA FOLIE.

Watermarks
I MADARET LIMOSIN FIN DANNONAY AUVERGNE ?ERRY 1742. Fleur de lis, crown. N♡DUFOUR. ?♡DE ROUEN. D·♥MALMENAIDE. ∧♉ MONGOL

Comments
This edition is closely modelled on the edition of 1751. The engravings are the same as those found in the 1751 edition. According to Hoefer, *Nouvelle Biographie générale*, 1856, vol 17, pp. 39–40, this edition was the work of Camille Falconet (1671–1762).

Locations
Brussels (R), Chicago (Ne), Columbia (U), Ghent (U), Gouda (Li), Illinois (U), London (BL, UC), Nancy (U), Orléans (BC), Paris (MA), Poitiers (M), Rotterdam (M), Strasbourg (U), Washington (P)

16. [red and black] / L'ÉLOGE / DE LA FOLIE, / TRADUIT DU LATIN D'ERASME, / *Par M.* GUEUDEVILLE. / Nouvelle Edition revuë et corrigée sur le Texte / de l'Edition de Bâle, / ET ORNÉE DE NOUVELLES FIGURES. / *AVEC DES NOTES*. / [engraved vignette of naked Truth playing with a naked child, and surmounted by the device — LUDENDO VERUM] / [unequal rules, thick-thin] / M.DCC. LVII.
In red: L'ELOGE / LA FOLIE, / GUEUDEVILLE. / ET ORNÉE DE NOUVELLES FIGURES. / double rule.

Formula
12° π1 2π² a⁸ b⁴ A–S⁸′⁴ T4 (–T4)
pp. [6] [xxiv] 1–222 xiii and xxiii misnumbered xii and xxii. 156 and 207 misnumbered 6 and 109. 208 has first digit printed upside down. Page numbers between rules except in T gathering.

Contents
π1, title; π1v, quotation from Erasmus; 2π1–2π2v, Explication des figures and Avis intéressant; a1–b1, Préface de l'éditeur; b2–b4v, Préface d'Erasme; A1–T3v, text. b1v is blank.

Signatures.
Half the leaves of each gathering signed to the right in roman numerals. b2, C4, D2, G3, I2, not signed. T3 is signed. In the signature Fij the i is printed upside down. 28 lines per page without notes.

Catchwords
On the verso of the last leaf of gatherings B, D, I, K, M, O, P, Q, S.

Running-title
L'ELOGE / DE LA FOLIE between rules except in T gathering where the rules are omitted. In this gathering the headlines are printed in larger type. At T3v the headline is misprinted LE'LOGE

Watermarks
G ♡LEGRAS; G♡DE ROUEN FIN NORMAND VEUVE; grapes. There are several dates which look like 1733, 1735, 1755 or 1758.

Plates, etc.
The fourteen plates are copies of those found in 1757 (no. 15). Those facing pp. 1, 20, 35, 68, 88, 90, 92 120 are reversed. The engraved title-page vignette, headpiece at A1 and tailpiece at T3v are copies and not signed, except that the headpiece at A1 bears the letters Br or Bt. There is a decorated initial O at A1.

Comments
This is a piracy of 1757 (no. 15) almost certainly originating in France.

Locations
Berne (BN), Ghent (U), Nantes (M), Rouen (M)

17. [red and black] / *L'ÉLOGE* / DE / *LA FOLIE,* / TRADUIT DU LATIN D'ERASME, / *PAR M. GUEUDEVILLE,* / Nouvelle Édition, revuë & corrigée sur le Texte / de l'Édition de Bâle, / *ET ORNÉE DE NOUVELLES FIGURES.* / AVEC DES NOTES. / [engraved vignette of naked Truth playing with a naked child, surmounded by the device — LUDENDO VERUM] / [unequal rules, thick-thin] / M. DCC. LXI.
In red: *L'ÉLOGE* / *LA FOLIE,* / *PAR M. GUEUDEVILLE,* / *ET ORNÉE DE NOUVELLES FIGURES.* / double rule

Formula
12° π1 2π² a⁸ b⁴ A–S⁸′⁴ T⁴ (–T4)
pp. [*6*] [xxiv] 1–222 147 and 218 misnumbered 137 and 812.

Contents
π1, title; π1v, quotation from Erasmus and Avis intéressant; 2π 1–2π 2v, Explication des figures; a1–b1v, Préface de l'éditeur; b2–b4v, Préface d'Erasme; A1–T3v, text.

Signatures
Half the leaves of each gathering signed to the right in roman numerals. 29 lines per page without notes.

Catchwords
Between gatherings

Running-title
L'ELOGE / DE LA FOLIE., except at T3v which reads L'ELOGE, & c.

Watermarks
G♡DE ROUEN FIN 1761. Grapes.

Comments
This is another edition modelled on the edition of 1757. The fourteen plates are those found in the 1757 piracy except that in the copy at Rotterdam the plate at p. 88 is not reversed and the plate at p. 130 is reversed. The small engravings are those found in the 1757 piracy. The plates have been given page numbers as references to compensate for the absence of such references in the Explication des figures.
This edition is not described in the *Bibliotheca Belgica* or the *National Union Catalog Pre-1956 Imprints*.

Locations
Cambridge (St.J.), Rotterdam (M), Troyes (M)

18. L'ELOGE / DE / LA FOLIE, / TRADUIT DU LATIN / D'ERASME, / PAR / Mr. GUEUDEVILLE. / [vignette of type ornament] / A BERLIN, / [rule] / AUX DEPENS DE LA SAGESSE. / M DCC LXI.

Formula
·8° π1 A–X^8 L^6 M–O^8
pp. [*2*] [1] 2–196 [*24*]

Contents
π1, title; A1–A3, Préface du traducteur; A3v–A6v, Préface d'Erasme; A7–N4v, text; N5–O8, Table des matières. π1v and O8v are blank

Signatures
$5 signed except L gathering where four leaves are signed. The L gathering has only six leaves. O7v is signed Dd2.

Catchwords
On every page

Running-title
L'ELOGE DE LA FOLIE / L'ELOGE DE LA FOLIE. Headline at A7v reads ELOGE DE LA FOLIE. There is a rule between the headlines and the text.

Watermarks
None visible

Plates, etc.
An engraved frontispiece with fancy border displaying a half-title beneath which are the portraits of Erasmus and More. There is a headpiece at A1, a decorated initial E at A1, and a tailpiece at N4v.

Comments
The location – A BERLIN – may be false. Certainly, the name of the publishing company, AUX DEPENS DE LA SAGESSE, is a piece of humour designed to contrast with the title of the work. The text is based on that of the edition of 1731 (no. 7).

Locations
Baltimore (JH), Brussels (R), Geneva (U), Rotterdam (M), Strasbourg (U), Toronto (RC), Wurzburg (U)

19. ENCOMIO / DELLA / PAZZIA, / COMPOSTO / IN FORMA DI DECLA- / MAZIONE / PER ERASMO, / E TRADOTTO IN ITALIANO. / [vignette of type ornament] / IN BASILEA, / [rule] / A SPESE DELLA SAVIEZZA. / M DCC LXI.

Formula
8° π1 A–X^8 Y^6 Z–2C^8 2D^2
pp. [*5*] 4–288 287–391 [= 393] [*23*] 289–291 are misnumbered 287–289. This error continues to the end except for 386 which is misnumbered 388

Contents
π1, title; A1, half title; A1v–A6, Préface du traducteur; A6v–B5, Préface d'Erasme; B5v–2B7, text; 2B7v–2D2v, Table des matières. π1v is blank.

Signatures
$5 signed centrally. B5 not signed. Only six leaves in Y gathering but five are signed. F3 and F5 missigned E3 and D5.

Catchwords
On every page

Running-title
L'ELOGE DE LA FOLIE / ENCOMIO DELLA PAZZIA

Watermarks
None visible

Plates, etc.
An engraved front. with fancy border displaying a half-title etc. Headpieces at A1v, A2, B5v, B6; tailpieces at B4v, B5, 2B6v, 2B7, 2D2v. Decorated initials at A1v and A2.

Comments
This edition was published by the same publishing house responsible for no. 18. In this edition the French and Italian versions are printed on opposite pages. The French text of this "Italian" edition is simply a reissue of the "Berlin" edition transposed to the left side of the book. The title-page vignettes are identical in both editions and the name of the fictitious publishing company has been translated into Italian. The engraved front. is the same in both editions. According to the *Bibliotheca Belgica* (E 939) the Italian translation of Gueudeville was judged by an editor in 1819 to be worthless. For more details of the Italian translations of this work see Beatrice Corrigan "Croce and Erasmus: The *Colloquies* and the *Moria* in Italy", *Erasmus in English*, 7 (1975), 21–25. The engraved front. of this edition is reproduced in this article.

Locations
Basel (U), Berne (BN), Brussels (R), Chicago (U), The Hague (R), Toronto (RC)

20. [red and black] / *L'ÉLOGE* / DE / *LA FOLIE,* / TRADUIT DU LATIN D'ERASME, / *PAR M. GUEUDEVILLE.* / Nouvelle Édition, revue &

corrigée sur le / Texte de l'Édition de Bâle. / *ET ORNE'E DE NOUVELLES FIGURES.* / AVEC DES NOTES. / [engraved vignette of naked Truth playing with a naked child, and surmounted by the device — LUDENDO VERUM] / [unequal rules, thick-thin] / M.DCC.LXVI.
In red: *L'ÉLOGE / LA FOLIE, / PAR M. GUEUDEVILLE. / ET ORNE'E DE NOUVELLES FIGURES;* / double rule

Formula
$12° \pi 1\ 2\pi^2\ a^8\ b^4\ A-S^{8/4}\ T^4\ (-T4)$
pp. [6] [xxiv] [1] 2–222

Watermarks
M G LEVANIER 1764 FIN NORMANDIE. Grapes 1765

Comments
Another edition modelled on the edition of 1757. In the copy at Rotterdam the frontispiece is in blue, green, yellow, pink and brown; The title-page vignette is also multi-coloured in pink and greeny yellow.

Locations
Ghent (U), Nantes (M), Rotterdam (M)

21. [red and black] / *L'ÉLOGE / DE / LA FOLIE,* / TRADUIT DU LATIN D'ERASME, / *PAR M. GUEUDEVILLE.* / Nouvelle Édition, revue et corrigée sur le / Texte de l'Édition de Bâle. / *ET ORNÉE DE NOUVELLES FIGURES.* / AVEC DES NOTES. / [engraved vignette of naked Truth playing with a naked child, surmounted by the device — LUDENDO VERUM] / [unequal rules, thick-thin] / M.DCC. LXXI.
In red: *L'ELOGE / LA FOLIE, / PAR M. GUEUDEVILLE. / ET ORNÉE DE NOUVELLES FIGURES.* / double rule

Formula
$12° \pi 1\ 2\pi^2\ a^8\ b^4\ A-S^{8/4}\ T^4\ (-T4)$
pp. [6] [xxiv] [1] 2–222. xix not numbered; xxi printed diagonally; 68 misnumbered 168; 183 not numbered.

Running-title
In the copy at Ghent the headline at a2 is incorrectly spaced — DEL' ÉDITEUR. In the copy at Rotterdam the headline at R8 is incorrectly spaced — DE LA ↔ FOLIE.

Watermarks
Grapes, FIN 1770. In the copy at Rotterdam the name G DE ROUEN appears in the plate between B9 and B10

Comments
Another edition modelled on the edition of 1757. In the *National Union*

Catalog Pre-1956 Imprints there is listed an edition dated 1772. On inspection, however, this appears to be the 1771 edition. The mistake in the date is due to a blob of ink on the title-page. This ink is fused with the period after the date, and makes the numerals LXXI. appear as LXXII

Locations
Caen (U), Ghent (U), Hamilton (McM), Paris (BN), Rotterdam (M), Rouen (M), Strasbourg (U)

22. L'ÉLOGE / DE LA / FOLIE, / *Composé en forme de Déclamation,* / PAR / ERASME, / *Et traduit* / Par M. GUEUDEVILLE, / Avec les Notes de GERARD LISTRE, / & les belles Figures de HOLBEIN. / *Le tout sur l'original de l'Université de Basle.* / NOUVELLE EDITION / *Revue, augmentée, & mise dans un meilleur ordre.* / [vignette of Mercury] / A NEUCHATEL, / Chez SAMUEL FAUCHE, Libraire du Roi. / [fancy double rule] / M.DCC.LXXVII.

Formula
8° *⁸ A–P⁸ Q⁴
pp. [*16*] [1] 2–234 [*14*] 158 and 188 misnumbered 178 and 187.

Contents
*1, title; *2–*2v, Avertissement; *3–*5v, Préface du traducteur; *6–*8, Préface d'Erasme; A1–P5v, text ; P5v–Q4v, Table des matières. *1v and *8v are blank.

Signatures
$4 signed to the right.

Catchwords
Between gatherings.

Running-title
L'ELOGE / DE LA FOLIE.

Watermarks
Not clearly visible.

Plates, etc.
Two engraved plates, six engraved folding plates, 75 half-page engravings. Headpieces at *2, *3 *6, A1; tailpieces at *2v, *5v, *8. Decorated initial J at A1.

Comments
The text of this edition is based on that of 1731. The fronts., folding plates and other engravings seem to be those found in the 1731 edition. The *Bibliotheca Belgica* suggests this is a false imprint but gives no details (E917). There seems no reason, however, to doubt the authenticity of this

edition. Samuel Fauche (1732–1803) was a well known publisher in Neuchâtel, and he did have the title of "Libraire du roi" (see *Dictionnaire historique et biographique de la Suisse*, Neuchâtel, 1926, vol III, p. 63). The 1777 edition listed by *The Nat. Union Cat. Pre-1956 Imprints* at Amherst college is, in fact, an edition in Latin and not the Gueudeville translation. The Union catalogue in Rotterdam lists a 1778 edition at Grenoble but this edition has not been found.

Locations
Berne (BN), Cambridge (U), Chicago (Ne), Cornell (U), Ghent (U), The Hague (R), Lille (M), Neuchâtel (P), Paris (BN), Rotterdam (M)

23. Erasme *L'Eloge de la folie. Traduction de M. Gueudeville, avec une notice biographique, les notes de Gérard Listre et un index des sujets traités.* Editions Verda, 11, Cité Dupetit-Thouars, Paris. 281 pp.

Comments
No date of publication is found in this edition but, in the *Bibliographie de Belgique* (1936), the edition is listed as being published in that year. In the edition itself the information is given that it was "Imprimé en Belgique. Des Presses de l'Union des Imprimeries S.A., A Frameries. Dir. V. Quenon." There is also a notice before the introduction that states "Ce livre a été traduit du latin par M. Gueudeville et contient les notes de Gérard Listre, le tout d'après le Manuscrit de Bâle. Traduction définitive publiée en 1777 à Neuchâtel, par Samuel Fauche, libraire du Roi."

Locations
Brussels (R, FU), Liège (U), Louvain (CU)

APPENDIX G.
L'Utopie

1(a) [red and black] / L'UTOPIE / DE / THOMAS MORUS, / *Chancelier d'Angleterre*; / Idée ingenieuse pour remedier au / malheur des Hommes; & pour leur / procurer une felicité complette. / *Cet Ouvrage contient* / *LE PLAN D'UNE REPUBLIQUE* / *dont les Lois, les Usages, & les Coutumes tendent* / *uniquement à faire faire aux Societez* / *Humaines le passage de la Vie dans* / *toute la douceur imaginable.* / REPUBLIQUE, QUI DEVIENDRA / infalliblement réelle, des que lès Mortels / se conduiront par la *Raison.* / *Traduite nouvellement en François* / Par Mr. GUEUDEVILLE, / & ornée de tres belles figures. / [vignette of type ornament] / A LEIDE, / Chez PIERRE VANDER Aa, / *Marchand Libraire, demeurant dans l'Academie,* / chez qui on trouve toutes sortes de livres curieux, comme aussi / de Cartes Geographiques, des Villes, tant en plan qu'en / profil, des Portraits des Hommes Illustres / & autres Tailles-douces. / [rule] / *MDCCXV.* / Avec Privilege.
In red: L'UTOPIE / THOMAS MORUS, / *LE PLAN D'UNE REPUBLIQUE* / REPUBLIQUE, QUI DEVIENDRA / Par Mr. GUEUDEVILLE, / PIERRE VANDER Aa, / *MDCCXV.*

Formula
12° *–5*^{12} 6*^{12} (–6*12) 7*^{4} (–7*4) A–O^{12} P^6 Q^{12} ^{2}A^{10} (–A10) B^4 C^8 (–C8) D^4
pp. [148] 1–4 [5–6] 7–10 [11–12] 13–44 [45–46] 47–92 [93–94] 95–98 [99–100] 101–104 [105–106] 107–122 [123–124] 125–132 [133–134] 135–146 [147–148] 149–162 [163–164] 165–168 [169–170] 171–210 [211–212] 213–222 [223–224] 225–236 [237–238] 239–300 [301–302] 303–322 [323–324] 325–348 349–372 [1–2] 3–48 325 misnumbered 225

Contents
*1, engraved title (verso blank); *2, printed title (verso blank); *3–*12v, épître à Jacques Emmeri; 2*–2*8v, préface du traducteur; 2*9–5*4, abrégé de la vie de Thomas Morus; 5*4v–5*9, préface de l'auteur; 5*9–5*10, Erasme à Froben; 5*10–6*4, Budé à Lupset; 6*4v–6*7v, Buslidius à Morus; 6*8–6*10v, Gilles à Buslidius; 6*10v–7*1v, Paludan à Gilles; 7*1v–7*2, vers de Paludan; 7*2–7*2v, Gérard Nivernois sur l'Utopie;

7*3, vers de C. Graphée; 7*3v, table de la division de cet ouvrage; A1—P6v, text; Q1—Q8, table des matières; Q8v—Q12v, catalogue, A1—D4, catalogues

Signatures
$7 signed to the right

Catchwords
On every page

Running-title
L'UTOPIE / LIVRE PREMIER [SECOND]

Watermarks
None visible

Plates
There is an engraved title as frontispiece, an engraved coat of arms, and sixteen other engravings distributed throughout the text. These engravings are unnumbered but form part of the gatherings in which they appear. The engravings portray:

A3r — the interior of the Eglise de Notre Dame at Anvers
A6r — the garden of the narrator
B11v — a farming scene
D11r — a harbour and rough seas
E2r — a harbour and a calm sea
E5v — an agricultural scene
F2v — Utopians playing a form of chess
F7r — a carpenter's shop
G2r — a refectory
G10v — slaves in chains
H1r — a procession of ambassadors
I10r — a ship
K4v — premarital inspection
K11r — a magistrate
N7r — a funeral pyre
O6r — a temple

Comments
In the collation I have assumed that the engraved title-page forms part of the first gathering, although I have not seen enough copies to be certain that this is the case.

    The engraving at K4v is by Bleyswick. All the rest are unsigned but, according to J. Lewine, *op. cit.*, p. 375, "a comparison of the composition suggests that all emanated from his hand."

Locations
Avignon (Ca); Brussels (R); Ghent (U); Leeds (U); Lyon (M); Paris (Ma); Rouen (M)

1(b) L'UTOPIE / DE / THOMAS MORUS, / *Chancelier d'Angleterre*; / Idée ingénieuse pour remedier au / malheur des Hommes; & pour leur / procurer une felicité complette. / *Cet Ouvrage contient* / *LE PLAN D'UNE REPUBLIQUE* / *dont les Lois, les Usages, & les Coutumes tendent* / *uniquement à faire faire aux Societez* / *Humaines le passage de la Vie dans* / *toute la douceur imaginable.* / REPUBLIQUE, QUI DEVIENDRA / infalliblement réelle, des que lès Mortels / se conduiront par la *Raison*. / *Traduit nouvellement en François* / Par Mr. GUEUDEVILLE, / & ornée de tres belles figures. / [vignette of hanging basket of fruit and leaves with a pendant on each side] / *A LEIDE,* /Chez PIERRE VANDER Aa, / *Marchand Libraire, Imprimeur Ordinaire* / de l'Academie & de la Ville, / demeurant dans l'Academie. / [rule] / MDCCXV. / Avec Privilége sous peine de 3000 florins d'amende & c. / contre les *Contrefacteurs.*

Comments

This is the first edition with a new title-page and the same *privilège* granted for *L'Eloge de la folie* on May 17 1715. The *privilège* occupies the verso of the title-page and the recto and verso of a leaf signed *2. The title-page seems to be a cancel. In 1961, the editors of the More bibliography, *op. cit.*, p. 29, had not seen this reissue, but in *Moreana*, no. 10 (May 1966), 31–32, R.W. Gibson described a copy he had found and that, for reasons unexplained, he had determined to be the first edition. My own inclination, however, has been to assign priority to the edition with the red and black title-page.

Locations

Berlin (S); Copenhagen (R); The Hague (ISG, R); Kiel (U); McMaster (U); Nantes (M); Neuchâtel (P); Valenciennes (M)

1(c) [red and black] / L'UTOPIE / DE / THOMAS MORUS, / *Chancelier d'Angleterre*; / Idée ingenieuse pour remedier au malheur des / Hommes; & pour leur procurer une / felicité complete. / *Cet Ouvrage qui contient* / *LE PLAN D'UNE REPUBLIQUE* / *dont les Lois, les Usages, & les Coutumes tendent* / *uniquement à faire faire aux Societez* / *Humaines le passage de la Vie dans* / *toute la douceur imaginable.* / REPUBLIQUE, QUI DEVIENDRA / infailliblement réelle, des que les Mortels se / con— duiront par la *Raison*. / *Traduite nouvellement en François* / par Mr. GUEUDEVILLE, / & ornée de tres belles figures. / [vignette of monogram of publisher?] A AMSTERDAM, / Chez R. & G. WETSTEIN. / [rule] / MDCCXVII.

In red: L'UTOPIE / *LE PLAN D'UNE REPUBLIQUE* / REPUBLIQUE, QUI DEVIENDRA / Par Mr. GUEUDEVILLE, / Chez R. & G. WETSTEIN.

Comments

At the auction on August 17 1716, Van der Aa sold his stocks and *privilège* of *l'Utopie*, together with those of *L'Eloge de la folie*, to R. and G. Wetstein who retained the engraved title-page but substituted a new printed one.

Locations
Basel (U); Columbia (U); Toronto (TF); Stockholm (R); Utrecht (U)

2. [red and black] / IDÉE / D'UNE / *REPUBLIQUE HEUREUSE*: / OU / L'UTOPIE / DE / THOMAS MORUS, / *Chancelier d'Angleterre.* / *Contenant le plan d'une République dont les* / *Loix, les Usages & les* *Coûtumes tendent* / *uniquement à rendre heureuses les Socie-* / *tez qui les* *suivront.* / Traduite en François / PAR MR. GUEUDEVILLE, / Et enrichie de Figures en Taille-douce. / [engraved vignette of Minerva with putti, signed B. Picart direxit] / A AMSTERDAM. / Chez FRANCOIS L'HONORE'. / MDCCXXX.
In red: IDÉE / *REPUBLIQUE HEUREUSE*: / THOMAS MORUS, / PAR MR. GUEUDEVILLE, / A AMSTERDAM. / MDCCXXX.

Formula
$12°$ π^2 $*^2$ $*-4*^{12}$ $5*^4$ $A-P^{12}$ Q^2
pp. [7] ii-ciii [*1*] 1–364

Contents
$\pi1$, engraved front., $\pi2$, title (verso blank); $*1-*2v$, épître à Guillaume Henri, duc de Saxe, etc.; $*3-*9$, préface du traducteur; $*9v-2*1$. préface de l'auteur; $2*1v-4*2$, abrégé de la vie de Thomas Morus; $4*2v-4*3$, Erasme à Froben; $4*3-4*8$, Budé à Lupset:$4*8-4*10v$, Buslidius à Morus; $4*11-5*1$, Gilles à Buslidius; $5*1-5*2v$, Paludan à Gilles; $5*2v-5*3$, vers de Paludan; $5*3v$, Gérard Nivernois sur l'Utopie; $5*4$, vers de C. Graphée; $5*4v$, table; $A1-P6v$, text; $P7-Q2$, table des matières.

Signatures
$7 signed to the right. Signatures $*1$ and $*2$ are repeated. $4*7$ is missigned $2*7$

Catchwords
On every page

Running-title
L'UTOPIE / LIVRE PREMIER [SECOND]

Watermarks
None visible

Plates
There is an engraved front. with place, date, and name of publisher, an engraved coat of arms, signed B. Picart f. 1730, and sixteen engraved plates distributed throughout the text. These sixteen plates are identical in appearance and distribution to those of the first edition.

Comments
The Wetsteins sold their rights to *L'Eloge de la folie* and *l'Utopie* to François

L'Honoré who brought out a new edition as described above. The layout of the text follows that of the first edition but this is not simply a reissue as the editors of the St. Thomas More bibliography, *op. cit.*, p. 32, would have it.

Locations
Bordeaux (U); Caen (U); Chicago (Ne); Copenhagen (R); Erlangen (U); Geneva (U); Ghent (U); Grenoble (M). The Hague (ISG, R); Leeds (U); Liège (U); London (BL); Louvain (U); Nancy (U); Nantes (M); Neuchâtel (P); Paris (Ar, BN); Pennsylvania (U); Princeton (U); Rochester (U); Rouen (M); Troyes (M); Yale (B).

ARCHIVES

France	Archives de Haute Normandie et du département de la Seine-Maritime	G 6342: Comptes de la fabrique de l'église paroissiale de St. Caude-le-Vieux de Rouen, 1597–1637
	Archives municipales, Rouen	Délibérations, 1389–1790
	Bibliothèque Nationale	D'Hémery, Journal de la libraire, ms. fr. 22156 (18/3/51); ms. fr. 22158 (8/2/53)
Holland	Centraal bureau voor genealogie, The Hague	Fiches de l'Eglise Wallonne
	Gemeentearchief, The Hague	Archief Waalse Gemeente, m. 101 Lidmaaten Register Waalse Kerk, 1632–1710, no. 1504. Notarieel archief. Inv. nos. 682, 1321, 1596, 2251 Rechtarchief 166
	Rijksarchief, The Hague	Staten van Holland 1572–1795, nos. 1654, 1667, 1671 Archief Staten-Generaal, Inv. no. 3761
	Gemeentearchief, Rotterdam	Extract uit de Registers der doden te Rotterdam

BIBLIOGRAPHY

ORIGINAL WORKS BY GUEUDEVILLE

1. *Les Motifs de la conversion de M. Gueudevile*, A Rotterdam, Aux dépens de l'Auteur, 1689.

2. *L'Esprit des cours de l'Europe* (called *Nouvelles des cours de l'Europe* from May 1701 to November 1703), La Haye et Amsterdam, François L'Honoré et al., 1699–1710, 19 vols.

3. *Remarques sur le mémoire que l'Ambassadeur de Moscovie présenta aux Etats-Généraux, le 9 février 1701*, translated into Swedish as *Anmårkningar öfwer den andra skriften som det Ryske Såndebodet i Haag har ingifwit til Herrar General Staterna i Holland den 9 Febr. Anno 1701* (see chapter three, note 47).

4. *Critique générale des Avantures de Télémaque*, A Cologne, chez les Héritiers de Pierre Marteau, 1700–1702 (in six parts).

5. *Dialogues des morts d'un tour nouveau*, A La Haye, T. Johnson, 1709.

COLLABORATIVE WORKS

6. *Atlas historique ou nouvelle introduction à l'histoire, à la chronologie et à la géographie ancienne et moderne,* A Amsterdam, L'Honoré et Châtelain, 1705–1720, 7 vols.

7. *Le Nouveau Théâtre du monde ou la géographie royale*, A Leide, chez Pierre van der Aa, 1713.

8. *Maximes politiques du Pape Paul III*, A La Haye, chez Henri Scheurleer, 1716.

TRANSLATIONS

9. *L'Eloge de la folie*, A Leide, chez Pierre van der Aa, 1713.

10. *L'Utopie*, A Leide, chez Pierre van der Aa, 1715.

11. *Les Comédies de Plaute*, A Leide, chez Pierre van der Aa, 1719.

12. *Les Colloques d'Erasme*, A Leide, chez Pierre van der Aa, 1720.

13. *Sur la noblesse et excellence du sexe féminin*, Leiden, chez Théodore Haak, 1726.

14. *L'Eloge de la fièvre quarte*, A Leide, chez Theodore Haak, 1728.

WORKS ATTRIBUTED TO GUEUDEVILLE

15. *Les Sentiments d'un officier flamand sur le mémoire que l'Ambassadeur de Moscovie présenta aux Etats-Généraux, le 25 janvier 1701*, translated into Swedish as *En Nederländsk officerares omdö och anmärkning öfwer en skrift som det Ryska Sändebodet den 25 Januarii 1701 til Herrar General Staterna i Holland har ingifwit Augående Ryssarnas nederlag wed Narwen* (see chapter three, note 47).

16. *Le Grand Théâtre historique ou nouvelle histoire universelle*, A Leide, chez Pierre van der Aa, 1703, 3 vols.

17. *Nouveaux Voyages de Mr. le Baron de La Hontan dans l'Amérique septentrionale*, A La Haye, Les Frères L'Honoré, 1703, 3 vols.

18. *La Quintessence des nouvelles*, La Haye et Amsterdam, 1711–1712? (see chapter three, note 60).

19. *Le Censeur ou caractères des moeurs de La Haye*, A La Haye, chez Henri Scheurleer, 1715.

20. *Les Eloges admirables des choses merveilleuses*, A Leide, chez Pierre van der Aa, 171? (see chapter seven, note 37).

21. E. Coulet, *L'Eloge de la goutte*, A Leide, chez Theodore Haak, 1728.

22. *Histoire abrégée et très mémorable du chevalier de la plume noire*, A Amsterdam, H. G. Löhner, 1744, translated into German as *Kurtzgefasste sehr merkwürdige Geschichte des Ritters von dem schwarzen Federbusche, Stallmeisters, und Herrn des ohngefähren Zufalls, des Glücks und der Ebentheuer*, Anno 1750.

LIST OF WORKS CONSULTED

Aa, A. J. van der. *Biographisch woordenboek der Nederlanden*, Haarlem, 1852–1878, 21 vols.

Barbier, A.-A. *Dictionnaire des ouvrages anonymes*, Paris, 1872–1882, 4 vols.

Bayle, P. *Dictionnaire critique et historique*, Rotterdam, 1697, 4 vols.

———— *Lettres choisies*, Rotterdam, 1714, 3 vols.

Bellanger, C. *et al. Histoire générale de la presse française*, Paris, 1969, 2 vols.

Bénézit, E. *Dictionnaire critique et documentaire des peintres*, Paris 1924.

Bibliographie de Belgique, Bruxelles, 1875–.

Bibliotheca Belgica, 2ème série, Gand/La Haye, 1891–1923, 27 vols.

Bibliotheca Erasmiana, Gand et Bruxelles, 1903–1950, 12 vols.

Biographie nationale de Belgique, Bruxelles, 1866–1938, 27 vols.

Bittner, L. and Gross, L. *Repertorium der diplomatischen Vertreter aller Länder..*, Zurich, 1936, 2 vols.

Camusat, D.-F. *Histoire critique des journaux*, Amsterdam, 1734.

Chaussy, Y., ed. *Matricula monachorum*, Paris, 1959.

Cherel, A. *Fénelon au XVIIIe siècle en France*, Paris, 1917.

Churchill, W.A. *Watermarks in Paper*, Amsterdam, 1935.

Cohen, H. *Guide de l'amateur de livres à gravures du XVIIIe siècle*, 6ème édition, Paris, 1912.

Correspondance entre Boileau Despréaux et Brossette, ed. A. Laverdet, Paris, 1858.

Corrigan, Beatrice. "Croce and Erasmus: The *Colloquies* and the *Moria* in Italy," *Erasmus in English*, 7 (1975), 21–25.

Dedieu, Joseph. *Le Rôle politique des Protestants français,* Paris, 1920.

Delcroix, M. "Le baron de Walef. Un Wallon face au soleil," in *Publications du centre méridional de rencontres sur le 17e siècle*, Marseille, 1975.

Delval, E. "Autour du *Télémaque* de Fénelon," *Mémoires de la Société d'émulation de Cambrai,* LXXXIV (1936), 133–215, and LXXXV (1937), 135–201, 211–212.

Depping, G. B. *Correspondance administrative sous le règne de Louis XIV,* Paris, 1850–55, 4 vols.

Dictionary of Canadian Biography, Toronto, 1966–1972, 5 vols.

Dictionnaire de biographie française, ed. M. Prévost et al., Paris, 1933–.

Dictionnaire des oeuvres littéraires du Québec, Montreal, 1978.

Dictionnaire historique et biographique de la Suisse, Neuchâtel, 1921–1933, 7 vols.

Eeghen, I. H. van. *De Amsterdamse Boekhandel (1680–1725),* Amsterdam, 1962–1978, 5 vols.

Enschede, A.-J. "Médaille commémorative d'un réfugié," *Bulletin de la Commission de l'histoire des Eglises Wallonnes*, I, 2ème série (1896), 179–185.

Erasmus, D. *Les Colloques d'Erasme, choisis, traduits et présentés par Léon-E. Halkin,* Québec, 1971.

———— *Opera omnia,* Amsterdam, 1969–1977, 8 vols.

Fassò, L. *Avventurieri della penna del seicento,* Firenze, 1923.

Fénelon, F. de S. de la M. *Oeuvres complètes,* ed. J. E. A. Gosselin, Paris, 1848– 1852, 10 vols.

———— *Les Aventures de Télémaque,* ed. A. Cahen, Paris, 1920, 2 vols.

Forehand, W. E. "Adaptation and Comic Intent: Plautus' *Amphitruo* and Molière's *Amphitryon," Comparative Literature Studies,* XI, no. 3 (September 1974), 204–217

Gachet d'Artigny, A. *Nouveaux Mémoires d'histoire, de critique et de littérature,* Paris, 1749–1756, 7 vols.

Gavin, J. A. and Walsh, T. W. "The *Praise of Folly* in Context: The Commentary of Girardius Listrius," *Renaissance Quarterly,* XXIV (1971), 193–209.

Georgi, Th. *Algemeinen Europäischen Bücher-Lexici,* Leipzig, 1742–1753, 3 vols.

Gibbs, G. C. "The role of the Dutch Republic as the intellectual entrepôt of Europe in the seventeenth and eighteenth centuries," *Bijdragen en Mededelingen betreffende de geschiedenis der Nederlanden,* LXXXVI (1971), 323–349.

———— "Some Intellectual and Political Influences of the Huguenot Emigrés in the United Provinces, c. 1680–1730," *BMGN,* XC (1975), 255– 287.

Gibson, R. W. and Patrick, J. M. *St. Thomas More, a preliminary bibliography of his works,* New Haven, 1961.

Goujet, C. P. *Bibliothèque française,* Paris, 1741–1756, 18 vols.

Greenly, A. H. "Lahontan: An Essay and Bibliography," *Papers of the Bibliographical Society of America,* XLVIII (1954), 334–389.

Haag, E. *La France Protestante,* Paris, 1846–1859, 9 vols., and 1877–1888, 6 vols.

Hatin, E. *Les Gazettes de Hollande et la presse clandestine au XVIIe et au XVIIIe siècles,* Paris, 1865.

———— *Histoire politique et littéraire de la presse périodique en France,* Paris, 1859.

Heawood, E. *Watermarks, mainly of the 17th and 18th centuries,* Hilversum, 1950.

Hoefer, F. *Nouvelle Biographie générale,* Paris, 1855–1866, 46 vols.

Jourdan, A.-J. L. ed. *Dictionnaire des sciences médicales,* Paris, 1820–1825, 7 vols.

Klaits, J. *Printed Propaganda under Louis XIV,* Princeton, 1976.

Knetsch, F. R. J. *Pierre Jurieu, theoloog en politikus,* Kampen, 1967.

Koeman, C. *Atlantes Neerlandici,* Amsterdam, 1967–1971, 5 vols.

Köpeczi, B. *La France et la Hongrie au début du XVIIIe siècle,* Budapest, 1971.

Kossmann, E. F. *De Boekhandel te 's-Gravenhage tot het eind van de 18e eeuw,* 's-Gravenhage, 1937.

La Barre de Beaumarchais, A. de. *Lettres sérieuses et badines,* La Haye, 1730– 1740, 12 vols.

Labrousse, E. *Pierre Bayle,* The Hague, 1963–1964, 2 vols.

218

———— *Inventaire critique de la correspondance de Pierre Bayle,* Paris, 1961.

La Chapelle, J. de. *Lettres d'un Suisse,* 1702–1709.

Lacoste, E. *Bayle, nouvelliste et critique littéraire,* Paris, 1928.

Lahontan, baron de. *Dialogues curieux,* ed. G. Chinard, Baltimore/Oxford, 1931.

———— *Dialogues avec un sauvage,* ed. M. Roelens, Paris, 1973.

Lamberty, G. de. *Mémoires pour servir à l'histoire du dix-huitième siècle,* La Haye, 1724–1734, 12 vols.

Le Bouler, J.-P. "Les emprunts de Rousseau à la Bibliothèque du Roi," *Annales Jean-Jacques Rousseau,* XXXVIII (1969–1971), 241–258.

Lebreton, T. *Biographie rouennaise,* Rouen, 1865.

Lenglet-Dufresnoy, N. *De l'usage des romans. . . par M. de C. Gordon de Percel,* Amsterdam, 1723, 2 vols.

Lewine, J. *Bibliography of Eighteenth-Century Art and Illustrated Books,* London, 1898.

Lichtenberger, A. *Le Socialisme au XVIIIe siècle,* Paris, 1895.

———— *Le Socialisme utopique,* Paris, 1898.

Lombard, A. *Fénelon et le retour à l'antique au XVIIIe siècle,* Neuchâtel, 1954.

Lottin, A. M. *Catalogue chronologique des libraires et des libraires-imprimeurs de Paris,* Paris, 1789.

Malssen, P.J.W. van. *Louis XIV d'après les pamphlets répandus en Hollande,* Amsterdam, 1936.

Marchand, P. *Dictionnaire historique,* Paris/La Haye, 1758–1759, 2 vols.

Margolin, J.-C. *Recherches érasmiennes,* Geneva, 1969.

Martin, H. G. *Fénelon en Hollande,* Amsterdam, 1928.

Mélèse, P. *Un homme de lettres au temps du grand roi: Donneau de Visé, fondateur du Mercure galant,* Paris, 1936.

Michaud, J. F. and L. G. *Biographie universelle, ancienne et moderne,* Paris, 1811–1828, 52 vols.

Molhuysen, P. C. and Blok, P. J. *Nieuw Nederlandsch biographisch woordenboek,* Leiden, 1911–1937, 10 vols.

National Union Catalog Pre-1956 Imprints, London/Chicago, 1968–1979, 555 vols.

Oursel, N.N. *Nouvelle Biographie normande,* Paris, 1886, 2 vols.

Paquot, J. N. *Mémoires pour servir à l'histoire littéraire des dix-sept provinces des Pays-Bas,* Louvain, 1765–1770, 3 vols.

Parguez, G. "A propos des pages de titre des livres anciens," *Revue française d'histoire du livre* (1971), 55–75.

Pfister, L. *Notices biographiques et bibliographiques sur les Jésuites de l'ancienne mission de Chine, 1552–1773,* Shanghai, 1934.

Phillips, M. M. "Erasmus and Propaganda. A Study of the Translations of Erasmus in English and French," *Modern Language Review,* XXXVII (1952), 1–17.

Pinot, V. *La Chine et la formation de l'esprit philosophique en France (1640–1740),* Paris, 1932.

Plautus, T. M. *Plaute,* ed. A. Ernout, Paris, 1932–1940, 7 vols.

Préclin, E. and Tapié, V.-L. *Le XVIIe siècle,* Paris, 1943.

Quérard, J. M. *Les Supercheries littéraires,* Paris, 1869–1870, 3 vols.

Radice, B. "Holbein's marginal illustrations to the *Praise of Folly,*" *Erasmus in English,* 7 (1975), 9–17.

Rechtien, J. G. "A 1520 French Translation of the *Moriae Encomium,*" *Renaissance Quarterly,* XXVII (1974), 23–35.

Riemens, K. J. *Esquisse historique de l'enseignement du français en Hollande du XVIe au XIXe siècle,* Leyde, 1919.

Roger, J. *Les Médecins normands du XIIe au XIXe siècle,* Paris, 1890, 2 vols.

Rosenberg. A. "The *Voyages et avantures de Jaques Massé* and the problem of the first edition," *Australian Journal of French Studies,* VII, no. 3 (1970), 271–288.

———— *Tyssot de Patot and His Work (1655–1738),* The Hague, 1972.

———— "An Eighteenth-Century French Translation of *Moriae Encomium.* Gueudeville's *L'Eloge de la folie,*" *Erasmus in English,* X (1979).

Rousseau, J.-J. *Discours sur les sciences et les arts,* ed. G. Havens, London, 1946.

Rowbotham, A. H. *Missionary and Mandarin: The Jesuits at the Court of China,* Berkeley, 1942.

Roy, J.-E. "Le Baron de Lahontan," *Transactions of the Royal Society of Canada,* 1st. ser., XII (1894), 63–192.

Sauvy, A. *Livres saisis à Paris entre 1678 et 1701,* The Hague, 1972.

Sayce, R. A. "Compositorial Practices and the Localisation of Printed Books, 1530–1800," *The Library,* XXI (March 1966), 1–45.

Sgard, J. ed. *Dictionnaire des journalistes, 1600–1789,* Grenoble, 1976.

Smith, D. W. "Helvétius, Voltaire and a French Pirate: Michelin of Provins," *Australian Journal of French Studies,* VII, no. 3 (1970), 289–298.

Stephen, L. and Lee, S. ed. *Dictionary of National Biography,* London, 1885–1901, 66 vols.

Tassin, R. P. *Histoire littéraire de la Congrégation de Saint-Maur,* Bruxelles, 1770.

Theobald, L. *The Censor,* London, 1715–1717.

Van der Haeghen, F. F. E. *Marques typographiques... des Pays-Bas,* Gand, 1894, 2 vols.

Yardeni, M. "Gueudeville et Louis XIV. Un précurseur du socialisme, critique des structures sociales louis-quatorziennes," *Revue d'histoire moderne et contemporaine,* XIX (1972), 598–620.

———— "Journalisme et histoire contemporaine à l'époque de Bayle," *History and Theory,* XII (1973), 208–229.

PERIODICALS

Bibliothèque ancienne et moderne
Bibliothèque britannique

Bibliothèque universelle et historique
Boekzaal
La Clef du cabinet des princes
L'Elite des nouvelles
L'Europe savante
Gazette
Histoire critique de la République des lettres
Histoire des ouvrages des savants
Journal de Trévoux
Journal des savante
Journal Littéraire de La Haye
Mercure galant
Mercure historique et politique
Nouveau Journal universel
Nouvelles de la République des lettres
Nouvelles Littéraires
La Quintessence des nouvelles

NOTES TO INTRODUCTION

1. Althought the term Holland should be more correctly reserved for the province of that name, I have adopted the common practice of using it to represent all the United Provinces of the Netherlands.
2. *Tyssot de Patot and His Work (1655–1738),* The Hague, 1972.
3. G. C. Gibbs, "Some Intellectual and Political Influences of the Huguenot Emigrés in the United Provinces, c. 1680–1730," *Bijdragen en Mededelingen betreffende de geschiedenis der Nederlanden*, XC (1975), 273.

NOTES TO CHAPTER I

1. See A.-J. Enschede, "Médaille commémorative d'un réfugié," *Bulletin de la Commission de l'histoire des Eglises Wallonnes*, I, 2ème série (1896), 179–185. The Rouen municipal archives contain references to a Pierre Gueudeville, "avocat à la Cour" in 1617, and his brother Thierry, "receveur général du taillon" (catalogue of the Archives municipales: Délibérations, 1389–1790, p. 295).

In the Archives de la région de Haute Normandie et du département de la Seine-Maritime (G 6342: Comptes de la fabrique de l'église paroissiale de St. Caude-le-Vieux de Rouen, 1597–1637), there is a reference to the burial of a Dom Jacques Gueudeville, religieux de Valmont, who died at the home of his brother, Nicolas Gueudeville, tapissier (1619). There are also references to other Gueudeville families in the Rouen parishes of St. Pierre-du-Châtel, Notre-Dame de la Ronde, and Saint Jean.

According to Haag, *La France Protestante,* 1855, vol. V, p. 382, "En 1660, on trouve un Gueudeville dans le consistoire de Basly, et en 1688, une Margueríte Gueudeville au nombre des Huguenotes détenues aux Nouvelles-Catholiques de Caen."

2. Although there are 900 registers relating to the civil records of some 35 parishes of Rouen at this time, these documents are uncatalogued and there is no index of baptisms. The standard biographies differ over the question of Gueudeville's year of birth. Michaud, *Biographie universelle,* 1817, vol. XVII, p. 35, and Hoefer, *Nouvelle Biographie générale,* 1858, vol. XXII, p. 478, give "vers 1650;" Lebreton, *Biographie rouennaise,* 1865, p. 173, gives 1652; Haag, *op. cit.,* Van der Aa, *Biographisch Woordenboek der Nederlanden,* 1862, vol. V, p. 165, and Oursel, *Nouvelle Biographie normande,* 1886, vol. I, p. 435, give 1654. On July 8 1671, when Gueudeville made his vows in the Benedictine monastery at Jumièges, his age was recorded as nineteen (see entry number 2801 in *Matricula Monachorum* ed. Dom Yves Chaussy, 1959). If this entry is correct, it means either that he was born in the latter half of 1651, i.e. when he became a monk he was nineteen and due to be twenty in the second half of the year, or that he was born in the first half of 1652. The monastic authorities, however, had a habit of rounding off ages to the nearest birthday (see, for example, the cases of Bessin, Alexandre, Martène, and Rivet de la Grange in R. P. Tassin, *Histoire littéraire de la Congrégation de Saint-Maur,* Bruxelles, 1770, pp. 479, 516, 542, 651). It is possible, therefore, that Gueudeville was born in the latter part of 1652, i.e. he made his vows when he was still only eighteen. I raise this possibility because, in the autobiographical preface to his *Les Motifs de la conversion,* Rotterdam, 1689, a book not mentioned by his biographers, Gueudeville states that, "je me fis moine, n'ayant guère plus de dix-sept ans, dans une abbaye de Bénédictins de la Congrégation de Saint-Maur, à cinq lieues de Rouen..." This would suggest he was born, at the latest, in the first half of 1654. It is conceivable that, so many years after the event, Gueudeville could have made a mistake of a year in his recollections, but unlikely that he would be out by two years, considering the importance of such an event in his life. Perhaps the explanation of this contradiction is that when Gueudeville wrote, "je me fis moine, n'ayant guère plus de dix-sept ans," he was referring to the time he first entered the monastery as a postulant, rather than to the date he officially entered the order. This, I think, is the source of the error in Haag, *op. cit.,* where it is stated, "A l'âge de 17 ans à peine, il entra dans la congrégation de Saint-Maur et fit profession dans l'abbaye de Jumièges." It looks as if Haag might have known *Les Motifs de la conversion,* although he does not mention it, but had not seen the *Matricula monachorum,* and thus took Gueudeville's year of birth to be 1654.

   To sum up this somewhat lengthy discussion, the best one can say, in the absence of further evidence, is that Gueudeville was most probably born some time in 1652.

The information that Gueudeville's father was a doctor is given by Bayle in his letter to Marais, March 6 1702 (see vol. II of his *Lettres choisies*, Rotterdam, 1714, p. 749). The name of Gueudeville does not appear in Jules Roger, *Les Médecins normands du XIIe au XIXe siècle*, Paris, 1890, 2 vols.

3. Preface to *Les Motifs de la conversion*.

4. Ibidem.

5. The archives of the monastery of Saint-Martin-de Sées (Archives de l'Orne, H938-1040) make no mention of Gueudeville.

6. Preface to *Les Motifs de la conversion*.

7. *De l'usage des romans. . . par M. de C. Gordon de Percel*, Amsterdam, 1734, vol. I, pp. 173—176.

8. In *Les Motifs de la conversion*, Gueudeville stated, "Il y a plus de douze ans que je suis détrompé sur l'Eucharistie, et depuis peu à peu aidé aussi par les livres du célèbre M. Jurieu, j'ai secoué les autres erreurs avec la prévention qui m'y attachait" (viii-ix). Later on in the work, in an unmistakeable reference to Jurieu, he says, "j'aurai toute ma vie obligation à un grand personnage que le ciel a donné à cette Eglise avec tant d'autres, et duquel je puis dire que les admirables écrits, après Dieu, m'ont illuminé" (p. 99).

9. For details of this "affair" see E. Labrousse, *Pierre Bayle*, The Hague, 1963, vol. I, pp. 227—229.

10. The fiches of the Eglise Wallonne provide the following information: Mariés à La Haye le 10 juin 1691, Nicolas Gueudeville et Marie Blèche. Baptisé à Rotterdam le 14 mai 1692, Marie Gueudeville, fille de Nicolas et Marie Blèche. Parrain : David de Caux; marraine : Marie de Cassel. Baptisé à Rotterdam le 29 janv. 1696, Anne Madeleine (1) et Marie (2) Gueudeville, enfants de Nicolas et Marie Blèche. Parrain (1) M. Basnage; marraine (1) Anne Madeleine Masclary. Parrain (2) le père; marraine (2) Marie Bunel.

Baptisé à Rotterdam le 13 oct. 1697, Pierre Gueudeville, fils de Nicolas et Marie Blèche d'Issoudun. Parrain : Bert d'Amsterdam; marraine : Christina van Herzèle de Nantes.

The Hague Municipal Archives have the following entry — "den 20 Mei 1691 ondertrouwden Nicolaas Guddeville jm van Rouen won te Rotterdam en Marie Bloche jd. van Issoudun en Berry, won. alhr. Getrouwd in de Fransche Kerk den 10 Juni 1691."

The Hague Municipal Archives (Archief Waalse Gemeente m. 101,

Lidmaten Register Waalse Kerk 1632–1710, no. 1504) also record that "Mademoiselle Marie Blocke de la Province de Berry s'est présentée à cette Compagnie pour témoigner le déplaisir qu'elle a d'avoir signé en France et demander la paix de l'Eglise ce qui lui a été accordé le 20 Juin 1689." The birth of Gueudeville's children is also recorded in the Municipal Archives of Rotterdam which supply additional information about the witnesses, and also record the death of an unnamed child, presumably either stillborn or dead before it could be given a name, on July 14 1698 (*Extract uit de Registers der doden te Rotterdam*). This entry also provides the information that Gueudeville was, at that time, living in Delftsevaart by the Krattebrug.

The information about Marie's residence with the Masclary family is found in a letter from Brossette to Boileau, December 20 1701 (see *Correspondance entre Boileau Despréaux et Brossette,* Paris, 1858, p. 97). The Masclary family is discussed in Haag, *op. cit.,* 1857, vol. VIII, pp. 304–305.

11. According to Lenglet Dufresnoy, *op. cit.,* after Gueudeville's death, his wife and daughter returned to France and embraced catholicism.

12. Letter to Marais, previously cited.
    For an account of the ways in which French refugees earned their living as teachers see K. J. Riemens, *Esquisse historique de l'enseignement du français en Hollande du XVIe au XIXe siècle,* Leyde, 1919.

13. *Lettres sérieuses et badines,* VIII, 2ème partie (1740), 248–249.

14. For details of Gueudeville's journalistic career see chapter three.

15. The critique of *Télémaque,* the *Atlas historique,* and the editions of Lahontan, are dealt with in chapters four, six and eight, respectively.

16. Algemeen Rijksarchief, Archief Staten Generaal, Inv. no. 3761, March 25 1706:

    Op de requeste van Nicolaes Gueudeville gewezene Religieus Benedictin van Congregatie van St. Maur; verzoekende dat haar Hoog Mogende geliefden hem Suppliant te accorderen een somme van twee honderd guldens, om hem te redden uit zijnen miserablen staat; is naar voorgaande deliberatie goedgevonden and verstaan, dat in het voorsz verzoek niet kan werden getreden, en werd dien volgende het zelve afgewezen.

17. In the previously cited letter to Marais, Bayle said he knew Gueudeville "assez particulièrement," and from a letter to the baron de Walef, February 12 1706, it is clear that he was still in close touch with Gueudeville.

224

18. These two works are dealt with in chapters five and six, respectively.

19. These two works are discussed in chapter seven.

20. See chapter six.

21. See chapter seven.

22. *Bibliothèque ancienne et moderne,* XXII (1724), 221–222.

23. See chapter seven.

24. *Op. cit.,* 222. Frédéric-Auguste Gabillon, about whom very little is known, was born in Paris where he became a monk. Regretting his loss of liberty he left the monastery, went to Holland and became a Protestant. He tried to support himself by working for publishers but amassed considerable debts. In order to escape his creditors he went to England where he passed himself off as Jean Le Clerc and, for a while, profited from the deception. Eventually he was unmasked and obliged to return to Holland where he instituted proceedings against Le Clerc, presumably on the the theory that attack is the best form of defence. He wrote violent anti-Catholic and anti-French diatribes but was unable to fulfil his ambition to be a minister in the Walloon Church. It is not known what became of him after about 1700 (see Michaud, *op. cit.,* vol. XV, p. 320).

25. J. N. Paquot, *Mémoires pour servir à l'histoire littéraire des dix-sept provinces des Pays-Bas,* Louvain, 1765–1770, 3 vols., vol. III, pp. 189–192, attributes this account to Lenglet Dufresnoy. There is no way of verifying the accuracy of this account which mistakenly identifies Van der Aa as a publisher of The Hague when he was the best known publisher in Leiden. Similarly, there is no way of verifying the following entry, dated 8/2/1753, that appears in d'Hémery's *Journal de la librairie* (ms fr. 22158, fol 8v–9r):

Le S. de St Auban [Aulan, Autun?] auteur très connu par ses couardises ayant été obligé de passer au service de la Compagnie des Indes a péri dans le vaisseau qui a fait naufrage. On m'a assuré que Gueudeville avait eu le même sort. Voilà deux bons sujets de moins.

I am grateful to Professor D. W. Smith for the above quotation.

26. Bayle, Letter to Marais; Le Clerc, *op. cit.*; Lenglet Dufresnoy, *op. cit.*

27. *L'Esprit des cours de l' Europe* (June 1699), 29.

28. *Ibidem* (August 1703), 140.

29. *Ibidem* (January-April 1709), 24.

30. *Ibidem* (March 1705), 258.

31. *Op. cit.,* 268–269.

32. *L'Esprit des cours* (September 1705), 340; (August 1706), 142.

NOTES TO CHAPTER II

1. LES / MOTIFS / DE LA / CONVERSION / DE / M. GUEUDEVILE, cy-devant / Religieux Benedictin de la Con- / gregation de S Maur, en France. / *Dans un Discours prononcé dans l'Eglise / Wallonne de Rotterdam, le* / 18. *Julliet* 1689. / [vignette of bowl of flowers] / A ROTTERDAM, / *Aux dépens de l'Auteur,* 1689.

   Formula
   8° *⁸ A-F⁸ G⁴
   pp. [16] 1–104

   Contents
   *1, title; *2–*3v, A... Mrs LES CONDUCTEURS DE L'EGLISE WALLONNE DE ROTTERDAM; *4–*6, AVIS AU LECTEUR, *6–*8, Priere avant le Discours; A1–G3v, text; G4–G4v, PRIERE APRES L'ACTION. *1v and *8v are blank. The only copy of this work known to me is at McMaster University, Hamilton, Ontario, where it is bound with *Histoire des tromperies des prestres et des moines de l'église romaine,* A Rotterdam, chez Abraham Acher, M.DC.XCIII. This latter work is attributed to Gabriel d'Emiliane.

   Les Motifs de la conversion, or some variant, was a common title in the seventeenth century, and was used by Protestants converting to Catholicism and vice-versa. Cf., for example, Daniel de Larroque's *Les Véritables Motifs de la conversion de l'abbé de la Trappe,* Cologne, Pierre Marteau, 1685, noted in Anne Sauvy, *Livres saisis à Paris entre 1687 et 1701,* The Hague, 1972, p. 139.

2. Lenglet Dufresnoy, *op. cit.,* p. 176, levelled a similar charge at the Protestants who accepted without question, but with no illusions, the hordes of *moines défroqués* who invaded Holland: "Mais on les reçoit; s'ils ne servent rien pour avancer l'honneur de la religion, ce sont au moins des sujets propres à augmenter les membres de l'état."

3. Innocent XI died less than a month after Gueudeville offered this dubious tribute.

4. In *L'Esprit des cours de l'Europe* (January 1705), 182, Gueudeville writes, "Si je n'étais Huguenot. . . "

NOTES TO CHAPTER III

1. L'ESPRIT / DES / COURS / DE L'EUROPE, / OÙ / L'on voit tout ce qui s'y passe de plus / important touchant la Politique, & en / général ce qu'il y a de plus remar- / quable dans les nouvelles. As far as I know, the only article devoted solely to this periodical is that of M. Yardeni, "Gueudeville et Louis XIV. Un précurseur du socialisme, critique des structures sociales louis-quatorziennes," *Revue d'histoire moderne et contemporaine*, XIX (1972), 598–620. There are some references to the journal in Yardeni's later article, "Journalisme et histoire contemporaine à l'époque de Bayle," *History and Theory*, XII (1973), 208–229, and in J. Klaits, *Printed Propaganda under Louis XIV*, Princeton U.P., 1976, especially chapters two, three and five. (I am grateful to Professor D. J. Roorda who first introduced me to this book). In B. Köpeczi, *La France et la Hongrie au début du XVIIIe siècle*, Budapest, 1971, pp. 391–395, there is a detailed study of the position taken by *L'Esprit des cours* on the relationship between France and Hungary from 1701 to 1710. References to the periodical are also found in E. Hatin, *Les Gazettes de Hollande et la presse clandestine au XVIIe et au XVIIIe siècles*, Paris, 1865, especially pp. 190–192; *Histoire politique et littéraire de la presse périodique en France*, Paris, 1859, vol. III, pp. 284, 298–299; E. Bourgeois and L. André, *Les Sources de l'histoire de France*, Paris, 1924, pt. 3, vol. IV, pp. 51–52; C. Bellanger et al., *Histoire générale de la presse française*, Paris, 1969, vol. I, p. 150; *Dictionnaire des journalistes*, ed. J. Sgard, Grenoble, 1976. My study is based on the copies of the periodical found at The Hague (R) and Paris (BN). Neither of these libraries possesses a complete set of first editions, and I am not aware of any library that does. Other libraries that have complete sets are Münster (U), Paris (Ar), Wisconsin (U). Partial sets, from 1699 to 1706, are held by Cambridge (U), Iowa (U), Lyon (M), Stockholm (R). Other sets, of varying degrees of completeness, are found in Carpentras (I), Copenhagen (R), Grenoble (M), Washington (LC), Wofenbüttel (HA), Zurich (C), and the university libraries of Erlangen, Göttingen, Kiel, Rostock, Wurzburg.

2. For an understanding of the tone and content of these political periodicals, it should be remembered that, when Gueudeville began publishing his journal, a war against France had just ended and another was about to begin. The Dutch, in fact, had been intermittently at war with France for some thirty years. In 1667, without a declaration of war, Louis XIV laid claim to the Spanish Netherlands, and French troops, led by Turenne, invaded the area. The Dutch formed an alliance with England and Sweden,

and peace was negotiated the following year, with France, the most powerful nation in Europe, retaining its gains in The Netherlands. By 1672, Louis XIV had succeeded in isolating the Dutch from their allies, and his troops invaded the United Provinces. But the Dutch held their own and were eventually supported by former and new allies. The war dragged on until 1679 when peace, again to the advantage of France, was signed at Nijmegen. Louis XIV next made plans to annex territories belonging to Austria. Since the Emperor was heavily involved fighting the Turks who were supported by France, Louis' prospects seemed bright. France made some gains at the expense of Austria and Spain, and, in 1684, a truce was signed at Ratisbon. By this time, French military and naval power were feared all over Europe. 1685 saw the Revocation of the Edict of Nantes which further exacerbated relations between France and the Protestant countries.

In 1686, in order to avert French domination of the nations of Europe and their overseas possessions, many of these nations, including Austria, the United Provinces, Spain, Sweden, The Palatinate, Saxony, Bavaria and Savoy, formed the League of Augsburg. In 1688, in a bloodless coup, William of Orange deposed James II and became king of England. Louis had already moved against the Emperor and occupied Cologne. In the ensuing battles, the French, forced to retreat, devastated the countryside. The war spread to many fronts. In 1690, in Ireland, James II was defeated at the battle of the Boyne and fled to France. In 1692 the French navy suffered a severe setback at the battle of La Hogue. However, the French made gains in The Netherlands and in Italy. By 1697 both sides were exhausted, in all senses, and a peace was negotiated at Ryswick.

The outstanding, unresolved issue concerned the rival claims of France and Austria to the Spanish throne. In 1698 there was drawn up the First Partition Treaty by which it was agreed that, on the death of Charles II of Spain, the interested parties would divide up Spain and its possessions in such a way as to maintain the balance of power. However, in 1699, one of the claimants, the Electoral prince, died, and a Second Partition Treaty was negotiated. This proved to be generally unsatisfactory to all parties, especially to Austria and Spain. In 1700, Charles died, leaving a will naming the duke of Anjou as heir to the throne. Louis decided to act on the will and not on the terms of the partition treaties. Meanwhile, war had broken out in the North, between Sweden and Poland, and was threatening to involve the rest of Europe. When Gueudeville began publishing *L'Esprit des cours de l'Europe*, therefore, all Europe was preparing for war. The popular attitude towards Louis XIV, outside France, was that he was an unscrupulous tyrant whose ambition was to establish a "monarchie universelle" in the manner of Alexander the Great and Charlemagne, and, more to the point, in the manner of Charles V and Philip II whose actions in the sixteenth century had made the

Spanish monarchy appear to be motivated by ambitions of a "monarchie universelle". See, for example, *La Monarchie universelle de Louys XIV traduite de l'italien de M. Leti. . . ,* Amsterdam, A. Wolfgang, 1698, 2 vols.

3. The most notable of the recent contributions in this field have come from G. C. Gibbs. See especially his articles, "The role of the Dutch Republic as the intellectual entrepôt of Europe in the seventeenth and eighteenth centuries," *Bijdragen en Mededelingen betreffende de Geschiedenis der Nederlanden,* LXXXVI (1971), 323–349, and, in the same journal, "Some Intellectual and Political Influences of the Huguenot Emigrés in the United Provinces, c. 1680–1730," XC (1975), 255–287. A study of the role of the monthly periodicals in reporting and commenting on the relationship between France and Hungary is found in B. Köpeczi, *op. cit.* The importance of these periodicals is also discussed in J. Klaits, *op. cit.*

4. G. C. Gibbs, art. cit., 348–349.

5. The copies of the first issue at The Hague (R) and Paris (BN) have a title-page bearing the name Les Frères L'Honoré. The copy at Stockholm (R) has Etienne Foulque, and the copy at Iowa (U) has François L'Honoré.

6. E.g., *Mercure historique et politique, contenant l'état présent de l'Europe, ce qui se passe dans toutes les cours; L'Elite des nouvelles de toutes les cours de l'Europe; Mémoires et Négotiations secrètes de diverses cours de l'Europe.*

7. Yardeni, art. cit., 218. In the case of *L'Esprit des cours* the section on France enjoys priority of position and greatest length until May 1701 when the section on Rome begins and continues to dominate the periodical until its demise in 1710. The first issue included articles on France, Rome, Poland, The Empire, Spain and England, in that order. It contained 120 pages, and this is roughly the length of all the monthly issues. When the journal began to appear every four months, from 1707, an issue contained about 240 pages. Other places dealt with over the years appear under the following headings – Bavaria, Berlin, Brandenburg, Brussels, Constantinople, Danzig, Denmark, Dresden, Great Britain, The Hague, Hanover, Italy, Lombardy, Lorraine, Madrid, Mantua, Moscow, Naples, Ottoman Empire, Portugal, Prussia, Savoy, Saxony, Scotland, Sweden, Switzerland, Turin, Venice, Vienna. At the end of each volume (i.e. every six months) there is a detailed index, except in vol. IV (January-June 1701).

   An examination of the format and contents of the *Mercure historique et politique* and of the ephemeral *L'Elite des nouvelles de toutes les cours de l'Europe* for the months immediately preceding the first issue of *L'Esprit des cours,* reveals to what extent Gueudeville's periodical followed established practice. The issues of the *Mercure historique* include articles on Rome, Italy, Turkey, Ethiopia, Egypt, Germany, Holland. Each issue contains about 120 pages, and an index is placed at the end of a six-month period, i.e. one volume. The issues of *L'Elite des nouvelles* from January to May have articles on Italy, Germany, France, Spain, England, Sweden, Denmark, Poland, Holland, and each issue contains about 120 pages.

For details of these two periodicals and their authors see Hatin, *Les Gazettes de Hollande...*, pp. 176–178, 189–190. Anne Sauvy, *Livres saisis à Paris entre 1678 et 1701*, The Hague, 1972, pp. 297, no. 823, suggests that *L'Elite des nouvelles* was not edited by Courtilz de Sandras, editor of the *Mercure historique*, but by his brother.

8. D.-F. Camusat, *Histoire critique des journaux*, Amsterdam, 1734, vol. II, p. 41: "Les préfaces des journalistes sont d'ordinaire assez uniformes. Ils promettent presque tous les mêmes choses." Some examples of this uniformity are: "Il n'y a rien après quoi nous courions avec plus d'avidité qu'après les nouvelles, et celles des mois ne sont pas moins impatiemment attendues que celles des semaines" (*Mercure historique et politique*, 1686); "Il n'y a rien de si amusant que les nouvelles; chacun même s'en montre si friand, que les plus habiles gens comme les autres y courent avec un empressement tout extraordinaire" (*L'Elite des nouvelles...*, 1698); "Il n'y a peut-être jamais eu de siècle si soigneux d'instruire le public de tout ce qui se passe de curieux dans le monde que le nôtre" (*Histoire abrégée de l'Europe*, 1686); "je n'ai cherché à dire du mal de personne" (*Mercure galant*, 1699); "on n'insérera pas... de satires personnelles" (*Bibliothèque universelle et historique*, 1686); "nous ne souhaitons pas de ces esprits satiriques qui ne s'attachent qu'à déchirer les réputations ou chagriner quelque particulier" (*Nouveau Journal universel*, 1689).

9. The copy of this issue at the Royal Library belongs to a series of later editions of the periodical. The title-page bears the date 1713. Similarly, the title-page of the issue for September 1699 bears the date 1708.

10. A comparison of the copies of this issue in The Hague (R) and Paris (BN) reveals a marked difference in compositorial practices. These differences also occur in several subsequent issues. Evidence of a demand for the periodical is also supplied by Anne Sauvy, *op. cit.*, who lists instances of the confiscation of numerous issues (see items 957, 966, 975 and 1062).

11. 390–412.

12. *Mémoires pour servir à l'histoire du dix-huitième siècle*, La Haye, 1724–1734, vol. I, p. 391. Very little was known about Guillaume de Lamberty (?-1733), especially the early years, before Luigi Fassò's *Avventurieri della penna del seicento*, Firenze, 1923, in which the author published the results of his researches into the correspondence of Gregorio Leti and the archives

of Milan and Geneva. According to Fassò, Lamberty's real name was Giovanni Gerolamo Arconati Lamberti. He was born in Milan, out of wedlock. During the course of his early years, first in Milan and then in Rome, he seems to have been involved in a variety of scandals including three murders, of which he was probably responsible for one, a stabbing, fathering an illegitimate child, and blackmail. He was also the author of several libellous manuscripts. For some of his misdeeds he was apprehended and spent time in prison from which he managed to escape. Altogether, then, he appears to have been an unsavoury and energetic individual, more like a character from fiction than real life. From 1674 to about 1685 his activities were centred in and around Geneva where he continued his nefarious activities. The Genevan authorities refused his repeated requests to embrace Calvinism, to get married and settle in Geneva, and they tried, in vain, to have him arrested and banished. In 1682, according to the archives, he was living in Geneva, probably with the status of "habitant", married and a Calvinist. Around this time he seems to have embarked on a new career as a spy, perhaps a double agent, since he became involved in a Spanish plot to foment a Protestant uprising in France and also in selling the secrets of the plot to the French ambassador, Gravel. He also proposed to Gravel's successor, Tambonneau, that he, Lamberti, would spy on the Dauphinois and the Milanese. This offer was refused.

After 1685, Lamberti disappeared from Geneva and turned up, the following year, in Amsterdam. From there he seems to have gone to London where he became secretary to Lord Portland, ambassador in The Hague until 1689. In 1691, passing through Rotterdam, he proposed to Bayle an Italian translation of the *Nouvelles de la République des lettres.* According to Joseph Dedieu, *Le Rôle politique des Protestants français,* Paris, 1920, pp. 244–247, Guillaume de Lamberty (as he was known although he signed his name "Lamberti de Saint Léo") was in charge of an espionage organization on behalf of England from about 1690 to 1715. Dedieu's evidence for Lamberty's spying before 1708 is meagre, and I have, unfortunately, been able to add little to substantiate it. Lamberty's name does not appear in the indexes to the printed Calendars of State Papers Domestic (1697–1702), or in the indexes to the Portland manuscripts in the Manuscript Dept. of the University of Nottingham Library. I have been unable to consult the HMC *Guides to Reports,* pt. II *Index of Persons* (1938, 1966) which have references to manuscripts, particularly the Cutts papers in HMC *Frankland-Russell-Astley* (1900). There is no reference to him in *Correspondentie van William III en van Hans Willem Bentinck, eersten graaf van Portland,* ed. N. Japikse, in *Rijks Geschiedkundige Publicatiën* ('s-Gravenhage, 1927–1937) 5 vols. In Bittner/Gross, *Repertorium der diplomatischen Vertreter,* vol. I, p. 76, there is reference to a Lamberty as agent and correspondent for Hanover in The Hague from 1706 to 1718. Some suggestion of espionage activities before 1708 has been given to me by Dr A. J. Veenendaal Jr., Bureau der Rijkscommissie voor Vaderlandse Geschiedenis, who, in the course of his magisterial edition of the correspondence of Heinsius, has come across a letter, dated August 23 1704, that envoy H. W. Rumpf sent from Stockholm to Heinsius' secretary, d'Alonne. With Dr Veenendaal's kind permission I quote the relevant extract. I have modernized the spelling here as everywhere else:

Vous savez, Monsieur, que je suis en correspondance avec M. Lamberty qui m'envoie tous les huit jours les nouvelles de La Haye en récompense de celles que je lui fais tenir d'ici. Quelques-uns de mes amis prétendent que je contreviens par là à la dite résolution et moi au contraire je soutiens que la défense d'entretenir un commerce de lettres avec d'autres personnes que celles du gouvernement, ne regarde que les secrétaires et les domestiques des ministres, et non pas les ministres mêmes, qui ne sauraient se dispenser de correspondre avec certains nouvellistes dont ils peuvent recevoir en échange de bons avis, pourvu qu'ils ne leur mandent rien, dont ils puissent faire un mauvais usage. M. Lamberty est un correspondant exact et curieux, qui a la bonté de se contenter de ma correspondance toute stérile et sèche qu'elle est; mais s'il ne m'était plus permis de lui écrire, il se lasserait bientôt de m'envoyer ses relations et je serais obligé de m'en rapporter aux gazettes et aux lettres du greffe, qui sont ordinairement un peu vieilles. . .

According to Fassò, Lamberty retired to Nyon in the Vaud where he was given permission to reside in 1718. In 1723, he sought and received the appointment as Resident for the Landgrave of Hesse-Cassel and for the king of Sweden for the republics of Berne and Geneva. In 1730—1731 he made an official visit to Geneva on behalf of the king of Sweden, and was received with full honours. He died on January 9 1733.

Until Fassò's publication it was thought that Lamberty was the author of only two works, the one mentioned at the beginning of this note that appeared in twelve volumes, and *Mémoires de la dernière révolution d'Angleterre*, La Haye, 1702, 2 vols. Fassò has argued, however, not altogether conclusively, that Lamberty was the author of several other works previously attributed to Gregorio Leti. Among these are, *Il Governo del duca d'Ossuna* (1678), the last three parts of *Il Divortio celeste* (1679) which include *Il Testamento di F. Pallavicino, L'Inquisizione processata* (1681), and *Vita del conte Bartolomeo Arese* (?).

For other references to Lamberty see E. Labrousse, *Inventaire critique de la correspondance de Pierre Bayle,* Paris, 1961, pp. 369—370.

I am grateful to my colleague Professor E. A. Walker for his clarification of certain sections of Fassò's book.

13. NOUVELLES / DES / COURS / DE L'EUROPE, / OU / L'on voit tout ce qui s'y passe de plus / remarquable sur la Politique & l'Intérêt des Princes.

14. Klaits, *op. cit.*, pp. 44–45. Klaits accepts Bayle's statement that the periodical reverted to its original title after d'Avaux's departure from The Netherlands, but the original title was not resumed until 1704.

D'Avaux evidently took great care to ensure that his complaints should remain informal, and that the matter should be settled quietly. In the 1701 resolutions of the States-General, both ordinary (States-General nos. 3344 and 3345) and secret (States-General no. 4610), there is no indication of any complaints by D'Avaux or Briord concerning the periodical. Nor is there any mention of the affair in the letters written by Briord, or in the correspondence of Coenraad van Heemskerck, extraordinary ambassador in France in 1701 (States-General no. 67931), or in the secret Lias Frankrijk (States-General no. 68641). I am most grateful to Mrs. M. C. J. C. Jansen-van Hoof of the Algemeen Rijksarchief for this information.

15. *Correspondance administrative sous le règne de Louis XIV,* ed. G. B. Depping, Paris, 1851, vol. II, p. 740. Complaints by foreign officials to the Dutch authorities about derogatory articles in the Dutch press were frequent, but not always effective. (See Hatin, *Les Gazettes de Hollande...* , pp. 93–101). In *L'Esprit des cours* for February 1700, 185–186, Gueudeville characterizes the role of an ambassador as that of "un honorable espion qui, à l'abri de son sacré et inviolable caractère, tâche de pénétrer dans le secret de l'état, observe toutes les démarches d'une cour, tient registre de tout ce qui se passe, en rend un compte exact à son maître et se formalise des moindres vérités qu'on ose publier contre son gouvernement."

16. In the May issue, The Hague (R) copy has a title-page with François L'Honoré, and the BN copy has Etienne Foulque. Apart from the difference in title-page both copies are identical, and both have running headlines that retain the old title, L'Esprit des Cours / de l'Europe, up to and including p. 241, after which the headline changes to Nouvelles des Cours / de l'Europe. This would suggest that by the time a new title had been adopted, well over half the issue (331 pp.) had already been printed. Copies with "Imprimé pour l'auteur" are found at Erlangen and the Library of Congress. A copy of the June issue that reintroduces the old title is in The Hague (R).

17. Jean Rousset, who took over the *Mercure historique* in 1724 (see the section on *Le Censeur* in chapter eight) complained that "tous les mois un misérable bouquiniste de Liège imprime en papier gris et avec des têtes de clous son Mercure qu'il sabre, châtre, rogne et défigure comme il lui plaît" (quoted by Hatin, *Les Gazettes de Hollande...* , p. 178). "French provincial printers seem to have reprinted the 'gazettes de Hollande' throughout the eighteenth century; nor were they alone in doing so. In the French-speaking parts of Switzerland, for example, the taste for the 'gazettes de Hollande'...

appears to have become firmly established during the War of the Spanish Succession, so firmly established, indeed, that after enduring a period of counterfeits, the city governement of Geneva was led in 1712 to offer to the highest bidder the obviously lucrative monopoly of their sole printing and publishing. A similar situation arose in c. 1723 and again in 1737 in Liège. . ." (Gibbs, art. cit., 334). Cf. Gueudeville's own comments on the suppression of anonymous publications: C'est ce qui arrive pour l'ordinaire à ces productions anonymes que l'on persécute avec tant de fureur. Le feu qui les brûle allume la curiosité de les lire, et leur cendre est comme une semence qui ne sert qu'à les multiplier. Que de satires seraient tombées d'elles-mêmes si on les avait négligées; au lieu qu'en leur faisant l'honneur de leur opposer les prisons et les galères on les immortalise, et on leur accorde beaucoup plus qu'elles ne demandent." (*L'Esprit des cours,* March 1700, 311).

18. Gemeente Archief 's-Gravenhage. Archief notarieel 19-10-73, Akte 66 IV, Inv. no. 1321. (See Appendix A).

19. See I. H. van Eeghen, *De Amsterdamse boekhandel* 1680–1725, Amsterdam, 1962–1978, vol. III, pp. 208–211.

20. Gemeente Archief 's-Gravenhage. Archief notarieel, Akte 31.12.1704[3], Inv. no. 1596). (See Appendix B).

21. Archief notarieel, fol. 463, Inv. no. 682. The disposition of Jonas L'Honoré's property was finally settled on May 19, 1706 (Archief notarieel, akte 19.5.1706 2, Inv. no. 1596. (See Appendix C). According to E. F. Kossmann, *De boekhandel te 's-Gravenhage tot het eind van de 18e eeuw,* 's-Gravenhage, 1937, p. 241, Jonas L'Honoré was declared bankrupt on October 28. Kossmann cites no document to support this date. There is, however, a document of that date (Recht Archief 166) in which a wigmaker, named Nicolaas Rougement, has a claim against Jonas L'Honoré and T. Johnson. This looks like the sort of claim that precipitates a bankruptcy, and would suggest that the bankruptcy, itself, occurred after that date. The problem is further complicated by the existence of a document dated March 17 1720 (Notarieel Archief, Inv. no. 2251) in which the date of the bankruptcy is cited as October 24.

I am deeply indebted to Drs. H. M. B. Jacobs of the Geemente Archief for all his help in obtaining this and other archival information.

22. *La Clef du Cabinet des princes de l'Europe,* IV (jan.-juin 1706) 67–68. For a recent account of this periodical and its role in the War of the Spanish Succession, see Klaits, *op. cit.,* pp. 77–85.

23. See chapter one, note 16.

24. The impression that L'Honoré published fewer copies of the periodical, once it began to be issued every four months, is strengthened by the observation that many libraries have sets from 1699 to 1706, but few have consecutive issues beyond that date (see note 3).

25. "Quant à la situation sociale de nos compagnons, c'étaient pour la plupart de pauvres hères, de déclassés, épaves de la grande ville. . . Clercs de basoche congédiés par le patron, officiers réformés, prêtres interdits. . ." (F. Funck-Brentano, *Figaro et ses devanciers,* Paris, 1909, p. 54, quoted by Yardeni, art. cit., 211, n. 16.) Gueudeville accurately portrays his plight in speaking of a banned book whose publisher had been arrested, and whose author, "homme sans aveu et sans emploi, en cela de notre grande confrérie, a pris la fuite. Nous autres petits peintres en charbon, ce n'est pas le jugement qui conduit le plus notre pinceau. Nous voudrions, comme des harlequins, faire rire pour du pain, au lieu que trop souvent nous faisons rire à nos dépens" (September-December 1707, 676). Cf. also — "Nous autres ouvriers et manoeuvres de Parnasse, il nous est permis de remplir nos feuilles au dépens de qui il appartiendra; le bon Apollon nous a donné ce beau droit pour nous dédommager de notre mauvaise fortune et de notre pauvre réputation" (January—April 1707, 46); and his reference to "notre gueuserie et la galère où nous ramons par une nécessité inévitable, sous peine d'être tirés à quatre famines, de produire nos feuilles par jour ou par mois. Si la faim nous initie aux mystères des cours, si elle fait notre vocation et notre professorat en politique. . ." (December 1704, 663).

26. *Op. cit.,* 275–276.

27. A good illustration of this type of informal transmission of information is found in a letter dated January 11 1704, in which Job de Wildt, secretary of the Amsterdam Admiralty, tells Heinsius that van Du Breuil, of the "Fransche courante", has provided information on the movements of a French naval squadron. De Wildt expresses reservations about the accuracy of this information (Heinsius archief, no. 958). Jean Tronchin du Breuil was born in Geneva and later moved to Paris whence, to avoid persecution, he left for Holland in 1683. From 1688 to 1690 he edited a bi-monthly journal and then took over the *Gazette d'Amsterdam* (see Hatin, *Les Gazettes de Hollande. . .* , pp. 157–158, 161–164). Tronchin enjoyed considerable respect as a journalist, and was noted for his moderation and relative impartiality in the reporting of news. I am grateful to Dr. A. J. Veenendaal, Jr. for drawing the de Wildt letter to my attention. For details of the espionage activities of Jurieu and his associates see Joseph Dedieu, *Le Rôle politique des Protestants français,* Paris, 1920, pp. 173–248.

28. "Toutes les relations de Paris ne sont pas Parisiennes. . . il y en a

d'Allemandes, de Grandes Bretonnes, de Hollandaises, enfin de tous les pays de la grande alliance. Mais aussi, toutes les relations qu'on publie en France pour étrangères ne le sont pas; il s'en trouverait maintes et maintes qui sont nées à Paris ou dans quelque autre endroit du royaume; car, en fait de nouvelles pendant une guerre, c'est un art très utile, et très usité, de savoir faire parler l'ennemi au désavantage de sa cause, soit dit par un petit écart en l'honneur de l'équité" (May—August 1707, 276).

29. ". . . vous avez toutes les gazettes flamandes dans le Mercure hollandais et les françaises dans le Mercure historique, Lettres historiques et l'Esprit des cours et. . . je crois que ce serait une dépense inutile que celle des gazettes" (Letter from Jean Louis de Lorme to J. P. Bignon, March 26 1708, quoted by Dr. I. H. van Eeghen, *op. cit.,* vol. I, p. 138).

30. On the relationship between journalism and history see Yardeni, art. cit., especially 208—220, and 615—617. Gueudeville frequently justified the staleness of his news on the grounds that accuracy was more important than novelty (August 1700, 152, November 1700, 556, September 1701, 627, March 1705, 270). The author of the *Mercure galant* used the same justification:

Je vous ai souvent dit qu'avant que mes lettres parviennent jusqu'à vous, les nouvelles qu'elles contiennent ne sont plus nouvelles, et que je ne prétends pas vous rien mander dont vous n'ayez déjà ouï parler. Mais je suis persuadé que je vous apprends souvent des détails des choses dont vous ne savez les nouvelles qu'en gros et souvent très imparfaitement. Cela ne doit pas vous étonner. Il se trouve de certains faits dont la vérité et les circonstances ne peuvent souvent être éclaircis qu'après plusieurs mois, et il y en a même dont il est difficile que la vérité soit bien développée qu'après plusieurs années. Un morceau d'histoire bien circonstancié, et dont la vérité est bien vérifiée, passe pour beau et nouveau, et même pour une chose rare. (December 1702, 9)

In any case, when Gueudeville's periodical began to be issued once every four months he was obliged to give up all pretence to be a purveyor of recent news — "il me semble qu'en matière de faits une vérité ancienne, mais conformée, doit faire beaucoup plus de plaisir que toutes ces faussetés naissantes qui, sujettes à se détruire elles-mêmes, ou à être démenties, passent par l'esprit comme un songe, et comme une illusion. Enfin je ne suis plus journaliste; je suis à présent une espèce de petit historien" (January—April 1707, 3).

31. Quoted by Yardeni, art. cit., 213. Letter to Minutoli, March 1 1675.

32. "Le roi de Pologne prétend que le gouverneur de Livonie en a mal agi avec les troupes saxonnes. Je n'en sais rien, cela peut être; mais les gens de bon

goût ne disconviendront point que c'est là un maigre sujet, et qu'une guerre appuyée sur un fondement si peu solide ne vaut guère mieux qu'une flamme en l'air. Mais moi-même, ne raisonnai-je point en l'air et en étourdi? Cela m'arrive souvent et c'est, je crois, l'un des plus beaux privilèges du caractère nouvelliste (September 1700, 323–324). "'On dit, on veut, on prétend, le bruit est, le bruit se répand, on conjecture', ce sont les mots essentiels de notre nouvellisme. Peut-on faire autrement, direz-vous? Non, sans doute, tant que le grand mystère de la politique ne sera pas plus révélé qu'il est; encore trop heureux d'avoir à faire à d'honnêtes gens qui ne veulent point nous tromper ni nous apprendre ce qu'ils ne savent pas." (October 1700, 408). "Ce que j'ai avancé le mois dernier sur une lettre, d'une émotion populaire à Naples, n'était pas vrai" (August 1706, 132). All the journalists were victims of wrong or misleading information, and all of them cautioned their readers against too great a reliance on the reports. Cf: "Il serait difficile de vous rien dire aujourd'hui de positif sur les affaires de la guerre, quoique toutes les nouvelles publiques soient remplies d'articles sur ce sujet; mais tout ce qu'elles rapportent n'est fondé que sur des *on dit, on croit, on est persuadé*, etc." (*Mercure galant*, January 1707, 398). "La Cour Impériale a fait de son côté de grandes avances pour le bien de la paix, et c'était sur de faux mémoires que j'avais dit quelque chose de contraire" (*Mercure historique*, December 1704, 635). "...plus de la moitié de ceux qu'on en a dit s'est trouvé faux...Dussé-je déplaire à ceux qui aiment qu'on les abuse en les flattant, je dois en faveur de la vérité connue, rétracter ce que j'ai avancé contre ses droits" (*La Clef du Cabinet des princes*, March 1706, 178).

33. "...que cette couronne ait eu du dessus la première année de la guerre présente, il n'y avait rien là de surprenant...Que la France se relevât de la fameuse et terrible journée d'Hochstedt il ne fallait pas non plus trop s'étonner. Mais qu'après les disgrâces de Barcelone, de Ramillies, de Turin, la France ait encore pu paraître dans la posture où nous venons de la voir?... Les Hauts Alliés, il est vrai, ont gagné beaucoup de terrain; mais qu'il leur coûte cher, et avec tout cela qu'ils sont encore loin du but!" (September–December 1707, 493–497). "Il est certain que les affaires de Catalogne et de Portugal paraissent dans une mauvaise situation pour les Hauts Alliés" (January–April 1708, 141). "Je débute par ne point dissimuler les bons succès de la France" (October–December 1708, 577).

34. "Si nos troupes, dit-on, avaient poursuivi leur avantage, une victoire complète ne pouvait leur échapper... Qu'on ait commis une faute, ou qu'on ait suivi les règles de la prudence... il est toujours certain qu'une déroute entière de l'armée ennemie aurait extrêmement bien influé sur la Grande Alliance... Le célèbre Général de nos bons et fidèles auxiliaires jugeait à propos de risquer le combat; mais comme cet excellent Capitaine n'a pas moins de modération, ni de sagesse que de valeur, il se désista d'une résol-

ution que son grand zèle pour la bonne cause lui avait inspirée, et il se rendit, non sans une noble répugnance, au sentiment de ceux qui croyaient cette entreprise devoir être funeste aux Hauts Alliés. Il était bien naturel que cet événement donnât lieu dans le monde à un schisme de pensée et d'opinion... Qu'on ait eu raison ou qu'on ait eu tort de ne pas attaquer les ennemis, sur quoi j'observe une parfaite neutralité, le reste de la campagne en Flandre a été peu de chose." (January 1706, 23–27).

35. "Avec un peu de satire on ne laisserait pas d'en faire quelque chose et l'on suppléerait à la stérilité de la matière; mais j'ai été contraint, pour des raisons essentielles, de renoncer tout à fait à cet odieux, à cet infructueux amusement, et comme il est assez de nouvellistes insipides, sans moi, le public, j'en suis sûr, ne tardera guère à me congédier" (October 1706, 364).

36. "Ce serait ici le lieu de décrire les mouvements des deux armées depuis le mois dernier; la matière est abondante; un esprit plus exact et plus laborieux que le mien trouverait de quoi se satisfaire. Les journaux publics sont bigarrés de relations, et qui voudrait les enfiler toutes, il y en aurait pour un juste volume. Quand j'aurai bien promené mon lecteur parmi ces campements, ces décampements, ces marches, ces contre-marches, ces lignes, ces routes, ces rivières, ces fourrages, ces escarmouches, ces partis, quel plaisir aura-t-il goûte? Je ne lui dirai rien que de sec et de mal digéré, car la spéculation militaire, non plus que la pratique, n'est pas mon fait; je ne lui apprendrai rien de nouveau, et il sera heureux s'il ne lui en coûte pas quelques bâillements soporatifs; enfin j'écris pour m'amuser et non pour fournir des matériaux à l'histoire" (September 1701, 582).

"Cette obligation de date me paraît bien onéreuse; n'est-on point assez mortifié de dire des faussetés sans avoir encore le chagrin de commettre des anachronismes. Que les grands historiens, que les savants et impitoyables critiques se chargent du soin de fixer exactement les époques; cette fatigue leur convient... mais pour un fantôme d'écrivain, pour un tisserand et un brodeur de gazettes? Oh, ne sue-t-il pas assez à démêler la vérité des faits sans exiger aussi qu'il soit un scrupuleux éplucheur de temps?" (March 1703, 295).

37. "... les journalistes publics de Hollande sont plus dignes de foi que celui de Paris; leur plume est moins bridée et, ne composant pas tous sur les mêmes mémoires, lorsqu'ils conviennent on ne peut moralement les soupçonner de supposition" (July 1702, 56).

"... les sages et trop aimables souverains sous le gouvernement desquels j'ai le bonheur de vivre, et d'écrire mes sentiments avec une raisonnable liberté..." (May 1703, 493).

38. Many of these documents are reproduced in Lamberty's *Mémoires pour servir à l'histoire du dix-huitième siècle.*

39. Humorous observations on fashions and hair styles are found, for example, in the issues of November 1699, 628, and September—December 1710, 493; remarks on women occur frequently and they are generally derogatory. See, for example, October 1699, 512, June 1700, 620, July 1704, 19, October—December 1708, 578; the evils of gambling are discussed in August 1699, 284; doctors and the healing arts are attacked in May—August 1707, 243; the problem of the freedom of the earth and private property is considered in August 1699, 249; the question of just wars is discussed in January 1706, 10; digressions on death are found repeatedly, especially in September 1699, 473, May 1703, 513, June 1705, 686, January—April 1707, 195 and September—December 1710, 500.

40. See chapter one, note 30.
    Not only was Gueudeville indebted to Bayle as his chief source of reference but, according to Hatin, *Histoire politique et littéraire de la presse en France*, vol. III, p. 299, "sa perpétuelle ironie et toute sa façon d'écrire sont une méchante caricature de la manière de Bayle dans ses Comètes."

41. Cf. Klaits, *op. cit.*, pp. 148—149;

    . . . modern readers can easily be misled by these apparently arcane allusions into judging them seemingly erudite works suitable only for an élite audience of scholars. In point of fact, classical references were a component of every stratum in seventeenth-century literary expression, and the popular literature of the day is replete with quotation from the ancients; indeed, much of the subject matter of popular fiction was filtered out of the classical corpus of history and mythology.

42. January 1706, 63. Cf. also:

    La religion et la politique, quelque opposition qu'il y ait entre elles, se tiennent souvent par la main, et se rendent mutuellement de bons offices. Quand la religion pourrait faire tout à la politique, la politique emprunte aussitôt le masque de la religion, et la contrefait si bien qu'il n'y a que les clairvoyants qui ne s'y méprennent point. Quand la politique peut nuire à la religion, la religion emprunte le pouvoir et la force de la politique, et elle les emploie si bien qu'on ne reconnaît plus sa simplicité, sa douceur, sa patience, sa générosité (August 1707, 274).

43. "C'est une chose étrange que la religion a été donnée aux hommes pour être le premier, le plus étroit et le plus indissoluble lien de leur société, et qu'il n'y a rien qui les divise ni qui les sépare davantage" (August 1699, 332). "Les Catholiques haïssent communément les Protestants; les Protestants de différente croyance se supportent encore moins. Les liens sacrés de la nature et la patrie sont entièrement brisés par l'animosité de la religion"

(April 1709, 128). "Qu'importerait-il à un Etat que la religion y fût uniforme, ou qu'elle ne le fût pas, si tous les hommes qui le composent faisaient le devoir de bons citoyens et de bons patriotes?" (April 1701, 446).

44. January—April 1708, 21.

45. References to the "Fénelon affair" occur in many of the issues of the first two years (see chapter four). For details of the "Chinese affair" see V. Pinot, *La Chine et la formation de l'esprit philosophique en France* (1640—1740), Paris, 1932; R. Etiemble, *Les Jésuites en Chine (1552—1773)...* , Paris, 1966. For bibliographical information see L. Pfister, *Notices biographiques et bibliographiques sur les Jésuites de l'ancienne mission de Chine, 1552— 1773*, vol. II, Shanghai, 1934; A.H. Rowbotham, *Missionary and Mandarin: the Jesuits at the Court of China*, Berkeley, 1942. References to the Jesuit missions in China are found frequently, but especially in December 1699, 767—776; August 1700, 128—130; September 1700, 246—254; September— December 1710, 460.

Of all the orders it was the Jesuits that Gueudeville most detested:

Cet ordre . . . a étendu la foi de Jésus Christ par celle du diable; il a exterminé le crime en le fomentant; il a sanctifié les actions les plus infernales par les bonnes intentions; il a fait fleurir la religion par les voies les plus fines et les plus intéressées de la politique; il a été au Pape contre le Roi, il a été au Roi contre le Pape; enfin, par cette riche devise, *à la plus grande gloire de Dieu*, il est parvenu à la plus grande gloire du monde... (June 1699, 24).

Gueudeville's attacks on monks and nuns in general occur throughout, but especially in August 1702, 172, 254; May 1703, 486; May—August 1709, 275.

46. "Les nouvelles qui nous viennent de cette extrémité du nord sont si sujettes à la variation et au contredit, qu'on ne peut les recevoir avec trop de circonspection . . . " (August 1702, 185).

47. The news of the Swedish victory over the Russians at Narva was received with amazement and, with the obvious exception of Russia's allies, with joy all over Europe. The Swedish ambassador to The Hague, Lilienrooth, officially reported the victory to the States-General on January 12 1701, and followed this up with a request for help in the struggle against Poland and Russia. On January 25 the Russian ambassador wrote to the States-General in an attempt to deny or at least diminish the magnitude of the Swedish victory. This document was supported by a conciliatory letter from the Czar. However, since Charles XII was bent on following up his advantage, and peace was out of the question, the Czar sought to purchase ships and

munitions in Amsterdam. On January 27 the Swedish ambassador asked the States-General not to comply with the Czar's request. In response to the Swedish note the Russian ambassador, on February 9, gave the Russian version of the battle of Narva, and claimed that the Swedes had won by a combination of treachery, trickery and good luck, and that their forces were much larger than had been reported. He also reminded the States-General of the long-standing friendship between the Russians and the Dutch, and asked them to honour their obligations to the Czar by ignoring the requests of the Swedish ambassador.

The Russian version of their defeat at Narva was the subject of much discussion and correspondence, and caused a great deal of amusement and derision among the various ambassadors in The Hague. Among the comments on the Russian notes were two anonymous pamphlets. The first one was entitled *Les Sentiments d'un officier flamand sur le mémoire que l'Ambassadeur de Moscovie présenta aux Etats-Généraux, le 25 janvier 1701*, and was dated Brussels, February 7 1701. The second was entitled *Remarques sur le mémoire que l'Ambassadeur de Moscovie présenta aux Etats-Généraux, le 9 février 1701*, and was dated Brussels, February 25 1701. According to Lamberty, *op. cit.*, p. 277, this second pamphlet was written by Gueudeville, at the invitation of the Swedish ambassador, for the amusement of the public. Only a few copies were printed, and I have been unable to find one. However, the text of the pamphlet is supplied by Lamberty (pp. 273–286). It is an analysis and rebuttal, in Gueudeville's satirical style, of the arguments of the Russian ambassador in his *mémoire* cited in the pamphlet's title. Both pamphlets were translated into Swedish and were probably published in Stockholm although they lack the date, place and name of publisher: (i) En/Nederländsk Officerares/OMDÔME/ Och / Anmårkning / Ôfwer en Skrift / som det Ryska Såndebodet / den 25 Januarii 1701 til herrar / GENERALSTATERNE / i Holland har ingifwet / Augående / Ryssarnas nederlag wed / Narwen; (ii) Anmårkningar / Ôfwer / Den andra Skriften / Som / Det Ryske Såndebodet / i Haag / har ingifwit / Til / HERRAR / GENERAL STATERNA / i Holland / den 9 Febr. Anno 1701.)

A copy of each pamphlet is available at the University Library, Göteborg, where both pamphlets are attributed to Gueudeville. It is possible that Gueudeville wrote them both, although, if so, one wonders why Lamberty did not mention this fact. Because the text of the first pamphlet is available only in a Swedish translation it is impossible to say anything on the basis of style. However, the treatment of the subject and the method of analysis are not unlike those employed by Gueudeville in the second pamphlet. It is always possible, of course, that Lamberty wrote the first pamphlet himself.

I am most grateful to Mrs. Olaug Smith for her translation of the first pamphlet.

48. Although, as I have suggested in chapter one, he almost certainly sided with Bayle in his quarrels with Jurieu, Gueudeville must have been receptive to both the style and content of Jurieu's anti-French and anti-Catholic pronouncements. He certainly subscribed to Jurieu's view of the social contract, and, like Jurieu but unlike Bayle, he supported the cause and actions of William III. While F.R.J. Knetsch, *Pierre Jurieu, theoloog en politikus der Refuge*, Kampen, 1967, does not entirely demonstrate that Jurieu is treated too harshly in E. Labrousse, *Pierre Bayle*, The Hague, 1963–1964, 2 vols., he does show that Jurieu's concern for the rights of the people was much more central to his philosophy than was Bayle's. In this respect, Gueudeville appears to be closer to Jurieu than to Bayle.

49. October 1699, 584; April 1701, 354; January 1700, 43.

50. October 1699, 583.

51. Yardeni, art. cit., 603.

52. "Cette couronne, à ce qu'on dit, a terminé le soulèvement des Camisards. . . Ce succès est aussi utile à la France qu'il est honteux et humiliant pour son monarque. Oui, la réduction des Camisards est avantageuse au gouvernement despotique. . . Par cet heureux événement la monarque respire, et se sent délivré de l'inquiétude du monde la mieux fondée. . . Il ne laisse pourtant pas d'être vrai que la moindre émeute est très dangereuse en France. . . il reste encore bon nombre d'honnêtes gens qui gémissent en secret de la calamité publique, qui déplorent tout bas l'aveuglement de leurs compatriotes, et qui embrasseraient avec un plaisir extrême une occasion favorable pour rétablir la monarchie sur l'ancien pied. D'ailleurs, le plus petit soulèvement dans un royaume opprimé sait ouvrir les yeux au peuple, et le fait réfléchir sur sa misère, sur sa honte, et sur sa lâcheté" (January 1705, 15–16).

53. January 1704, 23–24. Cf. also the following observation of Gueudeville, quoted by Köpeczi, *op cit.*, p. 589:

Les fauteurs de la puissance monarchique, le visage en feu, les yeux étincelants de bile, lanceront contre les Mécontents de Hongrie autant d'imprécations et d'anathèmes qu'on lance de bombes et de grenades pendant un siège. Les patrons du droit naturel donneront un tour de justice et de mérite à cette vraie ou prétendue rébellion; ils n'épargneront point les louanges et les éloges aux conspirateurs et ils donneront plus de bénédictions que n'en peut contenir le magasin d'un prince. Pour moi je souhaite tout bonheur à la bonne cause, quelle qu'elle soit, et je dois être neutre dans cette question (December 1703, 668).

54. The *Gazette* was founded in 1631 by Théophraste Renaudot, and inherited by his grandson Eusèbe, in 1679. *Le Mercure galant* was founded in 1672 by Jean Donneau de Visé, and continued under him until his death in 1710. This periodical eventually became *Le Mercure de France*. Claude Jordan, who began his journalistic career in Leiden and Amsterdam, founded *La Clef du Cabinet des Princes* in French-occupied Luxembourg in July 1704. Jean de la Chapelle's *Lettres d'un Suisse* appeared in the form of forty-eight anonymous pamphlets from June 1702 to January 1709. For details of the *Gazette* and *Le Mercure galant* see C. Bellanger *et al.*, *op cit.*, pp. 69 *et seq.* For information about the early career of Claude Jordan see Hatin, *Les Gazettes de Hollande...*, pp. 148—160. For information about La Chapelle, and the role of all four publications during the War of the Spanish Succession, see Klaits, *op. cit.*, especially chapters three and five.

55. September 1705, 337. De Visé referred to his fading sight in the issues of September and October—November 1703. In March 1706 he confirmed that he was blind.

56. Quoted by Pierre Mélèse, *Un Homme de lettres au temps du grand roi: Donneau de Visé, fondateur du Mercure Galant*, Paris 1936, p. 243.

57. July 1705, 167; January 1706, 35.

58. Quoted by Klaits, *op. cit.*, pp. 156—157.

59. The expression "C'est le chien de Jean de Nivelle qui s'enfuit quand on l'appelle," refers to the behaviour of one who slips away when he is wanted. Jean de Nivelle was summoned by his father, Jean II of Montmorency, to help Louis XI in his struggles with the Duke of Burgundy. Neither Jean nor his brother heeded the call, and their father disinherited them and termed them "chiens".

60. January—June 1706, 68.

61. His career was apparently not entirely at an end since, according to the preface to the October 4 1723 issue of *La Quintessence des nouvelles*, La Haye et Amsterdam, 1689—1730, in which the editor gives a history of the journal and its previous editors, Gueudeville had been temporarily in charge:

De ses mains la Quintessence est passée dans celles de Mme du Noyer, après avoir fait un court séjour sous la direction de M. Gueudeville. Je ne parlerai pas de celui-ci: ses écrits et sa réputation dans la république des lettres m'en dispensent.

Now, Mme du Noyer took over the periodical about 1712, so it looks as if Gueudeville was its editor from 1711 to 1712, unless he had a hand in it while he was still publishing his own journal. I have not seen any issues of the *Quintessence* during this period.

62. Baron de Lahontan, *Dialogues curieux entre l'auteur et un sauvage de bon sens qui a voyagé*, The Johns Hopkins Press, 1931, p. 39. For a discussion of the attribution of these dialogues to Gueudeville see chapter eight.

NOTES TO CHAPTER FOUR

1. For an account of the publication of *Télémaque* see A. Cherel, *Fénelon au XVIIIe siècle en France*, Paris 1917, pp. 24–25 and especially the bibliographical supplements. Cherel's observations are amplified and updated by A. Cahen in the introduction to his critical edition of *Les Aventures de Télémaque*, Paris 1920, 2 vols., especially li-lix and cii-cxxv. Fénelon's novel is based on the fourth book of the *Odyssey* in which Telemachus, the son of Ulysses, goes to visit Nestor in Pylos, and Menelaus in Sparta, to find out the whereabouts of his father who is wandering the seas at the mercy of Venus and Neptune, and trying to return home to Ithaca. The novel is divided into eighteen books which recount the adventures of Telemachus who is accompanied during his wanderings by Minerva disguised as the wise Mentor. In the first book, Telemachus and Mentor are driven by a storm to the isle of Calypso where, during the course of the next two books, Telemachus recounts his adventures in Sicily, Egypt and Tyre. In Book four there is a temporary cessation of the narrative while Mentor instructs his/her pupil. Then the account of the adventures continues, and we hear how Mentor rescued Telemachus from the island of Venus, and how they learned of the wise laws of Minos in Crete. In Book six the narrative is again interrupted. Calypso falls in love with Telemachus who loves the nymph Eucharis. As a result, Mentor and Telemachus are obliged to leave the island. Book seven is a digression concerning the cruel Pygmalion and the virtuous people of Boetica. Books eight and nine deal with the arrival of Mentor and Telemachus at Salentum which is in the process of being built by Idomeneus who had been exiled from Crete. Books ten to seventeen are taken up with the political and economic problems of Idomeneus, the advice of Mentor, the prowess of Telemachus, and the descent to Hades. At the end of Book seventeen Telemachus is betrothed to Antiope, daughter of Idomeneus. Book eighteen ends before Telemachus reaches his father.

2. Quoted by Cherel, *op. cit.*, p. 25.

3. *Histoire des ouvrages des savants*, June 1699, 276–278.

4. August 17, 1699. Quoted by the abbé Caron in his essay on the literary writings of Fénelon in *Oeuvres complètes de Fénelon*, ed. J.E.A. Gosselin, Paris, 1851, vol. I, pp. 136–137.

5. Mentioned in the Cahen edition, lix.

6. Extract from the *Journal* (1700) of the abbé Le Dieu. Quoted in A. Lombard, *Fénelon et le retour à l'antique au XVIIIe siècle*, Neuchâtel 1954, p. 92.

7. November 10, 1699. Quoted by Caron, art. cit., p. 136.

8. November 23, 1699. Quoted by Caron, art. cit., p. 137.

9. Quoted by Caron, art. cit., p. 137.

10. Quoted by Cahen, *op. cit.*, xxxviii, note 3.

    The editor of the 1719 edition of *Télémaque* was of the opinion that Astarbé, who is involved in a poisoning affair, was more a portrayal of Mme de Montespan than Mme de Maintenon. Gueudeville makes her seem a mixture of both these women. His description of her as "cette femme sans pudeur, qui possédait l'esprit du prince, et qui le faisait tourner en girouette au vent de son artificieuse ambition," is more in keeping with the reputation of Mme de Montespan; but he later says that "Astarbé était unie à Pygmalion par un mariage de conscience. . . le roi s'était démis de toute son autorité entre les mains de cette femme hypocrite. . . on ne pouvait désobéir à cette scélérate sans commettre un crime de lèse-majesté. . . enfin, étant l'âme et le mobile du gouvernement, l'ordre du roi était pour la forme, et celui de la reine cachée portait coup." (*Critique du premier tome*, pp. 119 et seq.) This latter description seems more applicable to Mme de Maintenon.

11. Fénelon's novel was published by Moetjens in five volumes: volume one, volume two, continuation of volume two, second continuation of volume two, and volume three. The first part of Gueudeville's work is a general introduction, and the next five parts follow the chronology of Fénelon's novel.

    The study of the various editions of the six parts of Gueudeville's work raises a number of bibliographical problems that, up to now, no one has tried to solve. My own attempts at dealing with these problems are presented in Appendix D.

    All references to the text are taken from edition number 5 which is the one most easily identifiable.

12. Faydit's work was entitled *La Télémacomanie, ou La Censure et critique du roman intitulé, Les Avantures de Télémaque Fils d'Ulysse, ou suite du quatrième livre de l'Odyssée d'Homère*, A Eleuteropole, Chez Pierre Philalèthe,

M. DCC. In the preface to this work, Faydit, who had been exiled to the provinces because of earlier clashes with the authorities, says that he published this work to show he was not the author of the earlier critique of *Télémaque* to which ' la malice du gazetier de Holland. . . attribue mon exil en Auvergne. . .'' The "gazetier de Hollande" was Gueudeville himself who, in the April 1700 issue of *L'Esprit des cours de l'Europe,* had written:

L'abbé Faydit a été relégué par une lettre de cachet à Riom en Auvergne. . . l'on prétend que cet ecclésiastique a fourni la matière de la foudre qui l'a frappé, par certaines vapeurs noires et malignes répandues dans plusieurs critiques qu'il a fait imprimer contre les ouvrages du temps. . . apparemment que ces ouvrages du temps, contre lesquels il s'est déchaîné sont du goût de la Cour, et que ne contenant rien qui ne flatte le gouvernement, le Prince les a pris sous sa protection. . . Monsieur l'Abbé Faydit n'est pas fort coupable, si l'on juge de sa faute par la punition; car il est exilé dans sa propre ville; et ce qui fait sa peine, ferait la joie de ceux qui ont été contraints de s'exiler eux-mêmes, hors du royaume, à condition qu'on leur permette de servir Dieu à leur manière (334–337).

The title-page of Faydit's work is reproduced in G. Parguez, "A propos des pages de titre des livres anciens," *Revue française d'histoire du livre* (1971), 70.

For details of Faydit see Hoefer, *op. cit.,* vol. XVII, p. 229.

13. Art. IV, May 1700. In the *Critique du second tome,* p. 160, Gueudeville quoted from Bernard's review — "et quand les partisans de Télémaque, gens redoutables et sans quartier, comme l'a dit depuis peu un habile écrivain. . ." In October 1700, Bernard published a largely unfavourable review of Faydit's book (Art. I, 384–390).

14. ". . . il faut bien que ce pauvre homme soit soupçonné d'être un esprit brutal, séditieux et infâme, puisqu'il avoue lui-même qu'il n'a publié sa Télémacomanie que pour assurer sa réputation contre le sentiment du public qui lui attribuait ces trois mauvaises qualités."

15. According to Caron, art. cit., p. 138, Gueudeville's reply is found in the *Critique du second tome*. My own impression, however, is that the passage quoted by Caron is in reply to an attack directed against Gueudeville's work by someone else. Gueudeville refers to him as "un cuisinier d'Esope et des fées" (p. 191) but I have been unable to identify him or his remarks. It seems more likely that the following section in the *Critique de la première et seconde suite du tome second* is in reply to the letter by the abbé G:

. . . vous voulez bien. . . que je vous apprenne comment j'ai reçu la lettre de notre illustre inconnu. . . Il m'accuse d'en vouloir à la personne de l'excellent auteur du Télémaque. . . L'auteur de la lettre y pense-t-il?. . . Bien loin de vouloir faire passer Monsieur de Cambrai pour un méchant homme, je voudrais que tout le genre humain conçût... que ce prélat est le meilleur des hommes... Je supplie donc mon spirituel et judicieux inconnu de me rendre un peu plus de justice... (pp. 127—130).

16. Saint-Rémy ends his preface with the following unsigned epigram:

G*** et F** ces critiques fameux,
Qui contre Télémaque ont fait mainte satire,
Depuis naguère ont un débat entre eux.
Votre style plaisant (dit l'un) est ennuyeux,
Le vôtre, répond l'autre, est d'un pédant crasseux.
Qui l'aurait jamais osé dire?
Ils ont trouvé moyen d'avoir raison tous deux.

In *Le Critique ressuscité* (p. 117) Gueudeville comments on this poem — "Pour l'auteur du sonnet, la reconnaissance m'empêche de vouloir le connaître; il doit m'en savoir quelque gré." According to the *Bibliothèque britannique*, XIX (1742), pt. I, 57, the author was a certain "Térond, excellent poète d'alors et bel esprit réfugié à la Haye." Perhaps this was a relative of François Térond, mentioned in Haag, *op. cit.*, vol. IX, p. 354.

17. Letter to Marais. See also the letter to the same, April 16 1705.

18. See Anne Sauvy, *op. cit.*, items 826, 924, 948, 959, and 1106.

19. G.B. Depping ed., *Correspondance administrative sous le règne de Louis XIV*, p. 744, August 23, 1702.

20. *Op. cit.*, vol. II, p. 275.

21. *Dictionnaire historique*, Paris, La Haye, 1758—1759, vol. II, p. 186, note 47. H.G. Martin, *Fénelon en Hollande*, Amsterdam, 1928, p. 46, refers to the influence of Gueudeville's criticism on the reception of *Télémaque* by Dutch critics.

22. *Nouveaux Mémoires d'histoire, de critique et de littérature*, Paris 1749—1756, vol. II, pp. 240—241. It should be remembered, of course, that any renegade Catholic was bound to be attacked unmercifully by the French critics.

23. Amsterdam 1770, vol. II, p. 339.

24. Michaud, *op. cit.*, vol. XVII, p. 35.

25. Art. cit., p. 138.

26. A. Cahen, *op. cit.*, lxi.

27. For the study of Faydit see *Mémoires de la Société d'émulation de Cambrai*, LXXXIV (1936), 133–215; for the study of Gueudeville see LXXXV (1937), 135–201, 211–212.

28. LXXXIV, 134.

29. Delval makes no mention of Cahen's excellent edition of *Télémaque*, and he did not consult *L'Esprit des cours de l'Europe*. He says that *Télémaque* was published at the beginning of May (LXXXIV, 135), unaware that the *Gazette d'Amsterdam* for May 1 announced its publication in April (Cahen, liii, note 3). He gives the date of publication of *Le Critique ressuscité* as 1704 instead of 1702 (LXXXV, 144 and 179). *L'Esprit des cours* was published in The Hague and, later, in Amsterdam, and was bound in nineteen volumes, not ten. The comte d'Avaux, as we have seen, was not successful in having it suppressed. Gueudeville was not the author of the works of the baron de Lahontan (not La Hotan, LXXXV, 138–141).

30. LXXXIV, 175; LXXXV, 148.

31. LXXXV, 192–194.

32. Cf. also:

> ... jamais matière ne fut plus abondante ni plus propre pour égayer un critique; presque à chaque pas on trouve de quoi badiner; mais comme je n'ai pas dessein de faire un livre, et que, d'ailleurs, je dois mon loisir à une plus solide occupation, je veux borner ma fade plaisanterie pour ce qui me reste, et je ne m'attacherai plus qu'aux endroits qui me paraîtront les plus dignes de réflexion (*Critique du premier tome*, p. 90).

> D'ailleurs, la remarque est superficielle, et n'est pas digne d'une plus longue discussion. J'en pourrais faire quelques autres aussi peu importantes.
> Mais c'est trop insister sur des bagatelles (*Critique du second tome*, pp. 145, 148).

33. In my study of Tyssot de Patot (p. 39), I pointed out that, although modern critics consider Tyssot's humour as coarse and vulgar, it was not so regarded in the circle in which he moved. Bayle, himself, enjoyed a good obscenity (see E. Lacoste, *Bayle, nouvelliste et critique littéraire*, Paris, 1928, pp. 39–40).

34. In referring to his *Critique du premier tome* Gueudeville wrote:

> Je conviens aisément... que ce petit ouvrage, qui n'est qu'un tissu de remarques satiriques et outrées, choque l'esprit d'un lecteur délicat par la

confusion et le galimatias qu'il n'est pas difficile d'y apercevoir. On y trouve des termes ambigus, des phrases louches, des expressions triviales: en un mot, c'est un visage difforme de soi-même, et qui offre des taches qui le rendent encore plus dégoûtant (*Critique du second tome*, p. 130).

35. In the *Critique du premier tome*, p. 82, Telemachus, walking behind Calypso, is described as admiring the beauty of her face and the sparkle in her eyes. In the *Critique du second tome*, p. 174, Aristodemus gives away, as a gift, the laws, the sacred foundation of the Cretan constitution, written in the hand of Minos himself. In the same part (p. 181), Venus, who has divine powers, fails to recognize the disguised Minerva. In the *Critique de la suite du second tome*, pp. 318 et seq., Gueudeville points out the philosophical nature and elevated style of the discourse attributed to a supposedly primitive and barbaric people. These and other examples are cited by Cahen in the notes to his critical edition.

36. See P.J.W. van Malssen, *Louis XIV d'après les pamphlets répandus en Hollande*, Amsterdam, 1936. Van Malssen does not refer to Gueudeville's criticisms of *Télémaque* but he does include *L'Esprit des cours de l'Europe* among the pamphlets.

37. LXXXV, 191.

38. Cf.:

Il [Louis XIV] a rasé ces temples qui défiguraient le culte dominant, et il a établi l'uniformité dans l'extérieur de la religion. Il a eu la joie de voir sa mission militaire efficace; le plus grand nombre a plié sous la barbarie du dragon, et ceux qui ont tenu ferme n'étaient regardés que comme une poignée de misérables... On confisque, on emprisonne, on traîne à la voirie, on enlève les enfants, en un mot, les ordres de S.M. Très Chrétienne sont exécutés par tout le royaume avec tant de ponctualité, qu'il ne s'agit plus que de faire bâtir de nouvelles prisons, ou de faire équiper de nouvelles galères pour abolir les restes de ce déplorable parti (October 1699, 517–518).

39. Cf.:

... un prince à qui l'on ne donne pas le temps de s'apercevoir qu'il est un homme; devant qui l'on tient incessamment un miroir trompeur; de quoi l'on canonise les vices, et qui n'entend retentir à ses oreilles que la louange et que l'applaudissement, a-t-il où placer chez lui cet excellent précepte de la morale, connais-toi toi-même?... un roi ne peut manquer de remplir bien ou mal son caractère, qui est de vivre pour les autres; s'il est bon il vit pour ses sujets; et dès qu'il est faible ou mauvais, il ne vit plus que pour ses flatteurs (June 1699, 74).

40. Art. cit., 192.

41. *Op. cit.*, vol. I, pp. 114–115, note 4, and pp. 122–123, note 2.

42. Cf. also:

> La conformité des sentiments tout humains du Télémaque avec les miens m'inspira la témérité de le paraphraser. Je n'ai pu le faire sans montrer selon ma faible portée le bon et le mauvais de l'ouvrage, mais au fond j'admire le livre plus que personne et je vénère encore plus l'auteur (*Le Critique ressuscité*, p. 117).

43. This is a reference to Louis XIV's continued and secret support of the Turks in their struggles with Austria.

44. Gueudeville refers here to the current contest for the Polish throne between Augustus and Stanislaus, mentioned in chapter three.

45. This is a thumbnail sketch of Louis XIV's amorous career, involving his escapades with Louise de La Vallière, Mme de Montespan, and others, and ending with his return to respectability in the care of Mme de Maintenon. The introduction of Charlemagne's name, at the end of the passage, is a good example of Gueudeville's satirical approach which is not very subtle.

46. Either Gueudeville's remark is purely general, and refers to the usual complaints by French ambassadors, or he is referring specifically to the French ambassador's objection to the article in *L'Esprit des cours de l'Europe* of April 1701, in which case, the date 1700 on the title-page of this part is false and should be 1701.

47. The reference to Louis XIV's "taille éminente" is ironic. Louis was small in stature and wore high heels to remedy the defect.

48. According to Delval, art. cit., 190, no reason is given for terminating the critique at this point, and for not dealing with the rest of Fénelon's novel. But Gueudeville clearly states: "Le peu d'espace qui me resterait à parcourir ne me fournissant aucun texte nouveau, je ne veux point pousser la redite jusqu'au bout" (p. 117).

NOTES TO CHAPTER FIVE

1. DIALOGUES / DES / MORTS, / *D'un tour Nouveau*; / Pour l'Instruction des vivans, Sur plusieurs matières / Importantes. / — *Facilis descensus Averno.* /

Sed revocare gradum, superasque evadere ad auras, / Hoc opus hic labor est. − Virg. AEn. VI. / [engraved vignette with the device NON SIBI SED OMNIBUS] / A LA HAYE, /Chez T. JOHNSON. / [rule] / M.DCC.IX. In red: DIALOGUES / MORTS, / Pour l'Instruction des Vivans, / A LA HAYE, M.DCC.IX.

Contents: *1, title, verso blank; *2−*3 v, dedication; *4−*12 v, preface; 1−469, text.

There is an engraved frontispiece showing Lucian and Fontenelle which, according to the British Museum Catalogue, is taken from an edition of Fénelon's *Dialogues des morts*. The dedication is to Henry de Cort, Baron de Walef (1652−1734) with whom Gueudeville was acquainted, probably through Pierre Bayle (see Bayle's letter to Walef referred to in chapter one, note 18). For details of this soldier-poet see M. Delcroix, "Le baron de Walef. Un Wallon face au soleil," *Publications du centre méridional de rencontres sur le 17e siècle*, Marseille, 1975. Although I have called the *Dialogues des morts* Gueudeville's last anonymous publication, it is, of course, eminently possible that he was the author of one or more of the many polemical works published anonymously at this time.

2. The BM catalogue does not identify the author. Kossmann, *op. cit.*, p. 208, attributes the work to Fontenelle, as does the card catalogue in the Leiden University library.
   T. Johnson's catalogue is in the *Journal Littéraire*, XI (1720).

3. Fontenelle's *Nouveaux Dialogues des morts* appeared in 1694, and Fénelon's *Dialogues des morts* in 1699.

4. Alcinoë and Aegialia (pp. 1−48); Alcmena and Myrrha (pp. 49−123); Apuleius and Agrippa (pp. 123−174); Heliogabalus and Diogenes (pp. 174−202); Julius Caesar and M. Junius Brutus (pp. 203−337); Caligula and Nero (pp. 338−469).
   The source of much of Gueudeville's information about these characters is Bayle's *Dictionnaire historique*.

5. Alcinoë was the daughter of Polybius, king of Corinth, and wife of Amphilocus. Because of her avarice she failed to pay the weaver, Nicandra, the amount she was owed. As a punishment Minerva caused Alcinoë to fall in love with Xanthus of Samos, a guest in her house. She left her husband and children and embarked for Samos with Xanthus. During the voyage she was overcome with remorse and drowned herself. Aegialia, in Gueudeville's version of the myth, was the daughter of Adrastus, king of Argos, and wife of her cousin, Diomedes. When Diomedes wounded Venus in the arm, during the siege of Troy, Venus avenged herself by turning Aegialia into a nymphomaniac. As a result of her passion for Cometes, son of Sthenelus,

she attempted unsuccessfully to kill her husband, who fled. Cometes then usurped Diomedes' throne.

6. In Gueudeville's version of the myth, Alcmena was the daughter of Electryon, son of Perseus and brother of Mestor. When the son of Pterelaus, king of the Taphian islands, laid claim to the kingdom of Mestor, his claim was rejected. Whereupon he invaded the kingdom and devastated it, killing all Alcmena's brothers in the process. Electryon determined on vengeance. Before setting out he left the country and his daughter in charge of Amphitryon, to whom he was related through Perseus. Amphitryon accidentally killed Electryon and, as a consequence, he and Alcmena were exiled. They made their way to Thebes where Alcmena agreed to mary Amphitryon on the understanding that he would avenge the death of her brothers. Creon, king of Thebes, refused to help Amphitryon until Thebes was rid of a plague of foxes. Amphitryon destroyed the foxes and, with the help of Comaetha, daughter of Pterelaus, avenged the brothers' death, after which he put Comaetha to death. The rest of the story concerning Jupiter's disguising himself as Amphitryon and sleeping with Alcmena who gave birth to Hercules, is too well known to need summarizing here. Myrrha was the daughter of Cinyras. Because of some transgression, Venus caused her to become infatuated with her father whom she tricked into sleeping with her. When Cinyras discovered the trick he tried to kill her, but she fled to South Arabia where the gods turned her into a myrrh tree. Adonis was born from the union of Cinyras and Myrrh. Myrrh's story plays no part in the dialogue and is referred to only at the very end.

7. Gueudeville is referring here to the well-known homosexual practices of the duke of Orléans, brother of Louis XIV, and of other noted courtiers of the day.

8. Henricus Cornelius Agrippa von Nettesheim (1487–1535) was famous, like his contemporary Paracelsus, for his cabbalistic writings and for his adventurous life. He began by pursuing a military career which he abandoned to take up the study of classical languages, medicine and philosophy. For a time he held a chair in Hebrew in Dole, but, after disputes with the authorities, went to England. From there he returned to Cologne, his birthplace, and taught theology. He also spent time in Italy, Germany, Belgium, Switzerland, always coming into conflict with the authorities because of his writings and pronouncements on magic, witchcraft, etc. He held various positions in royal houses in France and England. Although he acquired great fame or notoriety, and was judged either a sincere fanatic or a thorough charlatan, he never acquired material success, and died a pauper. Two of his works, *De incertitudine et vanitate scientiarum* (Cologne 1527) and *De nobilitate et praecellentia foeminei sexus declamatio* (Anvers 1529), were

252

translated by Gueudeville (see chapter seven). All the information in this dialogue about Apuleius and Agrippa is taken directly from Bayle's *Dictionnaire historique*. This includes not only the anecdotes but the quotations both acknowledged and unacknowledged.

9. Heliogabalus or Elagabalus (204—222) inherited, as a boy, the high-priesthood of the Syrian sun-god, Elagabal. His real name was Varius Avitus, but he assumed the name of the god according to custom. After the death of his cousin Caracalla, and through the intrigues of his mother, he was proclaimed Emperor under the name Marcus Aurelius Antoninus. Among his many indiscretions his devotion to the sun-god scandalized the Roman public. When his mother began to favour the aspirations of his cousin, Alexianus, Heliogabalus tried to assassinate him, but instead Heliogabalus and his mother were murdered by the praetorian guard.

10. Héliogabale. Te voilà donc fameux cynique. . .
    Diogène. Et toi infâme voluptueux. . . tu ne vaux guère la peine qu'on s'arrête.
    Héliogabale. . . . N'as-tu pas de chagrin d'avoir fait profession d'une vertu si bourrue?
    Diogène. . . . Mais toi, fameux efféminé, es-tu bien content d'avoir outré la mollesse, d'avoir poussé le plaisir des sens jusqu'à des excès monstrueux?
    Héliogabale. . . . Tu me débites là une morale joliment édifiante. Si je te tenais là-haut, je t'en ferais sentir toute la force par la main d'un bourreau (pp. 174—175).

11. This discussion about the right to revolt clarifies the apparent ambiguity of Gueudeville's attitude to revolution, noted in his partial condemnation of the Hungarian uprising and his unconditional support for the Cévennois (see chapter three, p. 43). According to Gueudeville, the Austrian domination of Hungary was of long standing and was legitimate.

12. This is a perceptive and valid comment on the Roman hierarchy in which patronage and obligation assumed almost Mafia-like proportions.

13. I have been unable to identify this historian. A likely candidate is Bossuet since Gueudeville characterizes him as "dévoué à la puissance monarchique parce qu'elle l'élevait aux premières charges et aux plus grands honneurs. Jugez par là de son désintéressement. . . enfin, jugez s'il pouvait faire plus de plaisir au maître dont il était un des principaux esclaves."

14. This technique is clearly derived from Bayle who, in the *Critique générale de l'Histoire du calvinisme de M. Maimbourg* and the *Nouvelles Lettres de*

l'auteur de la Critique générale, presents a series of letters in which the author sets out what will be the correspondent's objections to the arguments, and refutes them in advance.

15. See the section on Lahontan in chapter eight.

NOTES TO CHAPTER SIX

1. ATLAS / HISTORIQUE, / OU / NOUVELLE / INTRODUCTION / A l'Histoire, à la Chronologie & à la Géographie / Ancienne et Moderne; / Représentée dans de / NOUVELLES CARTES, / où l'on remarque l'établissement des Etats & Empires du / Monde, leur durée, leur chute, et leurs differens Gouvernemens; / La Chronologie des Consuls Romains, des Papes, des Empereurs, des Rois / & des Princes, &c. qui ont été depuis le commencement du Monde, jusqu'à présent: / Et la Génealogie des Maisons Souveraines de l'Europe. / Par Mr. C.*** / Avec des DISSERTATIONS sur l'Histoire de chaque Etat, / Par Mr. GUEUDEVILLE. / [engraved vignette, signed J. Goeree] / *A AMSTERDAM*, / Chez FRANÇOIS L'HONORE' & COMPAGNIE, / Pres la Maison de Ville. / [rule] / MDCCV.
In red: ATLAS / OU / INTRODUCTION / A l'Histoire, à la Chronologie & à la Géographie / Ancienne et Moderne; / NOUVELLES CARTES, / La Chronologie des Consuls Romains, ðes Papes, des Empereurs, des Rois / Par Mr. C.*** / Par Mr. GUEUDEVILLE. / *A AMSTERDAM*, / MDCCV.

2. Although the date on the title-page reads 1705, the Atlas was, according to practice, advertised in the September 1704 issue of *L'Esprit des cours de L'Europe*, and reviewed in November of that year in the *Histoire des ouvrages des savants*, art. VII, 483–499, and in the December issue of the *Nouvelles de la république des lettres*, art. I, 603–615.
   The Atlas was also advertised as being sold in Liège, by Daniel Monnal, in Maastricht by Jacques Delessart, and in London by J. Cailloué (see the December issue of *L'Esprit des cours*). It was also issued with title-pages announcing its availability in The Hague, chez Jonas L'Honoré, London, chez P. Varenne, and Berlin, chez Arnaud Dussarrat.
   The designation, volume one, did not appear on the title-page until the work was reissued with two more volumes in 1708. This is probably because there was originally no thought of proceeding beyond one volume.

3. The *Journal de Trévoux* (March 1705), art. XLVIII, 544, identifies Mr. C*** as "un nommé Chastelain qui s'est associé d'un libraire, et qui veut être auteur à quelque prix que ce soit." Dr. van Eeghen, *op. cit.*, vol. III, pp. 67–71, thinks this must be a reference to Zacharias Châtelain (?–1723) who, in 1700, was associated with the book dealer, Jean Malherbe.

It was Zacharias' daughter, Marthe, who married François L'Honoré, and it was his son, also called Zacharias (1690–1754) who took over the publication of later editions of the atlas. My only reason for hesitating to accept Dr. van Eeghen's convincing explanation is that the *Histoire des ouvrages des savants* (October 1708) art. II, 445–446, describes Mr. C.*** as having studied "ces sortes de matières pendant trente années." Now, as far as one can tell, Zacharias was a businessman and not a student of history, geography or chronology. It could be, of course, that he had always been interested in these subjects, and had finally decided to pursue them more seriously. Henri Châtelain (1684–1743), another son of Zacharias, was a pastor who lived in England and Holland. The *Dictionnaire de biographie française*, ed. M. Prévost et al., Paris, 1959, vol. 8, col. 787, recognizes that the author was not Henri Châtelain, but mistakenly attributes authorship to his brother Zacharias who, as we have seen, was not born until 1690, and was not involved in the project until later.

4. See Appendix E.

5. This information is provided in the prefaces to the various volumes. J.G. von Imhof (1651–1728) was a German historian and genealogist who published extensively in his field. For details, see Michaud, *op. cit.*, vol. XX, pp. 316–317. F.G.D. Bresler was also a historian and genealogist. He is referred to in the introduction to the second volume of the *Atlas* as "Sénateur de Conseil Royal de la Haute et Basse Silésie," and a former student of Mr. Budeus, professor at Jena. This is probably the same Bresler as the one referred to in the preface to volume five as "Ferdinand Louis de Bresler Conseiller de sa Majesté Impériale et Sénateur de Breslaw." Henri-Philippe de Limiers (?–1728) was born in The Netherlands where his French refugee parents had settled. He wrote many historical works and was also a journalist. For further details see the notice by M. Couperus in *Dictionnaire des journalistes 1600–1789*, ed. J. Sgard, Grenoble 1976. Limiers, like Gueudeville, also translated the plays of Plautus (see chapter seven).

6. *Histoire des ouvrages des savants* (1708), art. cit., 457.

7. These reviews are referred to in note 2.

8. Volume two was first mentioned in a catalogue of François L'Honoré in the January–April 1708 issue of *L'Esprit des cours.* In the following issue it was advertised as being "divisé en deux parties."

9. Cf. *L'Esprit des cours de l'Europe:*

La finance est la meilleure ressource du sexe galant. Une belle puise à pleines mains dans ces bourses toujours pleines et toujours ouvertes pour acheter un plaisir dont le marchand est souvent la dupe. Attraper un financier, c'est un exploit héroïque en coquetterie; et quand une femme a eu le bonheur d'en mettre un au nombre des ses conquêtes, c'est un amant qui fournit à tout, excepté à ce qu'il cherche le plus, et qui est ordinairement ce qu'on lui demande le moins (June 1700, 620).

Le beau sexe ne renonce pas aisément au luxe et à la vanité; comme rien ne le flatte plus que d'étaler ses appas, il aime avec attachement tout ce qui peut servir à le montrer... une femme n'est jamais si contente de soi que lorsqu'elle a fait une conquête; et quelque austère que soit sa vertu, elle ne peut se savoir mauvais gré d'être d'un mérite piquant (December 1701, 919–920).

Les femmes sont bien dangereuses à la société par deux endroits, par l'amour et par l'ambition. Par l'amour elles ont donné lieu à des guerres cruelles; la fameuse Hélène ne fut pas la première dont les charmes aient coûté des fleuves de sang... Elle ne fut pas non plus la dernière... Les femmes ne causent pas, à beaucoup près, tant de désordre par l'amour que par l'ambition. Une femme qui règne sur l'esprit du maître, et laquelle manque de lumières ou de droiture, quelles injustices, quelles violences, ne peut-elle pas lui faire commettre! (October–December 1708, 578–579).

10. Art cit. (October 1708), 445–458.

11. *Journal des savants* (July 1715), 106–113, Dutch edition; *Journal de Trévoux* (January 1716), Art. V, 45–97.

12. M. Gueudeville ne paraît pas fort content du public; il n'y découvre apparemment pas beaucoup de ces gens-là; mais en récompense, le petit nombre qu'il en aperçoit est, selon lui, fort respectable. "Monseigneur Public," dit-il dans la dissertation sur la Suède, "soit dit avec tout le respect dû à vos grandes, à vos vives, à vos profondes lumières, vous n'êtes nullement une personne contentable. Tâche-t-on de donner de l'esprit? Il y en a trop: Fi, le dégoûtant Phébusien! à quoi bon tout ce guindage? et que n'écrit-il comme on pense? Parle-t-on le naturel? C'était assurément bien la peine d'employer la plume et la presse pour nous dire si peu de chose! Monseigneur Public, voulez-vous me permettre de dire ce que je fais? Il était un villageois et son fils qui, révérence parler, avaient un âne en leur compagnie; ils montaient tour à tour la spirituelle bête, ils la laissaient aller seule, ils en vinrent jusqu'à la porter, et le tout sur le contrôle perpétuel des passants; à la fin, nos bonnes gens en firent à leur guise; et selon mon très petit et très infortuné moi, ils firent fort sagement. J'en fais de même, Sérénissime, mais ne serait-ce pas mieux dit, Obscurissime Prince, qui avez l'honneur de porter l'illustrissime nom de Public: je ris de votre arrêt de condamnation; j'en ris sur le droit que j'ai, et qu'on ne saurait m'ôter, d'en appeler à la cour des sensés, cour supérieure, et décisive en dernier ressort; c'est grand dommage que ce plus beau de tous les parlements ait si peu d'officiers! Oui, direz-vous, mais si vous n'écrivez pas mieux, nous ne vous achèterons point: tant pis pour le libraire, et tant mieux pour moi; j'en serai délivré plutôt de

votre dur esclavage, Monseigneur Public; en vérité, j'aimerais mieux être le dernier des manoeuvres, que d'avoir l'honneur de gagner ma vie avec vous. Pendant que je m'amuse à jaser, mon historien se morfond; çà, çà, il faut le citer, et il est grand temps: ayez donc le plaisir de me quitter pour un autre."

Ce qu'on vient de lire est une parenthèse que M. Gueudeville a insérée dans ce qu'il juge à propos de rapporter d'Albert de Mekelbourg qui succéda au roi Magnus en 1365. Albert, après un long règne fut obligé de renoncer à la couronne, ses sujets s'étaient révoltés contre lui, irrités qu'il voulait s'approprier le tiers des biens du royaume. On sera peut-être bien aise de voir ici de quelle manière le style comique de M. Gueudeville est employé à raconter un événement de cette espèce: "Les Suédois, se dépitant, travaillèrent sérieusement à se mettre sous une domination plus humaine; et ils s'y appliquèrent efficacement. Par "les Suédois", n'allez pas, s'il vous plaît, entendre toute la nation. Les fortunés, ne jugeant pas à propos de se ruiner pour la personne sacrée du Seigneur BON PLAISIR, entrèrent tous unanimement dans ce qui s'appelle, en morale despotique, révolte, rébellion, perfidie toute noire de la fumée d'enfer. Mais, les Suédois gueux, et chez qui la Hautissime, la Puissantissime Impératrice Fortune s'était brouillée avec mère Nature, avaient une vue bien opposée: Albert eut en eux les meilleurs soumis, les plus souples JOUGUEURS du monde: Quoi, sire, disaient-ils, à ce que je m'imagine, vous laisserez-vous ainsi maîtriser? Le divin titre de roi ne fonde-t-il pas un droit général? Que serait-ce donc que l'intérêt d'état, sinon le pouvoir arbitraire en essence et en espèce?

Ces Messieurs les Suédois pauvres avaient leur but: ils s'attendaient bien de participer au butin monarchique et de remplir leur vide des dépouilles des butinés. Les aisés de la nation sont pour la justice naturelle parce qu'ils sont pour le précieux coffre-fort; et les indigents tiennent pour le despotisme dans l'espérance d'adoucir leur condition. Ainsi, comme la moitié du genre humain se moque de l'autre, de même la moitié d'une nation détruit l'autre moitié: les uns brûlent de zèle pour la liberté parce qu'ils sont dans le bien-aise, les autres se remuent fort et ferme pour échapper des fers de la cruelle disette, et pour s'enrichir dans l'esclavage. Ainsi se forge la chaîne sociétaire. Malheureuse espèce, image corrompue de l'Etre parfait, faut-il que tu sois si contraire à toi-même! J'écris en bon républicain au moins; et si, je prends la liberté de vous assurer, avant de mourir, et par forme testamentaire, que je suis grand adorateur des bons monarques.

Ainsi cet amour du bien, cet intérêt du métal, qui donne chez les hommes tant d'occupation à la discorde, divisa le royaume de Suède et y alluma le feu d'une guerre sanglante. La cause des riches était la plus forte; aussi ce fut elle qui triompha. Les pauvres et faibles sujets de la tyrannie eurent le dessous: Albert est contraint de se retirer; revenant avec une armée il est battu, il est fait prisonnier; et n'ayant pu recouvrer la liberté qu'en renonçant juridiquement à la couronne, après un règne de vingt-trois ans, il retourne à son ancienne condition, et passe le reste de sa vie à Mekelbourg."

Il parle ensuite de la reine Marguerite, et après en avoir donné un portrait qu'il tire d'ailleurs, il dit "qu'assurément elle était belle et rare en coeur *féminin* cette Marguerite la Grande".

13. J. Mocquet, *Voyages en Afrique, Asie, Indes Orientales et Occidentales*, Paris, 1717 (first published in 1616). *Description de l'Afrique. . . traduit du flamand d'O.Dapper*, Amsterdam, 1686.

14. For a discussion of Gueudeville's role in the work of Lahontan see chapter eight.

15. December 1719, 616–627. Dutch edition.

16. LE NOUVEAU / THEATRE / DU / MONDE, / OU LA / GEOGRAPHIE ROYALE, / COMPOSÉE / DE NOUVELLES CARTES TRES-EXACTES, / Dressées sur les Observations de Messieurs de l'Academie Royale des / Sciences à Paris, sur celles des plus celebres Geographes, sur de / nouveaux Memoires, & rectifiées sur les Relations les plus / recentes des plus fidéles Voyageurs. / *Avec une* / DESCRIPTION GEOGRAPHIQUE ET HISTOR-IQUE / DES QUATRE PARTIES DE L'UNIVERS,/*Desquelles L'EUROPE en detail est écrite /Par* Mr. GUEUDEVILLE./& *Les trois autres Parties /Par* Mr. FERRARIUS. / Ouvrage qui donne une idée claire et facile de la Terre, & de ce qu'elle comprend / de plus considerable. / [engraved vignette] / A LEIDE,/Chez PIERRE vander AA, Marchand Libraire./[rule] /MDCCXIII.
In red: THEATRE / MONDE, / GEOGRAPHIE ROYALE, / *Avec une* / DES QUATRE PARTIES DE L'UNIVERS, / *Par* Mr. GUEUDEVILLE. / *Par* Mr. FERRARIUS./A LEIDE,/MDCCXIII.
A description of this work is found in Koeman, *op. cit.*, pp. 12–13.

17. Some of these works, described by Koeman, vol. I, pp. 1–2, as "spectacular", include the twenty-eight volume *Naaukeurige versameling der gedenk-waardigste zee-en-land reysen* (1706–1708), and the twenty-seven volume *Galérie agréable du monde*, completed in 1729. Koeman observes, however, that:

Van der Aa had optimistic ideas of the varied public demand for maps and prints. Also at that time, there was a tendency to rely on quantity rather than quality. The characteristics of the maps published by Van der Aa are:
   Firstly: lack of originality; and secondly: a horrible deformation of the subjects as a result of inadequate map projection. For instance, in several of his atlases and print books, Van der Aa shortened the distance between the parallels in order to put two maps, one above the other, on a single sheet.
   These cartographic oddities and the unattractive engraving of his maps make Van der Aa's products of little interest.

18. The section on Europe has sixty-six pages of text, and the other three sections occupy seventy-six pages.

19. The expression *"le mien* et *le tien"* derives from the writings of the baron de Lahontan (see chapter eight).

20. Gueudeville's attitude to the English seems to have changed from his unqualified hymns of praise in *L'Esprit des cours de l'Europe.* One must assume he had become somewhat disenchanted by the policies of the new government in England whose ambition was to terminate the War as quickly as possible, without regard for the allies.

21. Copies are available in the university libraries of Basel, Liège and Utrecht, in Stockholm (R), Madrid (N) and Michigan (WLC).

22. In a catalogue at the back of the 1717 reissue of Gueudeville's translation of More's *Utopia* (see chapter seven) the maps are advertised separately.

23. MAXIMES POLITIQUES / DU / PAPE PAUL III. / Touchant ses Démêlez avec / L'EMPEREUR CHARLES-QUINT, / AU SUJET DU / CONCILE DE TRENTE: / Tirées des Lettres Anecdotes de / DOM HURTADO DE MENDOZA, / Par Mr. AYMON, Theol: & Juriscons: / AVEC UN / PARALLELE entre le même Pape / & CLEMENT XI. / Sur diverses Matiéres du Tems présent; / ET DES / REFLEXIONS VIVES ET LIBRES / Par Mr. DE GUEUDEVILLE. / [vignette of type ornament] / A LA HAYE, / Chez HENRI SCHEURLEER, / Libraire proche la Cour, a l'Enseigne / D'ERASME. / [rule] / M.DCC.XVI.
In red: MAXIMES POLITIQUES / PAPE PAUL III. / L'EMPEREUR CHARLES-QUINT, / CONCILE DE TRENTE: / DOM HURTADO DE MENDOZA, / Par Mr. AYMON, Theol: & Juriscons: / & CLEMENT XI. / Par Mr. DE GUEUDEVILLE. / Chez HENRI SCHEURLEER,
Contents: *1, title (verso blank); *2—**1 v, preface; **2—**5 v Mendoza's credentials; **6—**9 v, table générale; **10—**12 v, catalogue des livres; 1—193, extracts from letters and reflections; 194—195, conclusion; 196—216, letter and reflection; 217—288, Parallèle des papes.
Copies are available at the university libraries of Cambridge, Columbia, Jena, Leiden, London, Regensburg, and Wolfenbuttel; at the municipal libraries of Amiens, Besançon, Lille, Nancy, Rouen; and in London (BL) and Paris (BN).

24. Jean Aymon was born into a Catholic family in Dauphiné in 1661. He was trained for the priesthood in Grenoble and Turin. He later spent time in Rome where he received the title of doctor of canon law. As a result of some disagreement with the authorities he wrote a scurrilous and obscene pamphlet attacking the Holy See. Returning to Grenoble he sought refuge with the bishop who pardoned him and granted him an ecclesiastical office. Aymon soon wearied of life in Grenoble and returned to Rome where, in

1687, he managed to obtain a minor post at the apostolic court. He then decided that his knowledge of the inner workings of the Catholic authorites might be useful to the Protestants being expelled from France under the Revocation of the Edict of Nantes. He made his way to Switzerland where he renounced his religion, after which he moved to Holland and settled in The Hague where he began publishing anti-Catholic tracts. In 1701 he became a Protestant minister, although he earned his living teaching mathematics, and was also supported by a pension from the States-General. In 1706, on the pretext of a desire to return to the fold, he went to Paris and was placed, by the Cardinal de Noailles, in the seminary for foreign missions. He was also given access to the Royal Library directed by Nicolas Clément. After a few months Aymon disappeared from Paris and turned up again at The Hague. It was then discovered that he had stolen from the library valuable manuscripts which he later published. He also stole other important works, but attempts by the French government to recover them failed. Aymon's pension was reinstituted and he carried on his publications against the Catholic Church. He died about 1720. For further details see *Haag*,[2] vol. I (1877), pp. 615–626.

25. Mendoza (1503–1575) was a Spanish statesman and historian. The picaresque novel, *Lazarillo de Tormes*, was once attributed to him. For details see Hoefer, *op. cit.*, vol. 34 (1861) cols. 950–955.

26. Paul III (1468–1549) was born Alessandro Farnese. He was created cardinal in 1493 and elected pope in 1534. His pontificate marks the transition from the Renaissance to the Reform papacy. The Council of Trent and the Roman Inquisition were inaugurated during his term of office. He was a skilled politician and a patron of the arts.

27. He died in 1721.

28. *Journal Littéraire*, VIII (1716), 237–240. The work was also reviewed in the *Nouvelles Littéraires* (1716).

NOTES TO CHAPTER SEVEN

1. This is the work in which Erasmus revived and rejuvenated the old rhetorical exercise that required one to defend the not normally defensible. Erasmus had many imitators, of whom one was Agrippa, mentioned in chapter five, and another, Insulanus Menapius. Gueudeville's translations of works by both of these Renaissance scholars will be discussed later in this chapter.

2. For details of these editions see Appendix F.

3. M.M. Phillips, "Erasmus and Propaganda. A Study of the Translations of Erasmus in English and French," *Modern Language Review*, XXXVII (1952), 7.

4. From Gueudeville' preface to *L'Eloge de la folie.*

5. Preface to *Les Motifs de la conversion.*

6. From Gueudeville's preface to *Les Colloques d'Erasme*, discussed later in this chapter.

7. *Journal littéraire*, I (1713), juillet et août, Art. XII.

8. *Bibliothèque ancienne et moderne*, VII (1717), Art. 6, 214—215.

9. *Op. cit.*, VI (1732), 209.

10. From the preface to the 1751 edition of *L'Eloge de la folie.*

11. From the preface to the Pierre de Nolhac translation of *L'Eloge de la folie*, Garnier-Flammarion 1964, (first edition 1927).

12. J.G. Rechtien, "A 1520 French Translation of the *Moriae Encomium*" *Renaissance Quarterly*, XXVII (1974), 24.

13. See Appendix G.

14. The first French translation was done by Jehan Le Blond d'Eureux in 1550, and entitled *La Description de l'isle d'Utopie.* . . A second edition of this translation, edited by Barthélémy Aneau, appeared in 1559. The Sorbière translation was a new one and was published by Jean Blaeu. For details of these three editions see *St. Thomas More, a preliminary bibliography of his works.* . . , ed. Reginald Walter Gibson and J. Max Patrick, New Haven, Yale U.P., 1961, pp. 24—27. For details of Jacob Emmery, baron van Wassenaer (1674—1724), burgomaster and magistrate of Leiden, official of the Dutch East India Company, see the *Nieuw Nederlands Biographisch Woordenboek*, vol. II, pp. 1526—1527.

15. Since it was the practice, in the publishing trade, that the one who wrote the dedication received payment for it, it is unlikely that Van der Aa would have asked Gueudeville to write it. It was, in any case, signed by Van der Aa.

16. A. Lichtenberger, *Le Socialisme au XVIIIe siècle*, Paris, 1895, p. 57, note 2, quotes another of Gueudeville's gratuitous comments: "Quand sera-ce

que le bon plaisir de Dieu fera de toute la terre une ronde et vaste Utopie? Je crains fort que ce grand ouvrage ne soit pas encore fini au jour du jugement" (p. 157).

17. November 1715, 548–549 (Dutch edition).

18. *Bibliothèque ancienne et moderne*, VII (1717), 210–214. There are no Gueudevillian neologisms in the passage on marriage, but elsewhere in the translation one finds such inventions as "s'utopier," "s'utopianiser," "cardinaline," "ultréquinoxiaux" amongst others.

19. April 1718, 81–108. In 1743, in a review of all Gueudeville's translations, Gachet d'Artigny, *op. cit.*, VI, 171, referred to the *Utopie* as "toujours le même mélange du style burlesque le plus bas, d'expressions triviales, de pensées fausses, ridicules, de plaisanteriés grossières. . ."

20. February 1776, p. 14. In discussing the various French translations the writer considered Gueudeville's "la meilleure traduction que nous ayons de l'Utopie. . ."

21. No new translation appeared until the one by M.T. Rousseau, *Tableau du meilleur gouvernement possible, ou l'Utopie de Thomas Morus*, Paris, 1780.

22. LES / COMEDIES / DE / PLAUTE, / *NOUVELLEMENT TRADUITES* / en *Stile Libre, Naturel & Naif*; / Avec des Notes & des Reflexions enjouées, / agreables & utiles, de Critique, d'Antiquité, / de Morale & de Politique;/ Par Monsr. GUEUDEVILLE. / *Enrichi d'Estampes en Taille-douce à la tête* / *de chaque Tome & de chaque Comedie.* /*DIVISE'ES EN DIX TOMES.* / [vignette of type ornament] / A LEIDE, / Chez PIERRE VANDER Aa; /*Marchand Libraire, Imprimeur Ordinaire de l'Université* /*& de la Ville, demeurant dans l'Academie.* / [rule] / MDCCXIX. / Avec Privilége sous peine de 3000 florins d'amende &c. /contre les *Contrefacteurs.*
In red: COMEDIES / PLAUTE, / GUEUDEVILLE. / *DIVISE'ES EN DIX TOMES.* /PIERRE VANDER Aa;/MDCCXIX.
Each volume has an engraved title-page in addition to the printed one, and a half-title. Each play, which is paginated and signed separately, has an engraved frontispiece. There is also an engraved frontispiece in volume one which applies to the whole set. Volume one also has preliminaries which include the translator's preface, a life of Plautus, and a table of contents. In addition, all the plays are preceded by a "Plan de la pièce," and a list of the *dramatis personae*, and are followed by "Réflexions." The plays are *L'Amphitrion* (vol. I); *L'Asiniaire* and *L'Aululaire* (vol. II); *Les Captifs* and *Le Curculion* (vol. III); *La Casine, La Cistelaire*, and *L'Epidique* (vol. IV); *Les Bacchides* and *La Mostellaire* (vol. V); *Les Ménechmes* and *Le Soldat*

fanfaron (vol. VI); *Le Marchand* and *Le Pseudole* (vol. VII); *Le Poenule* and *La Persane* (vol. VIII); *Le Rudens* and *Le Stichus* (vol. IX); *Le Trinumme* and *Le Violent* (vol. X).

At the end of the last volume are found "Les fragments des comédies de. . . Plaute, "Les obscénités qui se trouvent dans les comédies. . ." and the *Privilegie*. The copy at the Utrecht University library has, in volume one, a half-title that ends with the information: *Se vend / A LA HAYE, / Chez HENRY SCHEURLEER, / Qui en a acheté les Exemplaires et le Privilege. / MDCCXXVI*.

Copies are available at the Royal libraries in Copenhagen, The Hague, Stockholm; the university libraries in Columbia, Geneva, London, Louvain, Sorbone, Tubingen, Utrecht, Wofenbüttel; the municipal libraries in Abbeville, Besançon, Liège, Orléans; in Paris (Ar, BN, Ma), and London (BL). The sets at Brussels (R) and Namur (M) are incomplete.

23. This play, by Jean-Antoine Baïf, was published in his *Jeux* in 1573.

24. J. Rotrou, *Les Ménechmes* (1636), *Les Sosies* (1638), *Les Captifs* (1640); A. Mareschal, *Le Véritable Capitan Matamore* (1638), based on *Miles Gloriosus*. Molière's *L'Avare* and *Amphitryon* are the most famous of his borrowings, but critics have noted influences of Plautus in other Molière plays (see W.E. Forehand, "Adaptation and Comic Intent: Plautus' *Amphitruo* and Molière's *Amphitryon*," *Comparative Literature Studies*, XI, no. 3 (1974), 205, note 7). It is, of course, always difficult to say how much was due to the influence of antiquity and how much to the *Commedia dell'arte*. Another play based on the *Miles Gloriosus*, and entitled *Le Capitan*, was published anonymously in 1639, and a Provençal adaptation, by Charles Feau, was performed in Marseille about 1634. (See C.P. Goujet, *Bibliothèque Française*, IV (1744), p. 399).

25. This play, *Les Ménechmes*, was published, in 1714, in volume two of *Théâtre de Regnard*.

26. Coste's translation was reviewed in the *Nouvelles de la République des lettres*, (March and April 1716), Art. VIII. Coste replied in the next issue, Art. III, and also wrote to the editor of the *Histoire critique de la République des lettres*, XI, Art. XIV, who replied in XIII, Art. I, and XIV, Art. XI. Finally, some extracts from letters about Coste's translation were published in the *Journal de Trévoux*, (July 1716 and February 1717).

17. Limiers' work was entitled, *Les Oeuvres de Plaute, en latin et en français. Traduction nouvelle, enrichie de figures, avec des remarques sur les endroits difficiles, et un examen de chaque pièce selon les règles du théâtre*, A Amsterdam, aux dépens de la Compagnie, 1719, 10 vols.

Although the publications of Limiers and Gueudeville appeared in 1719, they were first announced in 1717 in the *Journal Littéraire*, IX, 485–486. Van der Aa had already acquired a *privilège* for the work in 1715, together with *L'Eloge de la folie* and *L'Utopie*.

The translations of Limiers and Gueudeville were reviewed in *L'Europe savante*, (1719), Art. III and IV, 203–238, and in the *Journal Littéraire*, (1720), Art. XI, 137–157. Limiers' work was also reviewed in the Dutch edition of the *Journal des savants*, (August 1719), 180–196. My examples of the translations are taken from these reviews.

28. There is no indication that Gueudeville consulted manuscript material. For help with the translation he probably used, *M. Accii Plauti Comoedia. Accedit commentarius ex variorum notis et observationibus. . . Ex recensione J.F. Gronovii*, Leyden, 1664.

29. The announcement, in the *Journal Littéraire*, (1717), of Gueudeville's forthcoming publication, drew attention to his affinities with Plautus: "Ceux qui connaissent le feu et la vivacité que M. Gueudeville a fait paraître ci-devant dans ses écrits, s'attendront à en trouver dans sa traduction d'un auteur dont le génie est assez conforme au sien à divers égards."

30. *Journal Littéraire*, (1720), 146.

31. As the reviewer in *L'Europe savante* pointed out (215), the tone of Gueudeville's translation is totally unsuitable in this situation where Amphitruo is extremely angry, and Sosia has good reason to be afraid of the outcome.

32. The most flagrant example of gratuitous dialogue occurs near the end of *Amphitruo*. When Amphitruo learns from Bromia that it is Jupiter who has slept with his wife, he says:

Pol me haud paenitet,
Si licet boni dimidium mihi dividere cum Iove. (1125)

This one remark prompts a whole diatribe in Gueudeville's translation:

Voilà donc le mot de l'énigme, voilà le secret du mystère, voilà le dénoue-ment de la pièce! N'en déplaise au Seigneur Jupiter, il peut se vanter de m'avoir fait bien du mal; et, sans parler des cornes divines dont sa Majesté suprême m'a fait présent, qu'est-ce que les ressemblances n'ont point fait souffrir à moi et à mon valet? En vérité le Lance-Foudre aurait bien épargné du trouble et du chagrin, s'il lui avait plu de s'abstenir d'un adultère, et garder mieux la foi d'époux à sa jalouse Junon. Mais chut. . . ce Dieu lascif et luxurieux pourrait m'entendre, car il n'ignore pas ce qu'il veut bien laisser échapper. Allons au plus sûr, et prenons-le sur un autre ton.

Par Pollux, je ne puis assez me féliciter. Le grand Jupiter m'a fait un honneur dont je ne saurais trop le remercier. Sa Seigneurie s'est abaissée jusqu'à vouloir bien être mon image vivante, prendre ma place de mari, en faire les fonctions, cultiver mon petit champ, peupler ma famille, tenir mon épouse en haleine. Que de biens à la fois! D'ailleurs, partager la moitié de son bien avec Jupiter; se peut-il rien de plus glorieux? Ma femme est à lui premier qu'à moi, et il conserve toujours sur elle le droit du Seigneur. Je dois donc passer à juste titre pour le plus noble cocu de la terre; et si jamais cocuage se tourne en puissant empire, je serai sans doute choisi pour en être le chef et pour le gouverner.

An example of a passage of which not one word is in the original is found in the prologue to *Amphitruo*. Gueudeville was most dissatisfied with Plautus' presentation of Mercury in the prologue. He felt that Plautus had failed to accord Mercury his proper status and dignity, and so he added the following lines:

Je n'ai que faire de vous décliner mon nom; il ne faut que regarder mon équipage. Y a-t-il ici quelqu'un qui puisse me méconnaître, et ignorer le rang que je tiens dans le Ciel? Silence donc, spectateurs; écoutez-moi des deux oreilles. Ce n'est pas pour vous le reprocher; Un Dieu n'est pas intéressé dans ses faveurs, il ne fait du bien que pour son plaisir; mais entre nous pourtant, vous ne disconviendrez pas que vous m'avez de grandes obligations.

33. It should not be forgotten, however, that Henri Scheurleer purchased the stocks and *privilège* for this edition (see note 22). This could be an indication of some interest in the work.

34. *Théâtre de Plaute*, Paris, 1831–1838, 9 vols. Quoted by A. Ernout in the preface to his edition, *Plaute*, Paris 1932–1940, 7 vols. All the quotations are taken from the Ernout edition.

35. Plaute, *La Marmite, traduction, notices, notes et dénouement de la pièce*, par Jean-Marie Courbon, Les Presses de l'Université de Québec, 1971, p. 5. I am grateful to Professors J.M. Bigwood and K.R. Thompson of the Department of Classics, University of Toronto, for their comments on this section.

36. LES / COLLOQUES / D'ERASME, / Ouvrage très interessant; par la diversité / des Sujets, par l'Enjoûment, et pour / l'Utilité Morale: / *NOUVELLE TRADUCTION*, / Par Monsr. GUEUDEVILLE, / *Avec des Notes, et des Figures très-/ingenieuses. /DIVISE'ES EN SIX TOMES. /TOME PREMIER,/* Qui contient, / *Les Femmes*. / [vignette of type ornament] / A LEIDE, / Chez PIERRE VANDER Aa, / & / BOUDOUIN JANSSON VANDER Aa, / Marchands Libraires. / [rule] / MDCC.XX. / Avec Privilége sous peine de 3000 florins d'Amende &c./contre les *Contrefacteurs*.

In red: COLLOQUES / D'ERASME, / GUEUDEVILLE, / TOME PREMIER, /
PIERRE VANDER Aa, BOUDOUIN JANSSON VANDER Aa,
Contents: title (verso blank; *1–*5, épitre dédicatoire à Frédéric, duc de
Gloucester; *5 v–*6 v, privilegie; **1–**8, préface du traducteur; **8–
7 v, Discours sur la vie d'Erasme; ***7 v–8 v, Lettre d'Erasme à
Frobenius; ***9–***11, Table des dialogues de chaque tome contenus
dans cet ouvrage; ***11 v–***12 v, catalogue des livres... chez Pierre van
der Aa; 1–272, text.

The other five volumes have the same title-page with the appropriate
volume numbers, preceded by a half-title. The texts of these volumes contain respectively, 192, 385, 394, 224 and 236 pages.

The contents of volumes two to six are entitled: Juger sainement et
utilement des choses; La Table, ou les Festins; Les Sottises du vulgaire
ignorant; Les trois principaux mobiles de l'homme: le culte, la nature
et l'art; Diverses matières, et instructions pour la jeunesse.

The privilege was granted on July 20, 1719 (Algemeen Rijksarchief,
Staten van Holland 1572–1795), and the book was advertised in the
Boekzaal, IX (November 1719), 621.

The edition is embellished, in the usual Van der Aa fashion, with an
unsigned, engraved coat of arms of Louis Frederick, duke of Gloucester,
to whom the work is dedicated. Louis Frederick (1707–1715), Prince of
Wales, was the eldest son of George II and Queen Caroline. He was created
duke of Gloucester in 1717 (see the *Dictionary of National Biography*, vol.
VII, pp. 675–678). There is also an engraved frontispiece by J. Schynvoet,
and sixty other unsigned engravings, "suivant les desseins d'un fort bon
maître, ayant imité en cela le célèbre HOLBEIN duquel les belles figures ont
servi d'un grand ornement à *l'Eloge de la folie*." The engravings are distributed throughout the six volumes. According to J. Lewine, *op. cit.*, pp.
169–170, these engravings are "in the style of Romain de Hooge or of
Harrewyn." In Victor Develay's three-volume translation of the *Colloquia*,
Paris, 1875, there appears the following judgement of the engravings: "Sans
aucun souci de l'exactitude historique, l'artiste s'est cru permis de faire
endosser parfois aux personnages d'Erasme les costumes du XVIIIe siècle,
et n'a su racheter cet anachronisme ni par le mérite de la composition, ni
par la variété des sujets qui se ressemblent tous dans leur uniforme mé-
diocrité." For a more detailed description see the *Bibliotheca Belgica*, vol.
V, pp. 197–203. According to the *Bibliotheca Belgica*, Gueudeville's work,
which is judged to be less a translation than a "paraphrase médiocre du
Colloquiorum opus d'Erasme," was probably based on the Elzevier edition
published in Leiden (1636), the Leers edition published in Rotterdam
(1693) and the French translation by Samuel Chappuseau published in
Leiden (1653). Other French translations are also noted in this volume.

Copies are available in Berne (N), London (BL), Paris (Ar, BN, Ma); the
Royal libraries in Brussels, Copenhagen and The Hague; the municipal

libraries of Besançon, Evreux, La Rochelle, Lyon, Montpellier, Mons, Nantes, Troyes, and Rotterdam; the university libraries of Basel, Berlin, Caen, Gent, Harvard, Illinois, Liège, Montpellier, Saarbrucken, Strasbourg, Utrecht, Wofenbüttel. The sets at Leeds and Leiden are incomplete. There is a complete set in Chicago (Ne).

37. In the *privilège* that Van der Aa acquired in 1715 for the publication of *L'Eloge de la folie*, *l'Utopie* and *Les Comédies de Plaute*, there is also reference to a work entitled *Les Eloges admirables des choses merveilleuses*. I have been unable to find any trace of this last work. Presumably it was, or would have been, a translation of *Admiranda rerum admirabilium encomia*, 1666 and 1667 (see T. Georgi, *Allgemeinen Europäischen Bücher-Lexici*, Leipzig, 1742—1753, vol. I, p. 14).

38. The *Bibliotheca Belgica* finds that "Les dialogues sont groupés arbitrairement en plusieurs décades soi-disant d'après leur contenu, dans un ordre complètement différent de celui adopté par l'auteur."

39. *Les Colloques d'Erasme, choisis, traduits et présentés par Léon-E. Halkin*, Presses de l'Université de Laval, Quebec 1971, pp. 11—13. For other comments on translations of the *Colloques* see J.-C. Margolin, *Recherches érasmiennes*, Geneva, 1969, pp. 123—161.

40. This extract is taken from volume three of the *Opera Omnia*, ed. L.-E. Halkin, F. Bierlaire and R. Hoven, Amsterdam, 1972, p. 277.

41. HENRI CORNEILLE / AGRIPPA / DE NETTESHEIM, / Sur la NOBLESSE, & EXCEL- / LENCE du sexe Feminin, de / sa PREEMINENCE sur l'au- / tre sexe, & du Sacre-/ment du MARIAGE./*Avec le Traittè sur l'incertitude, aussi | bien que la vanitè* / des SCIENCES & des ARTS. / Ouvrage joli, & d'une lecture tout a / fait agreable, traduit par le cele- / bre Sr. / M. DE GUEUDEVILLE. / TOME PREMIER. / [vignette of fruit and flowers] / *LEIDEN*. /Chez THEODORE HAAK, 1726.
In red: AGRIPPA / SCIENCES ARTS. / M. DE GUEUDEVILLE. / THEODORE HAAK, Contents: Title (verso blank); *1—*6v, préface du traducteur; *7—*10, index; *10v. conclusion; 1—6, lettre dédicatoire; 7—24, au lecteur; 25—31, lettre à Maximilien; 31—36, épitre dédicatoire; 36—206, text of Discours sur la noblesse, etc.; 207—429, text of chapters 1—29 of Discours sur l'incertitude. . . des sciences et des arts.
There are two engraved fronts, one is signed R. Blokh and is a portrait of Agrippa; the other, unsigned, shows the inventions of the arts and sciences in the process of being burned, and bears the device — LARVATA DETEGUNTER [*sic*] (enchanted things are being revealed).
HENRI CORNEILLE / AGRIPPA / DE NETTESHEIM, / Sur l'incertitude, aussi bien / que la vanitè / des SCIENCES & des ARTS. / *Ouvrage joli, &*

d'une lecture tout | a fait agreable, traduit par | le celebre Sr. | M. DE GUEUDEVILLE. / TOME SECOND. / [vignette of type ornament] / *LEIDEN.*/Chez THEODORE HAAK, 1726.

In red: AGRIPPA / SCIENCES ARTS. / M. DE GUEUDEVILLE. / THEODORE HAAK, 1726.

In some copies the word SECOND is printed as SECONDE.

Volume two contains chapters 30–71, and the pagination, continued from volume one, is 430–910.

The title-page of volume three is the same as for volume two except for the change of volume number and a different vignette of type ornament. This volume contains chapters 72–102, and runs from page 911 to 1350.

Although the title-pages bear the date 1726, the work was first advertised in the *Boekzaal*, XX (February 1725), 237.

42. Bayle dismissed Agrippa as a charlatan. In commenting on Agrippa's treatise on the vanity of knowledge, the *Journal des savants*, (March 1714) 263, described it as being "plus propre à amuser des écoliers qu'il ne peut être utile à une recherche sérieuse."

43. See Anne Sauvy, *op. cit.*, p. 321.

44. This was the translation by Arnaudin, *De la grandeur et excellence des femmes au-dessus des hommes*, Paris, 1713.

Arnaudin, in 1713, also had difficulties with the translation, but he solved them in a different way, and was commended in the *Journal des savants*, (1713), 49–50: "le traducteur ne s'est pas assujetti à rendre en français quelques phrases inutiles au sujet; il a cru avec encore plus de raison pouvoir changer, adoucir, et quelquefois retrancher certaines expressions que la politesse de notre langue ne souffre pas. . ." Gueudeville, of course, retained those expressions.

45. Rousseau's debt to Agrippa was advanced by Gustav Krueger, *Fremde Gedanken in J.J. Rousseaus erstem Discours*, Halle, 1891. In George R. Havens' critical edition of the discourse (Baltimore, 1946), it is argued that although Rousseau may have known, in a general way, of Agrippa's ideas, he did not read Agrippa until 1751 (see pp. 71–73). It is, of course, always possible that, although he did not borrow Agrippa's works from the Bibliothèque du Roi until 1751, he could have read them before that date.

46. Jean-Pierre le Bouler, "Les emprunts de Rousseau à la Bibliothèque du Roi," *Annales Jean-Jacques Rousseau*, XXXVIII (1969–1971), 255.

47. Au reste, si mon auteur est de bonne foi, s'il écrivait par persuasion, et si, sur quoi j'aurais bien de la peine à décider, son ouvrage n'est point un jeu d'esprit. . . (Préface du traducteur).

48. L'ELOGE / DE LA / FIEVRE QUARTE / Où il est doctoralement prouvé / I. *Que ceux qui ont le Bonheur d'avoir cete / Fièvre, ne peuvent trop s'en féliciter.* / II. *Que ceux qu'elle n'a pas honoré / de sa visite, ne peuvent la souhaiter / avec trop d'ardeur.* / Traduit du Latin / de / GUILLAUME MENAPE / En son vivant, Docteur en Mèdecine, / (apparemment.) / *Cherche qui veut,* / *Trouve qui peut.* / Par Monsr. GUEUDEVILLE. / [rule] / *A LEIDE,* / Chés THEODORE HAAK, / Libraire vis à vis de l'Académie / MDCCXXVIII.
In red: L'ELOGE / FIEVRE QUARTE / GUILLAUME MENAPE / GUEUDEVILLE. / THEODORE HAAK,
$12° *^5 A–D^{12} E^6$
Contents: *1, title (verso blank); *2–*5, Avertissement; A1–A6 v, Avertissement du traducteur; A7–E6, text.
pp. [10] 1–108
There are copies in Amsterdam (U), Darmstadt (U), London (BL), Paris (BN). The only copy I have examined is the one in Amsterdam where the text of the two *avertissements* is identical, although the type is different, the first one being in italics.

49. *Encomium febris quartanae, Guilielmo Insulano Menapio Grevibrugensi auctore; adjecta quoque est ejusdem quartanae febris curandae exactissima ratio, e doctissimis tam Graecorum quam Latinorum atque Arabum monumentis deprompta,* Basileae, ex officina Joanis Oporini, 1542. There were several editions during the seventeenth century, notably in 1636, in Leiden, where it was published together with a number of humorous treatises.

Guglielmus Insulanus Menapius (?–1561), also known as Guillaume Ménape, Guillaume L'Isle or de Lille, was a priest, orator, and medical doctor. Very little is known about him for certain. On the death of Erasmus he pronounced a funeral oration which was published in Basel, and later reproduced by Van der Aa in his 1706 edition of Erasmus' *Opera Omnia.* Menapius published other medical treatises and works on philosophy and history. For details see the *Biographie nationale de Belgique,* vol. 8 (1884–1885), col. 509–511.

50. AMUSEMENT / PHILOSOPHIQUE / TRÈS-SÉRIEUX-COMIQUE / HISTORIQUE, POLITIQUE, / CRITIQUE, SATYRIQUE, &c. / *MIS AU JOUR* / PAR MR. DE GUEUDEVILLE. / *EN DEUX PARTIES*: / Le GOUTEUX en BELLE-HUMEUR / ET LE / FÉBRICITANT PHILOSOPHE. / *Et sermone opus est modo tristi saepè jocoso.* / HORAT. / [vignette of type ornament] / A LA HAYE & a FRANCFORT sur Meyn. / AUX DEPENS DE LA COMPAGNIE. / M.D.CC.XLIII.

In red: PHILOSOPHIQUE / HISTORIQUE, POLITIQUE, / PAR MR. DE GUEUDEVILLE. / Le GOUTEUX en BELLE-HUMEUR / A LA HAYE & a FRANCFORT sur Meyn./M.D.CC.XLIII.

Copies are found in Paris (Ar); the municipal libraries of Avignon, Besançon, Lyon, Rouen; The Hague (R); the university libraries of Ghent, Göttingen, Lausanne, Leipzig, Louvain, Washington; Zurich (C). The title-page of Gueudeville's translation reads:

LE / FEBRICITANT / PHILOSOPHE: / OU / L'ELOGE / DE LA / FIEVRE-QUARTE; / Où IL EST DOCTORALEMENT PROUVE' / *Le Bonheur de l'avoir, les Avantages qui en resultent, & / que ceux qui ne l'ont point encore ne peuvent la / souhaiter avec trop d'ardeur.* / TRADUIT DU LATIN DE / *GUILLAUME MENAPE,* Savant Docteur en Medecine lorsqu'il vivoit; / PAR MR. DE GUEUDEVILLE. / *Ouvrage très serieux-comique.* / [engraved vignette signed B. Picart del. 1729, and surmounted by the device – VILIA DIVENDENS SCRUTA POPELLO) / A LA HAYE & à FRANCFORT sur Meyn,/ AUX DEPENS DE LA COMPAGNIE./M.D.CC.XLXXX.

In red: PHILOSOPHE: / FIEVRE-QUARTE; / *GUILLAUME MENAPE,* / PAR MR. DE GUEUDEVILLE. / A LA HAYE & a FRANCFORT sur Meyn,/M.D.CC.XLIII.

NOTES TO CHAPTER EIGHT

1. I do not intend to discuss the attribution to Gueudeville of some of the work of Vigneul-Marville (see, for example, the catalogue of the Bibliothèque Nationale), since there seems to be neither external nor internal evidence for such an attribution.

2. The first two volumes were reviewed in the *Histoire des ouvrages des savants,* (August 1702), Art. IV, 342–346. The third volume was first advertised in July 1703 in *L'Esprit des cours de l'Europe* where it was stated that "Les Frères L'Honoré donneront dans peu, le troisième tome des Voyages. . ." In the September issue it was advertised for sale, and was reviewed in the November issue of the *Nouvelles de la République des lettres.* Details of these and subsequent editions are given by A.H. Greenly, "Lahontan: An Essay and Bibliography," *Papers of the Bibliographical Society of America,* XLVIII (1954), 334–389. While Greenly did not solve the many bibliographical problems associated with the works of Lahontan, he did reveal the complexities and prepared the way for a definitive study. Such a study is currently in progress at Laval University, Québec, and is under the direction of Professor Réal Ouellet (see the article by Ouellet *et al.* in the *Dictionnaire des oeuvres littéraires du Québec,* Montreal, 1978, vol. I, pp. 533–543).

3. The quotation is from the detailed article on Lahontan by my colleague,

David M. Hayne, in the *Dictionary of Canadian Biography, 1701–1740*, University of Toronto Press, 1969, pp. 439–444.

4. The quotation is from an advertisement in the April 1705 issue of *L'Esprit des cours de l'Europe* in which it is announced that the new edition is "sous la presse." In the June issue it is announced as being on sale. Although, on the title-pages, this edition is described as a second edition, there had, in fact, been other editions in 1703, in French and English, and in 1704, in French (see Greenly, art. cit.), but none of these contained revisions other than the correction of errata.

5. The vitriolic and revolutionary nature of the revisions and additions was brought out by G. Chinard in his edition of the *Dialogues, op. cit.*, pp. 41–44, and by M. Roelens, *Dialogues avec un sauvage*, Paris, Editions sociales, 1973, pp. 66–70.

6. See the Avertissement to his *Recueil de voyages au nord*, Amsterdam, 1715–1727, 8 vols. Bernard is quoted by J.-Edmond Roy, "Le Baron de Lahontan," *Transactions of the Royal Society of Canada*, 1st ser., XII (1894), 121.

7. Art. cit., 221. A Lichtenberger, *Le Socialisme au XVIIIe siècle*, Paris, 1895, p. 54, thought Gueudeville was the author of the dialogues.

8. According to J.-E. Roy, art. cit., 127, this information derives from the German scholar, J.J. Brucker, and this was the view expressed by F.G. Freytag (*Analecta litteraria de libris rarioribus*, 1750) and J.A. Trinius (*Freydenker-Lexicon*, 1759).

9. There have been studies of the 1705 revisions but these have been concerned with such questions as narrative technique and historical veracity, and not with the problem of attribution. I refer particularly to two recent papers both delivered at conferences, and both, as yet, unpublished:
Hélène Vachon, "Les *Nouveaux Voyages* de Lahontan. Etude des variantes 1703–1705," and Judith C. Neave, "Lahontan and the Long River Controversy." I am most grateful to Dr. Neave for her help with my study of Gueudeville and Lahontan.

10. Quand je me figure un Marocain négocier à la cour de France, il me semble voir un Iroquois qui trafiquerait au milieu d'une colonie française; l'intérêt est le flambeau qui éclaire ces gens-là, aussi bien que le reste des hommes (*L'Esprit des cours*, June 1699, 40).

Les commissaires nommés par les rois de France et d'Angleterre au sujet du règlement des limites qui sont contestés entre les deux nations dans l'Amérique septentrionale, n'ont pu terminer leur affaire à fond. . . on s'est engagé de part à autre à retenir la férocité des Iroquois, et à les mettre dans la nécessité d'observer la paix entre eux. . . (August 1699, 253–354).

Si un Indien de bon sens, voyant disputer du pas à la procession ou à la communion, demandait de quoi il s'agit, et qu'on lui expliquât nettement la chose, n'inventerait-il point quelque nouvelle posture pour en mieux marquer son étonnement? (August 1699, 291).

11. This, at least, is the impression given by the preface to the English translation of 1703 (see Greenly, art. cit., 349), but perhaps some subterfuge is involved here.

12. "Tu me jettes là sur une ample et embarrassante matière" (1705, p. 234).

13. Hatin, *Les Gazettes de Hollande.* . . , pp. 191–192, quotes almost the whole of this passage which contains outstanding examples of the poor taste and obscenities of which Gueudeville's critics constantly complained:

En effet, quel rapport de l'union conjugale avec la puissance que les Vénitiens s'arrogent sur un espace de mer? La mer, je l'avoue, tient assez du naturel qu'on attribue aux femmes. . . mais en est-elle plus habile et plus propre à la génération humaine? Je ne crois pas que le doge s'avise jamais de caresser sa chère moitié: la copulation serait mortelle et la couche nuptiale serait infailliblement le tombeau du mari. . . Après tout, le mariage est d'une teneur bien fragile, et je ne m'étonne point qu'on le renouvelle tous les ans. L'épouse ne fait pas grand cas du marché, et, sans avoir égard à la persévérance inimitable de monsieur son mari, elle est toujours prête à se donner au premier venu. . . celui chez qui la munition se trouve la plus copieuse jouit de cette lubrique sans qu'elle fasse la moindre résistance.

14. In March, referring to the massacre of twenty-six unarmed Austrian soldiers by a troop of Hungarian rebels, Gueudeville writes:

Si l'on proposait à des Iroquois de deviner ce que l'on fit de ces pauvres gens, il n'y en a pas un, je le pose en fait, qui ne soutînt qu'on obligea ces malheureux Impériaux à suivre le détachement. Nos Iroquois, tout Iroquois qu'ils sont, auraient pourtant mal deviné: les vingt-six innocents furent massacrés (275).

When it suited his purposes, Gueudeville made the Chinese serve the role of noble savages:

Un Chinois instruit des prétentions du Pape, et à qui l'on conterait cette histoire, ne croirait-il pas deviner juste en disant que tous les princes catholiques prirent parti pour les Vénitiens contre Paul cinquième? Notre Chinois se tromperait néanmoins (December 1705, 604–605).

15. In the issue of May—August 1708 Gueudeville looked at the celebration of Mass through the eyes of a Huron:

> Quelle pourrait être l'origine de cette cérémonie? Car dans le culte romain il n'y a pas une minutie qui n'ait ses raisons; et un Huron qui en prendrait quantité pour des jeux et des postures de théâtre serait fort étonné qu'on lui donnât de tous ces mouvements une interprétation mystérieuse et sublime (222—223).

16. Although the humour is predominantly of the burlesque variety, Gueudeville does not miss the opportunity to indulge his love of the salacious. When Lahontan makes a brief reference to some Indian hospitality he was obliged to decline, Gueudeville develops the situation:

1703	*1705*
. . .sa première civilité fut de faire venir quantité de filles, entre lesquelles il nous pressait, moi et les miens, de choisir. La tentation aurait été plus forte dans un autre temps, le mets ne valait rien pour des voyageurs affaiblis de travail et d'abstinence, *sine Cerere et Baccho friget Venus.*	On nous amena par son ordre une troupe des plus belles filles du village, et le commode chef nous pressa fort obligeamment de choisir. Nous ne profitâmes point de ce maquerellage royal; nous remerciâmes civilement le prince de sa courtoisie, et outre que la fatigue et l'abstinence nous avaient épointé l'écharde, nous étions bien aises d'édifier ces sauvages par notre continence. A vous dire vrai, Monsieur, il y avait un peu de dégoût dans notre chasteté; cette prostitution nous fit mal au coeur, et nous aurions été bien autrement tentés, s'il y avait eu plus de peine ou de mystère (p. 221).

When Lahontan's prose is so pedestrian as to defy the introduction of humour, Gueudeville resorts to extravagance to enliven the proceedings:

1703	*1705*
Il en est aujourd'hui comme de tout temps, l'événement ne répond pas toujours au projet; tel s'imagine d'aller au but qui lui tourne le dos. C'est de moi que je parle, car au lieu de passer en France comme je vous l'écrivis il y a deux mois, il faut que j'aille au bout du monde, comme vous le verrez à la fin du récit de notre expédition (p. 92).	Si jamais homme a pesté contre sa malheureuse destinée, c'est moi. Il y a deux mois que je me repais de la douce idée du voyage de France. Figurez-vous avec quelle impatience j'attendais mon départ. Jamais amant transi n'a mieux trouvé les moments des jours, et les jours des années. Terminer des affaires importantes, travailler à ma fortune,

voir ma famille, mes amis, et vous, surtout, Monsieur, qui m'êtes si cher, toutes ces pensées me chatouillaient vivement l'imagination, et l'amant le plus passionné ne peut se représenter une jouissance avec plus de plaisir. Mais hélas! ces belles espérances sont évanouies; c'est comme si j'avais fait un agréable rêve, et mon bizarre destin, au lieu de me laisser embarquer pour La Rochelle, me relance au bout du monde. Avant que d'expliquer l'énigme, je veux vous tenir parole, et vous rendre compte de notre glorieuse campagne; préparez-vous à écouter de merveilleux événements (109–110).

17. LE GRAND / THEATRE / HISTORIQUE, / OU NOUVELLE / HISTOIRE UNIVERSELLE, / TANT SACREE QUE PROFANE, / DEPUIS LA CREATION DU MONDE, JUSQU'AU / COMMENCEMENT DU XVIII SIECLE: / Contenant une fidéle & exacte description de ce qui s'est passé de / plus memorable sous les quatre premieres Monarchies, des ASSYRIENS, / des PERSES, des GRECS, et des ROMAINS, comme aussi / des MONARCHIES qui leur ont succedé, / *Et ce qui concerne nommement le PEUPLE JUIF, & qui se trouve dans la* SAINTE ECRITURE *& ailleurs,* / Avec la Suite / DE L'HISTOIRE ROMAINE / *Sous les Empereurs d'Orient & d'Occident*: / La FONDATION, les PROGRES, les CHANGEMENS, la DECADENCE, / la RUINE, ou la continuation des Etats, Royaumes & Républiques de la Chrêtienté; / *Où l'on voit les Actions les plus remarquables* / DES PAPES, DES EMPEREURS, DES ROIS, ET DES / GRANDS CAPITAINES, / *Les invasions, les conquêtes, les révolutions des Infidéles:* les Progrés de l'EVANGILE, / *ses* PERSECUTIONS *& ses* TRIOMPHES: *la naissance, la durée, ou l'extirpation* / *des Hérésies: & en général tout ce qui concerne* / Les PAPES, & L'HISTOIRE ECCLESIASTIQUE. / *Le tout recueilli avec un grand choix des plus excellens Auteurs anciens et modernes,* / Et parsemé des particularitez les plus curieuses, et digeré dans un bon ordre CHRONO- / LOGIQUE, & de telle maniere que l'Histoire de chaque NATION considerable / & celle de l'EGLISE sont traittées à part. / OUVRAGES DIVISE'EN CINQ PARTIES, / *Avec des figures en taille douce, qui représentent les plus beaux endroits de l'Histoire,* / *Et des Indices des Livres, Periodes, Chapitres & Matieres.* / TOME PREMIER, / *Depuis la Création du Monde jusqu'à la mort de l'Empereur Auguste.* / [engraved vignette surmounted by the device: HAC ITUR AD ASTRA] / A LEIDE, / Chez PIERRE VANDER Aa, MDCCIII. / [rule] / *AVEC PRIVILEGE.*

In red: lines 3, 5, 7, 8. 15, 20, 21, 25, 30, 33 and PIERRE VANDER Aa. The five parts are in three volumes in folio. The title-pages of the other two volumes (three and five) bear the appropriate changes. The *Privilège* was obtained June 23 1702 (Algemeen Rijksarchief, Staten van Holland 1572–1795, no. 1654). The work was reviewed in the *Nouvelles de la République des lettres*, (January 1704) and in the *Histoire des ouvrages des savants*, (July 1704).

Copies are found at the university libraries of Baltimore (JH), Cambridge, Geneva, Ghent, Harvard, Iowa, Lausanne, Leiden, Liège, Montpellier, Nancy, Odense, Oslo, Princeton, Toulouse, Wurzburg; the municipal libraries of Besançon, Lille, Lyon, Nantes, Périgueux, Rouen; the royal libraries of The Hague and Stockholm; Boston (P), Chicago (Ne), Munster (L), Paris (Ar, BI, BN, Ma), Wolfenbüttel (HA), Zurich (C).

18. Andreas Lazarus von Imhof (1656–1704) was a counsellor at several European courts. The work, to which he contributed the first five volumes on which *Le Grand Théâtre historique* is based, was entitled *Neu-eröffneter historischer Bilder-Saal, des ist kurtze, deutliche und unpassionirte Beschreibung der Historia universalis, von Anfang der Welt bis auf unsere Zeiten...*, in seventeen volumes, of which the first three were published, 1692–1694, and the rest from 1694–1728 (see Michaud, *op. cit.*, vol. XX, p. 317).

19. As, for example, in the catalogue at the end of the *Nouveau Théâtre du Monde*, or the one at the end of the 1717 reissue of *L'Utopie*.

20. Art. XLVIII, 544.

21. Quérard, *Les Supercheries littéraires*, vol. II, p. 230c, says that Rogissart brought out the first edition of *Les Délices de l'Italie* in 1706. The authors are identified in the *privilège* as "le sieur de Rogissart et H*** (l'abbé Havard), according to Barbier, *op. cit.*, vol. I, col. 872.

22. See Kossmann, *op. cit.*, pp. 329–330.

23. *Le Misantrope* was published by T. Johnson. The author, Justus van Effen (1684–1735), was one of the most active journalists, editors, and translators of his time. He collaborated in the *Nouvelles Littéraires, Journal historique, Journal Littéraire*. He wrote in Dutch, French and English, translated works by Defoe, Swift and others, and was, for a time, secretary to the Dutch ambassador in London. For more details see *Nieuw Nederlands Biographisch Woordenboek*, vol. I, pp. 794–795.

24. *Nouvelles Littéraires*, I (January 1715), 21–23.

25. LE / CENSEUR, / OU / CARACTERES DES MOEURS DE LA HAYE, /
Par Mr. de G*** / MONTRE AUX HOMMES, UN HOMME VRAÏEMENT /
HOMME ET QUI VIVE SELON LA SAINE RAISON; / QU'ILS LE VOÏENT,
QU'ILS L'INTEROGENT; ET / S'ILS NE PEUVENT LE SUPORTER,
QU'ILS LE / FASSENT MOURIR. IL VAUT BEAUCOUP MIEUX / MOURIR
QUE DE VIVRE COMME EUX. *M. An-* / *tonin, réfl. Mor. Liv. X.S.* 20. /
[vignette of flowers and leaves] / A LA HAYE, / Chez HENRY SCHEURLEER,
à l'En- / Seigne d'Erasme. / [rule] / M.DCC.XV.
In red: CENSEUR, / DE LA HAYE, / A LA HAYE, / M.DCC.XV.
*⁴ A–2X⁴ (the 2X gathering is missigned X)
pp. [8] [1] 2–344 [8] (205 is misnumbered 305)
Contents: *1, title; *2–*4 v, épître; 1–344, text; [345–360], table des
matières.
Each issue ends with advertising material from the publisher.
Copies are found in Amiens (M), Chicago (Ne), The Hague (R), Nantes (M),
Nice (M), Stockholm (R), Wolfenbüttel (HA).

26. I have found no reference to his authorship by any of Gueudeville's contemporaries, but Quérard and Barbier, among others, identify him as the
author.

27. . . .étant inconnu et ayant pris toutes les précautions nécessaires pour
n'être point découvert, je n'ai point à craindre que les vicieux prennent
dans les irrégularités de ma conduite (car qui est parfait) des armes pour
combattre ma censure de leur vice.

Il est triste qu'on soit obligé de prendre tant de précaution pour faire sentir
tout leur faible à des hommes qui font parade de leur raison. Ils devraient,
s'ils sont si raisonnables, recevoir ces sortes d'avis d'une manière honnête
et en savoir gré à ceux qui les leur donnent (6–7).

28. Although an attempt was made to devote one issue to one topic, there are
many digressions and repetitions. Several issues are largely taken up by
letters from readers, of which some, if not all, could well be of the author's
own invention. Marriage is dealt with in numbers XVI and XXXII; fashion
(XIII, XVI); love and jealousy (V, VIII); gambling, etc. (XVIII, XIX);
attacks on religion (XXXV, XXXVIII); anecdotes (XVII, XL); Lahontan
references (XXXVI, XXXIX); criticism of "intellectuals" (III, XXIII, XXV,
XXVI).

29. One feature not previously dealt with by Gueudeville concerns references
to local affairs in The Hague, to names of places, and to activities such as
the *kermesses* (X, XI) and various social groups and activities (IX). There is
also occasional use of Dutch names and expressions, a practice not previously indulged in by Gueudeville.

30. Quoted by Hatin, *Les Gazettes de Hollande. . .* , p. 187. That *Le Censeur* was not well received is indicated in the review in the *Nouvelles Littéraires*, art. cit. The work was dedicated to Madame Postérité, and according to the review:

> Comme le public n'a pas aussi favorablement jugé de cet ouvrage qu'il a fait du *Misantrope*, un railleur a dit que lorsque l'auteur le présenta à Madame Postérité, cette dame lui répondit,
>> Censeur, malgré ta dédicace
>> Je te l'avouerai franchement
>> Ce livre qu'aujourd'hui je reçois en présent
>> Parmi les miens n'aura jamais de place.

31. Quoted by Hatin, *op. cit.*, p. 187.

32. For details see Haag, *op. cit.*, vol. IX, pp. 55–57.

33. Interestingly enough there was an English publication, entitled *The Censor*, modelled on the *Spectator*, that first began on April 11 1715, in *Mist's Journal* where it appeared three times a week until June 17 when it ceased publication. On January 1 1717, *The Censor* reappeared as an independent publication and was put out three times a week until June 1. The author was Lewis Theobald.

34. L'ELOGE / DE LA / GOUTE / Ouvrage Heroique, Historique, Po- /l:tique, Comique, Critique, Sati- / rique, Ironique, Veridique, / autres Epithetes / en *ique*. / [rule] / Par / ETIENNE COULET, / A.D.E.M. /(devinez)/ [vignette of wavy lines] / *A LEIDE*, / Ches THE'ODORE HAAK, / Libraire vis a vis de l'Academie /M.D.CC.XXVIII.
In red: L'ELOGE / GOUTE / ETIENNE COULET, / THE'ODORE HAAK, $12°*^6 A–F^{12} G^6$
Contents: $*1$, title (verso blank); $*2–3$ v, Au lecteur; $*4–*6$, Epître; $*6$ v, Avertissement; 1–141; text; [142–156], Table des matières. The initials A.D.E.M. that appear on the title page are referred to in the Avertissement where the author offers to explain them only to those who take away the A. I assume, therefore, that the initials stand for Docteur en Médecine. Perhaps the A stands for "Ancien."

35. LE GOUTEUX / EN / BELLE-HUMEUR: / OU L'ELOGE / DE LA / GOUTE. / OUVRAGE HÉROÏQUE / *Historique, Politique, Critique, Comique, Satyrique, Ironique &c.* / PAR LE SIEUR / ETIENNE COULET, A.D.E.M. / MIS AU JOUR / PAR MR. DE GUEUDEVILLE. / [engraved vignette signed B. Picart del. J. Besoet Sculp. with the device — ET AMARA LAETO TEMPERET RISU] / A LA HAYE & à FRANCFORT SUR Meyn. / *AUX DEPENS DE LA COMPAGNIE.* / M.D.C.C.XLIII.

In red: GOUTEUX / BELLE-HUMEUR: / GOUTE. / PAR MR. DE GUEUDEVILLE. / A LA HAYE & à FRANCFORT sur Meyn. / M.D.C.C. XLIII.

36. See Michaud, vol. IX, pp. 345–346; Hoefer, vol. XII, col. 168; and the *Dictionnaire des sciences médicales*, ed. A.-J.-L. Jourdan, vol. 6, pp. 532–534.

In reviewing *L'Art de conserver la santé des princes*, the *Journal des savants*, (February 1725) observed:

Nous ne connaissons point l'auteur de cet ouvrage. Il dit dans sa préface avoir composé un livre des maladies des artisans. Si le traité *de morbis artificum*. . . est de lui. . . il peut se vanter. . . d'avoir fait un bon livre. C'est un traité qui paraît sous le nom de Mr. Ramazzini, auteur connu et estimé dans la république des lettres. Nous n'approfondirons point cette énigme. . . (184–185).

37. It is possible that the publication, in 1727, of Louis Coquelet's *L'Eloge de la goutte* had something to do with Theodore Haak's decision to bring out a work with the same title. Apart from the titles the works bear little resemblance.

38. HISTOIRE / ABREGÉE, / ET TRES MEMORABLE, / DU / CHEVALIER DE LA / PLUME NOIRE, / *Ecuyer, Sire du Hazard, de la / Fortune, de l'Avanture* / &c. &c. &c. / [vignette of landscape with large tree in foreground and sun at top right. The vignette is circular and surrounded by the device — VENIENT SUO TEMPORE FRUCTUS] / A AMSTERDAM, / Chez *H.G. LÖHNER.* " MDCCXLIV.
In red: HISTOIRE / DU / PLUME NOIRE, / A AMSTERDAM, / MDCCXLIV.
Formula: 12° *² A–M¹² N¹⁰
Contents: *1, title (verso blank); *2–*2 v, preface; A1–N4, text; (N4 v– N10 v], catalogue des livres nouveaux.
pp. [4] [1] 2–295 [13]
Copies are found at the university libraries of Harvard, Illinois, Princeton and Tennessee.

The Löhner family came to Amsterdam from Cleves. On November 8 1743, were published the banns of a Hendrik Willem Löhner, aged thirty, from Cleves. His parents were dead, and he was attended by his brother-in-law, Jan Onkruyt. His fiancée, Willempje Wollimus, aged twenty-two, was from Amsterdam, and was attended by her mother, Jannetje Roos. He lived on the Prinsengracht and she on the Botermarkt. Both signed themselves as booksellers. On December 24 1743, Löhner, now married to Willemtje Wolmos [sic], daughter of Assuerus Wolmos, *varendsman*, was registered as a citizen. On March 30 1744, he was registered as a member of the booksellers' guild. Among his publications were the above, *De vermomde ont-maskerd* (1744), and, in 1746, Outhier's *Journal d'un voyage au Nord, 1736–1737*. He does not seem to have published anything in Amsterdam after 1746. I am indebted to Dr. van Eeghen for this information. It is not clear why his name appears as H.G. Löhner on the title-page of the *Histoire abrégée...* Perhaps the G. stands for Guillaume, a gallicization of Willem.

39. *Kurtzgefasste sehr merkwürdige Geschichte des Ritters von dem schwarzen Federbusche, Stallmeisters, und Herrn des ohngefähren Zufalls, des Glücks und der Ebentheuer... Anno 1750*. 208 p. There is no name of publisher or place of publication. A copy is available in Göttingen university library. Perhaps Löhner himself was responsible for the translation and publication of this edition.

40. See chapter one, note 10.

41. See chapter ten of my study of Tyssot de Patot, *op. cit.*, pp. 163–164.

INDEX OF PROPER NAMES

284